FRISIANS AND THEIR NORTH SEA NEIGHBOURS

FRISIANS AND THEIR NORTH SEA NEIGHBOURS

From the Fifth Century to the Viking Age

edited by

John Hines and Nelleke IJssennagger

THE BOYDELL PRESS

© Contributors 2017

All Rights Reserved. Except as permitted under current legislation no part of this work may be photocopied, stored in a retrieval system, published, performed in public, adapted, broadcast, transmitted, recorded or reproduced in any form or by any means, without the prior permission of the copyright owner

First published 2017
The Boydell Press, Woodbridge
Paperback edition 2023

ISBN 978 1 78327 179 5 hardback
ISBN 978 1 83765 130 6 paperback

The Boydell Press is an imprint of Boydell & Brewer Ltd
PO Box 9, Woodbridge, Suffolk IP12 3DF, UK
and of Boydell & Brewer Inc.
668 Mt Hope Avenue, Rochester, NY 14620–2731, USA

website: www.boydellandbrewer.com

A CIP catalogue record for this book is available
from the British Library

The publisher has no responsibility for the continued existence or accuracy of URLs for external or third-party internet websites referred to in this book, and does not guarantee that any content on such websites is, or will remain, accurate or appropriate

Typeset by Word and Page, Chester, UK

CONTENTS

List of Figures — vii
List of Tables — xi
Preface — xiii
Acknowledgements — xiv
Linguistic Conventions and Abbreviations — xv
Abstracts — xvi

Introduction: Frisians – Who, When, Where, Why? — 1
    John Hines and Nelleke IJssennagger

1. Palaeogeography and People:
Historical Frisians in an archaeological light — 5
    Egge Knol and Nelleke IJssennagger

2. The Anglo-Frisian Question — 25
    John Hines

3. Frisian between the Roman and the Early Medieval Periods:
Language contact, Celts and Romans — 43
    Peter Schrijver

4. 'All quiet on the Western Front?' The Western Netherlands and the 'North Sea Culture' in the Migration Period — 53
    Menno Dijkstra and Jan de Koning

5. Power and Identity in the Southern North Sea Area:
The Migration and Merovingian Periods — 75
    Johan Nicolay

6. How 'English' is the Early Frisian Runic Corpus?
The evidence of sounds and forms — 93
    Gaby Waxenberger

7. The Geography and Dialects of Old Saxon: River-basin communication networks and the distributional patterns of North Sea Germanic features in Old Saxon — 125
    Arjen Versloot and Elżbieta Adamczyk

8. Between Sievern and Gudendorf: Enclosed sites in the north-western Elbe–Weser triangle and their significance in respect of society, communication and migration during the Roman Iron Age and Migration Period — 149
    Iris Aufderhaar

9. Cultural Convergence in a Maritime Context: Language and material culture as parallel phenomena in the early-medieval southern North Sea region — 173
    Pieterjan Deckers

10. The Kingdom of East Anglia, Frisia and Continental Connections, *c.* AD 600–900   193
    Tim Pestell
11. A Comparison of the Injury Tariffs in the Early Kentish and the Frisian Law Codes   223
    Han Nijdam
12. Cultural Contacts between the Western Baltic, the North Sea Region and Scandinavia: Attributing runic finds to runic traditions and corpora of the Early Viking Age   243
    Christiane Zimmermann and Hauke Jöns

Index   273

FIGURES

Palaeography and People, *Egge Knol and Nelleke IJssennagger*
1.1 Palaeogeographical map of the northern Netherlands, *c.* 500 BC. — 7
1.2 Palaeogeographical map of the northern Netherlands, *c.* AD 800. — 8
1.3 The Frisian coastal area in the 8th century AD and the dates of conversion to Christianity. — 13
1.4 The distribution of Frisian regions around AD 1300. — 14
1.5 The 8th-century weapon grave of Antum. — 16

The Anglo-Frisian Question, *John Hines*
2.1 Rune-forms representing **a, æ, o** and **œ** in the Anglo-Saxon *fuþorc*. — 31
2.2 The reverse of the Schweindorf *solidus*. — 33
2.3 Copper-alloy brooches found in England and the Netherlands. — 35

'All quiet on the Western Front', *Menno Dijkstra and Jan de Koning*
4.1 Palaeogeographical reconstruction of the Netherlands in the early Middle Ages. — 54
4.2 Palaeogeographical reconstruction with the distribution of water- and place-names that derive from prehistoric or Roman times in the western Netherlands. — 60
4.3 Hand-made plain and decorated 'Anglo-Saxon' style pottery from the early-medieval cemetery of Rijnsburg-De Horn. — 63
4.4 The cruciform brooch from Katwijk. — 65
4.5 The perifical geographical position of the western Dutch coastal area in the Migration Period. — 69

Power and Identity in the Southern North Sea Area, *Johan Nicolay*
5.1 Equal-armed brooch from Dösemoor (Lkr. Stade). — 77
5.2 Geographical distribution of 5th-century 'Saxon-style' equal-armed brooches. — 78
5.3 Type-C bracteates from the coastal areas of the northern Netherlands and northern Germany. — 79
5.4 Geographical distribution of gold and silver bracteates belonging to *Formularfamilien* D7-10, and of those that cannot be assigned to any specific *Formularfamilie* (D-). — 80
5.5 Stylistic development of 'Jutlandic' brooches into regionally specific 6th-century brooches. — 82
5.6 Geographical distribution of 6th-century 'Kentish-style' keystone garnet disc brooches of Avent's Classes 1 and 2 and 'Frisian-style' disc-on-bow brooches of the Achlum type (white symbols). — 83

5.7 Close cultural affinities between regionally specific, filigree- and/or garnet-decorated high-status ornaments dating to the late 6th, or early decades of the 7th century. 84

5.8 Geographical distribution of garnet- and/or filigree-decorated ornaments with regional characteristics, dating to the late 6th, and early decades of the 7th century. 86

5.9 Hypothetical reconstruction of regional and supra-regional kingdoms along the southern North Sea coast around AD 500 and AD 600, and the political division of this area into territories belonging to larger political configurations around AD 804. 88

How 'English' is the Early Frisian Runic Corpus? *Gaby Waxenberger*

6.1 The distribution of the inscriptions that make up the Pre-Old English Corpus. 94
6.2 The distribution of the inscriptions that make up the Old English Corpus. 95
6.3 The distributions of inscriptions considered as part of the Frisian Runic Corpus. 97
6.4 The descent and periodization of Old Frisian according to Rolf Bremmer. 98
6.5 Characteristic rune-forms of the Old English *fuþorc*: the *ōs, āc, æsc* and *ōþil* runes, with diagramatic scheme of innovations in rune-form and adjustments to the order of the rune-row between the *fuþark* and the *fuþorc*. 100
6.6 The emergence of OE *ō*: phonology, and runic reflexes. 102
6.7 Key examples of the use of the *ōs* and *ōþil* runes in England and Frisia. 103
6.8 The treatment of West Germanic */a:/*: allophones and their runic representations; new phonemes and their runic representation. 108
6.9 The reflexes of Gmc *ai* in Old Frisian. 108
6.10 The sources of the long vowels /æ:/ and /a:/ in Pre-Old English and Pre-Old Frisian. 109
6.11 The Southampton (Hamwic) bone and its inscription. 112
6.12 Examples of the single-barred **h** rune. 118

Geography and Dialects of Old Saxon, *Arjen Versloot and Elżbieta Adamczyk*

7.1 The distribution of North Sea Germanic features in Old Saxon material against the background of the main river basins and peat bog areas. 130
7.2 Northern Germany, with *Münsterland* in the Westphalian Basin, the Teutoburger Wald, and the valley of the Weser-Aller *Urstromtal*. 135
7.3 The distribution of *i*-mutated forms in the word *stad-/sted-* in present-day place names and in Old Saxon onomastic material. 137
7.4 The distribution of forms with palatalized -*k*- in present-day place names. 139
7.5 The new runes *ōs* and *āc*. 141
7.6 The geographical distribution of forms with different root vowels in *stedi*, 'town' and *beki*, 'creek'. 145

Between Sievern and Gudendorf, *Iris Aufderhaar*

8.1 The location of the enclosed sites Heidenschanze and Heidenstadt at Sievern, Stadt Geestland, Cuxhaven-Gudendorf, and of the site of Spieka-Knill in the north-western Elbe–Weser triangle. 150

Figures

8.2	Bracteates from Sievern, Stadt Geestland: finds from 1999.	151
8.3	The Sievern/Land Wursten region: model of the function of the marsh and *Geest*-edge settlements as landing and trans-shipment sites.	153
8.4	Feddersen Wierde (Ldkr. Cuxhaven): jetty and waterfront revetment from Settlement Horizon 1c (first half of the 1st century AD).	154
8.5	Drawing of the landscape and monumental features at Sievern, Ldkr. Cuxhaven, around the year 1750 in MS *Palaeogentilismus Bremensis* of Martin Mushard.	157
8.6	Reconstruction of the palaeotopography of the *Geest* and marsh zones around Gudendorf-Köstersweg, Stadt Cuxhaven, in the first half of the 1st millennium AD.	160
8.7	Greyscale plot of the magnetometer survey of Gudendorf-Köstersweg.	162
8.8	General plan of excavation area 1/2014 at Gudendorf-Köstersweg.	163
8.9	Greyscale plot of the magnetometer survey of Spieka-Knill, Ldkr. Cuxhaven.	167

Cultural Convergence in a Maritime Context, *Pieterjan Deckers*

9.1	Distribution of organic-tempered pottery in assemblages of Merovingian-period date in western Flanders.	175
9.2	A comparison of typical structures from the Flemish coastal region and the Scheldt valley.	176
9.3	Houses from the Dutch coastland supported by wall posts rather than internal or external supports.	177
9.4	The linguistic koineization process from a social network perspective.	180
9.5	How petrographic analysis of 3rd- to 5th-century pottery demonstrates great variability in the Low Countries, corresponding to the linguistic 'patchwork' stage in the koineization process.	181

The Kingdom of East Anglia, Frisia and Continental Connections, *Tim Pestell*

10.1	The East Anglian kingdom and the Continent.	194
10.2	*Solidi* of Sigibert found in Suffolk and Norfolk.	196
10.3	The Balthild matrix found in Postwick, Norfolk.	198
10.4	Visigothic belt counter-plate from Caistor St Edmund; Frankish belt counter-plates from Paston and Scole; sword-chapes from Burnham Market and Diss.	200
10.5	Frankish belt-suites from Ipswich Buttermarket, grave 1306, St Mary's Stadium, Southampton, grave 3520, and Long Acre, London, grave J.	201
10.6	'Saint' brooch from West Acre; continental disc brooches from Kelling and Martham; bracelet fragment from Bracon Ash.	203
10.7	Examples of ansate brooches.	204
10.8	Distribution of ansate brooches of Type VIII.B and Type XII ansate brooches.	206
10.9	Proportions of *sceattas* by series from Bawsey and Caistor St Edmund.	210
10.10	Ship penny of King Æthelstan of East Anglia.	212
10.11	Frankish vessels recovered from 7th-century East Anglian burials.	213
10.12	Imported continental pottery found in East Anglia.	214
10.13	The distribution of imported continental pottery within the Kingdom of East Anglia.	216

Cultural Contacts between the Western Baltic, the North Sea Region and
Scandinavia, *Christiane Zimmermann and Hauke Jöns*

12.1 Groß Strömkendorf: the extent of the settled area and the position of the trading centre, the graveyard and the harbour basin. 248
12.2 Groß Strömkendorf: general plan of the graveyard. 250
12.3 Distribution of dated boat graves of the 8th and 9th centuries AD in northern Central Europe and Scandinavia. 251
12.4 Distribution of dated animal graves and depositions of animal bones of the 8th and 9th centuries AD in northern Central Europe and Scandinavia. 252
12.5 Distribution of *Grubenhäuser* of the 8th to 11th centuries AD with stone-built hearths, and their position in the house, in northern Central Europe. 254
12.6 Groß Strömkendorf: development of the trading centre, based on the distribution of *Grubenhäuser* and dendrochronologically dated wells. 255
12.7 Groß Strömkendorf: distribution of dirhams and *sceattas*. 258
12.8 Groß Strömkendorf: *sceattas* found during metal-detector surveys. 259
12.9 Groß Strömkendorf: fragment of a comb with a runic inscription. 260
12.10 Rune no. 1 in the Groß Strömkendorf inscription and comparative forms. 261
12.11 Rune no. 2 in the Groß Strömkendorf inscription and comparative forms. 262

The editors, contributors and publishers are grateful to all the institutions and persons listed for permission to reproduce the materials in which they hold copyright. Every effort has been made to trace the copyright holders; apologies are offered for any omission, and the publishers will be pleased to add any necessary acknowledgement in subsequent editions.

TABLES

3.1	The Proto-Germanic vowel system	47
3.2	The North and West Germanic vowel system	48
3.3	The Anglo-Frisian (= North Sea Germanic) vowel system	48
3.4	The Pre-Old Frisian vowel system	50
3.5	The vowel system of Low Countries Celtic around AD 200 (based on early British Celtic and northern Gaulish)	50
6.1	The periodization of the English and Frisian languages in the Middle Ages	96
6.2	The inscriptions considered as part of the Frisian Runic Corpus	99
6.3	Sound-changes in Pre-Old English and Pre-Old Frisian	101
6.4	An overview of the allograph types of the ōs rune in the Old English and Pre-Old Frisian Runic Corpora	106
6.5	An overview of the allograph types of the āc rune in the Old English Runic Corpus and the Pre Old-Frisian and Early Runic Frisian Corpora	114
6.6	Variants and developments of rune no. 6 in the rune-row: the **k** rune, or **c** (ċēn), in the Pre-Old English and Old English Runic Corpora	118
6.7	The distribution of variant types of the runes in Table 6.6 in Pre-Old English and Pre-Old Frisian inscriptions	119
6.8	The distribution of the single- and double-barred **h** rune in early English and Frisian inscriptions	120
6.9	The use of the āc rune for both /a:/ and /a/ in early Frisian and English inscriptions	120
7.1	The inventory of North Sea Germanic features and their attestations in the Old Saxon material	129
7.2	Geographical and diachronic distribution of North Sea Germanic features in Old Saxon	131
7.3	Synopsis of dating and spread of North Sea Germanic features in Old Saxon compared to Old Frisian	133
7.4	A selection of lemmas potentially containing the North Sea Germanic features in two varieties of Old Saxon, Old Frisian, and their equivalents in modern Low German and Frisian	134
9.1	A simplified overview of some of the different characteristics of the transmission of pottery production and house-building in early-medieval coastal Flanders	183
11.1	Injury tariff recorded among the Kamba (Kenya), early 20th-century	227
11.2	The structure of the injury tariff in the laws of Æthelberht of Kent	228
11.3	The structure of the injury tariff in the *Lex Frisionum*, Tit. XXII	230
11.4	Vernacular terms found in both the *Lex Frisionum* and the Old Frisian tariffs	230
11.5	Groupings of fingers in the Old East Frisian tariffs	236
11.6	Compensations for hand and fingers in the laws of Æthelberht of Kent and the *Lex Frisionum*	236

PREFACE

To celebrate the twentieth anniversary of the First International Symposium on Frisian Runes and Neighbouring Traditions, which met in January 1994 at the Fries Museum (Museum of Friesland) in Leeuwarden (The Netherlands), a second international conference devoted to the early-medieval Frisians and their neighbours was organized with a wider remit: to combine and integrate discussions of archaeology, history, historical linguistics, legal history and palaeogeography, as well as runology. The conference Across the North Sea: North Sea Connections from AD 400 into the Viking Age was held in the new premises of the Fries Museum in Leeuwarden from 5 to 8 June 2014.

Over the course of the twenty years from 1994 to 2014 many new insights had been gained that merited discussion in an international and multidisciplinary context, with a new generation of scholars able to contribute substantially. Although again held at the Fries Museum, the conference took place in the entirely new museum building that had been opened in the heart of Leeuwarden, the capital of Friesland, a province of the modern Netherlands, in 2013.

Both the new museum and this early major conference provided the opportunity to take stock of the *status quo* in research concerning the enigmatic Frisians, and related peoples and areas, in various disciplines. It also provided an opportunity for the collective exploration of possibilities, problems, lacunas and pressing issues for future scholarship, with the express purpose of stimulating and launching a new and effective round of research into Early Medieval Frisia. The multidisciplinary, international character and diachronic scope of the conference sought to promote a fully cross-disciplinary approach to enable understanding of the field to break free of over-specialized and constrained perspectives.

This publication is just part of the harvest of this event, and is intended to advance the appreciation of the long-distance and maritime contacts that were fundamental to the flourishing of the Frisian identity and culture throughout this period. By publishing a selection of papers that reflect the topics and current developments in them in English, making some discussions and data available to an international readership for the first time, we aim to stimulate the international study of the topics.

We sincerely hope that the conference, which the Fries Museum was happy to host, helped to establish and keep close and lasting relations with our modern neighbours from the North Sea area and beyond, in the museum world, the realm of academia and with the interested public.

The editors wish to thank their fellow members of the conference committee for all their work: Tim Pestell, Gaby Waxenberger, Kerstin Kazazzi and Han Nijdam, and above all Tineke Looijenga for her constant enthusiasm, determination, good humour and vision. Furthermore we thank all moderators, speakers, and participants for their contributions.

John Hines and Nelleke IJssennagger, June 2016

ACKNOWLEDGEMENTS

The conference was made possible by financial support from the Koninklijke Nederlandse Akademie van Wetenschappen (KNAW), Koninklijk Fries Genootschap, Groningen Research Institute for the Study of Culture (ICOG) University of Groningen, The Society for the Study of Medieval Languages and Literature, Cardiff University, Erasmus Mundus and Fries Museum, together with practical support from the Fryske Akademy, Groninger Museum and Terpencentrum Rijksuniversiteit Groningen (excursion).

This publication is made possible with funding from the Fries Museum in Leeuwarden, and a private donation.

LINGUISTIC CONVENTIONS AND ABBREVIATIONS

Every natural language has its own specific and defined inventory of sounds, amongst which both 'phonemic' (structural) and 'phonetic' (actual) distinctions may be identified. Sounds may be represented by the graphs of the International Phonetic Alphabet (IPA), with phonemes presented between square brackets […] and phonetic forms between slashes /…/. The presence of a colon after a graphic symbol represents the 'long' articulation of the sound in question. Angled brackets are used to represent spelt forms <…>.

It is also common practice to represent the typical sounds of early languages with italicized lettering. An asterisk before such a sound or word represents a form that is reconstructed rather than actually observed. In these circumstances long vowels are typically represented with either a macron (a horizontal line) or a circumflex accent above the graph. A single arrow < or > represents the direction of a sound-change: e.g. *u > y* means '*u* changes to *y*'.

Transliterations of runic inscriptions into the roman alphabet use **bold** type, where each letter in the transliteration should unambiguously represent a particular runic graph. Bind-runes, composed of two runic graphs ligatured, are represented by transliterations of the graphs concerned beneath a curved line bracketing them.

The following abbreviations are regularly used in this text:

acc.	accusative	neut.	neuter
fem.	feminine	nom.	nominative
gen.	genitive	pl.	plural
instr.	instrumental	sg.	singular
masc.	masculine	wk.	weak
Gmc	Germanic	OLF	Old Low Franconian
IE	Indo-European	ON	Old Norse
NSGmc	North Sea Germanic	OS	Old Saxon
NWGmc	North-West Germanic	PGmc	Proto-Germanic
ODu	Old Dutch	PIE	Proto-Indo-European
OE	Old English	Pre-OE	Pre-Old English
OFris	Old Frisian	Pre-OFris	Pre-Old Frisian
OHG	Old High German	WGmc	West Germanic

ABSTRACTS

Palaeogeography and People: Historical Frisians in an archaeological light
Egge Knol and Nelleke IJssennagger
Taking as its starting point the palaeography of the Frisian coastal landscape, the history and archaeology of Frisia and Frisians up to the Viking Age are set out in this introductory paper. We follow the historic Frisians from the first *terp* settlers into the Middle Ages, addressing the key questions of migration and repopulation after the Roman Era, the Frisians in a North Sea context, Frisian identity and Frisian culture, in light of the relevant archaeological and historical sources on Frisia. Chronologically the latest sources addressed are the Old Frisian law texts. Together, this provides an introduction to Frisia and an overall historical and archaeological framework for the volume.

The Anglo-Frisian Question
John Hines
'Anglo-Frisian' has long been a familiar concept in Early Medieval studies. Its use to reflect and label particularly close similarities in language, runographic practice, and material culture on two facing sides of the North Sea has become regular. This has not come about without exploration or explicit modelling of what form a special relationship between the Anglo-Saxon and Frisian populations and their cultures may have taken, although the habits of thought of earlier generations of scholars have, not surprisingly and perhaps too easily, tended to focus on the idea of an original stage of 'Anglo-Frisian unity'. This paper seeks to summarize the principal fields of evidence in relatively non-specialist terms, and emphasizes the extent to which convergence between the two areas can be observed within the Early Middle Ages as much as any divergence from some original common stock. It is argued therefore that the continuing inter-relationship of the populations either side of the North Sea, both in the Early Middle Ages and succeeding periods, requires and repays careful mapping and evaluation.

**Frisian between the Roman and the Early Medieval Period:
Language contact, Celts and Romans**
Peter Schrijver
The way in which languages usually expand their geographical range is at the expense of other languages: a community acquires a second language and in the course of time the second language may become the first and only language in the community. This language shift is usually driven by socio-political change. Language shift may leave distinct linguistic traces in the form of an 'accent': features of the language that has disappeared survive in the language that replaced it (e.g. a Welsh accent in the English of Wales). This paper addresses the question of whether the Frisian language contains traces of an accent that can be ascribed to a language that preceded it. It turns out that there is some evidence in favour of the hypothesis that the Frisian language arose when

a population that spoke a Celtic language switched to speaking Germanic. That evidence is mainly based on changes in the vowel system which occurred at the earliest stages of the Frisian language.

'All quiet on the Western Front?'
The Western Netherlands and the 'North Sea Culture' in the Migration Period
Menno Dijkstra and Jan de Koning

Based on the latest historical, palaeogeographical and archaeological evidence, this study clearly demonstrates that the Dutch western coastal area was not occupied by Anglo-Saxon groups during the 5th-century *adventus Saxonum* as the *terp* region of Friesland and Groningen was. It had become a periphery of no international interest. The few Anglo-Saxon-style pots and brooch present are datable to the 6th century, and were the result of growing contacts between the western and the surrounding *terp* region, the Dutch central river area, and England too. Only from the 7th, or even the late 6th century onwards, with political interest from the Frankish and Frisian kings, did the region find its way back on the international stage. Some lines of thought of how the 'North Sea Germanic' dialect fits into these developments are also briefly discussed.

Power and Identity in the Southern North Sea Area:
The Migration and Merovingian Periods
Johan Nicolay

In early-medieval times, the southern North Sea area found itself in between the Late Roman Empire and Frankish kingdom to the south, and the Scandinavian kingdoms to the north-east. Throughout the 5th to 7th centuries AD, its coastal areas saw the formation of regional and larger kingdoms – following the migration of the 'Anglo-Saxons'. After the identity of elite networks was first expressed by imitating 'Saxon' and Scandinavian status symbols, the 6th and early decades of the 7th centuries alternatively saw the expression of regional identities. Within Kent, the northern Netherlands and later also East Anglia and the western Netherlands, a mixture of Scandinavian and Frankish influences resulted in the production of regional-style ornaments, each making the extent of individual networks or kingdoms visible. After the incorporation of these networks into even larger networks under Carolingian, Mercian and Danish rule, the former kingdoms became invisible – remaining only as archaeological finds of gold and silver.

How 'English' is the Early Frisian Runic Corpus? The evidence of sounds and forms
Gaby Waxenberger

This paper deals with the earliest runic inscriptions in Frisia and England, in light of the earliest sound changes which effected the long vowels of the languages used there in their Pre-Old English and Pre-Old Frisian stages. The sound-changes of Pre-Old English (*c.* AD 400–600) are used as a framework in order to reveal how the Frisian runes and the sound values they represent may be correlated. Certain rune-forms are examined in addition, in order to shed more light on the characteristics of the Frisian corpus. The early runic inscriptions of the Frisian Corpus can thus be demonstrated to be congruent with the Pre-Old English Corpus both in the underlying sound changes involving long vowels and the runic forms employed.

The Geography and Dialects of Old Saxon: River-basin communication networks and the distributional patterns of North Sea Germanic features in Old Saxon
Arjen Versloot and Elżbieta Adamczyk

The West Germanic language group is traditionally divided into North Sea Germanic (Old English and Old Frisian) and Continental Germanic (Old Low Franconian and Old High German). The position of Old Saxon within this West Germanic language continuum is ambiguous: on the one hand, it shares various innovations with Old English and Old Frisian; on the other, it has many traits in common with Old High German. The North Sea Germanic characteristics are more abundant in the minor Old Saxon texts, especially those associated with Eastphalia than in *Heliand*, *Genesis* and other sources from the region of Essen and Werden. This implies that the 'coastal' features were more widespread in the Old Saxon dialects of the deep south-east inland than in the dialects of the south-western regions, closer to the coast. This rather unexpected distribution of linguistic characteristics is the focus of the present paper, which offers a detailed mapping of a range of North Sea Germanic features in the Old Saxon material. The patterns resulting from the mapping confirm the assumed dialectal contrasts in Old Saxon. The aim of the paper is to account for the attested distribution of linguistic features. The explanation is sought in the ancient traffic networks which, given the poor overland traffic conditions, overlapped with river basin networks. More specifically, the central and south-eastern regions stayed in direct contact with the Frisian-speaking region on the North Sea littoral through the rivers Ems, Weser and Elbe, while the south-western regions were in close contact with the continentally oriented Franconians in the Rhine Valley. The inland extension of the North Sea Germanic linguistic features can therefore be interpreted as a reflection of communication networks, which developed along the lines of economic and political contacts, and was directed by the travel networks of those days.

Between Sievern and Gudendorf: Enclosed sites in the north-western Elbe–Weser triangle and their significance in respect of society, communication and migration during the Roman Iron Age and Migration Period
Iris Aufderhaar

Waterways provided the most favourable conditions for communication and transport of goods in the 1st millennium AD. Research focusing on archaeologically identifiable structures indicates that these waterways were firmly controlled during this period. In the Elbe–Weser triangle this is most clearly evident in the area of Sievern. The topography and infrastructure of the settlement cluster suggest that during the first half of the 1st millennium AD its residents controlled and protected both overland routes and especially waterways along the estuary of the River Weser. The centre of this region seems to have been located in the hinterland represented by two sets of rampart systems. Between 2013 and 2015 the Lower Saxony Institute for Historical Coastal Research investigated on further fortified sites in this area from the first half of the 1st millennium AD. The article provides an overview of the premises and initial results of the project.

Abstracts

Cultural Convergence in a Maritime Context: Language and material culture as parallel phenomena in the early-medieval southern North Sea region
Pieterjan Deckers

This contribution draws the parallel between developments in linguistic and material-cultural expressions (notably, domestic architecture and pottery) of the communities around the southern North Sea between the 6th and 8th centuries AD. It is argued that a proposed process of linguistic koineization forms a fitting model for a broader 'North Sea Culture' that gradually emerged from the demographic and cultural reconfiguration of the Late Roman Period; a process of convergence that was cut short (if not entirely halted) by the growing political centralization from several cores around the North Sea in the 8th century. The differing rates at which the cultural traditions studied here converged can be explained by referring to the properties of these traditions and their transmission from one generation to another.

The Kingdom of East Anglia, Frisia and Continental Connections *c.* AD 600–900
Tim Pestell

As the nearest political entity across the North Sea from Frisia, it was inevitable that the kingdom of the East Angles should share with it cultural and economic links. While our understanding of any diplomatic connections is hampered by a lack of documentary evidence for both Frisia and East Anglia, it is clear that the latter enjoyed widespread relationships with the Continent. This paper summarizes the available historical evidence for East Anglia's continental connections and then investigates and analyses the contribution material culture studies can play in developing this picture, especially through the study of jewellery, coinage and pottery. The conclusion is that strong links can be seen between East Anglia and the Low Countries, but that these shifted over time, doubtless relating to vicissitudes in the political and economic fortunes of both areas.

A Comparison of the Injury Tariffs in the Early Kentish and the Frisian Law Codes
Han Nijdam

Since the turn of the millennium, the antiquity of Germanic law has enjoyed renewed attention from scholars such as Patrick Wormald and Lisi Oliver. A special role is assigned to so-called compensation tariffs as encountered in the early-medieval *Leges Barbarorum*. This paper addresses the question of whether it is possible to reconstruct a Proto-Anglo-Frisian tariff, given the close linguistic and cultural affinity between Anglo-Saxon and Frisian law. To this end, the Anglo-Saxon Law of Aethelberht (*c.* AD 600) has been compared with the Frisian *Lex Frisionum* (8th-century) and the younger Old Frisian compensation tariffs (13th-century). Although the two tariff traditions show a degree of closeness to one another when compared with the other Germanic traditions, it is impossible to reconstruct a common ancestor to these two tariff traditions. It is suspected that a compensation tariff was seen as an identity marker, so that each society endeavoured to have its own set of regulations.

Cultural Contacts between the Western Baltic, the North Sea Region and Scandinavia: Attributing runic finds to runic traditions and corpora of the Early Viking Age

Christiane Zimmermann and Hauke Jöns

Early-medieval trading centres in the North Sea region and the western Baltic can be conceived of as meeting places of people from different cultures, and as places of language contact. This is of particular significance when it comes to reading and interpreting runic inscriptions from these places. Against this background, the paper discusses a runic inscription on the fragment of a comb from the Early Viking Age trading centre at Groß Stömkendorf which has been identified with the emporium *Reric* that is mentioned in the Frankish Annals under the year AD 808. Manufacturing details point to the fact that the comb was either produced in the North Sea area or manufactured by a craftsman who was familiar with the traditions of comb-making in that area. By discussing and evaluating the extant data for the reading and interpretation of the new runic find more general questions of attributing inscriptions to runic corpora are addressed and the methods applied reconsidered.

INTRODUCTION

Frisians – Who, When, Where, Why?

John Hines and Nelleke IJssennagger

Wherever and whenever present-day scholars attempt to analyse and discuss a named 'people' of the Early Middle Ages such as our 'Frisians', they are dealing at one and the same time with a phenomenon that was thoroughly real and of great significance in its own time and yet also one that is intrinsically slippery and deceptive, if not downright illusory, in key respects. It has now long been the familiar and conventional understanding of the peoples of that period – often referred to as *nationes* in contemporary Latin sources, and nowadays frequently as 'ethnic groups', in connection with a phenomenon of 'ethnogenesis' – that they are constructions, formations which were dynamically adapted to needs and opportunities provided by changing circumstances, while what these groups certainly were not is substantially solid and fixed entities that lived purely organically and reproduced themselves naturally, generation succeeding to generation. Indeed, a recent study implies that a necessarily endless process of identity-formation is a feature of history and archaeology we can handle with more confidence than we ever should think in terms of the presence and functioning of completed ethnic identities (Pohl 2013).

Of a significance equal to the questions listed in the title above for the definition of the focus of the present volume, therefore, has to be the historical context in which the attempt is made to present and examine 'the Frisians', and their neighbours. The principal chronological range is a period of four to five centuries, from the beginning of the 5th century AD into the 9th: a long period, falling between the end of the maintenance of effective Roman imperial rule in western Europe and the impact of the Scandinavian Viking expansion and incursions that began at the end of the 8th century. Of course, evidence from both before and after that period sheds light upon aspects of it, and is included here too where appropriate. The 5th century was, however, indisputably at the heart of a convulsion in Europe, marked primarily by the collapse of the Roman Empire in the West. The consequences of that fall were massive, both socially and economically. Across western Europe, the Roman structures of government were replaced by 'barbarian' kingships – mostly Germanic in terms of language, albeit several had Turkic elements too. Economically, a sophisticated system of specialized production and distribution, both through markets and in accordance with administrative and military demand, crumbled away, to be replaced by a system much closer to a subsistence-level strategy and so dominated all the more by agrarian landholding as the basis of personal power (Wickham 2005, esp. 56–124, 303–79).

This was not a total collapse, however. The eastern Roman Empire based in Constantinople carried on, and rose in power, now unchallenged by any western rival. Ideologically, the Church survived the collapse of the western Empire remarkably well, and commenced a process of successful missionary expansion, first in the west and north of Britain and in Ireland, and soon amongst the Germanic peoples, within what had been the Empire and subsequently beyond its old borders. A 'Late Antique' component was thus a significant element in the reconstruction of life and culture within the former western Empire, and it was equally to be a major factor in the development of Germanic Europe beyond the old frontier lines of the Rhine and the Danube, together with the newly emergent Anglo-Saxon England.

Historical sources that we have from the pre-Viking centuries of the Early Middle Ages are consistent in reflecting a schematic perspective that saw the north-western Europe of that period in terms of a plan inhabited by named groups, some of whom – for instance Franks, Angles, Saxons, Danes and Frisians – appear quite regularly, and in seductively stable terms territorially, while others (for instance the Boructuari and the Warni) appear in more fleeting and historically marginal terms. With direct support from early-medieval sources in some cases, modern scholars have found some attractive scope for associating named groups of that age with language varieties and/or distinctive features of material culture. Even though the concept of the 'culture group' thus becomes one that can readily be added to, and even interchanged with, the 'ethnic' group, such associations are not deployed merely to reify the identities in question in a naïve way; they are rather themselves consistently embedded into the understanding that they are elements in the sort of continuing and dynamic process of constant redefinition and assertion of identity.

As the name of a *natio* or ethnic group, *Frisii* were known to two major Roman authors, Pliny the Elder and Tacitus, as early as the 1st century AD. Pliny also refers to a group called the *Frisiavones*, a name which recurs in several Latin inscriptions from the Empire and was incorporated in the name of a cohort *I Frisiavonum* that served in Britannia (Galestin 2007/8). There are further references to the *Frisii* in Latin and Φρίσιοι in Greek from the 2nd and 3rd centuries AD; then in the 6th century Procopius and Venantius Fortunatus refer to contemporary Φρίσσονες and *Fresones* respectively. Manifestly the root of the ethnonym had survived, and was still associated with a population in essentially the same area of north-western Europe, north of the Rhine and bordering the North Sea (for relevant maps, see Figs 1.1–1.3 and 4.1–4.2, *infra*). However there is now a clear scholarly consensus, almost unanimity, that it could not then refer to a population that was simply and directly descended from the people to whom either of the 1st-century names were attached. The Frisians must thus have been virtually a type-example of a people that had to have been entirely recreated, and in a sense, reinvented.

Historical references to the group multiply in the 7th and 8th centuries, reflecting the recognition of an extensive Frisian kingdom, for which the non-historical term *Magna Frisia* ('Great Frisia') is sometimes used in modern historiography, emphasizing the perception that the range of a politically independent Frisian territory and people was greatest at this point. In the 8th century, the Frisian lands were progressively conquered and annexed to the nascent Carolingian Empire. At this juncture we find references to a *citerior Fresia* which appears to have extended south of the Rhine to the mouth of the River Scheldt and across the Rhine mouth into Holland, and a *Frisia ulterior* further north and east. In most circumstances, however, we lack precise indications of the extent and boundaries of the territories understood to be the parts of early-medieval Frisia, and consequently it is extremely helpful to be able to refer to the clear evidence provided by the *Lex Frisionum* of *c.* AD 800. In this text, Frisia extends from the River Zwin on the northern edge of medieval and modern Flanders to the River Weser, which flows through Niedersachsen in Germany to the North Sea, but it is divided into three parts. West Frisia lies between the Zwin and the Vlie, and thus comprises the provinces of Zeeland and both South and North Holland in the modern Netherlands. Central Frisia (or Middle Frisia) lies between the Rivers Vlie and the Lauwers, and thus is essentially the modern Dutch province of Friesland. East Frisia lies between the Lauwers and the Weser, and thus incorporates the area of Germany still known as Ostfriesland, as well as the province of Groningen in the Netherlands (for the rivers, see especially Figs. 1.1–1.3, *infra*).

Not surprisingly, in light of the flat and low-lying topography of the whole area, a series of waterways was thus used to define and frame early-medieval Frisia, and its internal structuring into three parts. The River Lauwers is similarly also used to refer to areas with which particular manuscript traditions of the Frisian law codes are associated. 'Westerlauwers' is the tradition of the area west of the Lauwers, and thus principally of West and Central Frisia as described above, while 'Oosterlauwers' is the East Frisian area. Both within these larger divisions and within the modern provinces there are smaller discrete areas such as Westergo and Ostergo within Friesland, and important towns and central places such as Dorestad, Wijnaldum, Rijnsburg and Domburg. Specific parts within the area of what can validly be referred to as early-medieval Frisia may also be referred to as the *terp*-area and the clay district, for self-evident reasons.

The papers in this volume present a series of empirical studies of how the population of these Frisian regions changed, and how the people lived, through the earliest centuries of the post-Roman, Early Middle Ages. It is conceived as a collection of evidence subjected to up-to-date analyses which add to our insight and understanding of the way in which the people known to history as the Frisians made use of the resources of their lands and the sea, and how they interacted with their neighbours. While the papers are fully informed by the theoretical issues noted earlier, the major focus and the emphasis of this volume lie upon methodological demonstrations of how to interpret the particular evidence each chapter presents, not the furtherance of a strictly conceptual debate. Every effort has consequently been made in the writing and editing of the papers to ensure that specialist approaches are adequately explained for readers approaching the subject from some different background to be able to understand the material. But no scholarship is free of theoretical implications, and at the very heart of both this volume, as of the conference from which it springs, lies a recognition of how essentially Frisian identity functioned within the relationship between the population of the coastal lands of north-western Europe and those of the surrounding world. Being Frisian was something that was made clear in relation to and in distinction from (although not necessarily in sharp contrast with) the different identities of the neighbouring peoples: primarily the Franks to the south and the (Old) Saxons to the east by land, and also to the various Anglo-Saxon groups and kingdoms over the sea in southern and eastern England, and to those of Scandinavia across the sea and along the coasts to the north and north-east. Hence the relevance of the attention given to the Frisians' neighbours around the North Sea in this volume.

There are multiple ways in which the papers in this volume are inter-related. A recurrent theme, however, is not just that there are observable and significant similarities of development between Frisians at any given time and their neighbours, but also how influence may lead to convergence no less than contact can stimulate divergence. We have sought to arrange the volume in a manner most consistent with the overarching principles and vision presented above, rather than to structure it. After introductions to the region and its study, the papers are grouped, as far as practicable, alongside one another in geographically and chronologically consistent relationships. They are not separated into sections by academic disciplines; this would be directly contrary to the aspirations of the whole initiative that has produced this book, and in fact several of these contributions are successfully multi-disciplinary in contexts as well as cross-disciplinary in spirit. Accordingly, we are confident that methodologically this collection represents something of considerably wider interest to early-medieval studies than a group of specialized papers relevant to 'Frisian Studies' alone. This is the light in which we encourage our readers to explore its contents.

References

Galestin, M. C. 2007/8. '*Frisii* and *Frisiavones*', *Palaeohistoria* 49/50, 687–708.

Pohl, Walter 2013. 'Strategies of identification: a methodological profile', in *Strategies of Identification: Ethnicity and Religion in Early Medieval Europe*, ed. W. Pohl and G. Heidemann (Turnhout), 1–64.

Wickham, Chris 2005. *Framing the Early Middle Ages: Europe and the Mediterranean, 400–800* (Oxford).

1

Palaeogeography and People

Historical Frisians in an archaeological light

Egge Knol and Nelleke IJssennagger

The story of Frisia and the Frisians is one of a changing landscape, people, identity and name, as well as one of constant connections across the North Sea. For an understanding of the pre- and proto-historical Frisians and their archaeological traces, we first consider the changing landscape that they inhabited. We then look into the historical and archaeological sources that can tell us something about them, before turning to their connections across the North Sea.

The Frisian landscape and its use

In the course of recent millennia, the geomorphology of the Netherlands has seen major changes. An insight into the contemporary landscapes is indispensable to understanding the physical environment of the peoples who at different times considered themselves to be Frisians, or were so labelled by others, and what opportunities it offered. This was understood as early as the 16th century, when maps were drawn showing the Low Countries as they were believed to have been in the Roman Period. In recent decades an important research tradition has arisen in the Netherlands of compiling palaeogeographical maps, representing past landscapes on the basis of all available geological, paedological, archaeological and historical evidence. Such maps by definition are continually 'work in progress'. Every new excavation revealing archaeological or geological evidence, as well as detailed studies of archaeological or historical data, prompts adjustments to them. But, broadly speaking, the current maps are well substantiated (Vos 2015).

Geographically, the coastal zone of historical Frisia in the Netherlands can be divided into two different parts: the Holland coast in the west, and the northern Netherlands (see also Dijsktra and de Koning, this vol.). In the west, the interior is protected by a sturdy belt of sand dunes. However, in the northern part of the west, most of the dune belt has been eroded away by the sea (Woltering *et al.* 1999; Dijkstra 2011). Initially, the mouth of the Rhine cut through the dunes at Katwijk, and further north a breach appeared at the Marsdiep, possibly in the 10th century AD. Although the Rhine mouth offered opportunities for controlling waterborne traffic, the great emporium of Dorestad evolved a considerable distance upstream (van Es 1990; van Es and Verwers 1980; 2009; 2015). The cores of what later became the islands of Texel and Wieringen consisted of Pleistocene boulder-clay outcrops. Extending inland from the dune belt were vast expanses of marshland which were difficult to exploit. Early-medieval settlement was therefore initially restricted to the dunes, the banks of rivers like the Rhine and Meuse, and to some sandy outcrops of Pleistocene origin.

In the north of the Netherlands, by contrast, the interior was open to the sea. The barrier of a chain of islands with sand dunes protected the shallow, tidal Wadden Sea, which to the south was bordered by an extensive zone of saltmarsh (Vos and Knol 2015). The great bio-productivity that characterizes the Wadden Sea environment made this fertile region a highly attractive place to live. From as early as 600 BC, it formed the largest area of natural pasture in Europe (Nieuwhof 2006; 2010; Bazelmans *et al.* 2012; Schepers 2014). The saltmarsh was dissected by watercourses: tidal inlets as well as small streams that drained the interior. The saltmarsh merged into a brackish marsh which in its turn bordered on extensive fenland. These marshy fens in due course gave rise to inaccessible peat bogs, which eventually expanded to cover much of the Pleistocene uplands, now the province of Drenthe. Apart from a few rivers, there were some sandy ridges that allowed communication between the coastal saltmarsh and the habitable parts of the Pleistocene interior (Fig. 1.1). This broad division of the landscape into tidal flats, saltmarsh, brackish marsh and peat bog bypasses the local differences within these zones. Relative elevation, the influence of sea water or fresh water from the interior, and intensity of grazing, all affected the land and the possibilities for exploitation. It has transpired that in periods of increased population pressure the margins of the marshlands were brought under cultivation; after drainage these offered good opportunities for arable farming (de Langen 2011). However, drainage also caused oxidation and shrinkage of the peat. Such surface subsidence made the land vulnerable to flooding and might even result in marine transgressions. Various tidal inlets in today's Wadden Sea area in fact directly resulted from the former exploitation of the peatland margins. Indeed the changes to the Dutch coastal zone are in most cases attributable to anthropogenic processes (Vos and Knol 2015).

The saltmarsh in the northern Netherlands offered easy access to the sea. Intermittently, mostly in winter, it would be flooded. The settlers were well adapted to this regime. They built their homes on man-made settlement mounds, the *terpen* or *wierden* described below. The wide saltmarsh was overgrown with grasses and other vegetation resistant to occasional flooding. As the saltmarsh grasses were rich in protein and highly nutritious, the landscape was eminently suited to stock farming. As long as one managed to herd one's offspring and livestock on to the *terp* when a storm was brewing, this was a good place to make a living. Recovered bones show that cattle and sheep were the principal livestock. Cattle would be brought in to the farm at night. Hunting, fishing, and shooting or trapping birds supplied a minor part of the diet. Hunting may nevertheless have fulfilled an important social function (Fig. 1.2).

Palaeogeography and People

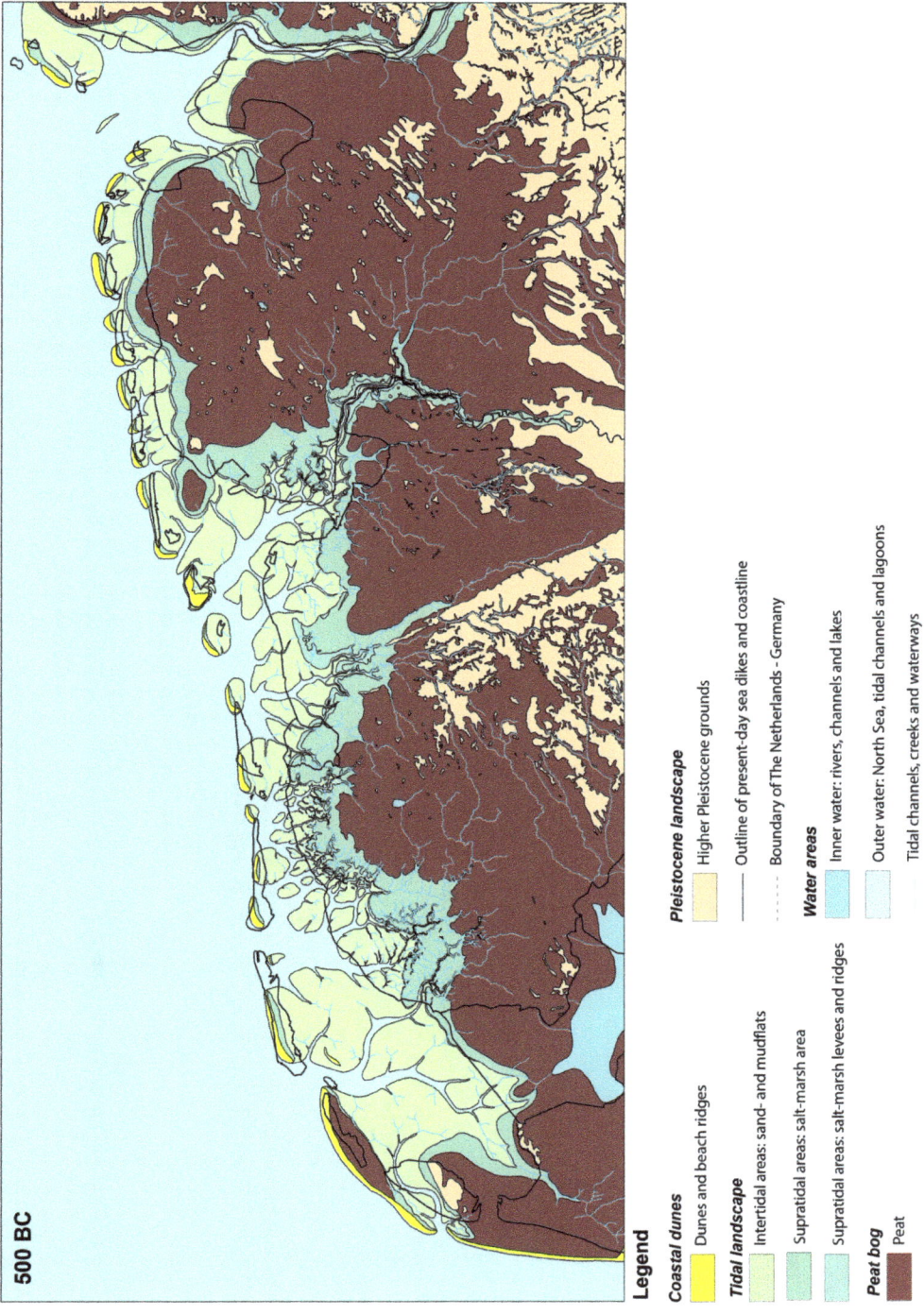

Fig. 1.1. Palaeogeographical map of the northern Netherlands, *c.* 500 BC. By Peter Vos and Egge Knol.

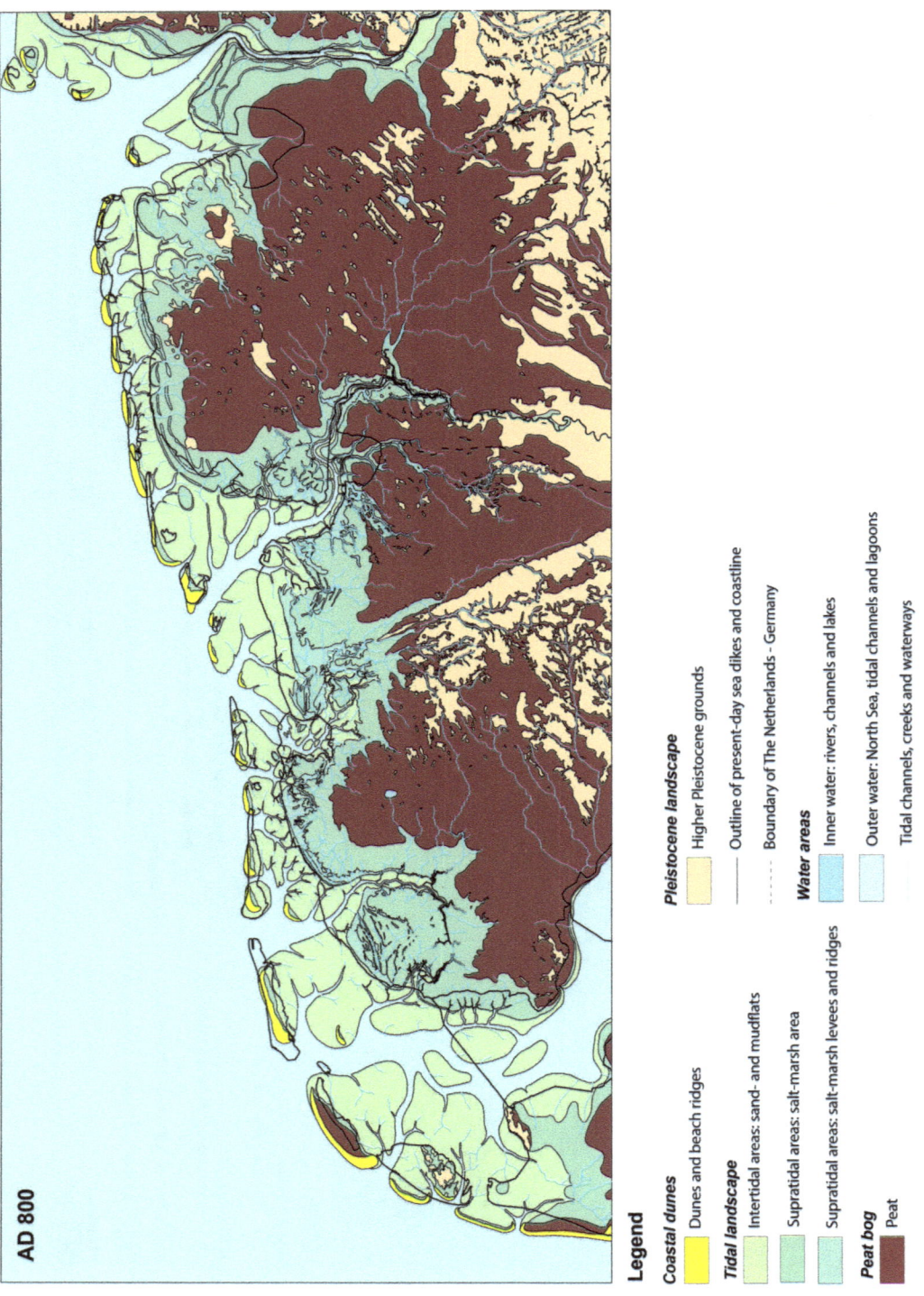

Fig. 1.2. Palaeogeographical map of the northern Netherlands, c. AD 800. By Peter Vos and Egge Knol.

Protected by low banks around higher parts of the saltmarsh, and on the flanks of the dwelling *terps*, small fields could be successfully tilled for crops (Bazelmans 2005; Prison 2009). As trees tolerate salt water poorly, there were just a few on the *terps*, and timber had to be imported from the interior uplands. Dung was not needed as a fertiliser, so it could be dried and used for fuel (Nieuwhof and Woldring 2007). In some parts of the region this practice survived into the 20th century; in the north German 'Halligen' area, dung served as fuel until the 1960s (Lengsveld 1998, 66–9). Excavations such as those at Ezinge, Leens and Foudgum have shown that people occupied large, aisled farmhouses with byres to accommodate dozens of cattle. The walls were built of wattle and daub, and in later times of turf (Waterbolk 1991; van Giffen 1940; de Langen 1992). Recently a turf-built house was erected by way of experimental archaeology, showing that these houses could make quite comfortable dwellings (Postma 2015). Freshwater provision was a perennial problem in this briny land, but ponds and wells generally offered sufficient water (Nicolay 2010; 2015). Beyond the saltmarsh, in the peat-bog margin, were wetlands, where mosquitoes would have thrived. Malarial fever may well have been endemic there (Knottnerus 2002).

For transport on land, the coast dwellers used carts with discs and spoked wheels. In summer, the clay tracks were firm and easily passable. Presumably the watercourses were crossed with simple plank bridges. Meanwhile people were quite familiar with waterborne transport. In recent years excavations have uncovered fragments of boats at numerous sites, but an entire boat is still on the archaeologists' wish-list. Just across the German border, a 4.7 m long fragment of a Late Iron-age logboat recently came to light (Thiemann and Kegler 2013). In the 8th-century cemetery of Dunum in Ostfriesland a body was interred in one half of a boat, which still measured 2.90 m in length (Siegmüller and Peek 2015). In the cemetery of Solleveld in South Holland a 7th-century grave in the shape of a boat was constructed out of fragments of a clinker-built vessel (Waasdorp and Eimermann 2008). Moreover, iron clinker nails, characteristic of clinker-built craft, have turned up in early-medieval contexts at various recent excavations (Brouwers, Jansma and Manders 2015).

From the first Frisians to new Frisians

Frisians as a group of people and Frisia as a geographical (and cultural) area are two different things that do not always coincide. On the one hand we have written sources mentioning Frisians, on the other hand we have sources mentioning Frisia. In addition, we have the coastal area that we currently know as *Frisia*, with its rich archaeological remains. The question is how at various points in time these connect or coincide. It is clear that over the ages, the names *Frisia* and *Frisian* have been used in various ways to refer to different people and specific areas. This is reflected by the modern use of *Friesland* as a name of a province, which is only part of the area historically known as Frisia.

From archaeological sources it has become clear that, succeeding a transient Neolithic population, the first settlers in the coastal area of the northern Netherlands arrived from the interior and neighbouring areas around 600 BC. They settled on the higher ridges in the tidal landscape, building their houses on platforms made from sods. Over the centuries, individual platforms were widened and raised, creating *terps* on which villages evolved (Bazelmans *et al.* 2012, 116–18). New *terps* were created as the land extended seawards with younger sediments. The extension and alteration of the *terps* in some areas continued up to around AD 1000. However, occupation was not always continuous.

Of the *terps*, which in Friesland are known as *terpen*, in Groningen as *wierden* and in Germany as *Wurten* or *Warften*, many are still present, but many others were quarried away in the 19th and 20th centuries for their fertile soil, particularly in Friesland and Groningen. This has industry produced a huge amount of archaeological finds and evidence, also in comparison to the German coastal area, where the *terps* largely remained intact. In Friesland, many of these objects were collected by the Fries Genootschap (Frisian Society) and housed in the Fries Museum (Frisian Museum) in Leeuwarden or by the Groninger Museum in Groningen, where they still form part of the core collection. Today, some of the *terps* still are distinct landmarks, a case in point being Hogebeintum. This *terp*, which used to be about 9 m high, was the highest in Friesland. The main reason why a remnant is still standing is the fact that the church and churchyard were on top of it – besides a number of houses that are still inhabited. Other *terps* were all but completely levelled, but when excavated may still provide archaeological evidence, particularly about their structure and the development of the *terps*. The Terpencentrum at the Groningen Institute of Archaeology (University of Groningen) has undertaken a number of excavations of the these steep-sided remnants in recent years.

The first time an area inhabited by Frisians is mentioned in the written sources is in Roman texts from the 1st and 2nd centuries AD, which describe the coastal zones of the Continent and its inhabitants (e.g. Pliny the Elder, *Naturalis historia*, iv.29 (15), xvi.2–4: Tacitus, *Germania*, 34.1: Rives 2002; Ptolemy, *Geographica*, 2.11.7: Stevenson 1932; cf. Bazelmans 2009 for a discussion). Famous is Pliny the Elder's description of the tidal-dwelling *terp* region as an environment truly belonging to neither land nor sea:

> There twice in each period of a day and a night the ocean with its vast tide sweeps in a flood over a measureless expanse, covering up Nature's age-long controversy and the region disputed as belonging whether to the land or to the sea. There this miserable race occupy elevated patches of ground or platforms built up by hand above the level of the highest tide experienced, living in huts erected on the sites so chosen, and resembling sailors in ships when the water covers the surrounding land, but shipwrecked people when the tide has retired, and round their huts they catch the fish escaping with the receding tide. (trans. H. Rackham 1952)

Pliny does not, however, call these unfortunate people who inhabit this twilight zone Frisians, but the Greater and Lesser *Chauci* (*Naturalis historia*, book 16:I). He was a Roman army officer. He would have noticed the remarkable opportunaties of the rich marsh if he had been of agrarian stock. The Roman authors referred to the Germanic population along the southern North Sea coast in a number of ways, e.g. as the *Frisii*, *Frisiavones*, *Cananefates* and *Chauci* (Nieuwhof 2015, 26–8; Galestin 2007/8, 687). The *Frisii* are usually regarded as the Frisians proper, whereas the *Frisiavones* are thought to have been people living within the Roman Empire in a Romanized society (Galestin 2007/8). Although the statements of the classical writers cannot be taken at face value, putting all the information together it appears that the *Frisii* and the *Chauci* inhabited the Dutch coastal area, both of which in turn could be subdivided into *minores* and *maiores* tribes. From west to east, the *Frisii minores* lived along the western coast (Noord-Holland), the

Frisii maiores on the central northern coast (Friesland and Groningen), the *Chauci minores* between the rivers Ems and Weser and the *Chauci maiores* (Nieuwhof 2015, 26–7; Galestin 2007/8, 692). How far the territories of these tribes extended inland is uncertain, but the story of the Frisian leaders Verritus and Malorix – bearing Celtic names (see Schrijver, this vol.) – relates how they travelled to Rome around AD 58 to discuss settlement on the banks of the Rhine. The two leaders are said to have moved to the Rhine with their families to settle there, but the land belonged to the Romans (Tacitus, *Annales*, XIII, 54). Archaeologically it is almost impossible to establish these boundaries or to test the historicity of these stories. Yet it may be pointed out that pottery traditionally recognized as belonging to the *Chauci* has also been found in the vicinity of Utrecht (Taayke 2007, 334–6; Galestin 2007/8, 693). Possibly, people from this group had crossed the Rhine, moving southward, which primarily indicates that groups of people and their territories, names and identities were dynamic and in constant flux.

A habitation hiatus?

Between these references and the references to Frisians in the Merovingian Period, there is a lacuna. The 4th century particularly is a 'dark age' with very little evidence. On the basis of archaeological traces, or rather the lack of them, a hiatus in the occupation of the *terp*-area is now postulated for this century, after which the coastal area became inhabited again in the 5th century. This idea is based not only on the absence of archaeological remains from the 4th century, but also on a change in material culture – including settlement structure and burial rites – in the following period (Knol 2009). The material remnants from the later period are usually considered 'Anglo-Saxon' in style or nature, and may be connected to the Anglo-Saxon migration. However, it is probably an oversimplification to state that 'Frisian' material culture made way for 'Anglo-Saxon' material culture, as has sometimes been done, and this is one of the reasons why the idea of an occupation hiatus has led to much discussion. Not only is the question of ethnic identity in relation to the material culture in the coastal zone debated; so too are the extent to which the population declined – does lack of traces automatically mean lack of people? – and the possible reasons for an abandonment (Nieuwhof 2013, 53–5). Recent studies have shown that there must have been many local differences in terms of habitation and depopulation in the Migration Period. Most likely, the area was not completely deserted but the population declined substantially – some perhaps moving across the North Sea, and to the south – leaving space for new settlers. In addition, there are differences in the extent of population decline throughout the southern North Sea coastal area. It seems to have been most intense in Westergo and Oostergo in current Friesland, whilst in parts of Groningen more traces of surviving occupation can be found. It appears that continuity was most marked in the eastern coastal area, whilst true discontinuity can most convincingly be proposed in the west (Nieuwhof 2013; Taayke 1996, V, 193). This discontinuity (and its variability) seems to have been due to a combination of social, political and environmental conditions (Nieuwhof 2013, 78).

The people who (re)populated the coastal area from the 5th century onwards are again called Frisians, but they must have been largely different people from the first Frisians who raised the dwelling *terps* (Knol 2009; Gerrets 2012; Nicolay 2005; Bazelmans

2009). However, the 'new Frisians' were originally coastal dwellers too, just like the first Frisians, and must have had much in common with them. It appears that the bulk of them came from various places along the North Sea coast (Knol 2009; Nicolay 2005). Although becoming 'Frisians', they retained close links with their homelands well into the 6th and 7th centuries (Knol 2009, 127). This is clearly reflected in the archaeological material, such as the prestige goods from this period found in the *terps*, which are discussed at length by Johan Nicolay in this volume. This socio-cultural network in which 'Frisians', 'Anglo-Saxons' and others were connected and functioned must have been important in the formation of identity as well as for its expression in material culture.

Bazelmans has argued that after the repopulation of Frisia, 'Frisian' was used more as a political term than an ethnic one, instigated by the Frankish people living further south (Bazelmans 2009). Indeed, whereas in Roman times many different Germanic groups were recognized, including the *Frisii*, once Frisia became incorporated into the Frankish realm at the time of Charlemagne, the whole coastal region (including the former Chaucian area) up into Germany was essentially made into one area called *Frisia*. The borders of this area are described in the *Lex Frisionum*, one of the *Leges Barbarorum* (Nijdam, this vol.). It was Frisian customary law codified on the command of Charlemagne just before AD 800. It defines the area in which it applied as stretching from the River *Sincfal* – now Zwin, on the border between Belgium and the Netherlands – in the south-west, up to the River Weser in Germany in the north-east. Despite most of the laws being in force throughout this Frisian area, there were three sub-areas in which some of the laws applied and some did not. From west to east, these extended up to the Vlie, between the Vlie and Lauwers, and east of the Lauwers.

Early-medieval Frisia

In the course of the Early Middle Ages, the coastal zone of the northern Netherlands became increasingly densely populated (Fig. 1.3). In due course most of the old *terps* were reoccupied. In this period the dead were either cremated – the ashes being buried in urns – or interred. Bodies might be buried in coffins made of hollowed logs (cf. Hines, this vol.). They were buried fully attired, and often provided with further grave goods. A representative example of such a cemetery, in use between AD 400 and 725, was excavated at Oosterbeintum (Knol *et al.* 1995–6). In these cemeteries the graves of horses and dogs may also be encountered (Prummel 1993).

Late-medieval sources often speak of the ancient Frisian kingdom, and even have pictures of the old Frisian kings' coat of arms (Bruch *et al.* 1956). Unfortunately there are very few contemporary written sources that offer any further information about such a kingdom. Just a few rulers are known by name, and the area and scope of their power is uncertain. They would have had their geographical bases, which may well have shifted around in the course of time, but such sites are known only in part. The leaders are sometimes referred to as kings, sometimes as dukes. We know just three of these leaders by name: Aldgisl, Radbod and Bubo (Halbertsma 2000; van Egmond 2005). Presumably the various regions were independent, while occasionally collaborating under a greater chieftain (Nicolay 2014, 346–66). For corroboration of this idea archaeology is indispensable, but it is historical tradition which delineates the various

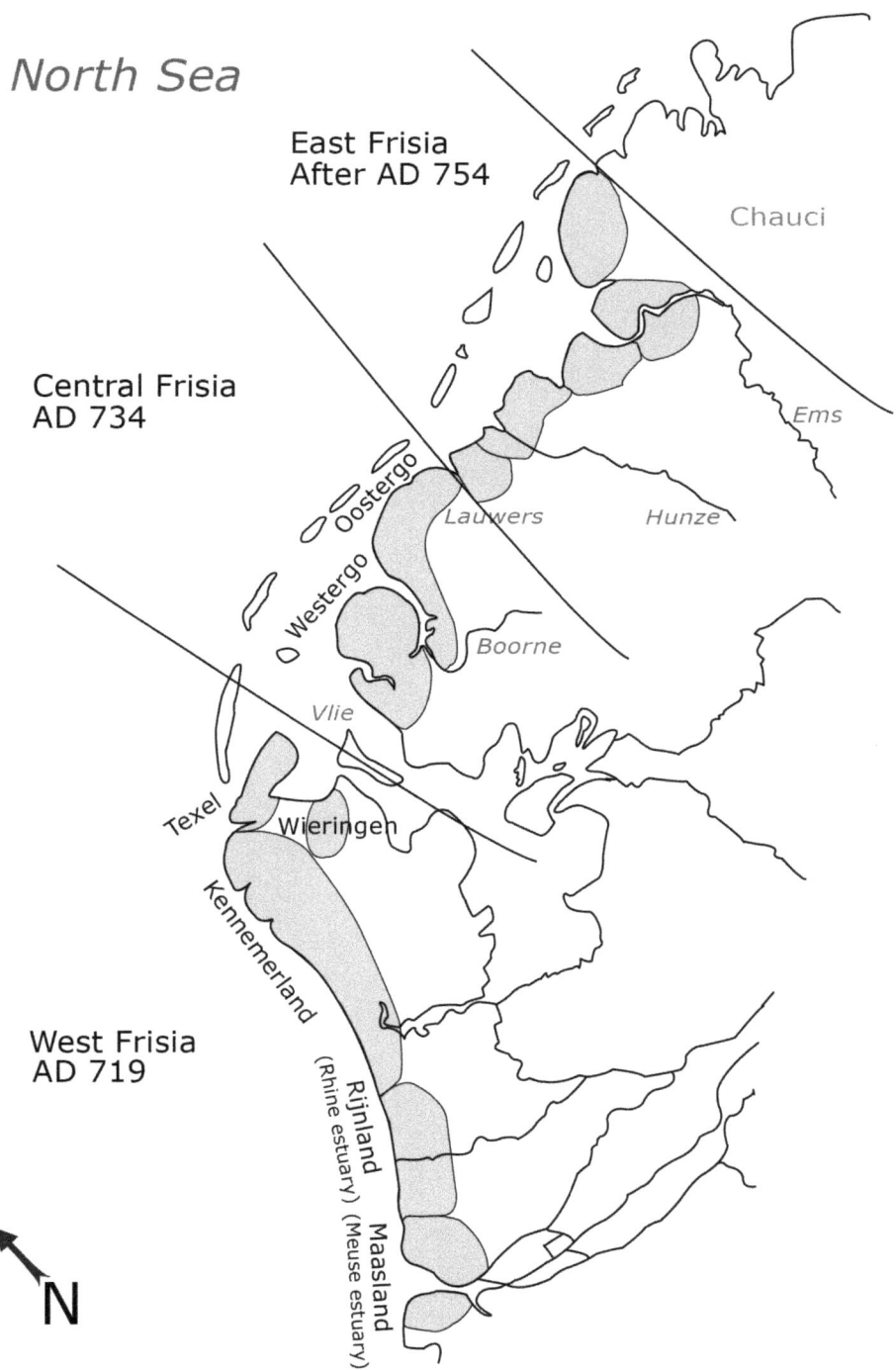

Fig. 1.3. The Frisian coastal area in the 8th century AD and the dates of conversion to Christianity.

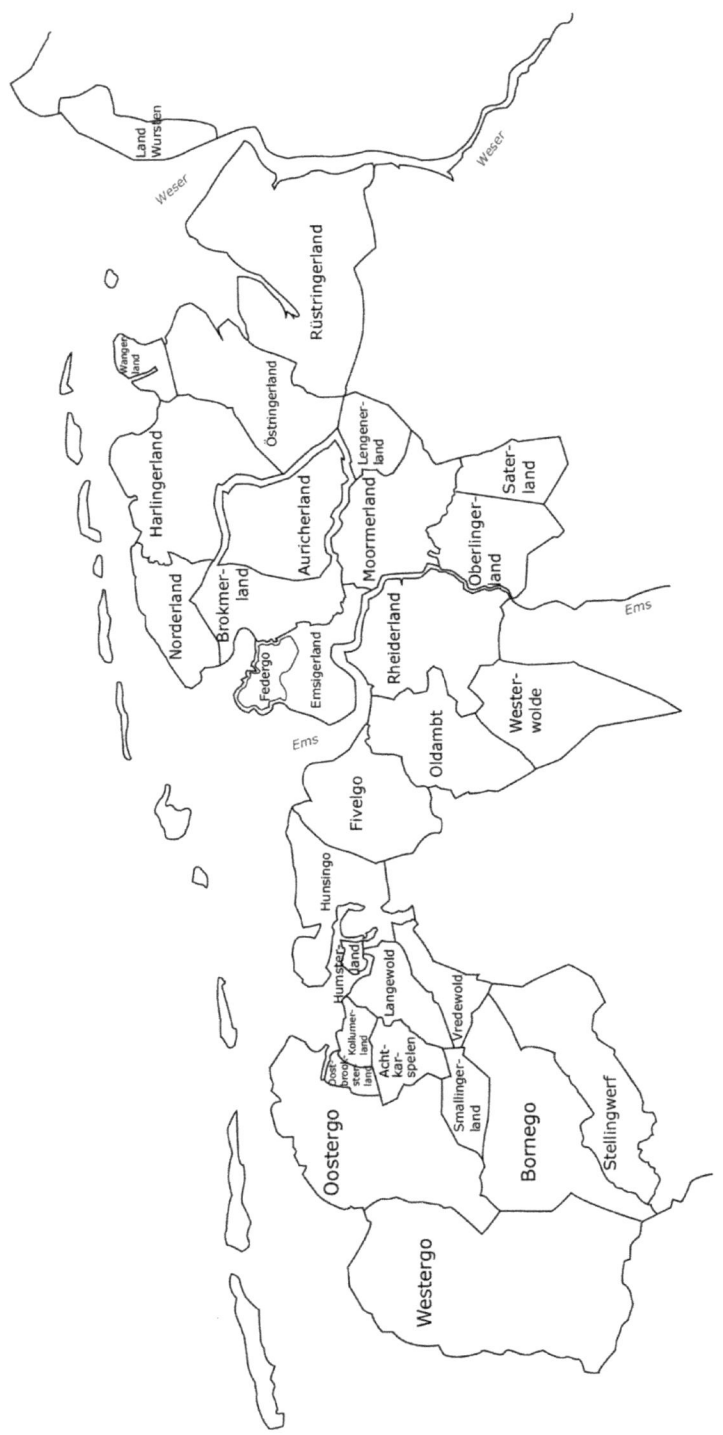

Fig. 1.4. The distribution of Frisian regions around AD 1300.

regions (Heidinga 1987). Scant Carolingian-period references to Frisian regions can be matched up with territories mentioned in later sources.

In 786, Charlemagne charged the missionary Liudger with converting the pagan regions of Hugmerchi, Hunusga, Fivilga, Emisga, Federitga and the island of Bant (Halbertsma 2000, 287–8). Liudger was made bishop of Münster in 805, and was given permission to add these territories to his diocese. In time, they formed a separate deanery, which survived up to the late 16th century as an enclave among other dioceses. As a result, this missionary region is well documented. The named areas, now in the province of Groningen, are known today as Humsterland, Hunsingo, Fivelingo, Eemsgo and Federgo, respectively, while the island of Bant in the Wadden Sea has long since been lost to the waves (Haarnagel 1979).

It is from these territories that in the 9th century people began to colonize the peat-bog margins. By the 10th century this colonization resulted in a doubling of the inhabited area and the emergence of new regions to be added to the diocese of Münster (e.g. Achtkarspelen, Langewold, Vredewold, Duurswold, Oldambt, Reiderland, Brokmerland, Auricherland, Moormerland and Oberledingerland: Slofstra 2008; de Langen 2011) (Fig. 1.4). Similar developments can be identified in neighbouring Friesland and North and South Holland, where the sources mention ancient regions such as Oostergo, Westergo, Sutergho, Wieringen and Kennemerland (Künzel et al. 1989, 204, 274–5, 336, 344, 393–4, 399–400). These recorded territories coincide with concentrations of 8th-century findspots. Heidinga has termed them 'nuclear regions' (Heidinga 1987). Each of them will have been ruled by leading families. It was they who determined the distribution of imported goods and, conversely, what should be done with the agricultural surplus, which is sure to have arisen. Periodically, the leading families must have had to reaffirm their power. On the basis of the distribution of early-medieval finds of gold and silver, Nicolay suggests some locations of these leading families' power bases (Nicolay 2014, figs. 13.2, 13.3 and 13.4). Another possibility is to examine historical sources that mention later royal estates, which are likely to go back to confiscated property of defeated Frisian leaders (Blok 1974, 72–9; Noomen 1990; 2007). On the evidence of the jewellery and other kind of prestige goods that have been found, the Frisian elite was well connected with Scandinavia, England and the Frankish realm. These finds include gold coins, brooches, bracteates, bronze vessels, cowrie shells, ivory and wheel-thrown pottery. Small-long brooches and annular brooches typical of England but seldom found on the Continent are quite common in Frisia (Knol 1993, 198–201; Hines, this vol.).The close contacts between the Frisian and English elites made it logical that English missionaries should come over to convert their Frisian brothers and sisters to Christianity.

The missionaries were aware that they should aim high: once the elite were converted, the common people would generally follow suit. Liudger understood that each of Frisia's small territories had its own petty chieftain, who was independent. One day he visited a prominent lady, Meinsuit, at her residence on the *terp* of Helwerd (Mol 2004; Noomen 2005, 69–70). How we should like to see the layout of that house! As the story goes, she had invited a famous blind bard to liven up the occasion. Liudger managed to convert the aged singer, Bernlef, who then miraculously regained his eyesight (Diekamp 1881, 30–1; Halbertsma 2000, 292–7). It can hardly be coincidental that the monastery of Werden later owned quite a lot of land just south of Helwerd. Helwerd itself is a modest-sized *terp*, but it lies not far from Kloosterwijtwerd (the name of which refers to its monastery, *klooster*) and the large *terp* of Usquert, the later site of a deanery church. The *Vita Ludgerii secunda* reveals that Liudger returned from Frisia with a great deal of treasure. In the course of his missionary activity he may well have got hold of old votive offerings to the pre-Christian deities (Nieuwland 1991, 28). Naturally this gold will then be missing from the archaeological record.

This of course raises the question of whether the archaeological record reveals anything at all about this dimly observable elite, and leaves us wondering about the graves of that social class. In terms of burial ritual, something remarkable continued in the 8th century. Throughout Frisia, we find graves containing weapons: often a sword, sometimes a long *seax*, sometimes both, and occasionally a shield boss. Glass drinking vessels also belong to such assemblages, as well as horse gear and horse and dog burials. By contrast, the preceding centuries saw very few weapon graves (Fig. 1.5).

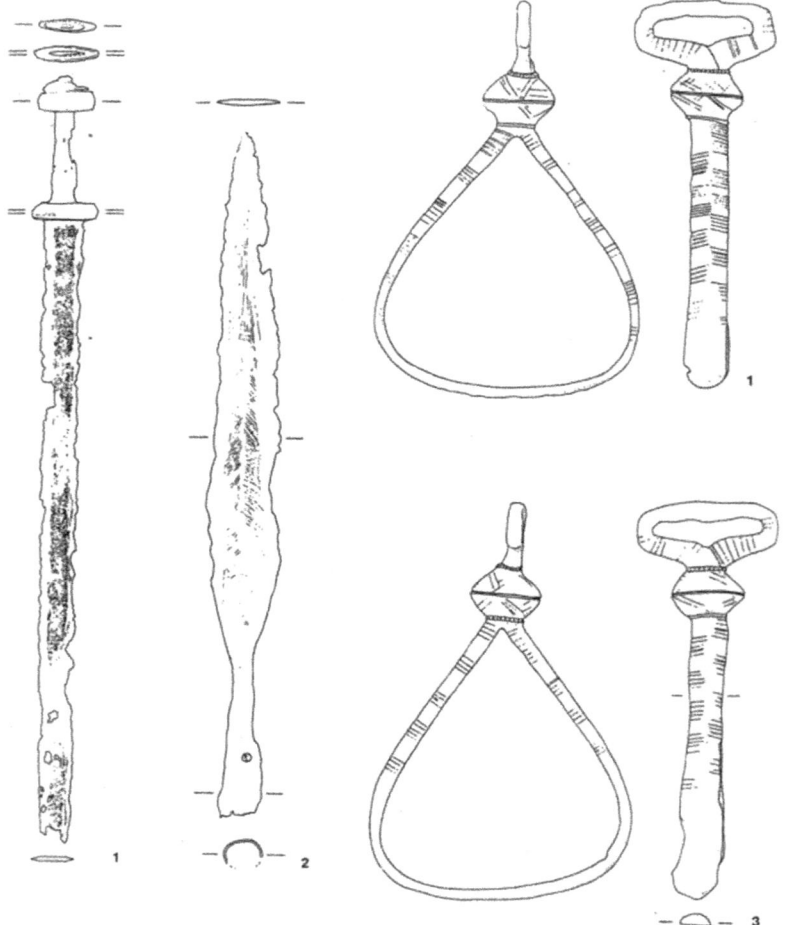

Fig. 1.5. The 8th-century weapon grave of Antum. Drawings H. J. M. Burgers (Archeologisch Instituut Vrije Universiteit) from Miedema 1983, fig. 136.1, fig. 137.2 and fig. 140.1–2.

Merovingian Period specimens are much less frequently found than Carolingian weapons, although their chances of archaeological survival should be roughly equal. There must be a reason for this change; possibly it was prompted by the Carolingian Frankish occupation of Frisia. People may have felt a need to express, in their funerary rites, the martial prowess of the deceased and his family (Knol and Bardet 1999; Knol 2001). In numerous cemeteries we find several contemporary graves containing weapons. In the western Netherlands, between the rivers Meuse and Rhine, the situation is fairly similar. At Valkenburg (South Holland) an early-medieval weapon grave was uncovered beneath the church; at Rijnsburg an unusual buckle turned up, and in Katwijk-Klein Duin the tip of a horn with bronze mounts. Unfortunately these cemeteries had also been disturbed, and rather haphazardly excavated a century ago (Dijkstra 2011, 223–45).

The coastal territory of the Frisians was criss-crossed with watercourses and rivers. Adjusting to such an environment required good means of waterborne transportation, and these made it possible to engage in commerce. From the 8th and 9th centuries especially there is a great deal of evidence of Frisian traders visiting emporia along the coasts of the North Sea and the Baltic. The written sources do not, however, offer much information regarding the provenance of these Frisian traders in terms of the various Frisian territories such as the emporium of Dorestad and its surroundings, the estuary of the Rhine and Meuse in the western Netherlands or the saltmarsh regions of the northern Netherlands and northern Germany. Presumably the hub of their activity lay at Dorestad.

Frisia and Frisians in the Viking Age

Although the Viking Age (*c.* AD 800–1050) is not a formally recognized archaeological period in Dutch archaeology, there are good reasons for distinguishing and defining a Viking Age in Frisia (between the rivers Zwin and Weser) on historical grounds, and for looking into Frisia's place in the Viking world in both an archaeological and a historical sense (IJssennagger 2013; 2015). Having been incorporated into the Frankish realm by the end of the 8th century, Frisia became a border zone at the margin of the empire, facing Denmark and the other, Scandinavian and Insular, Viking regions. As a region with traditionally close links to the pre-Viking Scandinavian and the Anglo-Saxon worlds, however, it was also a culturally intermediate zone between the Christian continental and the non-Christian Viking worlds (Lund 2006; IJssennagger 2013). As such, Frisia was a strategic region within the North Sea Viking world.

The first time Frisia was affected by Viking activity was in the year 810, when Danish Vikings attacked the Frisian coast – devastating all the islands – and imposed a tribute on the Frisians in response to a political conflict with the Franks (*Annales regni Francorum* 810: ed. Rau 1977, 94). Expansion of the Danish and Frankish realms led to rivalry over Frisia, Saxony and other areas, which continued into the 10th century (Henstra 2012, 195–6). Some have even called Frisia a 'no-man's land' between the two rival political powers (Reuter 1991, 69). For the two centuries following AD 810, the whole Frisian coastal area, as well as the sites on the rivers including the famous trading town of Dorestad and the Frankish realm beyond it, were subject to regular Viking attacks and demands for tribute. In addition, the Frankish rulers granted a number of Frisian coastal areas in fief to Danish warlords, from about 826 to 884. This provides the framework for Viking Age Frisia.

Written sources

Most of the information on the Viking Age in Frisia is provided by contemporary Frankish annals and chronicles, such as that relating to the 810 attack. These Latin sources shed light on where and when Viking attacks in Frisia occurred. Sometimes they provide details – true or false – of the number of people involved, of who were in charge and what the outcome was. For instance, in the entry for 873 in the *Annales Bertiniani*, *Annales Xantenses* and the *Annales Fuldense*, we read that a Viking leader named Rodulf, who previously raided in the British Isles ('across the sea'), and his war-band were raiding Oostergo when Rodulf met his death. According to the Frankish sources either 500 or 800 Vikings died with him, after which the remaining Vikings departed with the ships. The numbers in the sources should not be taken on face value, as is implicit in the variance between 500 and 800 casualties on the Danish side.

The Frankish sources also inform us about the granting of areas in fief or benefice to Danish warlords. These were pagan or converted Danes of one royal family in the 9th century (Coupland 1998). The benefices primarily concerned Walcheren in Zeeland, Dorestad and the surrounding area, Kennemerland including Wieringen and Texel in North Holland (West Frisia) and Rüstringen in Ostfriesland. Others parts of Frisia continued to be ruled by Christian Frankish or Frisian counts; for instance, Central Frisia, consisting of Oostergo and Westergo, and eastern Frisia, covering the modern provinces of Groningen and Drenthe, was not given in benefice, as far as we know.

Information concerning Frisia and Frisians in the Viking Age, on the other hand, is provided by Scandinavian and Insular sources as well – some of which are contemporary and some of which are recorded at a later date. They provide examples of Frisians in the context of the North Sea world, and information on Vikings coming from or via Frisia, travelling across the North Sea and taking part in activities in the British Isles. The Icelandic *Egils saga Skalla-Grímssonar*, about the 9th-century Viking hero Egill, describes how he and his comrade 'go viking' in Frisia (ch. 49 and 69 (70); ed. Nordal 1933; trans. Scudder 1997). Despite many heroic elements which may not be historical, the description of the Frisian landscape and of the Vikings and Frisians jumping across small watercourses when chasing each other is very realistic for Frisia.

Given that in this period there was no indigenous tradition of writing in Frisia apart from some runic inscriptions in Anglo-Frisian, one of which is dated to the 9th century (Knol and Looijenga 1990), the earliest sources in Old Frisian to reflect Viking activities are the Old Frisian law texts from the 12th century onwards (see the discussion by Nijdam, this vol.). A poetic description of Viking attacks and the Frisian's duty to defend the Frisian coast both against the 'flood of wild Vikings' and against the salty sea is preserved in a number of different law texts, and represents a collective memory of Viking Age events that had probably been orally transmitted (Vries 2007; IJssennagger 2013, 81).

Material traces

Archaeology has started to contribute more to the image of this period since the discovery of the Westerklief hoards in 1996 and subsequently (Besteman 2006/7). For a long time, these and the scattered finds primarily of jewellery and dress-accessories from Dorestad and the river area were the only material traces of a Viking Age in Frisia (Willemsen 2009). Today, the contribution of archeology mostly takes the form of small finds of items such as jewellery and dirhams by metal detectorists, as well as occasional finds during excavations such as the Borre-style buckle found in the ring-fortress of Domburg (Ufkes 2011). However, finds are still few and far between, particularly in comparison with other areas of Viking activity. This is mostly due to the different character of Viking Age activity in Frisia and, say, England, but may partly also be attributable to the former lack of a national finds-recording system in the Netherlands comparable to the Portable Antiquities Scheme in Britain. Happily, such a system has now been set up.[1]

Metal-detected finds increasingly point to cross-North Sea connections rather than just Viking activity in Frisia itself. This goes hand in hand with a shift in focus from finding evidence of Vikings in Frisia, to looking into Frisia during the Viking Age. A case in point is the recent find of a fragment of a Hiberno-Scandinavian broad-band arm-ring of late-9th- or early-10th-century date on the Isle of Texel (IJssennagger 2015; see Sheenan 2011 for the most concise information on the arm-rings). Being the first find of this type in the Netherlands, and even the first of this type outside Scandinavia and the British Isles, it is a striking find. The arm-ring was presumably made in the Irish Sea region, whilst the inspiration for the type must have come from southern Scandinavia. The transfer of the prototypes and the context for the development of the Hiberno-Scandinavian broad-band type are thought to relate to the Great Army and their connections with Denmark, England, Ireland and possibly Frisia.

In addition, finds that may be connected to Viking activity in Frisia may not always be recognized as such. This can be exemplified by the silver hoards that were deposited in the northern Netherlands (Central Frisia) in the Viking Age, and that coincide with Viking activity (Knol 2005; Coupland 2006). Being mixed hoards, they are different in character from the usual Carolingian Period hoards. Equally, they cannot be recognized as Scandinavian hoards in the way the Westerklief hoards can, as they do not contain any Viking silver. However, if such a mixed hoard containing continental silver were found in Scandinavia, it would immediately be classified as a Viking hoard and the result of Viking activity. As Knol (2005; 2010) and Coupland (2006) suggest, we should therefore view the silver hoards in Frisia in relation to Viking activity.

Across the sea

Throughout the Viking Age, there is substantial evidence for trade between on the one hand the Frisian area, through emporia like Dorestad, Walichrum and subsequently Tiel, and on the other, the Scandinavian and English emporia. It meant a lot of travelling back and forth across the sea and probably great numbers of Frisians were

---

[1] Under the title PAN: Portable Antiquities of the Netherlands, https://www.portable-antiquities.nl.

involved in this. As a maritime-oriented nation they at least possessed the skills and equipment for doing so.

The activity of Rodulf and his war-band mentioned above is a further example of how Vikings travelled across the North Sea between Frisia and the British Isles. It is clear that Viking war-bands, mostly from southern Scandinavia but probably recruiting warriors along the way, visited Frisia because it was a strategic region: hence the attacks, the extraction of tribute and the benefices. From here the war-bands travelled across the North Sea to England and Ireland, and vice versa. It is assumed that part of the famous Great Army active in England from 865 onwards joined up from or via Frisia, which provides an interesting context for the find from Texel. The men in the army need not have been Frisians, but could have been Vikings who had made a name in Frisia (McLeod 2014, 132–58; Bremmer 1981, 78). In addition, war-bands that had been part of the Great Army came to Frisia after their campaigns in England. This is the case for the Danish Godfrid and his men, who in 879 came to the Continent, raided, commended himself to Charles the Fat, and in 882 was given a Frisian benefice. This was the last Danish fiefdom in Frisia.

The idea that Frisians joined Viking war-bands on their campaigns – in England or elsewhere – has earlier been expressed on the basis of one of the Old Frisian law codes. The passage states that if a Frisian man is captured by Vikings and forced to join them, he shall be considered innocent since his Viking activities were performed under duress. The passage implies that Frisians might also join the Vikings voluntarily (Samplonius 1998, 98; Jesch 2004, 257). This 13th-century recollection of 9th-century events and their impact on the Frisian coastal area marks the chronological end of our historical Frisians in an archaeological light.

References

Primary sources

Annales Regni Francorum, ed. Reinhold Rau, 1972, Quellen zur Karolingischen Reichsgeschichte ii (Darmstadt).
Egils saga Skalla-Grímssonar, ed. Sigurður Nordal 1933, Íslenzk Fornrit II (Reykjavík).
Egil's Saga, trans. Bernard Scudder 1997 (ed. Svanhildur Óskarsdóttir, 2004) (London).
Tacitus, *Germania,* trans. J. B. Rives 2002 (Oxford).

Secondary sources

Bazelmans, Jos 2005, 'Die Wurten von Dongjum-Heringa, Peins-oost und Wijnaldum-Tjitsma: kleinmaβstäblicher Deichbau in ur- und frühgeschichtlicher Zeit des nördlichen Westergo'. In *Kulturlandschaft Marsch. Naturgeschichte Gegenwart*, Schriftenreihe des Landesmuseums für Natur und Mensch 33, ed. M. Fansa (Oldenburg), 68–84.
Bazelmans, Jos 2009, 'The early-medieval use of ethnic names from classical antiquity: the case of the Frisians'. In *Ethnic Constructs in Antiquity. The Role of Power and Tradition*, ed. T. Derks and N. Roymans (Amsterdam), 321–38.
Bazelmans, Jos, Henny Groenendijk, Gilles de Langen *et al.* 2009, 'De late prehistorie en protohistorie van holoceen Noord-Nederland', *Nationale Onderzoeksagenda Archeologie,* chapter 12 (Leeuwarden).

Bazelmans, Jos, Dirk Meier, Annet Nieuwhof, Theo Spek, and Peter Vos 2012, 'Understanding the cultural historical value of the Wadden Sea Region. The co-evolution of environment and society in the Wadden Sea area in the Holocene up until Early Modern Times (11,700 BC–1800 AD): an outline', *Ocean & Coastal Management* 68, 114–26.
Besteman, Jan C., with contributions by Gert Rispling and Simon Coupland. 2006-7, 'A second Viking silver hoard from Wieringen: Westerklief II', *Jaarboek voor munt- en penningkunde* 93-4, 5–80.
Bremmer Jr., Rolf H. 1981, 'Frisians in Anglo-Saxon England: a historical and toponymical investigation'. In *Fryske Nammen*, ed. N. R. Århammar, W. T. Beetstra, Phillipus.H. Breuker and J. J. Spahr van der Hoek (Leeuwarden), 45–94.
Brouwers, Wil, Esther Jansma and Martijn Manders 2015, 'Middeleeuwse scheepsresten in Nederland: de Vroege Middeleeuwen (500–1050)', *ArcheoBrief* 19(3), 6–24.
Bruch, H., K. M. van der Kooi, H. M. Mensonides, K. Sierksma and J. Visser 1956, *De Fryske flagge. Rapport en advys fan de kommisje ta bestudearring fan de Fryske flagge* (Leeuwarden).
Coupland, Simon 1998, 'From poachers to gamekeepers. Scandinavian warlords and Carolingian kings', *Early Medieval Europe* 7(1), 85–114.
Coupland, Simon 2006, 'Between the Devil and the Deep Blue Sea'. In *Coinage and History in the North Sea World, c. AD 500–1250: Essays in Honour of Marion Archibald*, ed. Barrie Cook and Gareth Williams (Leiden), 241–66.
Dijkstra, Menno F. P. 2011, *Rondom de mondingen van Rijn en Maas. Landschape en bewoning tussen de 3e en de 9e eeuw in Zuid-Holland, in het bijzonder de Oude Rijnstreek* (Leiden).
Es, Wim A. van 1990, 'Dorestad centred'. In *Medieval Archaeology in the Netherlands: Studies presented to H. H. van Regteren Altena*, Studies in Prae- En Protohistorie 4, ed. J. C. Bestemann, J. M. Bos and H. A. Heidinga (Assen and Maastricht), 151–82.
Es, Wim A. van, and W. J. H. Verwers 1980, *Excavations at Dorestad 1 The Harbour: Hoogstraat 1* (Amersfoort).
Es, Wim A. van, and W. J. H. Verwers 2009, *Excavations at Dorestad 3 Hoogstraat 0, II-IV*. (Amersfoort).
Es, Wim A. van, and W. J. H. Verwers 2015, *Excavations at Dorestad 4 The Settlement on the River bank Area* (Amersfoort).
Egmond, Wolfert van 2005, 'Radbod van de Friezen, een aristocraat in de periferie', *Millennium, tijdschrift voor middeleeuwse studies* 19 (1), 24–44.
Galestin, Marjan C. 2007/2008, '*Frisii* and *Frisiavones*', *Palaeohistoria* 49/50, 287–708.
Giffen, Albert E. van 1940, 'Een systematisch onderzoek in een der Tuinster wierden te Leens', *Jaarverslagen van de Vereniging voor Terpenonderzoek* 20(4), 26–115 (and fig. 1–28).
Haarnagel, W, 1979, 'Burcana archäologisches und landschaftsgeschichtliches'. In *Reallexikon der Germanischen Altertumskunde* 4, 114–17.
Halbertsma, Herre 2000, *Frieslands Oudheid. Het rijk van de Friese koningen, opkomst en ondergang* (Utrecht).
Heidinga, H. Antonie 1987, *Medieval Settlement and Economy north of the Lower Rhine* (Assen).
Henstra, Dirk Jan 2012, *Friese graafschappen tussen Zwin en Weser* (Assen).
IJssennagger, Nelleke L. 2013, 'Between Frankish and Viking. Frisia and Frisians in the Viking Age', *Viking and Medieval Scandinavia* 9, 69–98.
IJssennagger, Nelleke L. 2015, 'A Viking find from the Isle of Texel (Netherlands) and its implications', *Viking and Medieval Scandinavia* 11, 127–42.
Knol, Egge 1993, *De Noordnederlandse kustlanden in de Vroege Middeleeuwen* (Groningen).
Knol, Egge 2001, 'Carolingian weapons from the Northern Netherlands, particularly from the cemetery of Godlinze'. In *Kingdoms and Regionality, Transactions from the 49th Sachsensymposium 1998 in Uppsala*, ed. B. Arrhenius (Stockholm), 115–20.
Knol, Egge 2005, 'Gold und Silber aus Marsum – karolingische Schatzfunde in den Niederlanden'. In *Die Macht des Silbers: karolingische Schatze im Norden*, ed. E.Wamers and M. Brandt (Regensburg), 112–18.

Knol, Egge 2009,' Anglo-Saxon migration reflected in cemeteries in the northern Netherlands'. In *Foreigners in Early Medieval Europe: Thirteen International Studies on Early Medieval Mobility*, ed. D. Quast and H. W. Böhme (Regensburg), 113–29.

Knol, Egge 2010, 'Frisia in Carolingian times'. In *Viking Trade and Settlement in Continental Western Europe*, ed. I. Skibsted Klæsøe (Copenhagen), 43–60.

Knol, Egge, and Xandra Bardet 1999, 'Carolingian weapons from the cemetery of Godlinze, The Netherlands'. In *In Discussion with the Past, Archaeological Studies Presented to W. A. van Es*, ed. H. Sarfatij, W. J. H. Verwers and P. J. Woltering (Zwolle–Amersfoort), 213–25.

Knol, Egge, Wietske Prummel, Hilde T. Uytterschaut, Menno L. P. Hoogland, Wil A. Casparie, Gilles J. De Langen, Evert Kramer, and Jaap Schelvis 1995–6, 'The early medieval cemetery of Oosterbeintum (Friesland)', *Palaeohistoria* 37/38, 245–416.

Knol, Egge, and Tineke Looijenga 1990, 'A tau staff with runic inscriptions from Bernsterburen (Friesland)'. In *Aspects of Old Frisian Philology*. Amsterdamer Beiträge zur älteren Germanistik 31-2, ed. R. H. Bremmer, G. van der Meer and O. Vries, 226–41.

Knottnerus, Otto S. 2002, 'Malaria around the North Sea: a survey'. In *Climatic Development and History of the North Atlantic Realm: Hanse Conference Report*, ed. G. Wefer, W. H. Berger, K. Behre, E. Jansen (Berlin–Heidelberg), 339–53.

Künzel, Rudi E., Dirk P. Blok and J. M. Verhoeff 1989, *Lexicon van Nederlandse toponiemen tot 1200* (Amsterdam).

Langen, Gilles J. de 1992, *Middeleeuws Friesland* (Groningen).

Langen, Gilles J. de 2011, 'De gang naar een ander landschap'. In *Gevormd en omgevormd landschap van prehistorie tot middeleeuwen*, ed. M. Niekus (Assen), 70–97.

Lund, Niels 2006. 'Friesland og vikingerne', *Fireogtyvende tværfaglige vikingesymposium, Hikuin*, 7–16.

Lengsveld, Klaus J. ed. 1998. *Halligleben um 1900* (Heide).

McLeod, Shane 2014, *The Beginning of Scandinavian Settlement in England. The Viking 'Great Army' and Early Settlers, c. 865–900* (Turnhout).

Mol, Hans 2004, 'De dood van Bonifatius: gevolg van een verkeerde kersteningsstrategie?', *Fryslân* 10(3), 16–20.

Nicolay, Johan A. W. 2010, 'De nederzettingssporen en hun fasering'. In *Terpbewoning in oostelijk Friesland. Twee opgravingen in het voormalige kweldergebied van Oostergo*, Groningen Archaeological Studies 10, ed. J. A. W. Nicolay (Groningen), 94–131.

Nicolay, Johan A. W. 2014, *The Splendour of Power: Early Medieval Kingship and the Use of Gold and Silver in the Southern North Sea Area (5th to 7th Century AD)*, Groningen Archaeological Studies 28 (Groningen).

Nicolay, Johan A. W. 2015, 'Het kwelderland als cultuurlandschap: een model'. In *Graven aan de voet van de Achlumer dorpsterp*, ed. J. A. W. Nicolay and Gilles de Langen (Groningen), 205–21.

Nieuwhof, Annet 2006, 'Changing landscape and grazing: macro-remains from the *terp* Peinseast, provincie of Friesland, The Netherlands', *Vegetation History and Archaeobotany* 15, 125–36.

Nieuwhof, Annet 2010, 'Living in a dynamic landscape: prehistoric and proto-historic occupation of the northern-Netherlands coastal area'. In *Science for Nature Conservation and Management: the Wadden Sea Ecosystem and EU Directives. Proceedings of the 12th International Scientific Wadden Sea Symposium in Wilhelmshaven, Germany, 30 March - 3 April 2009*, Wadden Sea Ecosystem No. 26, ed, H. Marencic *et al.* (Willemshaven), 173–8.

Nieuwhof, Annet 2013 'Anglo-Saxon immigration or continuity? Ezinge and the coastal area of the northern Netherlands in the Migration Period.', *Journal of Archaeology in the Low Countries* 5 (1), 53–83.

Nieuwhof, Annet 2015, *Eight Human Skulls in a Dung Heap and More. Ritual Practice in the Terp Region of the Northern Netherlands 600 BC – AD 300*, Groningen Archaeological Studies volume 29 (Groningen).

Nieuwhof, Annet, and Henk Woldring 2007, 'Botanische Resten'. In *De Leege Wier van Englum. Archeologisch onderzoek in het Reitdiepgebied*, Jaarverslagen van de Vereniging voor

Terpenonderzoek 91, 160–76.
Nieuwland, Jeannette 1991, "De Friezen gedenken zijn wonderbare daden" De functie van wonderen in de Friese kersteningstijd. *Utrechtse Historische Cahiers* 12 (1), 1–103.
Noomen, Paul N. 1990, 'Koningsgoed in Groningen. Het dominiale verleden van de stad'. In *Groningen 1040, Archeologie en oudste geschiedenis van de stad Groningen*, ed. J. W. Boersma, J. F. J. van den Broek and G. J. D. Offerman (Bedum), 97–144.
Noomen, Paul N. 1999, 'De goederen van de abij Echternach in de Friese landen', *Jaarboek voor middeleeuwse geschiedenis* 2, 7–37.
Noomen, Paul N. 2005, 'Kerstening en kerkstichting in Friesland', *Millennium. Tijdschrift voor middeleeuwse studies* 19 (1), 61–72.
Noomen, Paul N. 2007, 'Winsum in de Vroege Middeleeuwen'. In *Winsum 1057–2007*, ed J. Tersteeg and R. Alma (Winsum), 65–87.
Postma, Daniel 2015, *Het zodenhuis van Firdgum. Middeleeuwse boerderijbouw in het Friese kustgebied tussen 400 en 1300* (Groningen).
Prison, H. 2009, 'Von Prielen und Sielen. Ein kaiserzetiliches Siel?', *Archäeologie in Niedersachsen* 12, 127–9.
Prummel, Wietske 1993, 'Paarden en honden uit vroeg-middeleeuwse grafvelden'. In *Het tweede leven van onze doden. Voordrachten gehouden tijdens het symposium over het grafrituel in de pre- en protohistorie van Nederland op 16 mei 1992*, Nederlandse Archeologische Rapporten 15, ed. E. Drenth, W. A. M. Hessing and E. Knol (Amersfoort), 53–60.
Reuter, Timothy, 1991, *Germany in the Early Middle Ages, c. 800–1056* (London).
Schepers, Mans 2014. 'Reconstructing Vegetation Diversity in Coastal Landscapes'. Ph.D. dissertation, University of Groningen (Groningen).
Sheehan, John 2011,'Hiberno-Scandinavian broad-band arm-rings'. In *The Cuerdale Hoard and Related Viking-Age Silver and Gold from Britain and Ireland in the British Museum*, ed. J. Graham-Campbell (London), 94–100.
Siegmüller, Annette, and Christina Peek 2015, 'Das Bootgrab aus dem frühmittelalterlichen Gräberfeld von Dunum, Ldkr. Wittmund', *Nachrichten Marschenrat zur Förderung der Forschung im Küstengebiet der Nordsee* 52, 46–8.
Slofstra, Jan 2008, 'De kolonisatie van de Friese veengebieden (ca. 900–1200)'. In *Diggelgoud, 25 jaar Archeologisk Wurkferbân: Archeologisch onderzoek in Fryslân*, ed. K. Huisman, K. Bekkema, J. M. Bos, H. de Jong, E.Kramer and R. Salverda (Leeuwarden), 206–30.
Taayke, Ernst 2007, 'Recensie van Peter Schmidt, Die Keramikfunde der Grabung Feddersen Wierde', *Westerheem* 56, 334–6.
Thiemann, B., and Jan F. Kegler 2013, 'Das Boot im Damm – ein frühmittelalterlicher Einbaum aus Jemgum, Ldkr. Leer (Ostfriesland)', *Siedlungs- und Küstenforschung im südlichen Nordseegebiet* 36, 235–47.
Ufkes, Adrie. 2011, *Een archeologische opgraving in de vroegmiddeleeuwse ringwalburg van Domburg, gem. Veere (Z.)*, ARC-publicaties 223 (Groningen).
Vos, Peter C. 2015 *Origin of the Dutch Coastal Landscape: Long-Term Landscape Evolution of the Netherlands during the Holocene, Described and Visualized in National, Regional and Local Paleogeographical Map Series* (Groningen).
Vos, Peter C., and Egge Knol 2015, 'Holocene landscape reconstruction of the Wadden Sea area between Marsdiep and Weser', *Netherlands Journal of Geosciences* 94 (2), 157–83.
Vries, Oebele 2007, *Asega, is het dingtijd?* (Leeuwarden–Utrecht).
Waasdorp, J. A., and E. Eimermann 2008, *Solleveld. Een opgraving naar een Merovingisch grafveld aan de rand van Den Haag*, Haagse Oudheidkundige Publicaties 10 (Den Haag).
Waterbolk, H. Tjalling 1991, 'Ezinge'. In *Reallexikon der Germanischen Altertumskunde* 8(1/2), 60–76.
Willemsen, Annemarieke 2004, 'Scattered across the Waterside: Viking Finds from the Netherlands'. In *Vikings on the Rhine: Recent Research on Early Medieval Relations between the Rhinelands and Scandinavia*, ed. R. Simek and U. Engel (Wien), 65–82.

Willemsen, Annemarieke, and Hanneke Kik ed. 2010, *Dorestad in an International Framework: New Research on Centers of Trade and Coinage in Carolingian Times* (Turnhout).

Woltering, Philippus J., J. C. Besteman and J. F. van Regteren Altena 1999, 'Early Medieval North Holland Surveyed. The Hollands Noorderkwartier Sheet: Early Middle Ages of the Archaeological Map of the Netherlands.' *Berichten Rijksdienst voor het Oudheidkundig Bodemonderzoek* 43, 361–70.

2

The Anglo-Frisian Question

John Hines

A major issue in mid-19th-century European politics was the 'Schleswig-Holstein question', of which the later British Prime Minister and former Foreign Secretary Lord Palmerston is famously alleged to have said:

> Only three people were completely acquainted with the truth: the Prince Consort, who is dead; a German professor, who is in a lunatic asylum; and I, who have forgotten all about it.

The disputed matters in fact involved the succession to the dukedoms of Schleswig and Holstein, and the conflicting interests of the Danish crown and Prussian/German nationalists. The anecdote of Palmerston's quip is, alas, probably apocryphal: it emerged in the earlier twentieth century, when, not least in the shadow of the Great War, it was intellectually fashionable to caricature the Victorian statesman as a laconic patrician (Grant Robertson 1918, 156; Strachey 1921, 308; cf. Lorne 1892, 210 and 221–2). The Anglo-Frisian question may not be as arcane as the Schleswig-Holstein question, nor as amenable to exploitation for either political or satirical ambitions of this scale. Nonetheless the analogy is more than merely playful, in that clarifying what exactly the problem *is*, is indeed the key issue.

Of course, there cannot be just *one* question, or *one* answer. On the contrary, even the most superficial idea of what might be meant by the Anglo-Frisian question is likely to involve recognition of the fact that close similarities between England and Frisia, two areas only around a hundred sea-miles apart across the North Sea, exist in quite diverse features of the populations and their cultures: their language; aspects of their material culture; their early laws; and more. An initial proposal for how to formulate the question could therefore be whether there is any deeper explanation for these similarities other than proximity. Is there, very simply, anything special in the relationship, either in terms of its origins or in terms of its role? After all, both England and Frisia have long been equally close neighbours to the French people and state, and to the Francophone Continent, yet with clear contrasts in most of the cultural characteristics which can be claimed to show some degree of 'Anglo-Frisian' relationship.

While recent and new finds, new techniques and recent and new research continually advance our understanding of this relationship, which involves substantial areas of land and a major period of history, it is still primarily the initiative of asking for the Anglo-Frisian question to be defined and discussed at all that is the really new and the most important factor for a volume such as the present one. It is genuinely surprising that this topic has not been more fully investigated before now. Across a range of separate academic disciplines, there has been no shortage of recognition of remarkably close parallels between England and her 'Frisian' neighbours in the closest lands along and behind the coasts of the opposite side of the North Sea. The history of the Germanic and English languages – called philology in English; *historische Sprachwissenschaft* in German, which is not quite the same as our 'historical linguistics' – uses the term 'Anglo-Frisian' for a series of distinctive features found in these two members of the Germanic language family which could be explained by an ancestral stage at which these were part of a single, undifferentiated, language variety within Germanic (Strang 1970, 376–88; Nielsen 1981; 1998, 42–57; Stiles 1995; Kortlandt 2008). The term Anglo-Frisian is also used in the study of runic writing (e.g. Bammesberger 1991; 1996; 2005; Page 1999, 16–21, 43–4; Düwel 2008, 71–87), but not for exactly the same reasons as those for thinking of Old English and Old Frisian as once having formed a homogeneous linguistic unit. *Angelsaksisch* has been used as a regular term to describe a style and set of finds in Dutch archaeology, particularly pottery (Boeles 1951, 235; van Es 1967, 310–17; Knol 1993, 53–5). Historians have to deal not only with the similarities in the Old Frisian and Old English laws (Lendinara 1997; Nijdam, this vol.), but also with tantalizing associations of the name of the Frisian people with England – for instance in Procopius of Caesarea's Byzantine history, and in place-names – and with the weight of Anglo-Saxon Church involvement in the conversion of Frisia in the 8th century (Dijkstra and de Konig, this vol.; Talbot 1954; Wood 2001; Mayr-Harting 1991, esp. 262–73).

The very first more focused 'Anglo-Frisian question' that needs to be addressed, then, is why this wealth of evidence for a genuinely close connection between these peoples and cultures has not led to the level of comparative and integrated scholarly research one could expect. It is relatively easy to identify what one may call 'infrastructural' factors that have created a barrier. There have never been more than a tiny handful of centres of Dutch studies in the United Kingdom. British historical and cultural studies concerned with the Continent have tended to be dependent upon the study of the continental languages, and this has directed attention elsewhere. The infamous monoglottalism of the British is exaggerated – and indeed is a regrettable by-product of the fact that the English language has become the international *lingua franca* – but British scholars can usually at best be expected to be able to use French, German, Italian or Spanish historical and archaeological publications, but very rarely Dutch-language material (which will similarly be accessible in relatively few libraries).

All of this being recognized, we might still have expected the key agenda for research in early Anglo-Saxon studies over the past two generations to have encouraged a serious engagement with Frisian studies and Frisian archaeology: not only the continuing debate over the origins of Anglo-Saxon England in a putative 'Migration Period', but perhaps above all the increasing sophistication of studies and modelling of settlement evidence and its environmental and ecological contexts (Hamerow 1994; 2004; Härke 2011; Rippon et al. 2014; 2015; Jones 1996, 186–243; Bloemers and van Dorp eds 1991, esp. 265–360; Vos 1999; Zimmermann 1999). Here, in fact, one may to some extent point the critical spotlight in a different direction for a while, and note how the particular and really rather local traditions of *terpenonderzoek* have not always been closely engaged with international research traditions (see further Knol and IJssennagger, this vol.), while a divided orientation in Dutch early-medieval archaeology, between a focus on the Late Antique *limes* and the influence of the Frankish successor states on the one hand, and the more autonomous subsistence and settlement strategies of the northern areas of the Netherlands on the other, has tended to dissipate collective scholarly focus far more than, say, the rivalry between period-specific specialists such as Romanists, prehistorians and medieval (and later) archaeologists has in Britain.

None of these, however, are major hurdles to overcome, and to identify them as the principal practical issues to be recognized and addressed is not to imply they are excuses, either for not having dealt with these issues in the past, or for not dealing with them in the immediate future. The key point to emphasize is that the field of Anglo-Frisian studies is underdeveloped not because of intrinsic obstacles to progress but simply because there has been a lack of sufficient focus upon it. That focus needs to be concentrated; it needs to be international; and it needs to be collaborative. This is precisely what the current volume seeks to initiate and to stimulate.

The language question

It is interesting in itself that the topic of linguistic similarities and relationship between Old and Middle English on the one hand and Old Frisian on the other appears an appropriate place to start, because it illustrates how very hard it is for cultural history and scholarship not to regard language as truly essential to identity: if two groups of people are very closely related in language, we tend to assume they are very closely connected historically and culturally, and possibly or even probably genetically related as well. It would be consistent with that principle that the origin of the idea of a special Anglo-Frisian branch of Germanic is attributed to a Dutch scholar, Franciscus Junius filius – son of the professor of theology at Leiden, born in 1591 – who would have had access to the Frisian language in order to be able to observe the parallel (Breuker 1990). He was not alone in developing the theory, with other Dutch scholars, Vlitius in the 17th century and Halbertsma in the 19th, making vital early contributions (Nielsen 1981, 40–7; Halbertsma 1836). It would, however, greatly over-simplify matters to postulate that close proximity to Frisian as a living language could be the only context in which this scholarly observation could have been made. For the observation to have been embodied in the learned writings of a European antiquary, that might be true; but one of the most important aspects of the very nature of language is that a natural language is used by every community, everywhere, and that where people come into contact, they develop ways of talking to one another (Lyons 1968, 39).

Middle Dutch speakers, usually referred to as Flemings, were present in medieval England and Wales, with what appears to have been a substantial settlement in Pembrokeshire (*Brut y Tywysogion*, s.a. 1105: Williams ab Ithel ed. 1860, 80–3) and a recognizable émigré community in London. Middle Dutch literature was mined or even plagiarized as a source in Middle English – most famously, the Miller's Tale in Chaucer's *Canterbury Tales* has its closest analogue in the Flemish *boerde* set in Antwerp, *Heile van Beersele* (Hines 1993, 112–13, 238–47). Infamously, there was a massacre of Flemings in London by the rebels during what is popularly termed the Peasants' Revolt of 1381, and the brief chronicle record we have of this tells us that the victims were identified as being the men who could not say 'bread and cheese' but *'case and brode'* (*kaas en brot*) (McLaren ed. 2002, 173 n.122; Spindler 2012). The fact that essentially the same grim anecdote is used of the early-16th-century anti-Hapsburg Frisian rebel Grutte Pier, distinguishing Frisians from Hollanders by their ability to say *'Bûter, brea en griene tsiis'* in order to spare them, implies that the employment of this shibboleth was common folklore around and between these dates (IJssennagger 2013). It is nonetheless also implied that, in 14th-century London, the Flemings were understood not to have assimilated linguistically, and to be identifiable by their language. Also comparable, although in fact contrary as an anecdote, is a fascinating moment in one of 'Gulliver's Travels', by Jonathan Swift, which comes just after Gulliver has escaped from Japan (Swift 1726, part III, ch. XI). He is picked up by a Dutch ship, and casually mentions that he had studied medicine in Leiden and could speak with the crew in sufficiently fluent Dutch to pass as a gentleman of Gelderland. The fictional character Gulliver thus represents exactly the same sort of middle-class and professional career ambition that brought Franciscus Junius to the service of the earl of Arundel in 1621. Above all, the tale and its historical parallel illustrate very nicely the pragmatic and historically dependent sociolinguistic terms in which we should consider any and every phase of language history.

A thorough review of the earliest detectable relationship between the English and Frisian languages was undertaken by the Danish scholar Hans Frede Nielsen in 1981 (Nielsen 1981, esp. 103–54). He demonstrated in overwhelming quantitative terms how especially close is the relationship between Old English – namely the English of the Anglo-Saxon, pre-Norman Conquest period – and Old Frisian when compared with any other relationships between Old English and both the continental and the Scandinavian Germanic languages. Nielsen focused on details of the languages within two of the fundamental structural components of any language: the stock of sounds that the language uses (its phonological system), and the inflexions that are added to words to identify how they fit into meaningful sentences (which is part of the morphological system). Over nearly fifty pages, he presents and analyses 77 special parallels between Old English and Old Frisian – about one-third of which are also found in Old Saxon but the majority of which specifically distinguish Old English and Old Frisian. These parallels vary, in fact, between what we might call truly systematic features – for instance regular and invariable sound-changes, such as the palatalization of an initial *k*-sound which produced the difference between the German and Dutch words *Käse* and *kaas* and English and Frisian *cheese* and *tsiis* – and what we may regard as one-off phenomena, such as the fact that Old English and Frisian alone have *less* or *lessa* and *least* as the comparative and superlative forms of the adjective *little* (this paradigm has now been confused with those of the adjectives *few* and *small* in modern English) rather than forms corresponding to *minder* and *minste* as in Dutch (cf. Norwegian *mindre*, *minst*; German *mindest*).

We should not undervalue the interest and importance of such isolated phenomena, and another such can indeed be added to Nielsen's 77 examples. Old English and Old Frisian alone have the noun 'heart' as a feminine noun: *seo heorte* and *thiu herte*. Other Germanic languages have or had this as a neuter noun: e.g. German *das Herz*, Dutch *het hart*, Norwegian *hjertet*. The philologist can deduce that this noun was originally one of a rare group of neuter *n*-stem or 'weak' nouns in prehistoric common Germanic, along with just three other words: the words for 'eye', **augan*, 'ear', **auran*, and 'cheek', **wangan*. Plainly, this special grammatical set distinguished a group of physical sites and locations of particularly personal sense and thought or emotion within the human body. It is, however, a common fate of unusual paradigms to be absorbed by more common patterns, and in most cases these nouns have changed, in time, to conform to the inflexional patterns of the more common *a*-stem neuter nouns. In some form of Anglo-Frisian *Sprachbund*, however, **hertan* passed instead to join the more numerous and formally very similar feminine *n*-stem class – a path also followed later in Middle High German by *wange*, so that we now have German *die Wange* rather than what we would expect to have become **das Wange*.

In the 13th to 15th centuries, as a Middle English noun, *he[o]rte* can retain its historical grammatical gender, which was otherwise systematically replaced in grammatical structure by the marking of 'animacy' or 'inanimacy' of nouns and pronouns. This is not merely strikingly reflected but also affectively exploited in a literary characterization of the heart, the seat of emotion, as essentially feminine, in, for instance, the text known as the *Ancrene Wisse* or *Ancrene Riwle*, an early-13th-century guide for anchoresses, female recluses:

> **Her biginneð þe oþer dale, of þe heorte warde þurh þe fif wittes**
> *Omni custodia serva cor tuum, quia ex ipso vita procedit.* 'Wið alles cunnes warde, dohter,' seið Salomon, 'wite wel þin heorte; for sawle lif is in hire, ȝef ha is wel iloket.'
>
> **Here begins the second part, of the keeping of the heart through the five senses**
> *With every form of custody, guard your heart, because life derives from it.* 'With every form of keeping, daughter,' says Solomon, 'guard your heart well, for the life of the soul is within her, if she is well observed.'
>
> (*Ancrene Wisse*, part 2: Millett ed. 2006, 20)

One cannot simply point to any direct counterpart in older Frisian texts, before the feminine and neuter nouns merged in the dominant Modern West Frisian branch. It is nonetheless tempting to wonder whether the gender connotations of a feminine *herte* could have had any influence in the free adaptation and appropriation of the hagiographical legend of the palm knight of Lisbon into the story of Poptatus, defender of Flemsburg against the Saracens, in the *Gesta Fresonum* (Bremmer 2009, 181–3). In this version a palm tree grows from the grave of Poptatus's martyred body, and is found to be rooted in his heart – and it is explicitly interpreted as a sign of the strength of the lioness (*lauwe*), apparently displacing the serpent of Moses' rod. Precisely because the common grammatical form has deep historical roots, one need not even consider any question of literary influence between medieval English and Frisian literature. However, rather than the affective personification of the heart being merely an elegant stylistic conceit, philologically we can show how it draws upon and makes use of a distinct Anglo-Frisian grammatical peculiarity. However mechanical the explanation of how that form came into existence may be, it was something that could be used in the rich way it is, clearly in Middle English literature and perhaps also in the literary construction of a Frisian historical hero, and which was not possible in any other branch of Germanic. Anglo-Frisian thus had a stylistic potential which technical language history alerts us to.

The runic question

Potentially an important source of insight into the earliest stages of the distinct Old English and Old Frisian languages is, of course, the small and challenging corpus of early runic inscriptions (Bammesberger 1996; Looijenga 1996; Page 1996; Parsons 1996). This is a collection of material that has been growing quite energetically in England in recent years, as a result of metal-detecting activity and the reporting of finds encouraged by the Portable Antiquities Scheme and the Treasure Act of 1996. The Netherlands and Frisia have not seen a similar growth – more, it would appear, because the early Frisian inscriptions are typically on organic materials such as wood or bone than because of differences in heritage management organization.

The original runic alphabet is known, by making a word of its first six letters, as the *fuþark*. It is common in runological circles to talk of an Anglo-Frisian *fuþorc*, identified by the introduction of a set of new runes which themselves reflect changes in the languages being written that were characteristic of Old English and Old Frisian (Waxenberger, this vol.). The vowel *a* shifted and diverged in pronunciation according to the sounds around it in different words, producing, in different contexts, a 'fronted' sound æ, or a nasalized vowel ã, which usually eventually becomes ō (a long vowel) and so merges with existing examples of ō of different phonological history, while in some circumstances it either stayed unchanged as *a* or even changed back to *a* from æ or ã (Schrijver, this vol.). This is manifestly more than a little confusing, and one may quite reasonably suspect that people trying to represent their language while writing in runes in England and Frisia between the 5th century and the 8th century could also be somewhat confused (Campbell 1959, §§126–69; Hogg 1992, §§5.3–5.40; Bremmer 2009, §§29–35, 39–41).

Such changes do, however, seem to be represented in a very neat and regular way in Anglo-Frisian runic writing. The original *a*-rune had the Germanic name **ansuz* (Fig. 2.1a). In this name, because of its phonetic context, the initial *a* became ã (phonetically [ɔ̃:]) and then ō, and the place of this rune is taken in the fuþark by a developed form represented by Figure 2.1b with the name ōs, which is exactly how the word and name **ansuz* came to be pronounced in Old English. Usually, the *a* or ã (it had short and long forms) inherited by Old English and Frisian were 'fronted' to æ or ǣ, and the old form of the rune (Fig. 2.1a) came to stand for æ and was given the name æsc. Another rune with a similar form appears for the sound *a* (Fig. 2.1c): it is suspected that this form may have been constructed out of the two runes **a** and **i** (cf. Fig. 2.1d) because one of the sources of new examples of the vowel ā was the former diphthong (two vowels pronounced in the same syllable) *ai*. The new rune had the name āc, meaning 'oak', itself deriving from a word that had had that diphthong, **aik-*: the diphthong is still preserved in German *Eich*, Norwegian *eik* and Dutch *eik*; it has been monophthongized in English āc, although

Fig. 2.1. Rune-forms referred to in the text. a: the original *ansuz-rune; b: the ōs-rune; c: the āc-rune; d: the original *ansuz-rune with the īs-rune, **ai**; e: the *oðil-rune.

the long vowel has turned into yet another diphthong in Modern English *oak*. It now appears in Frisian as *ēk* (cf. Nielsen 1995; Parsons 1996; Schrijver, this vol.).

The overwhelming majority of runologists find it inconceivable that these similar and apparently perfectly co-ordinated developments are not interrelated and so effectively simultaneous, whether they were intelligently designed or were the outcome of natural evolution (Bammesberger 1991; Page 1999, 42–4). There is scope for considerable doubt, however, and there are plausible alternative models of the sequence of development. Phonetically, the conventional view of the relative sequence of the so-called 'Primitive Old English' sound-changes are that the shift of *a* to *ã* before a nasal consonant and a spirant consonant must have taken place before the fronting of *a* to *æ* because otherwise there would be or could be no *a* before a nasal to become *ã* (Campbell 1959, §§131–2). It is possible, conversely, that the change *a*> *æ* took place *except* before a nasal consonant, which preserved the primary *a*, which in many cases appears itself to have taken on a nasalized articulation (Campbell 1959, §§127–30; Hogg 1992, §§5.3–5.6). From the runological evidence, however, the *ōs* rune first appears on a bracteate found at Undley in Suffolk dated to the later 5th century, and by the beginning of the 6th century there is another example on a scabbard fitting from Chessell Down, Isle of Wight (Hines 1990, 438–9). Our earliest examples of the *āc* rune, by contrast, appear about a hundred years later, and in a rather different context.

The earliest quite securely and closely dated examples of the *āc* rune are on a comb fragment from Amay in Belgium, dated by type and context to the end of the 6th or beginning of the 7th century, and on a gold coin, the **skanomodu** *solidus* in the British Royal collection. This coin may be dated, partly by type but more confidently by gold fineness, no later than the early 7th century (Williams and Hook 2013, esp. fig. 3). There are also examples of the *āc* rune on two further finds of *solidi* from what may be called the Frisian area: the **hada** *solidus* from Harlingen and the **wela[n]d** *solidus* from Schweindorf (Berghaus and Schneider 1967; on the reading of the Schweindorf *solidus*, see further below). Significantly, all three of these coins were cast in a mould, not struck. Inferences concerning the date of these coins can be based upon measurements of gold fineness, which has been observed to have declined substantially, although not necessarily uniformly and consistently, between the late 6th and the late 7th century, and the type (or, strictly, size) of the coins. The **skanomodu** *solidus* has the highest measured gold content, at 90.5% (Williams and Hook 2013, fig. 3 no. 3). As yet unpublished and incompletely processed figures for the Harlingen and Schweindorf *solidi* indicate a range of readings of *c.* 50–73% gold, implying that the gold quality of the these two coins is parallel to that represented in the southern English Crondall hoard, datable to *c.* AD 640 (Williams and Hook 2013, 67–70, esp. fig. 7). Together with the fact that these three coins are the relatively large *solidi* rather than the smaller counterparts, one-third of the weight of the *solidus*, the *tremisses*, it is unlikely that any of them is from any later than the first half of the 7th century (Grierson and Blackburn 1986, esp. 90–7, 135–8; Blackburn 1991).

Meanwhile it is not only type that suggests that the **skanomodu** *solidus* similarly had a Frisian origin, but two distinctive linguistic features: the vowel *ā* in the element **skano-**, 'bright', representing the Frisian development of West Germanic *au* to *a* (hence *age*, 'eye', and *brad*, 'bread'), and the unusual ending *-u* on a neuter noun *mōd-*, meaning 'mind' or 'mood'. It has been suggested that we might read this as a woman's name with a feminine ending, but this would not contradict a Frisian character; meanwhile, this is, in fact, another word that appears as a neuter in English and Frisian alone; in all other Germanic languages it is masculine. Apparently the same *-u* ending is definitely represented on what we would expect to be *a*-stem masculine nouns in **kabu**, 'comb', and **adugisulu**, the personal name *Adgils*; possibly also in **habuku**, 'hawk', and the **æniwulufu** of another coin, a *tremissis* with a gold content of about 50% (Blackburn 1991, 143–4; Nielsen 1996; Nedoma 2014). The *āc* rune, to focus upon the immediate subject of discussion, then turns up on a series of English coins dating from the middle of the 7th century onwards: firstly the gold **desaiona** *tremisses*, then the pale-gold **pada** *tremisses*, and finally the silver **pada** and **epa** *sceattas* (Metcalf 1993–4, 42–79). Around the middle of the 7th century this rune was also used in the signature of the craftsmen who had repaired a brooch found in a grave at Harford Farm near Norwich: **luda gibœtæ sigilæ**, 'Luda repaired the brooch' (Hines 2000; cf. Bammesberger 2003).

It is also important to note that the inscription on the **skanomodu** *solidus* uses the original **ōþil* rune, not *ōs*, for *o*: in the earliest definitely English inscriptions, by contrast, this rune (Fig. 2.1.e) consistently represents the fronted mid-vowel *œ* (Waxenberger, this vol.). There are as yet no examples of *ōs* in Frisia dated before the 8th century (Looijenga 2003, 299–328). Of course, we are dealing with a very small number of finds here, and it is very likely that the available evidence presents anything but a complete picture. Nonetheless, what evidence we have is unquestionably as consistent with the idea that Anglo-Frisian unity in runic writing practice was something that was gradually achieved by a process of *con*vergence from the 5th century to the 8th as it was something primal, the starting point that was gradually lost through a process of *di*vergence over the same period. Just as languages have to be considered in terms of their contexts, and how they are used, so too such runological convergence is not just linguistic and graphical but also, significantly, a matter of where the runes were actually used. England seems to follow Frisia in the production of runic coins. Inscribed combs are a striking feature of the continental and Frisian use of runes, yet we only have one of these from England: a fine although incomplete example from close to the important monastic site of Whitby, North Yorkshire, with the thoroughly Christian text in Latin and Old English: **d[æ] us mæus god aluwaludo helipæ cy-**, 'May my God, God Almighty, help Cy . . .' (Page 1999, 164–5).

The *-u* ending of *a*-stem or strong nouns in the nominative and accusative cases singular – possibly in the case of both the masculine and neuter genders – is quite consistent in the earliest runic Frisian and perhaps found once in runic Old English in **flodu** on the Franks Casket. In relation to this feature, special notice is required of a matter of debate that has recently arisen concerning the Schweindorf *solidus*. It was originally understood

Fig. 2.2. The reverse of the Schweindorf *solidus*. Scale 2:1. Photo: Christina Kohnen. © Ostfriesische Landschaft. Reproduced by kind permission.

that the runic text on this coin provided a further example of an *a*-stem noun with an ending in -*u*, in a masculine personal name *Welandu*, spelt **weladu** in runes with the common non-representation of the nasal *n* in a consonant cluster. Tineke Looijenga, however, has cogently noted that the putative **u**-rune at the end of this name (written from left to right) may have been written, not as part of the horizontal row of runes but rather as a roman-script capital V in a garbled inscription imitating lettering that would be found on the Roman coin that is the ultimate archetype of this piece, a *solidus* of Theodosius II (AD 402–50) (Fig. 2.2; Looijenga 2013; cf. Berghaus and Schneider 1967). The graph in question is certainly of the right size for this interpretation, only half the height of the otherwise consistently sized five runes of **welad**. We cannot confirm this argument by identifying a direct model in roman script for the non-runic text on the Schweindorf *solidus*. However, a numerous series of *solidi* of Theodosius, including a type with a standing portrayal of the emperor alongside a smaller figure of Victory that is the prototype of the Schweindorf design, has the reverse legend VICTORIA AUGUSTORUM with a V in just this position. A complicating factor is the fact that the Harlingen *solidus* is a less degenerate imitation of precisely the same design, and could very well have been an intermediate model. This has its runic lettering in a different position on the reverse, and no V in that position – but it does have the letters VI in exactly the right style on the opposite side of the design, below the figure of Victory. Altogether, the reading **welad** does seem rather more secure than the previously accepted **weladu**.

The archaeological question

The relevant archaeological evidence consists of the material evidence of artefactual finds from this period in England and Frisia; the evidence of buildings, settlements and sites; and indeed the material evidence for the whole context of landscape and culture within which these also belong. Archaeology is a rich source of insight, not least because it represents the totality of the material circumstances that underlie and coordinate so many different, more specialized fields of past culture and of modern scholarship. Inevitably, archaeology will offer the best description of the general context that we can access when the historical sources are very few and very selective – as is the case with the 5th to 9th centuries in England and Frisia. This does not mean, of course, that archaeological analysis and interpretation are themselves easy, clear and problem-free: far from it. All the same, if we take a very broad perspective upon the half-millennium of the immediately post-Roman Early Middle Ages in England and the northern Netherlands, what is immediately striking is that we are faced with two genuinely similar cases of near total collapse and reconstruction. One of the most radical and even daring historical hypotheses that has come to be widely and seriously accepted within the past thirty years is the idea that Frisia, especially the northern *kustlanden*, was effectively abandoned and then repopulated between the 4th and 6th centuries AD (Gerrets 1999, 333; Knol and IJssennagger, and Dijsktra and de Koning, this vol.). Comparably, in the south and east of Britain, directly opposite across the North Sea, we have the utter collapse of the Roman provinces of Britannia and their replacement, by the late 6th century, with the earliest attested small Anglo-Saxon kingdoms. Schrijver argues (this vol.) that in Frisia, as in England, this transition and repopulation was the context of the expansion of the West Germanic language zone into an area formerly indigenously Celtic-speaking.

In the case of England, the question of whether the transition from Roman Britain to the Anglo-Saxon culture was achieved with a high degree of continuity of population and settlement – with material culture, language and sense of identity being changed under the influence of a new intrusive elite, replacing the continental and Mediterranean Romans – or there was a dramatic replacement of population; perhaps even a demographic collapse, and depopulation and repopulation, similar to Frisia – has been much argued over, to the point, in fact, that we are rather weary of the argument now, even though the problem is still as important as ever (Hamerow 1994; Härke 2011). From the very beginning of the Early Middle Ages in the 5th and 6th centuries, both England and Frisia also saw a process of development which involved the growth of the state and the establishment of the power of the Church. Were we simply to compare and contrast England and Frisia as wholes, we should emphasize how these experiences, and the level of regional success and power achieved through these processes, were very different; but in fact it is possible to see that the relatively marginal status of the coastal heartlands of medieval and modern Friesland is quite similar to the conditions we find in some large, less central regions in England: for instance the south-west, the half of Wessex referred to as 'beyond Selwood', and in Lincolnshire, the old Anglian kingdom of Lindsey (e.g. Higham 2008; Costen 2011; Green 2012). In the 9th and 10th centuries AD, both nations suffered dislocation because of the attentions, activities and presence of Viking Scandinavians: although, interestingly, once again the Vikings' impact was much more disruptive in the supposedly more developed kingdom centres of Northumbria, Mercia, Wessex and Kent than it was in the south-west, in Lindsey or in Frisia.

There are, however, also important and close parallels in terms of specific forms of finds and archaeological sites, which also point to an especially close interrelationship between Frisia and England in the Early Middle Ages, and which shed further light on the complexity of the relationships involved (Myres 1948; Hills 1996; Hines 2002). From the 5th and 6th centuries we have parallels in pottery, both in respect of forms and fabric; there are sometimes parallels also in the form of relatively humble copper-alloy brooches worn by women (Fig. 2.3). We can find examples of parallels representing every

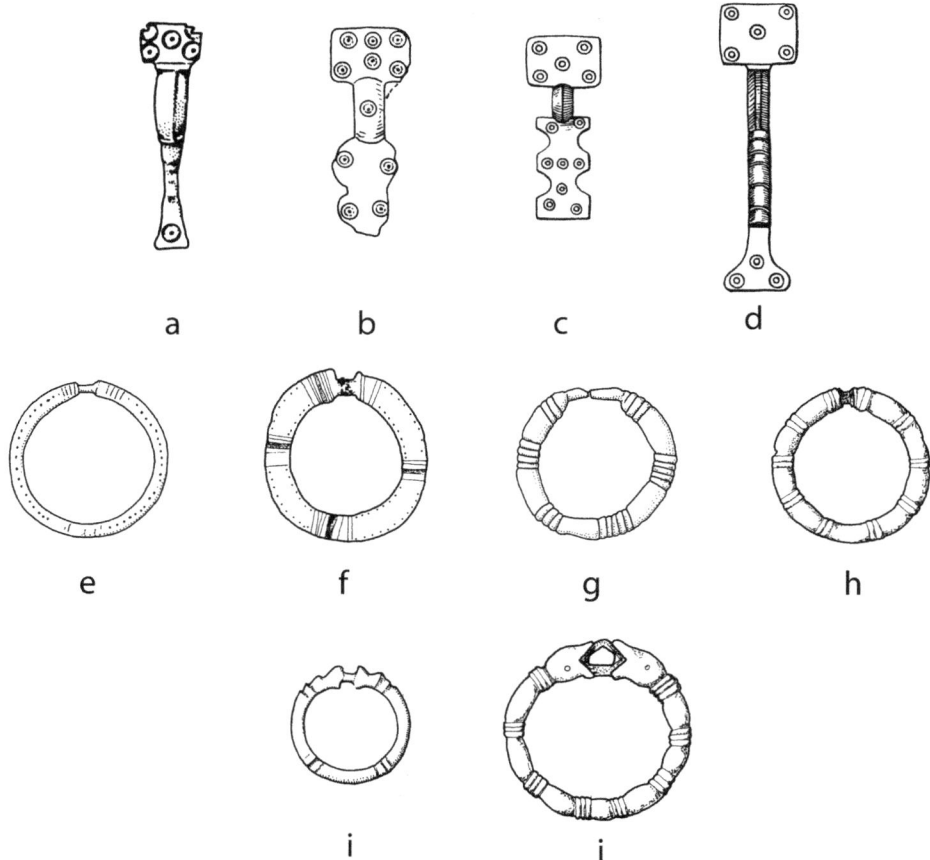

Fig. 2.3. Copper-alloy brooches found in England and the Netherlands. a–d: small long brooches. a: Hogebeintum, grave 47; b: Oosterbeintum, grave 360; c–d: Bifrons (Kent); e–j: annular brooches. e: Hogebeintum, grave 47; f: Whetton Hills (Staffordshire); g: Rhenen, grave 669; h: Cleatham (Lincolnshire), grave 15; i: Anjem; j: Londesborough Collection, British Museum, probably from Yorkshire. Drawn by the author, a–b, e, g and i after Knol 1993. Scale 1:1.

conceivable pattern of contact or influence. There are what we call imported Frisian brooches in England, such as examples of the 'Domburg Type' from Wharram Percy in Yorkshire (Ager 1992; cf. Deckers, this vol.). There are aspects of pottery, and types of brooch such as the 'small long' (Fig. 2.3a–d), and 'annular' or ring brooches (Fig. 2.3e–j), where all the evidence we have would suggest an Anglo-Saxon origin exported to the Netherlands. There are other types where it may well be that England and Frisia equally show the reception of types developed within a much wider North Sea cultural zone, including Niedersachsen immediately to the east and Jutland – but when a particular form of cruciform brooch is known in just two examples from Germany and three from Denmark, against 11 from Frisia and 14 from England it is difficult not still to see the Anglo-Frisian relationship as something particularly meaningful and substantial (cf. Martin 2015, 26, 121 and 175).

A dramatic new parallel emerged in 2016 with the excavation of what appears to have been primarily an 8th-century cemetery at Great Ryburgh in Norfolk, quite possibly monastic, in which the great majority of the deceased were interred in split and hollowed oak log coffins (Hilts 2016). This style of burial was previously unrecorded in Anglo-Saxon England, but had been identified at a number of cemeteries in the Frisian zone from as early as the 6th century and certainly up to the date of the Great Ryburgh cemetery (Knol 1993, 176). Much more detailed information on the latter site is to be awaited, but the possibility that some specifically ecclesiastical relation between East Anglia and the northern Netherlands is reflected here is an intriguing one (see next section, and Pestell, this vol.)

A further group of archaeological finds allows us to look much more directly at the business dealings of the populations of England and Frisia – and other areas around the North Sea and down the English Channel – rather than having to try to work out the story represented by the form and distribution of archaeological finds like detectives attempting to reconstruct events from a handful of clues. Coinage that was in use either side of the North Sea has already been referred to in relation to the runic evidence; by the late 7th century and through the first half of the 8th century England and Frisia were truly using a single currency, in the form of the stubby silver *sceattas* (Grierson and Blackburn 1986, 149–54, 164–89; Metcalf 1993–4). We can follow the transition from a debased gold coinage to the first silver coinage equally clearly in both areas, with the Dorestadt Madelinus pale-gold and silver forms standing as exact counterparts to the same sequence of debasement and replacement in the English **pada** coinage. Moreover, we can examine in detail the principal sites in which these coins were being produced and used: the trading *emporia* or *wic* sites, Wijk-bij-Duurstede (Dorestad) and Medemblik in the Netherlands, and Southampton, London and Ipswich (Old English *Hamwic*, *Lundenwic* and *Gipeswic*) in southern and eastern England (Nicolay 2014, 36–61). As Jan Bestemann has noted, it is really in the context of these sites and the trading network between them that the almost definitive association of Frisian identity with maritime trading was generated, and fixed particularly in Carolingian times (Bestemann 1990, esp. 105). 'Frisian' is now the label we attach to the North Sea coastal trading sites of the same essential and simple layout as Medemblik, not only at Emden at the mouth of the Ems but as far away as Ribe in Jutland: a site where the material culture is otherwise firmly rooted in the traditions and identity of Jutland (Feveile 2006, 75–6; Skre 2007, 344–7). Contact can lead people to copy or adopt some details from those they meet at the same time as they preserve other details which are local and become distinctive; and in some cases they may positively emphasize and cultivate certain local differences in order to resist homogenization. This process may be traced in material culture and language history alike.

A historical overview

The historical evidence for these areas in the periods concerned can only be described as 'sparse', as already noted: although of course by studying and discussing the special forms of evidence for language, literacy and material life, in effect we write more, or new, history. The surprisingly few textual references we have to Frisia and Frisians in Anglo-Saxon sources, both historical and literary (the distinction between these two is not an easy one to maintain), are worth reflective consideration. We have 8th-century narrative historical writing from within the Anglo-Saxon Church, and this, as we would expect, reflects the English involvement in the ecclesiastical colonization of the Netherlands as well as of northern Germany (Westfalen and Niedersachsen). Eighth-century saints' lives, for instance, provide essential details as well as the usual pious hagiographical fantasies about the successes and struggles of missionary bishops: Wilfrid and Boniface, both of them in Frisia quite briefly, although Boniface returned to the north of Frisia as a very old man, actively seeking martyrdom; and Willibrord, first bishop of Utrecht – in fact archbishop of Utrecht – but compelled to withdraw southwards to Echternach, now in Luxembourg (Talbot 1954, esp. 1–66; Wood 2001, 79–122). The report in Eddius's *Life of Wilfrid* that this ambitious Northumbrian bishop was openly welcomed by King Aldgisl of the Frisians at the end of the 670s (Eddius Stephanus, *Vita Wilfridi*, XXV–XXVI: trans. Webb 1965, 158–9) indicates how political and cultural developments were being carefully orchestrated within an informed and sophisticated network bridging the two sides of the North Sea. The Venerable Bede, writing down to the early 730s, could give information on most of these missionary attempts; he also provides the illuminating story of a Frisian trader attempting to buy a noble Northumbrian prisoner of war, Imma, as a slave in London, only to find that no fetters will stay fastened on a man who has a brother who is a priest who can pray for him (Bede, *Historia Ecclesiastica*, IV.22).

In Old English poetry, the epic *Beowulf* not only famously recalls the death of the Scandinavian king Hygelac (Chochilaicus) on a raid on Frisia, but also retells the story of the battle at Finnsburh, amongst the Frisians and in their territory (Fulk *et al.* 2008). This too is very probably an 8th-century poem (Neidorf ed. 2014), although even there these events are set in a distant past – indeed, very likely the 5th and 6th centuries, just when Anglo-Saxon England and (West) Germanic Frisia were establishing themselves. These archaic traditions, which are poetic rather than historical (Biggs 2014), are also echoed in the Old English poetic curiosity *Widsith* (lines 27 and 45). It is interesting to contrast these somewhat specialized and purposeful notions of the place of Frisia in the Anglo-Saxon conceptual horizon with the late-9th-century context of King Alfred the Great's Winchester. Here was produced a translation of Orosius's *Historia contra paganos* ('History against the Pagans'), in which the geographical survey of Europe had a contemporary sketch of Germanic northern Europe added to it (§I.i), covering north of the Danube and east of the Rhine, including the words:

> ... the Thuringians, and north of them are the Old Saxons, and to the northwest of them are the Frisians. On the west of the Old Saxons is the mouth of the River Elbe and Friesland.
>
> (Bately ed. 1980, 12; author's translation)

While the explicit location of the Old Saxons east of the mouth of the Elbe is rather problematic, this passage effectively attributes the entirety of the North Sea coastal strip in what is now Germany to Friesland; in other words, the Frisians, for the late-9th-century West Saxons, were that coastal population. In the *Anglo-Saxon Chronicle* for the year 897, reporting King Alfred's last battles with Viking raiders, we are told of how Alfred personally commissioned a new type of warship, according to neither a Frisian model nor a Danish one but as his own genius best devised:

> Then King Alfred ordered the building of longships against the Viking ships. These very nearly twice as long as the others: some had 60 oars, some more. They were both swifter and more stable and higher than the others. They were modelled neither on Frisian or Danish [ships] but as seemed most useful to Alfred himself.
>
> (Earle and Plummer (eds) 1892, MS A, *s.a.* 897; author's translation)

These were tested in a successful battle in the Solent, but we then learn of a number of distinguished, and indeed individually named, Frisians who fell in Alfred's service there. Their names are anglicized as Wulfheard, Æbbe and Æðelhere: the combined and unseparated English and Frisian casualties numbered 62.

The difference in focus we encounter in these various sources – from different centuries, and representing their own particular contexts – does not just represent for us as modern cultural historians how fragmentary and skewed our sources are, and therefore how incomplete our picture must be. Rather, the multiplicity of glimpses and situations involved is itself a realistic representation of the dynamically varied state and significance of Anglo-Frisian relations in the earliest centuries of the Middle Ages. We do not have to justify a real interest in the Anglo-Frisian question by invoking an intimate, deep historical kinship between the groups. There is some evidence that there was such a thing, and it did not get forgotten, although perhaps it did drift into the mists of legendary – and rather muddled – epic history, as represented in *Beowulf* and *Widsith*. Similarly Han Nijdam shows (this vol.) that there are illuminating similarities between the very early legal traditions of England and Frisia that shed complementary light on how law functioned in similar early-medieval societies rather than identifying a common starting point in the form of a 'proto-Anglo-Frisian legal system'.

Nor, conversely, should we suggest that attention to the question of Anglo-Frisian relationships is vindicated and validated primarily by the important consequences of those connections and interactions: again, this can be held to be true to a degree; but it is not all that matters. Rather it is the fact that there clearly was a continuing relationship across the North Sea from the 5th century to the end of the 9th, and beyond, and that it is the diversity and practical relevance of that relationship which really matter and which deserve our attention. We can see how these links, and reactions to these links, contributed to the development of the economy, the construction of politically organized and self-conscious societies, the consolidation of the Church, and the continuous reconstruction of identity itself, in both England and Frisia. It was not so much inheritance as a practical interrelationship in the Early Middle Ages that made Anglo-Frisian unity meaningful.

References

Primary Sources

Ancrene Wisse. Millett, Bella ed. 2005–6, *Ancrene Wisse: A Corrected Edition of the Text in Cambridge, Corpus Christi College, MS 402, with variants from other manuscripts*. 2 vols., Early English Text Society OS 325–6 (Oxford).

[ASC] *Anglo-Saxon Chronicle*. Plummer, Charles and John Earle 1892, *Two of the Saxon Chronicles Parallel* (Oxford).

Bately, Janet ed. 1980, *The Old English Orosius*, Early English Text Society SS.6 (Oxford).

Bede, *Historia Ecclesiastica Gentis Anglorum*. In Bertram Colgrave and Sir R. A. B. Mynors ed. and trans. 1969, *Ecclesiastical History of the English People* (Oxford).

Fulk, Robert D., Robert Bjork and John Niles ed. 2008, *Klaeber's Beowulf: Fourth Edition* (Toronto).

Swift, Jonathan 1726, *Gullivers Travels into several Remote Nations of the World* (London).

Williams ab Ithel, John ed. and trans. 1860, *Brut y Tywysogion; or, The Chronicle of the Princes* (London).

Secondary Sources

Ager, Barry 1992, 'Discussion'. In 'Non-ferrous metal objects', A. Goodall. In *Two Anglo-Saxon Buildings and Associated Finds. Wharram, A Study of Settlement on the Yorkshire Wolds VII*, G. Milne and J. D. Richards (York), 47–9.

Bammesberger, Alfred 1991, 'Ingvaeonic sound changes and the Anglo-Frisian runes'. In *Old English Runes and their Continental Background*, ed. Alfred Bammesberger (Heidelberg), 389–408.

Bammesberger, Alfred 1996, 'Frisian and Anglo-Saxon runes: from the linguistic angle'. In *Frisian Runes and Neighbouring Traditions*, Amsterdammer Beiträge zur älteren Germanistik 45, ed. A. Quak and T. Looijenga, 15–23.

Bammesberger, Alfred 2003, 'The *Harford Farm brooch* runic inscription', *Neuphilologus* 87, 133–5.

Bammesberger, Alfred 2005, 'Das *fuþark* und seiner Weiterentwicklung in der anglo-friesischen Überlieferung'. In *Das fuþark und seine einzelsprachlichen Weiterentwicklungen*, ed. A. Bammesberger and G. Waxenberger (Berlin), 179–87.

Berghaus, Peter, and Kurt Schneider 1967, *Anglo-friesische Runensolidi im Licht des Neufundes von Schweindorf (Ostfriesland)*, Arbeitsgemeinschat für Forschung des Landes Nordrhein-Westfalen Heft 134 (Wiesbaden).

Bestemann, Jan C. 1990, 'North Holland AD 400–1200: turning tide or tide turned?' In *Medieval Archaeology in the Netherlands: Studies Presented to H. H. van Regteren Altena*, Studies in Prae- En Protohistorie 4, ed. J. C. Bestemann, J. M. Bos and H. A. Heidinga (Assen and Maastricht), 91–120.

Biggs, F. M. 2014, 'History and fiction in the Frisian raid'. In *The Dating of Beowulf: A Reassessment*, ed. L. Neidorf (Cambridge), 138–56.

Blackburn, Mark 1991, 'A Survey of Anglo-Saxon and Frisian coins with runic inscriptions'. In *Old English Runes and their Continental Background*, ed. A. Bammesberger (Heidelberg), 137–89.

Bloemers, J. H. F., and T. van Dorp ed. 1991, *Pre- & Protohistorie van de Lage Landen* (Houten).

Boeles, Pieter C. J. A. 1951, *Friesland tot de elfde eeuw*, 2nd edn ('s-Gravenhage).

Bremmer, Rolf 2009, *An Introduction to Old Frisian: History, Grammar, Reader, Glossary* (Amsterdam).

Breuker, Phillipus H. 1990, 'On the course of Franciscus Junius' Germanic studies, with special reference to Frisian'. In *Aspects of Old Frisian Philology*. Amsterdamer Beiträge zur älteren Germanistik 31–2, ed. R. H. Bremmer, G. van der Meer and O. Vries, 42–68.

Campbell, Alastair 1959, *Old English Grammar* (Oxford).

Costen, Michael D. 2011, *Anglo-Saxon Somerset* (Oxford).

Düwel, Klaus 2008, *Runenkunde*, 4th edn (Stuttgart).

Es, Wim van 1967, 'Wijster: a native village beyond the Imperial frontier 150–425 A. D.', *Palaeohistoria* 11, 28–595.
Feveile, Claus 2006, *Ribe Studier. Det ældste Ribe: Udgravninger på nordsiden af Ribe Å 1984 – 2000*. 2 vols (Århus).
Gerrets, Danny A. 1999, 'Conclusions'. In *The Excavations at Wijnaldum: Reports on Frisia in Roman and Medieval Times: Vol. 1* , ed. J. C. Bestemann, J. M. Bos, D. A. Gerrets, H. A. Heidinga and J.de Koning (Rotterdam), 331–42.
Grant Robertson, C. 1918, *Bismarck* (London).
Green, Thomas 2012, *Britons and Anglo-Saxons: Lincolnshire* AD *400–650* (Lincoln).
Grierson, Philip and Mark Blackburn 1986, *Medieval European Coinage with a Catalogue of the Coins in the Fitzwilliam Museum, Cambridge. 1: The Early Middle Ages (5th to 10th Centuries)* (Cambridge).
Halbertsma, Joost H. 1836, 'IV. Friesic', In *The Origin of the Germanic and Scandinavian Languages and Nations*, J. Bosworth (London), 35–80.
Hamerow, Helena 1994, 'Migration theory and the Migration Period'. In *Building on the Past*, ed. B. Vyner (London), 164–77.
Hamerow, Helena 2004, *Early Medieval Settlements: The Archaeology of Rural Communities in Northwest Europe 400–900* (Oxford).
Härke. Heinrich 2011, 'Anglo-Saxon immigration and ethnogenesis', *Medieval Archaeology* 55, 1–28.
Higham, Robert 2008, *Making Anglo-Saxon Devon: Emergence of a Shire* (Exeter).
Hills, Catherine 1996, 'Frisia and England: the archaeological evidence for connections'. In *Frisian Runes and Neighbouring Traditions*, Amsterdammer Beiträge zur älteren Germanistik 45, ed. A. Quak and T. Looijenga, 35–46.
Hilts, C. 2016, 'Great Ryburgh: a remarkable Anglo-Saxon cemetery revealed', *Current Archaeology* 322, 18–24.
Hines, John 1990, 'The runic inscriptions of Early Anglo-Saxon England'. In *Britain 400–600: Language and History*, ed. Alfred Bammesberger and A. Wollmann (Heidelberg), 437–55.
Hines, John 1993, *The Fabliau in English* (Harlow).
Hines, John 1996, 'Coins and runes in England and Frisia in the seventh century', In *Frisian Runes and Neighbouring Traditions*, Amsterdammer Beiträge zur älteren Germanistik 45, ed. A. Quak and T. Looijenga, 47–62.
Hines, John 2000, 'The runic inscription on the composite disc brooch from grave 11'. In *Excavations on the Norwich southern Bypass. Part 2: The Anglo-Saxon Cemetery at Harford Farm, Caistor St Edmund, Norfolk*. East Anglian Archaeology 92, ed. K. Penn (Gressenhall), 81–2.
Hines, John 2001, 'The role of the Frisians during the settlement of the British Isles'. In *Handbuch des Friesischen*, ed. H. H. Munske, N.Århammer, V. F. Faltings, J. F. Hoekstra, O. Vries, A. G. H. Walker and O. Witts (Tübingen), 503–11.
Hogg, Richard M. 1992, *A Grammar of Old English. Vol. 1: Phonology* (Oxford).
IJssennagger, Nelleke 2013. 'Grut, Grutter, Grutste Pier'. In *Topstukken uit het Fries Museum* (Leeuwarden), 169–71.
Jones, Michael E. 1996, *The End of Roman Britain* (Ithaca).
Knol, Egge 1993, *De Noordnederlandse kustlanden in de Vroege Middeleeuwen* (Groningen).
Kortlandt, F. 2008, 'Anglo-Frisian', *NOWELE* 54/55, 265–78.
Lendinara, Patrizia 1997, 'The Kentish laws'. In *The Anglo-Saxons from the Migration Period to the Eighth Century: A Ethnographic Perspective*, ed. J. Hines (Woodbridge), 211–44.
Looijenga, Tineke 1996, 'On the origin of the Anglo-Frisian runic innovations'. In *Frisian Runes and Neighbouring Traditions*, Amsterdammer Beiträge zur älteren Germanistik 45, ed. A. Quak and T. Looijenga, 109–22.
Looijenga, Tineke 2003, *Texts and Contexts of the Oldest Runic Inscriptions* (Leiden).
Looijenga, Tineke 2013, 'Die goldenen Runensolidi aus Harlingen und Schweindorf'. In *Land der Entdeckungen: Die Archäologie des friesischen Küstenraums*, ed. Jan F. Kegler (Emden), 430–1.

Lorne, the Marquis of 1892, *Viscount Palmerston, K. G.* (London).
Lyons, John 1968, *Introduction to Theoretical Linguistics* (Cambridge).
McLaren, Mary-Rose ed. 2002, *The London Chronicles of the Fifteenth Century: A Revolution in English Writing* (Cambridge).
Martin, Toby 2015, *The Cruciform Brooch and Anglo-Saxon England* (Woodbridge).
Mayr-Harting, Henry 1991, *The Coming of Christianity to Anglo-Saxon England*, 3rd edn (London).
Metcalf, D. Michael 1993–4, *Thrymsas and Sceattas in the Ashmolean Museum Oxford*. 3 vols (London).
Myres, John Nowell Lynton 1948, 'Some English parallels to the Anglo-Saxon pottery of Holland and Belgium in the Migration Period', *L'antiquité classique* 17, 453–72.
Nedoma, Robert 2014, 'Voraltfriesisch -**u** im Nominativ und Akkusativ Singular der maskulinen a-Stämme', *Directions for Old Frisian Philology*, Amsterdamer Beiträge zur älteren Germanistik 73, ed. R. H. Bremmer, S. Laker and O. Vries, 343–68.
Neidorf, Leonard ed. 2014, *The Dating of* Beowulf: *A Reassessment* (Cambridge).
Nicolay, Johan A. W. 2014, *The Splendour of Power: Early Medieval Kingship and the Use of Gold and Silver in the Southern North Sea Area (5th to 7th Century AD)*, Groningen Archaeological Studies 28 (Groningen).
Nielsen, Hans F. 1981, *Old English and the Continental Germanic Languages* (Innsbruck).
Nielsen, Hans F. 1995, 'The emergence of the *os* and *ac* runes in the runic inscriptions of England and Frisia: a linguistic assessment'. In *Friesische Studien II*. NOWELE Supplement Volume 12, ed. V. F. Faltings, A. G. H. Walker and O. Wilts (Odense), 19–34.
Nielsen, Hans F. 1996, 'Developments in Frisian runology: a discussion of Düwel & Tempel's runic corpus from 1970'. In *Frisian Runes and Neighbouring Traditions*, Amsterdammer Beiträge zur älteren Germanistik 45, ed. A. Quak and T. Looijenga, 123–30.
Nielsen, Hans F. 1998, *The Continental Backgrounds of English and its Insular Development until 1154* (Odense).
Page, Raymond I. 1996, 'On the baffling nature of Frisian runes' In *Frisian Runes and Neighbouring Traditions*, Amsterdammer Beiträge zur älteren Germanistik 45, ed. A. Quak and T. Looijenga, 131–50.
Page, Raymond I. 1999, *An Introduction to English Runes*, 2nd edn (Woodbridge).
Parsons, David 1996, 'The origin and chronology of the Anglo-Frisian runes'. In *Frisian Runes and Neighbouring Traditions*, Amsterdammer Beiträge zur älteren Germanistik 45, ed. A. Quak and T. Looijenga, 151–70.
Quak, Arend, and Tineke Looijenga ed. 1996, *Frisian Runes and Neighbouring Traditions*. Amsterdamer Beiträge zur älteren Germanistik 45.
Rippon, Stephen J., Adam Wainwright and Chris Smart 2014, 'Farming regions in medieval England: the archaeobotanical and zooarchaeological evidence', *Medieval Archaeology* 58, 195–255.
Rippon, Stephen J., Adam Wainwright, Chris Smart and Ben Pears 2015, *The Fields of Britannia* (Oxford).
Skre, Dagfinn 2007, 'Dealing with silver: economic agency in south-western Scandinavia AD 600–1000. In *Means of Exchange*. Kaupang Excavation Project Publication Series 2, ed. D. Skre (Aarhus), 343–55.
Stiles, Patrick V. 1995, 'Remarks on the "Anglo-Frisian" thesis'. In *Friesische Studien II*, NOWELE Supplement Volume 12, ed. V. F. Faltings, A. G. H. Walker and O. Wilts (Odense), 177–220.
Strachey, Lytton 1921, *Queen Victoria* (New York).
Strang, Barbara M. H. 1970, *A History of English* (London).
Talbot, C. H. 1954, *The Anglo-Saxon Missionaries in Germany* (London).
Vos, Peter C. 1999, 'The Sub-Atlantic evolution of the coastal area around the Wijnaldum-Tjitsma terp'. In *The Excavations at Wijnaldum: Reports on Frisia in Roman and Medieval Times* vol. 1, ed. J. C. Besteman, J. M. Bos, D. A. Gerrets, H. A. Heidinga and J. de Koning (Rotterdam), 33–72.
Webb, J. F. trans. 1965, *Lives of the Saints* (Harmondsworth).
Williams, Gareth, and Duncan Hook 2013, 'Analysis of gold content and its implications for

the chronology of the Early Anglo-Saxon coinage'. In *Sylloge of Coins of the British Isles 63. British Museum Anglo-Saxon Coins Part I: Early Anglo-Saxon and Continental Coins of the North Sea Area, c. 600–760* , ed. A. Gannon (London), 55–70.

Wood, Ian 2001, *The Missionary Life: Saints and the Evangelisation of Europe 400–1050* (Harlow).

Zimmermann, Haio 1999, 'Favourable conditions for cattle farming, one reason for the Anglo-Saxon migration over the North Sea?' In *In Discussion with the Past: Archaeological Studies presented to W. A. van Es*, ed. H. Sarfatij, W. J. H. Verwers and P. J. Woltering (Amersfoort), 129–44.

3

Frisian between the Roman and the Early-Medieval Periods

Language contact, Celts and Romans

Peter Schrijver

Language and history

Languages expand and contract over time and space. For obvious reasons, this phenomenon attracts linguists, who study language change and its mechanisms. What is less familiar is that this study, apart from its contribution to purely linguistic matters, can yield information which is relevant to historians and archaeologists. This article deals with one type of information: demographic history. More specifically, this contribution centres around the fact that languages spread in two ways:

1. As a result of the propagation of the genes of their speakers – that is, by the multiplication of children speaking the language of their parents and migrating into a new area. If in a previously inhabited area a language primarily spreads in this way, speakers of that language join and often replace speakers of a previously existing language. The result is demographic discontinuity. An example is the expansion of European languages, particularly English, in North America at the expense of Native American languages.

2. As a result of the acculturation of people who previously spoke another language. In this case, it may require only a small number of speakers migrating into a new area in order for the natives to adopt that language and, ultimately, often to abandon their native language. The result of this type of language expansion is demographic continuity. An example is the expansion of French in modern-day Brittany at the expense of Breton.

Normally, the expansion of a language is a blend of both mechanisms, one outweighing the other as a matter of degree. In the case of the expansion of European languages at the expense of Native American languages, demographic replacement strongly outweighed acculturation (cf. Padel 2007, 228–9). In the case of French and Breton, the situation is the reverse (cf. Ternes 2011, 436–9).

The expansion of Latin in the Western Roman Empire is a well-known example of a language that spread primarily as a result of acculturation, although it should be added that it went hand in hand with a minor expansion of people from central Italy. In this particular case, Latin was so successful that it replaced almost all other native languages on Western Roman territory. On the basis of historical information we know that the success of Latin was connected to the fact that Roman society was by and large open to newcomers and that a command of Latin boosted upward social mobility, which in a general sense is one of the most powerful motivators for people to change their traditional behaviour, linguistic or otherwise. This generalization allows us to surmise that in cases of language expansion where historical evidence for social settings is largely lacking, such as the spread of Germanic in Britain between the 5th and 8th centuries at the expense of Celtic and Latin, fluency in the incoming language apparently boosted the social mobility of British natives, whose original languages were Celtic and Latin.

In particular instances, it is possible to argue on purely linguistic grounds and in the absence of relevant historical or archaeological evidence that the expansion of a language resulted primarily from acculturation rather than replacement. That is possible if the language that disappeared as a result of acculturation left traces in the language that succeeded it in the form of a 'foreign' accent in pronunciation or syntax. Modern examples of this phenomenon are abundant, such as a Welsh accent in the English of Wales or a Scots Gaelic accent in Hebridean English. In the course of time, such accents may persist and even wholly replace their unaccented counterparts, as I have argued for the origins of English (based on a variety of Germanic with a Celtic accent), the origins of Dutch and German (based on varieties with different Latin accents), and the origin of the Germanic language family as a whole (based on a variety of North-Western Indo-European with a Fennic accent).[1] These accents usually enter languages as a result of bilingualism and subsequent language shift, i.e. in the course of time, a population shifts from using one language to another. What is especially interesting is that by tracing language shifts in the past, it is possible to identify population continuity across linguistic discontinuity, as explained above.

In this light, the present article explores the earliest history of the Frisian language, chronologically between the Roman Period and the Early Middle Ages, and geographically between the estuaries of the Rhine and Ems.

'Frisian' in the Roman Period

The Latin name *Frisii* is attested from the 1st centry AD, when it denoted a tribe that inhabited the estuary of the Rhine and the area to the north-east up to the estuary of the Ems.[2] Almost nothing is known about their language or languages. A few onomastic data indicate the presence of a Celtic-speaking population in the area. The Frisian kings who visited Rome under the emperor Nero are called *Verritus* and *Mal(l)orix*. Both names make sense in Celtic, *Verritus* meaning 'strong runner' (Celtic **wer-*, 'super, eminent', which is very frequent in Gaulish personal names, and **ret-*, 'to run', as in Old Irish

---

[1] See Schrijver 2014 on all of these examples, and Knol and IJssennagger, this vol.
[2] See Ramat (1976, 18–43) on the Frisii of the Roman Period.

reithid, 'runs') and *Malorix*, 'praise king' (Celtic *mālo-, 'praise', as in Middle Welsh *mawl*, 'praise', and the frequent personal name element *-rīx*, 'king', as in many Gaulish names ending in *-rix* and in Old Irish *rí*, Middle Welsh *ri*, 'king'). These names are typically 'Old Celtic' forms and do not betray any dialectal peculiarities.

Other names do show a striking peculiarity: a place-name element **hel-* is present in the Roman name of the Maas estuary, *Helinium*, as well as in a number of modern hydronyms, which show a small concentration in present-day Friesland, e.g. *de Hel*, *Lytse Hel*. The most likely etymology of this element connects it to British Celtic **hel-*, 'marshland, estuary', as in the medieval Cornish river name *Heyl* and in Modern Welsh *hêl*, 'moor, marsh, meadow along a river'. All of these reflect Proto-Indo-European *selos, 'marsh'. All show the development of initial **s-* to *h-*, which is well known from British Celtic but not from Germanic. The name *Helinium* indicates that the development had already occurred by the time the name was first recorded, in the first century AD. By this time, the change had already affected British Celtic in the sense that all words starting with *s + vowel had a variant starting with *h-* if the preceding word ended in a vowel (so-called Celtic lenition).[3] It is typical of British Celtic, and apparently of the variety of Celtic responsible for the *hel* names in the Low Countries, that the variant with *h-* was generalized.

A similar development of *s to *h, but with subsequent loss in the position between vowels, may account for the Dutch county names *Drenthe*, older *Threant* (820, copy 10th century), from pre-Germanic **Tri-sant-*, which is strikingly similar to Romano-British *Trisantona*, which survives in British river names such as *Trent, Tarrant, Trannon*.[4] The meaning of this name, and therefore its etymology and Celticity, is unknown, but the existence of similarly formed *Tuihanti* (AD 222–35: Künzel *et al.* 1988, 353), the oldest known form of the Dutch county name *Twente*, strongly suggests that they stem from compounds of the numerals **dwi-*, 'two', and **tri-*, 'three', followed by an unknown word **sant-*. The development of the initial **d-* and **t-* of these numerals to *t-* and *th-*, in *Tuihanti* and *Threant*, respectively, betrays the later Germanicization of these forms. The development of *s to *h is certainly not Germanic.

From this scanty material the conclusion may be drawn that it is possible that a Celtic language that closely resembled British Celtic was spoken between the estuaries of the Rhine and Ems during the Roman Period. The general assumption is that south of the rivers Maas, Waal and Rhine, Celtic was spoken at least until the early Roman Period, possibly beside Germanic. The idea that Celtic was present further to the north has never been seriously entertained. Yet this is what the onomastic material bears out. At the same time, a note of caution is in order: linguistic material for this period is very sparse and scattered, so that it is hazardous to generalize on the basis of a few names. The Celtic personal names *Verritus* and *Malorix* may easily have spread amongst a

---

[3] Compare the Romano-British river name *Sabrina*, whose *s-* was retained long enough for it to pass into Latin and thence into English, where it ultimately yielded *Severn*, while its Welsh equivalent, *Hafren*, was inherited from British Celtic. See Schrijver (1995a) on the *Hel-* names and Schrijver (1995b), 377–83) on the complex details of the change from **s-* to *h-* in British Celtic, which started out as an ordinary case of lenition.

[4] Rivet and Smith (1982, 476–8). Old Dutch *Threant* is strikingly similar to Bede's 8th-century name for the Trent: *Treenta, Treanta*.

non-Celtic-speaking population, as personal names have a habit of crossing linguistic boundaries. Finally, the resemblance of the three toponyms (modern *Hel(-)*, *Drenthe*, *Twente*) to Celtic words may be accidental precisely because they number only three.

It is clear that we need more evidence to convince us that Celtic was spoken among the *Frisii* of the Roman Period. A useful test would be to find out whether medieval Frisian, which quite clearly is a Germanic language, shows traces of a Celtic 'accent', which would betray a possible shift of a Celtic-speaking to a Germanic-speaking population. This 'accent' would show itself in the form of a convergence of the sound structure of early-medieval Frisian to that of Celtic. Convergence results from the fact that speakers of Celtic who learn to speak Germanic replace Germanic sounds that are alien to Celtic with their closest counterparts in Celtic. And it results from the fact that those speakers use Celtic phonotactic rules rather than their Germanic counterparts (phonotactic rules state that particular sounds occur only in particular phonetic environments).

There is a complication involved in finding a Celtic accent in Frisian. The Celtic that was spoken in the Low Countries during the Roman Period has left so few traces that it is impossible to determine the details of its sound structure. Hence we are ill-informed about the ways in which it may have resembled or differed from the only slightly better-known Celtic dialects of northern Gaul and eastern Britain, which died out before the Middle Ages. Much more is known about the Celtic dialects of western Britain because those dialects survived and became the modern Celtic languages Welsh, Cornish and Breton. But it is not at all clear that western British Celtic is a reliable proxy for Low Countries Celtic. Our scanty knowledge of eastern British Celtic and northern Gaulish rather suggests that they resembled one another closely and were quite different from western British Celtic.[5] What I have therefore selected as a proxy of Low Countries Celtic is a conservative stage of Celtic that had undergone sound changes that are attested in Gaulish and/or British Celtic up to the 2nd century AD (further details below). I have excluded from my proxy later sound changes shared by eastern British Celtic and northern Gaulish because these were influenced by spoken Latin, which probably did not play a significant role in the area between the estuaries of the Rhine and Ems, which is north of the *limes*.[6]

Having established a proxy for Low Countries Celtic, it is now possible to find out whether Frisian really converged with Celtic. That is the subject of the next section.

Sound change in Germanic and the origin of Frisian

In order to find out whether the Germanic language that we know as Frisian was influenced by a Celtic dialect, it is necessary to trace the different stages of development of the sound system between the Proto-Germanic ancestor language (PGmc) and Pre-Old Frisian of the Early Middle Ages (Old Frisian as attested in medieval texts belongs to the

---

[5] That it is a reliable proxy was the supposition of Schrijver (1999). Meanwhile, it has turned out that western British Celtic underwent strong influence from late spoken Latin and may have differed substantially from eastern British Celtic. The latter's sound structure probably resembled that of northern Gaulish and Irish (Schrijver 2014, 49–53, 87–93).

[6] Those later sound changes involve the diphthongization of $*\bar{\imath}$, $*\bar{u}$ to *ei*, *ou* respectively, and the diphthongization of $*\bar{e}$, $*\bar{o}$ to *ie*, *ua* respectively (Schrijver 2014, 49–52).

later Middle Ages). Since these stages are prehistoric stages, they can be recovered only by linguistic reconstruction, which is performed by applying the so-called 'comparative method' to the medieval Germanic languages. The comparative method was developed by a group of late-19th-century German linguists called the Neogrammarians. More than a century since its discovery, the method has turned out to be an exceptionally powerful tool.[7]

In this survey, I concentrate on changes in the vowel system, which underwent numerous developments. The consonant system, by contrast, remained remarkably stable between PGmc and OFris. It will be addressed briefly in the next section, where we shall see that it is very similar to 1st-century AD Celtic. Hence if a form of Celtic that is similar to British Celtic came into contact with Germanic in the north of the Low Countries, as the development of *s to h that was discussed in the previous section suggests it may have done, that contact would have had little or no effect on the consonant system of Germanic. Remember that we are looking for a Celtic accent in Frisian and that an accent can only arise if the sound system of Celtic differed from that of Germanic, so that Celtic learners of Germanic had difficulty in pronouncing Germanic. While the consonant system is not very informative,[8] the vowel system offers a much better opportunity to trace the effects of language contact because it changed radically over time.

As I have argued elsewhere, PGmc itself resulted from intense contact with speakers of the Balto-Finnic branch of the Uralic language family (Schrijver 2014, 158–79). The PGmc vowel system can be reconstructed as shown in Table 3.1.[9]

Table 3.1. The Proto-Germanic vowel system[†]

long vowels		short vowels		diphthongs
ī	ū	i	u	ai, au, eu, iu
ē	ō	e	a	
ǣ	ā			

[†]u is the phonetic symbol that approximates to the vowel in English *ooze*.
æ is the phonetic symbol for the vowel in English *hat*.
The merger of pre-Germanic *ā and *ō post-dates Proto-Germanic (Schrijver 2014, 180-2, with references).

Subsequently, Germanic began to split up gradually into a number of dialects. North and West Germanic shared a two-way development of long vowels, depending on whether they occurred in stressed (i.e. first) or unstressed (i.e. non-first) syllables (Table 3.2; Schrijver 2014, 180–96).

---

[7] See Durie and Ross (1996) on the comparative method. A short introduction is offered by Schrijver (2014, 5–11).
[8] One exception, palatalization of velars, will be addressed in the next section.
[9] The tables show the usual representation of vowels according to the way in which they are articulated: the horizontal axis indicates the degree to which the tongue is protracted (far left, position of e.g. English *ee* in *meet*), at-rest position (middle, position of e.g. English *u* in *but*) or retracted (right, position of e.g. English *oa* in *oak*). The vertical axis indicates the degree to which the lower jaw is dropped: topmost = mouth almost closed (closed position of e.g. English *ee* in *eel* or *oo* in *ooze*), bottom = mouth opened maximally for pronunciation (open position of e.g. the two different pronunciations of English *a* in *bad* and *hall*).

Table 3.2. North and West Germanic†

stressed long		unstressed long		short	
ī	ū	ī	ū	i	u
ē	ō	ē	ō	e	o
ā		ǣ	ɔ̄	a	

† ɔ is the phonetic symbol for the vowel in English (not American English) *dog*.

By the 4th or 5th century AD, approximately, an Anglo-Frisian branch of Germanic had formed, which simplified the long-vowel system by adopting the 'unstressed long' vowel system in stressed syllables as well (Table 3.3). All other North and West Germanic dialects, i.e. Scandinavian and Dutch-German, by contrast generalized what had been the 'stressed long' system in unstressed syllables. Anglo-Frisian is also known by the name of North Sea Germanic.

Table 3.3. Anglo-Frisian (= North Sea Germanic)†

long vowels		short vowels		diphthongs
ī	ū	i	u	ai, au, eu, iu
ē	ō	e	o	
ǣ	ɔ̄	a		

†The stage represented in Table 3.3 dates from before differentiation between English and Frisian sets in, so before breaking, a/i-mutation, and monophthongization of *au, *ai.

In the ensuing period, Anglo-Frisian begins to gradually break apart into an English and a Frisian branch. This break-up was effectuated by sound changes that are superficially similar but differ on details in either branch (Bremmer 2011, 27–36; Stiles 1995; Nielsen 1985). The reader who feels overwhelmed by the following host of sound changes may want to proceed directly to the next section!
1. *ɔ̄, and *ō merge as *ō (the development affects English and Frisian in the same way, so it may have already occurred at the Anglo-Frisian stage, which is presented in Table 3.3).
2. In Frisian, diphthongs open their close second members:
2a. *au > *aɔ > OFris ā. The development is first attested in the Frisian Runic name *Skanomodu* on a *solidus* in the British Museum, therefore possibly found in Britain and dated to c. AD 575–610 (cf. Hines, this vol.; Waxenberger, this vol.): the first member of the name reflects older *skauna-, 'clean, beautiful' (Dutch *schoon*, German *schön*, Old English *scean-*).
Contrast the development of *au via *æɔ and ultimately to ēa in Old English (OE).
2b. *eu > *eɔ > OFris iā (OE ēo)
2c. *iu > *iu/io > OFris iō/iū (OE īo)
2d. Opening also affects *ai, which via *aæ became Frisian ǣ. This latter stage is attested in two words of the Westeremden B runic inscription: *hæmu*, later OFris *hēm*, 'home(stead)', and *æh*, 'has', later OFris *āch*. This earliest Frisian ǣ subsequently split into OFris ā or ē or short ă depending on the phonetic context: ā arose before preserved back vowel in

the following syllable and before velar fricative, while *ē* developed before a word-final single consonant and as a result of *i*-umlaut; short *ă* arose before a consonant cluster (de Vaan 2011).[10] The **ai* that became Pre-OFris **ǣ* pushed the pre-existing Anglo-Frisian **ǣ* towards **ē*, with which it merged.

In OE, **ai* developed differently: it became *ā*, which if it was affected by *i*-umlaut developed into *ǣ*.

3. In Frisian, short **a* became *æ*. This development may well have affected the **a* in **ai* before that became Frisian *ǣ* (above, 2d), in which case the intermediate stage was **æi*. But the fronting of **a* to **æ* certainly did not affect the **a* in **au* before that yielded Frisian *ā* (see 2a, above) because it is hard to envisage how **æu* subsequently could have become *ā*.

Contrast the situation in English: here, too, short **a* was fronted to *æ*, but in English fronting affected **au* > **æɔ* > *ēa* rather than **ai* > *ā*. The background of this difference probably is chronological: fronting of **a* to *æ* affected English when **ai* had already become *ā* so that it could no longer be affected by the fronting. In Frisian, by contrast, it was **au* that had already become **ā* before fronting of **a* to *æ* affected the language. So fronting hit English and Frisian when they were already slightly different from one another.

4. The velar obstruents *k* and *g*, *gg* were palatalized to **tʃ* (as in English *chin*) and **j*, **dʒ* (as in *yawn*, *jaw*), respectively, if they preceded or followed front vowels (the Anglo-Frisian vowels that effectuated palatalization were long and short **i*, **e*, **æ*). This change affected both English and Frisian, but the exact conditions differ in detail in either language. For instance, in word-final position in OFris, only **g* was palatalized, and only after **æ*, **e*, as in **dæg* yielding OFris *dei*, 'day' (see Laker 2007 for a detailed treatment).

5. *i*-umlaut: a back vowel turns into the corresponding front vowel if the following syllable contains **i*, **ī* or **j*. An example is **badja*, 'bed', which became OFris *bedd*. The development affects all medieval Germanic languages, but details of its application differ considerably from language to language and, especially in the case of Dutch, from dialect to dialect. *i*-umlaut in English and Frisian is strikingly similar but occurred later in time than developments which affected Frisian in a different way from English (such as the palatalization of velars (above, 4), and the fronting of **a* to **æ* (above, 3), which itself probably followed the rise of **ā* from **ai* in English but from **au* in Frisian). That means that *i*-umlaut cannot belong to the Anglo-Frisian proto-stage of Table 3.3 but occurred later. As a result of *i*-umlaut, Frisian (and English) acquired the rounded front vowels **ȳ*, **ø̄* (which in Frisian merged at some unknown point of time and ultimately became OFris *ē*), and **y* (which became OFris *e*).[11]

6. Labio-velar mutation and breaking (Bremmer 2009, 33–6) produce a diphthong *iu*, which joins the pre-existing **iu/io* (see 2c)

Developments (1) to (6) give rise to the vowel system presented in Table 3.4.

---

[10] De Vaan argues for an initial Frisian stage **ā* rather than **ǣ*, which is probably incorrect in view of the Westeremden B evidence.

[11] *y* symbolizes the vowel of French *mur, pure*, while *ø* represents the vowel in French *peuple*.

Table 3.4. The Pre-Old Frisian vowel system

long vowels			short vowels			diphthongs
$\bar{\imath}$	$\bar{y}$	$\bar{u}$	i	y	u	$iu, e\mathit{ɔ}$
$\bar{e}$ ‡	($\bar{\textit{ø}}$)†	$\bar{o}$ °	e		o	
$\bar{æ}$ ¤	$\bar{a}$ §		$æ$			

† $\bar{\textit{ø}}$ possibly had already merged with $\bar{y}$, both resulted from *i*-umlaut
‡ $\bar{e}$ developed from Anglo-Frisian *$\bar{e}$ and *$\bar{æ}$
¤ $\bar{æ}$ developed from Anglo-Frisian *ai
§ $\bar{a}$ developed from Anglo-Frisian *au
° $\bar{o}$ developed from Anglo-Frisian *$\bar{o}$ and *$\bar{ɔ}$

Results

This concludes the presentation of the sound changes that occurred between Anglo-Frisian and Pre-Old Frisian during the period that covers approximately the Late Roman Period and the very early Middle Ages. Simply put, the consonant system changed very little while the vowel system changed a lot. One may ask why that was and why the vowel system changed in the direction that it did. It is at this point that we may return to the thought experiment that was introduced at the end of the second section of this paper, and ask ourselves whether it makes sense to regard the Pre-OFris sound system as the result of the introduction of a Celtic accent. Remember that a Celtic accent should betray itself by a convergence of the Germanic sound system with that of Celtic, as speakers of Celtic who learnt Germanic replaced unfamiliar Germanic sounds with their closest Celtic counterparts.

The Pre-OFris vowel system of Table 3.4 shows striking similarities to our proxy of 2nd-century Low Countries Celtic, which, as explained at the end of section 2, combines the developments of early British Celtic with those of Gaulish (Table 3.5).[12]

Table 3.5. Low Countries Celtic around AD 200
(based on early British Celtic and northern Gaulish)

long vowels			short	
$\bar{\imath}$	$\bar{y}$	$\bar{u}$	i	u
$\bar{e}$		$\bar{o}$	e	o
$\bar{æ}$		$\bar{ɔ}$		a

Both vowel systems have seven long and six short vowels that are situated at approximately the same positions in the diagram. There are indeed small differences as well. Where Pre-OFris has long *$\bar{a}$,[13] Celtic has *$\bar{ɔ}$, which phonetically lie close to one

---

[12] More particularly, this type of Celtic had *$\bar{ɔ}$ from earlier *$\bar{a}$; *$\bar{æ}$ from earlier *ai; *$\bar{y}$ from earlier *$\bar{u}$; *$\bar{o}$ from earlier *ou; and *$\bar{u}$ from earlier *oi. See Jackson (1953, 694) on the early date of these developments in British Celtic; Schrijver (1998–2000, 136–7) on *$\bar{a}$ > *$\bar{ɔ}$ in northern Gaulish.

[13] In Schrijver (1999, 24–5), I attempted to argue that Frisian and English *$\bar{a}$ arose much later, but this is doubtful. The present account presupposes that *$\bar{a}$ arose independently in English and Frisian (see (2) above) but earlier than fronting of *a (3), palatalization (4) and *i*-umlaut (5); this chronology is more in line with general thinking about the chronology of sound changes (e.g. Stiles 1995).

another. Where Pre-OFris has *æ, Celtic has very similar *a*. In both cases, the Pre-OFris variant was more strongly fronted (i.e. produced with protracted tongue) than its Celtic counterpart. More substantial are two other differences: Celtic lacks short *y*, which arose as an innovation in Frisian (and English); and Frisian possessed the diphthongs **iu*, **eo* (see (2), above), which Celtic lacked at the time. What is important is that the the general picture is that the Pre-OFris vowel system is so similar to that of Celtic that we may hypothesize that the similarity resulted from convergence. Indeed, this is what we would expect if Celtic speakers were switching to Germanic by the Late Roman Period.

The small differences between the Pre-OFris and Celtic vowel systems require an explanation as well. One possibility is that they are artefacts of an imperfect proxy: Low Countries Celtic may have differed slightly from British Celtic and Gaulish around AD 100. In particular, it may have possessed slightly more fronted counterparts of **a* and **ɔ̄* than British Celtic did. Additionally, Pre-OFris may not represent a pure Celtic accent but rather a compromise between a pure Celtic accent and 'native' Germanic, which arose as the dialects of former Celtic speakers and native Germanic speakers merged to become Pre-OFris.

I have already addressed the fact that the consonantal system underwent very little change between the PGmc and the Pre-OFris stages: the main exception is the rise of **tʃ* and **dʒ* by palatalization (see (4) above). The consonantal system that Celtic possessed by the first to second century AD was very similar to that of Anglo-Frisian: in particular, both had a system of double and single plosives (consonants of the type *p, t, k, b, d, g* which are produced by a sudden release of the air stream) as well as voiceless and voiced fricatives (consonants of the type *v, f, s, z*, which are produced by compressing the air stream in such a way that turbulence arises). Both Celtic and Anglo-Frisian possessed the following consonants: **pp – *p – *b – *f – *v; *tt – *t – *d – *θ – *ð; *kk – *k – *g – *x – *γ*.[14] British Celtic lacked **tʃ, *dʒ*, however.

A comparison of vowel systems (Tabs. 4 and 5) and the consonantal systems of Pre-OFris and Celtic indeed suggests that a convergence had taken place: the consonantal systems of Celtic and Anglo-Frisian were very similar to begin with, while the vowel system of Pre-OFris resulted from changes that made it closely similar to the Celtic vowel system, even though convergence was not complete.

On the basis of these observations, we may conclude that it is a reasonable hypothesis that the area between the estuaries of the Rhine and Ems contained a Celtic-speaking population during the Roman Period (as the onomastic data suggest, above) and that this population shifted to speaking Germanic, which by the introduction of a Celtic accent became Pre-OFris.

It is interesting to contrast the linguistic history of the Frisian area with the linguistic history of the area south of the lower Rhine, where the Dutch language arose. As I have argued elsewhere (Schrijver 2014, 122–57), Dutch resulted from a language shift by an

---

[14] Some phonetic symbols may require explanation: **θ* is *th* in English *think*; **ð* is *th* in English *then*; **x* represents *ch* in Scottish *loch*, Dutch *lach*; **γ* is Southern Dutch *g* in *goed, mogen*. Voiceless fricatives at this stage existed but were phonotactically rare. They are not to be confused with the voiceless fricatives that arose much later as a result of British Celtic spirantization. Older voiceless fricatives are those that resulted from **sr-, *spr- (> *fr-); *-str- (> *-θr-); *kt, *pt (> *xt)*. Voiced fricatives had arisen by lenition of voiced plosives and became phonemic when geminate voiced plosives became single.

originally Latin (rather than Celtic) speaking population to Germanic. Hence it is possible to state that the difference between Dutch and Frisian was the result of different socio-political events on either side of the Roman *limes*.

References

Bremmer, Rolf H. 2011, *An Introduction to Old Frisian* (Amsterdam–Philadelphia).
Durie, Mark, and Malcolm Ross ed. 1996, *The Comparative Method Reviewed: Regularity and Irregularity in Language Change* (Oxford).
Jackson, Kenneth H. 1953, *Language and History in Early Britain* (Edinburgh).
Künzel, Rudi E., Dirk P. Blok, and J. M. Verhoeff 1988, *Lexicon van Nederlandse Toponiemen tot 1200* (Amsterdam).
Laker, Stephen 2007, 'Palatalization of velars: a major link of Old English and Old Frisian'. In *Advances in Old Frisian Philology*, Amsterdamer Beiträge zur älteren Germanistik 64, ed. R. H. Bremmer Jr., S. Laker and O. Vries, 165–84.
Nielsen, Hans F. 1985, *Old English and the Continental Germanic Languages* (Innsbruck).
Padel, Oliver 2007, 'Place-names and the Saxon conquest of Devon and Cornwall'. In *Britons in Anglo-Saxon England*, ed. N. Higham (Woodbridge), 215–30.
Ramat, Paolo 1976, *Das Friesische* (Innsbruck).
Rivet, A. L. F., and Colin Smith 1982, *The Place-Names of Roman Britain* (London).
Schrijver, Peter 1995a, 'Welsh *heledd*, *hêl*, Cornish *heyl, 'Latin' *Helinium*, Dutch *Hel-*, *zeelt*', *NOWELE* 26, 31–42.
Schrijver, Peter 1995b, *Studies in British Celtic Historical Phonology* (Amsterdam–Atlanta).
Schrijver, Peter 1998/2000, 'The Châteaubleau Tile as a link between Latin and French and between Gaulish and Brittonic', *Études celtiques* 34, 135–41.
Schrijver, Peter 1999, 'The Celtic contribution to the development of the North Sea Germanic vowel system, with special reference to Coastal Dutch', *NOWELE* 26, 31–42.
Schrijver, Peter 2014, *Language Contact and the Origins of the Germanic Languages* (New York–London).
Stiles, Patrick 1995, 'Remarks on the "Anglo-Frisian" thesis'. In *Friesische Studien II*, NOWELE Supplement Volume 12, ed. V. F. Faltings, A. G. H. Walker and O. Wilts (Odense), 177–220.
Ternes, Elmar 2011, 'Neubretonisch'. In *Brythonic Celtic – Britannisches Keltisch*, ed. E. Ternes (Bremen), 431–530.
Vaan, Michiel de 2011, 'West-Germanic *ai in Frisian', *Amsterdamer Beiträge zur älteren Germanistik* 67, 301–14.

4

'All quiet on the western front'?

The Western Netherlands and the 'North Sea Culture' in the Migration Period

Menno Dijkstra and Jan de Koning

For a long time, the only claim the western Netherlands had to participation in the 5th-century *adventus Saxonum* was based upon a handful of Anglo-Saxon pots in three cemeteries in the Rhine estuary. Recent research, however, dates these pots to the 6th century, thus beyond the initial period of migrations from Old Saxony (*Niedersachsen*) to Britain. Together with other differences in material culture, this clearly reveals a contrast to developments in the *terpen* area of Friesland and Groningen. The internal partition in the *Lex Frisionum* into three parts also points to regional differences (see further Knol and IJssennagger, and Nijdam, this vol.). Even within the region of West Frisia, the modern provinces of North and South Holland, regular archaeological distinctions can be found. Bazelmans (2009, 332-3) has already pointed to the fragmented ethnicity the different coastal regions must have had, following the crisis in habitation they all went through between the late 3rd and early 6th century AD.

At the same time there were some shared characteristics in the Frisian coastal region, such as brooches of the Domburg Type (Deckers, this vol.). How does this all add up to a coherent picture of the habitation history of the Dutch west coast in the Migration Period? In this paper a general outline is presented of the recent research of both authors as part of the former 'Frisia Project', taking an interdisciplinary approach (Dijkstra and van der Velde 2011; Dijkstra 2011; de Koning 2003; 2012).

An introductory warning about geographical terminology is required, however. In German studies present-day Friesland is called 'West Frisia', to distinguish it from the German East and North Frisia (e.g. Bos 2001, 490 and map 1). This is confusing, because in the Early Middle Ages the littoral of the western Netherlands was known as Frisia as well, and its inhabitants as *Fresiones* or *Fresiones occidentales* (West Frisians). The name *Holland* did not come into regular use until *c.* 1100, reserving the name *West-Friesland* for the northernmost part of Holland until the present day (Blok 1969). Consequently we prefer to refer to modern Friesland as Middle Frisia (Fig. 4.1).

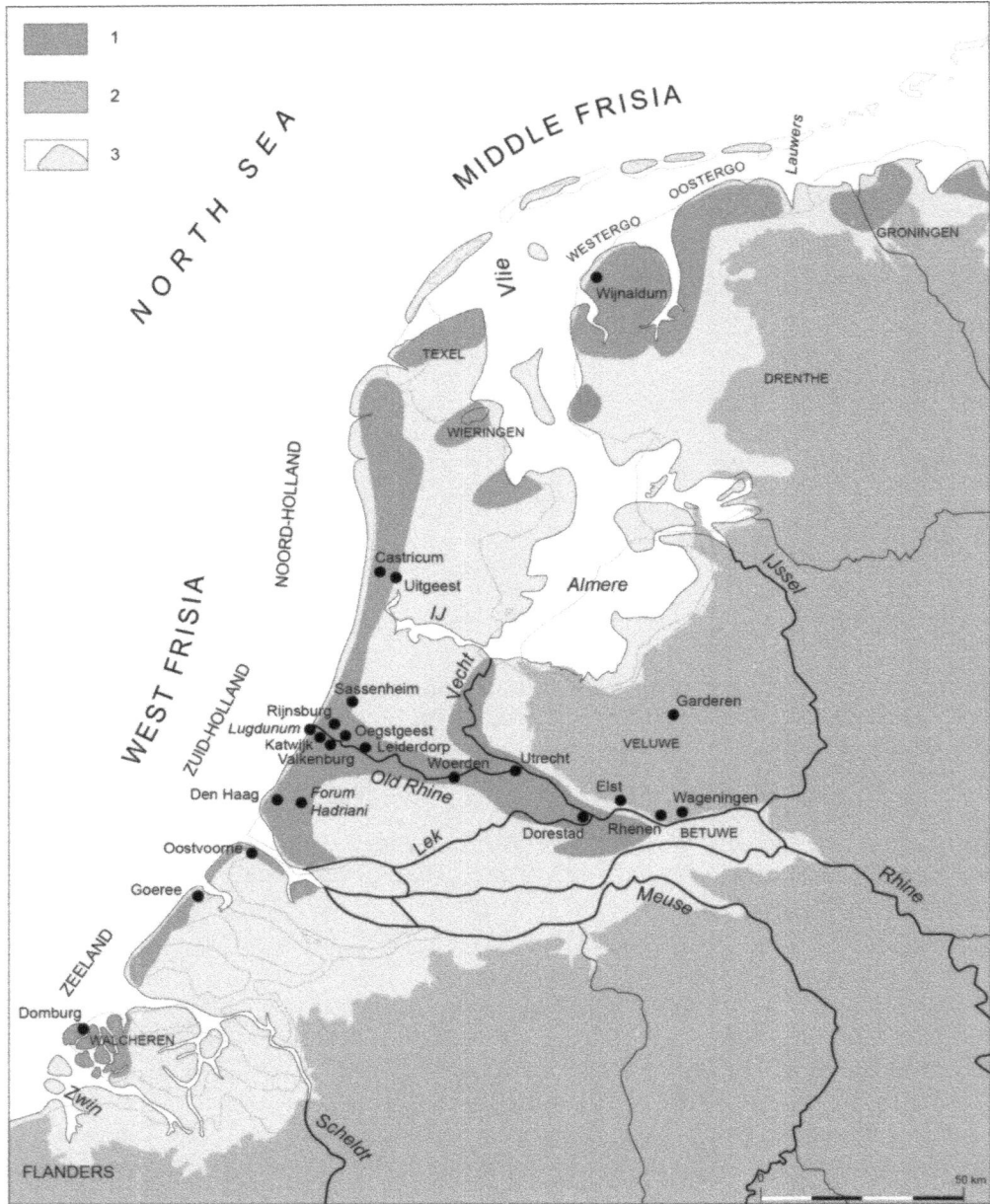

Fig. 4.1. Palaeogeographical reconstruction of the Netherlands in the Early Middle Ages (7th–8th centuries AD). 1: 'Frisian' habitation area; 2: sandy Pleistocene hinterland; 3: the (mainly) Holocene coastal plain.

A short historiography of the Migration Period in the western Netherlands

No indigenous origin myth or habitation history for the Early Middle Ages has survived for the western Netherlands. The first thoughts on the subject were put to paper at the end of the 13th century, in the context of the political status of the Count of Holland (Floris V). Based on 'old books' such as the early-5th-century *Historiae adversus paganos* of Orosius, late-medieval historians deduced that the Dutch coast had been inhabited by Saxons. They inferred that the name 'Frisians' was given by the Romans in AD 363, after a victorious battle in this 'freezing' country. For the historians, after all, the names for the 'Lower Saxons' and Frisians who lived along the coast of Holland were interchangeable, because Frisians still lived in the north of the county of Holland and in the Frisian *terp* region. Thus the Saxons who, according to Bede, had migrated to England, were also Frisians (Anonymous/Melis Stoke, *Rijmkroniek van Holland*, lines 76–8; Burgers 1999, 168–9).

A variation to the story was introduced in the 14th century by Johannes de Beke. 'Slavs who were called Wilten' conquered Holland and, together with the Frisians, were defeated by Valentinianus in 363 (*Croniken van den Stichte van Utrecht end van Hollant*, III–VI). The introduction of the Wilten was prompted by the place-name Wiltenburg near Utrecht, and the folk etymology Bede gave in his early-8th-century *Historia Ecclesiastica Gentis Anglorum*, V.11. Other well-known stories, such as that of the year 789 in the *Annales Einhardi*, or Charlemagne's wars against the Slavs and *Wiltzi*, convinced late-medieval writers of this interpretation (Schönfeld 1935). To complicate things even further, a later chronicler stated that the Slavs and Wilten were actually Danes (*Kronijk van Holland*, VII: pre-1409).

After a phase in the 15th century in which the embellishment of the past was enhanced by attributing the founding of cities to legendary persons and the myth of Trojan ancestry, the Batavian myth developed as a result of the rediscovery of classical texts. According to this, the Batavians were regarded as the founders of the Dutch struggle for independence (Tilmans 1987, 194–8). In the 19th century this view came to be replaced by the Frisian myth. The Frisians could boast of being one of the few peoples that had survived from the Roman Period to the present day. Historical sources such as the *Lex Frisionum* and remnants of the Frisian language and toponyms made it clear that, after the Romans left, the Frisians took their chance to take possession of the Dutch coastal region as far as Zeeland and Utrecht, under the leadership of illustrious kings like Aldgisl and Radbod (e.g. Dirks 1846; cf. Halbertsma 2000, esp. 298–316).

At the beginning of the 20th century, however, archaeologists entered the debate, on the basis of the material culture they discovered in various early-medieval cemeteries. Holwerda, archaeologist of the National Museum of Antiquities in Leiden (RMO), supported the view that the Frisians had spread over Holland and Zeeland, but let the Frankish and Saxon urns found at Rijnsburg and Katwijk speak for themselves: the strategic position of the Rhine estuary led to a dominant occupation by Franks in that zone, amid Saxon elements, for whom this only was a staging post on the way to England (Holwerda 1914, 47–9; 1925, 225–61).

In Frisia, the archaeologist Boeles concluded on the basis of 'Anglo-Saxon' brooches and urns found that the early-medieval Frisians were not the same as those of the Roman Period, because large groups of Angles and Saxons settled in Frisia around the middle of the 5th century. The remaining Frisians amalgated into an 'Anglo-Frisian' entity, extending itself in the western Netherlands in the 7th century (Boeles 1927; 1951). This theory met with a great deal of criticism, but archaeological research of the last two decades has supported Boeles' perception of discontinuity of settlement along a large section of the Dutch coast. According to Bazelmans it is possible that migrants from the north named themselves after the Frisian area in which they settled (cf. Gerrets 1999). Bazelmans, however, considers it more likely that the name 'Frisia' was reintroduced by the Franks in the 7th century when, together with their familiarity with the classical ethnographic tradition, they again became politically interested in the northern periphery of their kingdom (Bazelmans 2001; 2009).

Historical evidence

Raids by Frankish and/or Saxon pirates mentioned by classical writers are the only scant sources of information about the Low Countries in the Late Roman Period, but with no clear geographical location of their homelands given (de Boone 1954; Hiddink 1999, 223–5). Earlier tribes which are locatable in the north-western corner of the continental Roman Empire, such as the *Cananefates* and *Frisiavones*, are heard of no more. The last time the Frisians are mentioned is in 297, when imperial eulogists state they were defeated and settled, together with *Chamavi* and Franks, in northern Gaul (*Panegyrici Latini* 8 (5), cited in de Boone 1954, 15). There then follows a deafening silence for almost three centuries. On the few occasions Frisians are mentioned in the 4th to 5th centuries, it is the classical canon speaking, not reality. Even the Frisians in *Beowulf* are anachronistic, since the poem is a composition of the 8th or even 10th century, adjusted to the context of its time, not a trustworthy historic narrative (Bazelmans 2009, 329–30; cf. Hines, this vol.).

The Byzantine historian Procopius was the first to mention Frisians again, *c.* AD 550, in his bewildering statement that Britain is inhabited by three nations with a king: the *Angiloi, Frissones* and *Brittones* (*De Bellis*, VIII.20.6–8). As Bremmer has noted (1990, 354), it is strange that in later sources Frisians are not known as an important English political entity at all. Some scholars see these Frisians as a reference to those Saxons who used Frisia as a bridgehead to migrate to Britain (taking some ethnic 'Old Frisians' along) (Boeles 1951, 225; Campbell 1991, 31; Myres 1989, 47–8). Bartholomew agrees, stressing the tripartite literary formula that Procopius used. Besides the indigenous Britons, he knew of the Angles, as part of a Frankish embassy to the emperor Justinian in Constantinople (*De Bellis*, VIII.20.7–10). To find another tribe who could plausibly be associated with the immigration, therefore, he fell back on the old classical canon and found the opposite littoral of Frisia to fit best (Bartholomew 2005, 27). Given the poor knowledge of Procopius and his generation about the peoples that lived around the North Sea at that time, however, we do not believe, as Bartholomew did, that Procopius satisfied his readers' expectations by citing the Anglo-Saxons twice under different names. His Byzantine audience was probably just as ignorant about Saxons as he was. It is unlikely that the Franks introduced the Frisians to Procopius. The Merovingians knew about

Saxones, from the Continent as well as (maybe) in Britain (Springer 2003, 17–18), but they probably had not felt the need to name them as a third party either, since the Angles already fufilled the purpose of stating their claim to rule Britain.

Procopius leads us to refute another problematic proposition: the presence of Warni and Heruli in the Dutch delta. Attempts by de Boone in the 1950s to locate them in the Netherlands, using historical and archaeological evidence, had previously been found unsubstantiated, notably by Russchen, but these tribes still find their way into local history books (de Boone 1951; Russchen 1964; 1967, 33–7; for a summary of the controversy see Dijkstra 2011, 345–9). The main argument for placing the Warni in the Netherlands was the legend, dated around 540, of the scorned Anglian fiancée from Britain and the Warnish prince Radigis. He preferred to marry his step-mother, the Frankish princess Theudechild, a sister of king Theudebert I. The Anglian princess and her brother sailed to the Continent with a vast army, captured Radigis and compelled him to marry her after all (Procopius, *De Bellis*, VIII.20.1–41).

After hearing this entertaining story from Herulian informants or a Frankish delegation at the Byzantine court, Procopius put it to paper. He writes that the Warni lived 'beyond the Ister [Danube] and as far as the northern ocean along the Rhine, which separates them from the Franks and other peoples who live in that region', and that the battle with the Anglian princess took place 'not far from the sea shore and the mouth of the Rhine' (*De Bellis*, VIII.20.2 and 33). Writing this in far-away Byzantium, in a stereotypical, classical literary style, and with only a very crude idea of the peoples living there, interchanging Thuringians and the related Warni (Boeles 1958; Russchen 1964; 1979, 21 and 28; Springer 2006, 278; Dijkstra 2011, 348–9), this cannot be taken seriously as a localization of the Warnish tribe in the Netherlands. It is more probable that the Anglian fleet set sail for the Elbe or Weser region, to attack the Warni in their plausible homeland in Central Europe, near the Thuringians. There is even the possibility that Procopius erroneously mixed the North German Angles with those in Britain. Procopius also probably saw no conflict with presenting the Frisians as likely immigrants earlier in his chapter, because they lived in Britain now, not along the Dutch shores.

As for the Heruli, their presumed presence in the Low Countries is mainly based on de Boone's opinion that they co-operated in a Late Roman army unit *Herulorum et Batavorum* (de Boone 1951, 49). But, as Ellegård says, this concerned Heruli stationed with Batavians in Austrian Passau (*Castra Batava*). Another segment of the Herulians remained an independent group and existed with some success until *c*. 560, but not in the Netherlands (Ellegård 1987).

Not until the second half of the 7th century are the Frisians mentioned again in early-medieval Frankish sources. The *Vita* of Saint Eligius of Noyon (588–660), written by the friend of Eligius, Bishop Dado of Rouen († 683), and re-edited in the course of the 8th century (Lebecq 1983, vol. 2, 47), mentions the hostile reception of the Christian faith 'in Flanders and Antwerp' by 'Frisians and Suevi and other barbarians coming from the seacoast or distant lands' (*Vita Eligii*, 2.3). Apart from mentioning Flanders and Antwerp for the first time, one can still see the reuse of the classical ethnographic tradition. The name Frisian had become a self-fulfilling prophecy, and the *Suevi* must have been the learned name for the local name for the 'sea-people', still known today as *Zeeuwen*: an appropriate name for a region that is dominated by the sea (Halbertsma 2000, 56). The learned interpretation of *Suevi* causes confusion, however, about whether or not we are dealing with *Suebi* or *Suevi* mentioned by classical authors or Gregory of Tours (*Hist.* II.2 and V.15 and 41). The name *Suevi* was still used in the *Annales Vedastini*, describing a Viking attack in this region in 880. The later *Zeeuwen* is the name for inhabitants of the county (now province) of *Zeeland* (first mentioned in 1254). The Germanic word for 'sea', **saiwi*, resembles *Suevi*.

The 'new Frisians' we encounter in the 7th and early 8th centuries are mentioned in the context of the struggle for power between Frankish and Frisian kings and renewed Christian missionary activities. Under the Carolingians, the name Frisian turns out to be applied to the entire Dutch coastal area, thus adding an official *gens* to the Carolingian Empire. How far this represents an older policital Frisian entity is discussed below.

Habitation history of the western coastal area in the late 3rd to 6th centuries AD on the basis of archaeology

The physical landscape and discontinuity of population numbers

Recent archaeological and palaeogeographical studies shed more light on habitation along the coast of Holland in the Migration Period (cf. Knol and IJssennagger, this vol.). Situated in a vast holocene delta, it is the physical landscape that sets the scene. It was characterized by several rows of cultivated low dunes along the coast, divided by the estuaries of the rivers Meuse, Old Rhine and the 'Oer-IJ', a former northern branch of the Rhine and Vecht. The dune area and the hinterland towards Utrecht–Dorestad were separated by huge impassable peat areas, with small streams that drained into the main rivers. The wilderness of the peat beds was to be settled only from the 10th century onwards, although improved drainage made this even possible from the early 8th century in the areas around Medemblik and Texel in the northernmost part of North Holland (Bazelmans *et al.* 2004, 20). This meant that habitation was limited to the relatively high ground of the dunes and river banks. Needless to say the rivers were important life-lines for communication and transport with the outside world.

There is a persistent image in the literature that the whole of the Dutch coast became uninhabitable in the 4th to 5th centuries owing to extensive inundation by the sea, caused by the 'Dunkerque II transgression'. This dramatic model has nowadays been replaced by a more nuanced one, the 'process approach', which takes into account regional developments in relation to available flood-basin storage capacity and tidal range (Vos 2015, 8–11 and 41–4). Zeeland had drawn the shortest straw, however; the extensive peats eroded into intertidal sand- and mud-flats, except for some settlements in the dunes along the sea coast, like Domburg (possibly *Walichrum*). The region could only be used again from the 9th century onwards, when saltmarsh levees and ridges developed above the storm surge level (Vos and van Heeringen 1997, 67–9, and Enclosure II, maps 13–14). The northern *terp* region of Groningen-Friesland suffered not from increased marine floodings but from an ever higher silted-up cap ridge along the coastline, preventing drainage of its hinterland (Nieuwhof 2011, 62–3).

North and South Holland also suffered a deterioration of the natural drainage sytems, partly caused by human action; the surface of certain cultivated peat domes, which were artificially drained in Roman times, began to sink. This made them swampy and liable to flooding, especially in the Meuse estuary (Dijkstra 2011, 38–9). Even though the water discharge of the Old Rhine gradually decreased during the Roman Period, being steadily redirected in the south-western direction of the Hollandse IJssel and Lek, the river flood frequency and the magnitude of floods probably increased. This was caused by intensified deforestation and agricultural land-use in the continental hinterland of both the Rhine and the Meuse (van Dinter 2013, 13–14). But gradually the situation changed for the better. At some point between *c.* 470 and 550 an extreme high-water event must have caused the Old Rhine to form a new watercourse, resulting in much better drainage and new scope for exploitation of the levees (Brijker and van Zijverden 2011, 17).

Overall, people managed to make a living in the delta for thousands of years, learning to live with the problems and potential of the water. Arable farming was possible in stretches of the dunes and levees, but with large areas suitable for meadows available, the most important aspect of farming was the husbandry of cattle and sheep.

Worsening drainage was a major factor in the drop of population noticeable in the archaeological record. Other factors that must have stimulated people to seek their fortune elsewhere were probably the over-exploitation of the landscape for the provisioning of the Roman army (Groenman-van Waateringe 1983) and political turmoil. Inter-tribal raids on unprotected, small-scale communities close to the sea must also have been a stimulus to leave (Bazelmans 2009, 332). For South Holland, the estuaries of the Rhine and Meuse and the adjoining dunes, it is estimated that in the period AD 260–450 the population fell by about 90% compared with the Roman Period. The number of people thus shrank from about 10,000–16,000 (including the military apparatus, *vici* and the small town of *Forum Hadriani*) to maybe a few hundred. These inhabitants were living primarily on the higher parts of the river banks, especially in the few Roman forts that still functioned, such as Valkenburg (*Praetorium Agrippinae*) and Brittenburg (*Lugdunum*). For two sites along the sea shore south of the Meuse, Oostvoorne and Goeree, the function as forts remains uncertain, let alone their role in the *litus Saxonum*. It seems clear, however, that in the almost depopulated coastal region, only the safeguarding of the important junctions of the long-distance military infrastructure was required (Bazelmans *et al.* 2004, 13 and 16; Dijkstra 2011, 71–5).

The dune area shows less habitation activity in the Late Roman Period. The market town of *Forum Hadriani* did not survive and was never heard of again. The place-name *Foreburg* (modern *Voorburg*) mentioned in the 8th- or 9th-century property list of the Bishop of Utrecht points to some continuity of habitation, but probably as a more or less rural settlement. The Roman ruins finally vanished from sight until their rediscovery in the early 19th century by Professsor C. Reuvens. Prehistoric water names and a few place-names (apparently also based on water names) which survived into medieval times point to a continuity of habitation to some extent (Fig. 4.2). The drop in population and the survival of some prehistoric names can also be seen in North Holland. Since archaeological visibility in this region is less hampered by modern city extensions, there are even a few known sites of the 4th–5th century AD, such as Dorregeest and Castricum-Oosterbuurt (de Koning 2003; 2012, 21–2; Bazelmans *et al.* 2004, 26–7). In the central river

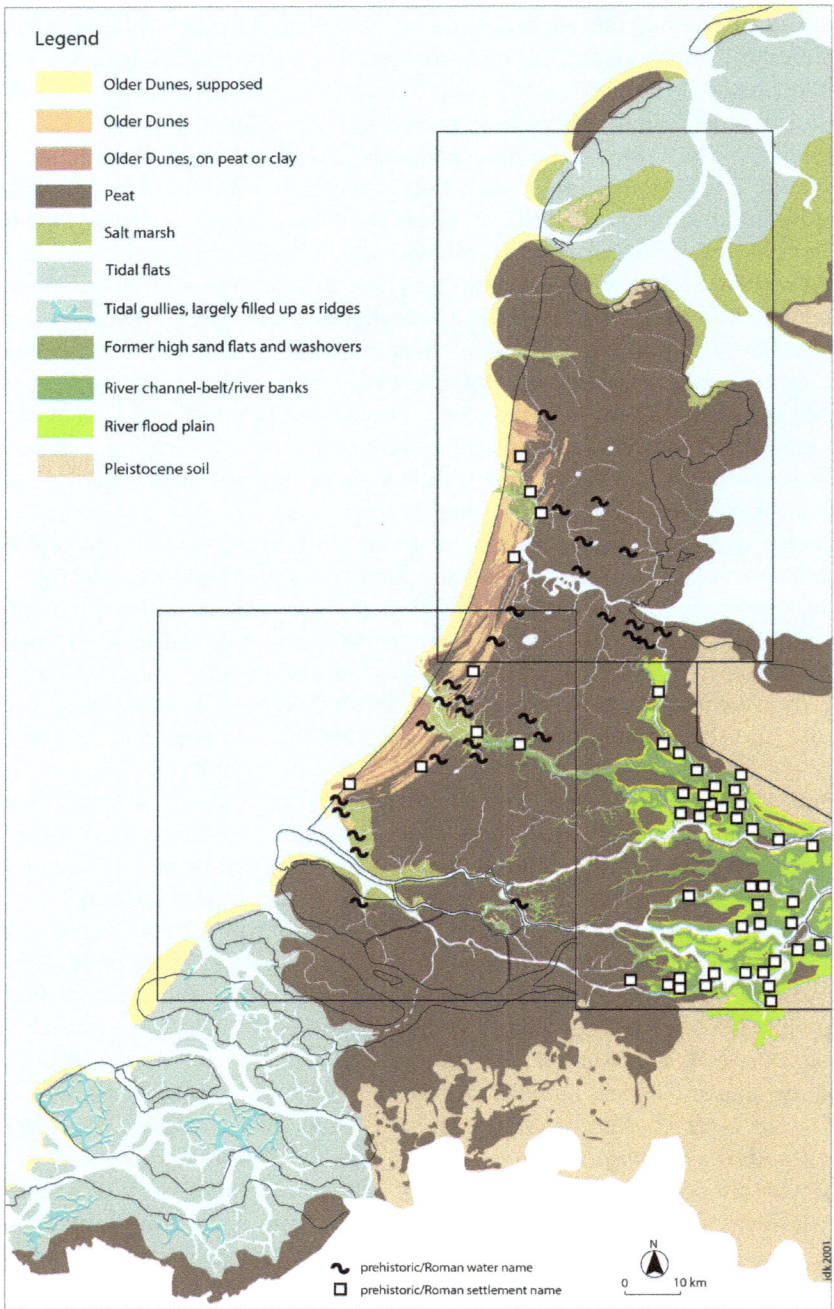

Fig. 4.2. Palaeogeographical reconstruction with the distribution of water- and place-names that derive from prehistoric or Roman times in the western Netherlands (no inventory of water-names in the central river area is available). Based on Henderikx 1986, Bazelmans *et al.* 2004, Dijkstra 2011 and de Koning 2012.

area of the Netherlands (up the Rhine from Woerden onwards), both archaeological finds and the quantity of surviving place-names point to more continuous habitation in the Late Roman Period. The presence of relatively high levees certainly helped in this case (Henderikx 1986; Dijkstra 2011, 80–1; van Dinter 2013, appendix 1).

The decline of population must have been worse in the *terp* region. In the province of Friesland, habitation in the second half of the 3rd and 4th century was reduced to virtually nil; even prehistoric place-names did not survive. Groningen seems to have been less thoroughly depopulated than Friesland (Nieuwhof 2011).

South and North Holland show a steady growth of population from about AD 450/500 onwards. Based on a reconstruction of the number of contemporary settlements, the population of South Holland grew to an estimated 1,800–2,400 people in the Merovingian Period (c. AD 450–750) and about 2,400–3,100 in the Carolingian Period (c. AD 750–900). It is supposed that comparable numbers should apply in North Holland, which is about the same size. The estimate of 3–5 people per square kilometre for both provinces is typical for habitation in sandy regions elsewhere in the early-medieval Netherlands (Dijkstra 2011, 102–8). In theory, the western coastal region could have generated the calculated population growth by itself from the surviving inhabitants of the 4th century, but this is of course unlikely. Networks of marriage, family relations and consequent property interests must have generated migration of peoples from and to surrounding areas. It is through the archaeological study of material culture that we try to find out more about the cultural affinities and the possible ethnic identity of the people(s) living in the western Dutch littoral.

Material culture and (ethnic) identity

Finds such as pots and brooches were long regarded as ideal mirrors of people's cultural and ethnic identities. Nowadays archaeologists realize that this view was in fact a product of the 19th century, when nation states and the people living in them were perceived as unitary entities, of one biological descent, with an invariable character and unchanged cultural traditions. Influenced by sociology and anthropology, ethnicity is now viewed as a dynamic phenomenon that changes over time according to the historical social context. It is important to realize that typical markers of ethnicity, like descent, territory, language, law, clothing, ceramics and so on, can be constructions, are not used as markers in every case, and may even appear in contradictory situations (see, e.g., Daim 1982; Geary 1983; Pohl 1991; Bazelmans *et al.* 2005, 23). Furthermore, ethnicity is only one form of identity that people use, alongside class or gender for example. In the Roman and Early Medieval Periods ethnicity usually mattered in a military-political context, generated by elite groups who sought a god-given legitimacy for their power, and a common identity to bind their followers (Wenskus 1961).

What cultural picture emerges for the western coastal area in the Migration Period? It may be no surprise that the distribution and dating of various finds show that the region lay within a continuum of influences from surrounding areas. The architectural tradition of longhouses belonged to the northern, 'Germanic', world, but with a positioning of entrances typical of the area between the Vlie and the Flemish coast (Dijkstra 2011, 202–5). Less is known about the early-medieval building tradition in the *terp* region of

Friesland and Groningen, however, owing to the limited archaeological information, the extensive use of sods and general lack of wooden structures, which could be the products of extensive reuse.

The cemeteries in South Holland, datable to the first half of the 6th century to the greater part of the 7th century, contained cremations as well as inhumations orientated in various directions (notably south–north and south-west–north-east, or vice versa, since the position of the head is not always documented from excavations of the early 20th century) and partly with crouched bodies. The similarities with the central river area as well as the *terp* region, and indeed Anglo-Saxon cemeteries, again show a connection to the northern world.

But there are differences from the northern world as well. In the Merovingian Period, cemeteries and settlements in South Holland show a very high percentage of wheel-thrown pottery, up to 80 to 100%, just like the central river area. These wares were for the most part imported from the Frankish hinterland. The favourable geographical position down the Rhine and Meuse is the main reason for this abundance of imported pots. The local hand-made wares consist mostly of plain, undecorated cooking pots, tempered either with chopped grass or gritted stone. This kind of pottery was used commonly in the north-western 'Germanic' world, showing how international pottery styles can develop. This seems also (partly) true for the decorated pots in 'Anglo-Saxon' style. The decorations must have had some symbolic and religious meaning, of which ethnicity could be a part. The few decorated pots (or fragments) in 'Anglo-Saxon' style are only found in the cemeteries of Rijnsburg–de Horn (7 pots, Fig. 4.3), Den Haag–Solleveld (4), known as 'Monster' in older publications, and in settlement contexts like Oegstgeest–Nieuw Rhijngeest (2), Leiderdorp (1) and in the ruins of the town *Forum Hadriani* (1) (Dijkstra 2011, 265–6 and fig. 6.33; for Leiderdorp: Dijkstra *et al.*, in prep.). Note that the cemetery of Katwijk-Klein Duin is not mentioned: only three undecorated urns were found there (Dijkstra 2011, 238). Two of these have three (pierced) lugs, which we do not count as decoration. Further inland, a handful of decorated Anglo-Saxon-style pots are also known, notably from the cemeteries of Garderen in the Veluwe region and along the Lower Rhine in Elst (7), Rhenen (10) and Wageningen (5) (Garderen: de Boone 1970–1; Elst: Verwers and van Tent 2015; Rhenen: Wagner and Ypey 2011; Wageningen: van Es 1964).

Striking is the absence from West Frisia of early, 4th- to 5th-century types of Anglo-Saxon pottery, such as beakers, wide *Schalenurnen* and lavishly decorated *Buckelurnen*. Based on the accompanying wheel-thrown wares and the footplate of a brooch found in one of the urns in Den Haag-Solleveld, the western Anglo-Saxon pots can be dated to the 6th or the greater part of the 7th century (Dijkstra 2011, 247–8 and 350).[1] This is strengthened by their apparent absence from 7th-century settlement contexts, and radiocarbon dates of cremated bone in the urns recently published by Lanting and van der Plicht (2009/2010, 141, 145 and 149). We disagree, however, with their arguments for ignoring a second peak of a bimodal distribution of 1 sigma (68%) probability *c.* cal. AD 525–600/640, and so dating almost all of these pots in the area of the first peak, *c.* cal. AD

---

[1] Because of its striking resemblance to a 'Frankish' brooch with a rectangular headplate found in Katwijk-Zanderij, the Solleveld brooch can be dated to *c.* 520–70.

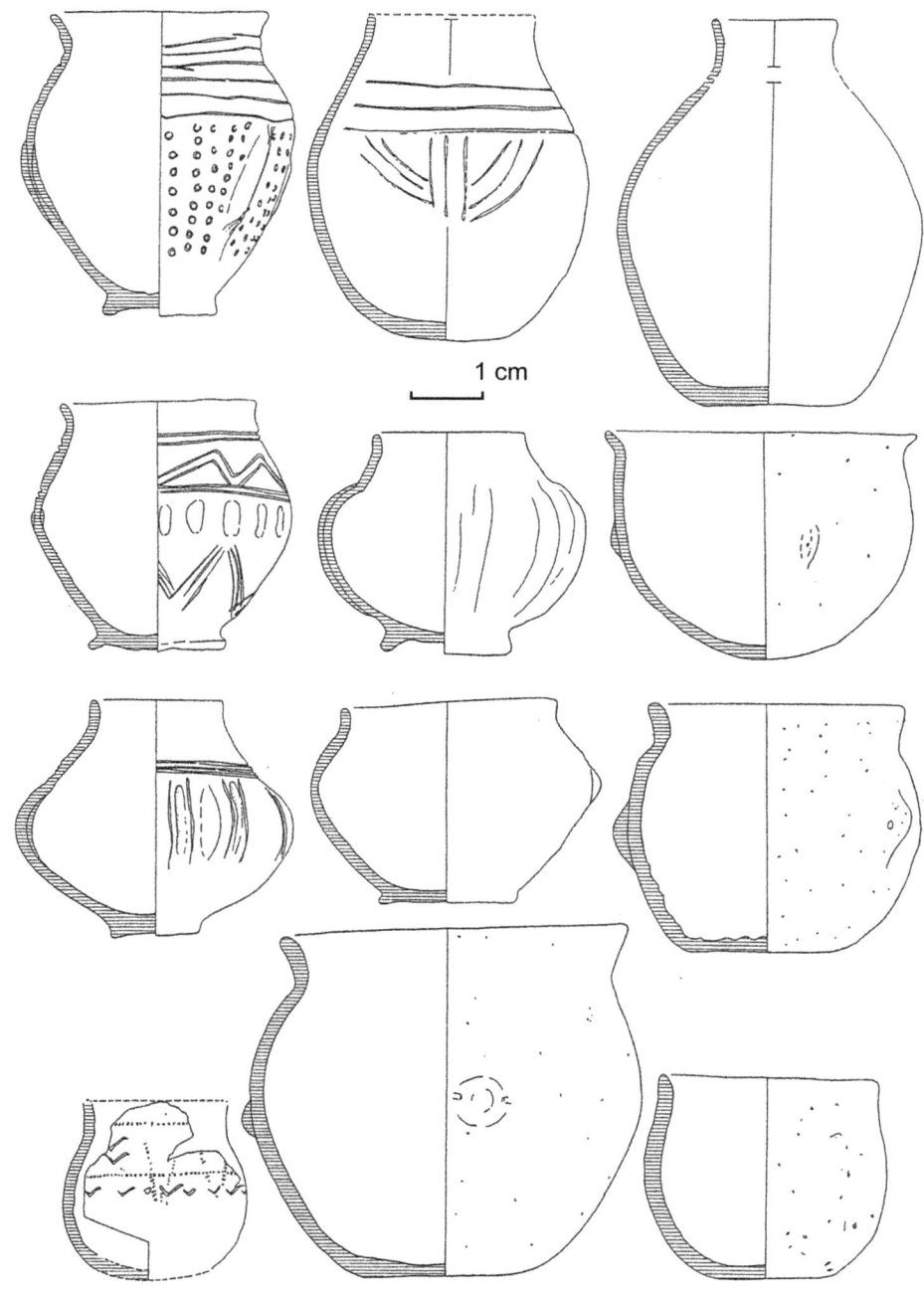

Fig. 4.3. Hand-made plain and decorated 'Anglo-Saxon' style pottery from the early-medieval cemetery of Rijnsburg-De Horn (collection RMO). Scale 1:4.

400–525. This preference was guided by their idea of historical developments, positing that the Anglo-Saxon pots were superseded by Frankish wheel-thrown pottery as soon as *Frisia citerior* was conquered by the Franks in the first half of the 6th century (Lanting and van der Plicht 2009/2010, 78, 131, 134; 2011/2012, 376–9). This is a rather peculiar way of reconstructing the past, whereby material culture keeps pace with supposed military and political developments and a Frisian can change into a Frank as soon as he holds a *francisca* axe!

It is in any case striking that other typically 5th-century 'Saxon' inspired finds, like Scandinavian-type bracteates, supporting-arm, saucer, equal-armed and cruciform brooches, are also absent from West Frisia (Nicolay 2014, 347). Only one example of a cruciform brooch is known from the settlement of Katwijk–Zanderij and this seems a plain, unclassifiable type, possibly datable *c.* AD 475–560/570 on the basis of the rounded triangular terminal which can be found as a component in Martin's group 4 (Fig. 4.4) (cf. Knol 2008, 298; Reichstein 1975; Martin 2015, 66 and 128). Thus, the few Anglo-Saxon style influences in West Frisia (and also, for the main part, further upstream along the Rhine for that matter) point to some cultural exchange with typical Anglo-Saxon elements from surrounding regions in the 6th or possibly the 7th century. It seems implausible to explain the presence of these few pots as imported trade goods or gifts; they are rather fragile, and worth less than metal objects (Krol 2006, 18). There are several other possible (simultaneous) explanations, certainly when one takes into account the fact that handmade ceramics were probably made by women. Firstly, they could have been developed by taking over a new style from outside amongst the few people left along the coast. Secondly, such pottery could have been introduced by brides from surrounding regions like the *terp* region, England, or the central river area. And thirdly, it could have been made by a small number of immigrants from the aforementioned areas (Dijkstra 2011, 354). Either way, the material culture gives no indication that, in the 5th century, West Frisia was chosen by Anglo-Saxon settlers from the Elbe–Weser area as a new home. Only at a later stage, in the 6th century, are Anglo-Saxon influences visible in part of the material culture. Of course, such influence may have been more extensive; nothing stopped either ethnic new Frisians or Anglo-Saxons using imported, wheel-thrown pottery from the Frankish Rhineland, simply because they were easy to obtain. But we suppose the influence from the Frankish hinterland was just as important.

Interestingly, the place-name of the village of Sassenheim, situated on a dune ridge north-west of Leiden, could be additional evidence for a very modest presence of ethnic Saxons in the estuary of the Old Rhine. This toponym means 'homestead of Saxons' (Künzel *et al.* 1988, 189, 315 and 396). The recorded forms are *Hostsagnem* and *Westsagnem* (8th–first half of the 10th century), *Sasheim* or *Saxheim* (first half of the 11th century). East and West *Sagnem* were probably situated opposite each other on separate dune ridges. Such a name only makes sense amidst other, non-Saxon folk. Another option is a first element derived from a personal name *Sahso* or *Saxo*, but does this really change things? This kind of personal name would still have stood out for outsiders. The same can be said for other toponyms which may refer to tribal names, like Saaksum (AD 802–17 *Sasheim*), Englum (AD 1251 *Ingaldum*), both in Groningen, and Engelum (AD 1335 *Anglum*) in the eastern part of Westergo. The names of Saaksum and Englum could be further evidence that Groningen was less depopulated in the 4th century.

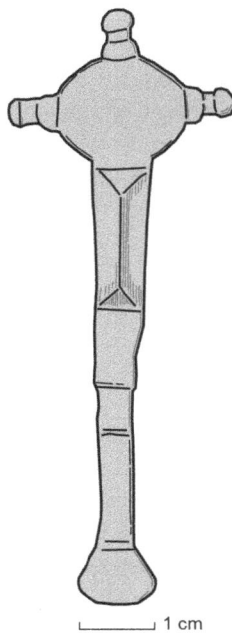

Fig. 4.4. The only known cruciform brooch from the western Dutch coastal area to date, found in Katwijk and probably datable to the late 5th or greater part of the 6th century. Redrawn after Knol 2008, fig. 14.6.

Thus, the Frisian coastal lands were not so much of a unity in every respect. Nicolay (2014) has also noticed a division in the way silver and gold objects were used. In socially and politically stable areas like West Frisia these objects were almost never buried as ritual hoards or used as grave goods but remained in circulation. In the more unstable *terp* region, however, such symbolic objects were handled in quite the opposite way. This division also reinforces the proposition that the internal partition into three zones in the *Lex Frisionum* was based on cultural differences east and west of the Vlie.

But even within the region of West Frisia there are notable cultural differences. In North Holland no early-medieval cemeteries have been found except for a possible small group of urns in Texel (Bazelmans *et al.* 2004, 26). It seems that the people kept to the almost invisible grave ritual known from the Iron Age onwards, with isolated inhumation graves and other, unknown ways of disposing of the dead (for instance non-interred cremation, or exhumation?). A second difference is that decorated Anglo-Saxon ceramics are lacking. Finally, a few settlements in North Holland show a variation of the building tradition, whereby longhouses are two-aisled instead of one- or three-aisled. This may be a prolonged tradition from Roman times (Bazelmans *et al.* 2004; Dijkstra 2011, 271–2).

Clearly, there was contact between the neighbouring coastal regions too, especially from the 6th century onwards. This is shown not only by some of the Anglo-Saxon pottery but especially by the distribution of brooches of the so-called Domburg Type, datable *c.* 525–650. Their core distribution is confined to the coastal areas which are traditionally seen as Frisian. In the relatively small border area that Frisia was, they could have functioned as an ethnic marker to outsiders, notably Franks. Conversely their primary significance may have been directed at insiders, for instance as a marker of married women or as amulets, creating a typical geographical distribution only by the nature of being nearest neighbours in the coastal lowlands. The distribution of Domburg brooches is almost identical with that of Frankish wheel-thrown pottery along the coast. Both items must have been spread through the same (commercial) network. Another possible ethnic unifier we have to discuss is language.

The relationship with the 'North Sea Germanic' dialect

Linguistic studies identify a series of sounds and words along the littoral of the southern North Sea which do not fit in the development from Lower Frankish to modern Germanic languages, including Dutch. They do, however, fit with phenomena in modern Frisian and English, as well as (largely extinct) dialects of the provinces of Flanders, Zeeland and North and South Holland, and to a lesser extent along the north-west German coast and part of the German and Dutch hinterland. This old dialect is named North Sea Germanic (NSGmc, also known as 'Ingvaeonic': a rather confusing name derived from Tacitus's *Germania*).

This is not the place to go into the linguistic peculiarities of NSGmc, but there is not much clarity about its background, spread and date of origin. On the whole, scholars assume an origin in the north-western coastal regions of the Continent prior to the *adventus Saxonum*, when the speakers of this variant were in closest contact. After the migration to England, NSGmc divided into several dialects on both sides of the North Sea. Schrijver has recently sought an explanation in another direction (Schrijver 1999; 2000; this vol.). Because the vowel system of NSGmc is similar to British Celtic spoken around AD 500, it seems probable that people also spoke some variety of Celtic along the coasts of Flanders, Holland and Friesland. These inhabitants later spoke in a Germanic tongue, but did not lose their Celtic accent. The first germanicization of 'North Sea Celtic' could have taken place with the arrival of Batavians and Cananefates in the late 1st century BC. A second phase of germanicization was brought about by migrating Saxons and 'new Frisians' on both sides of the North Sea.

Kuhn, on the other hand (1955), argued for an origin *after* the migration. Intensive overseas contacts and trade resulted in a North Sea Culture, with common linguistic ties. This hypothesis was countered by the argument that the linguistic similarities between English and the Dutch coast are so strong that they must date from before the *adventus Saxonum*. Another argument is that NSGmc elements do not gradually reduce from the English littoral into the hinterland, something one would expect if NSGmc developed in a later stage (Stiles 1995, 183). Ultimately, in the course of the Early Middle Ages NSGmc developed into Old Frisian, Old English, Old Saxon and Old Low Franconian.

It is questionable, however, how a relatively hypothetical reconstruction of the linguistic evolution along the coasts of the North Sea can contribute to the archaeological and historical debate about the formation of (ethnic) identity. According to Hines (1990, 33), linguistic details of *c.* AD 400 may already have been obscured by *c.* AD 600. A dangerous network of circular arguments based on others' disciplines is a pitfall. If there was already a linguistic continuum *before* the depopulation of the greater part of the continental North Sea littoral, the origin of immigrants in the *terp* region or in West Frisia cannot be determined on linguistic grounds. The migrants were from the same NSGmc region.

Based on the habitation history outlined above there are three possible scenarios to explain the presence of NSGmc in the western Netherlands:
1. It was spoken before the Migration Period and survived the drop in population in the 4th to late 5th centuries.
2. It was introduced during the late 5th to 6th centuries under the influence of socio-cultural contacts and/or migrations with/from neighbouring coastal regions along the southern North Sea coast.
3. It appeared in the 7th century under the political influence of a Frisian confederacy of petty kingdoms.

This is not the place to go into detail concerning the linguistic implications of these scenarios. They are presented solely as further food for thought for the historical linguists.

Although contacts and exchange across the North Sea flourished, a Frisian language developed from the NSGmc dialect in the 8th century. A 'nationalization' of language varieties was probably responsible for this; it was in the interest of the Frisians in power to mark off the distinctiveness of their territories in language variety (Hines 1995, 54–9). Relicts of Frisian in the western Netherlands can still be found, mostly in toponymy, on the 'old land' of dune ridges and levees, and especially near the mouth of the Old Rhine (Blok 1958; 1959a). Ultimately, in the 12th to 13th centuries, Low Franconian gained more and more influence in the county of Holland, although in North Holland, north of the IJ stream, Frisian was spoken much longer. There is no evidence that Low Franconian gained influence because of immigration of farmers from the Utrecht river area during the peat reclamations in Holland (Blok 1959b, 24–6; van Bree 1997, 21–34).

The relation of the western coastal region to early-medieval Frisians

How were the inhabitants of the western coastal area related to the early-medieval Frisians? This is of course a difficult question to answer, since our sources do not speak for themselves, let alone the inhabitants. Certainly in the initial period of the 5th and 6th centuries AD, the inhabitants of the coastal area of Holland would have formed a heterogeneous though interrelated group with various ethnic backgrounds: a residual population from the area itself supplemented by 'Franks' from the central riverine area, 'new Frisians' from the northern coastal area and perhaps a number of 'Anglo-Saxons' from England. In any event, repopulation did not depend on a wave of migration from Middle Frisia, as envisaged by older generations of historians. In the sphere of politics, it can be supposed that various elite networks were active in the different regions. Some of the aristocracy may have worked their way up to become (petty) kings, demonstrating their military, political and religious authority to their *Gefolgschaft*. The spheres of influence of these minor kingdoms fluctuated along with their success. In the case of the assumption of political power by a Frisian king, his subjects were considered as belonging to the *gens* of the Frisians, notwithstanding any underlying, sub-regional ethnic self-definition.

One wonders if the reappearance of the Frisians can be dated back to the decades around the year 600. According to Nicolay, the distribution of the jewellery of royalty or their retinue datable to *c.* AD 580–630 in Wijnaldum and the cemetery of Rijnsburg and Katwijk indicates the presence of kingdoms in the *terp* region and the western Netherlands respectively (Nicolay 2014, 357–9), both areas that were part of Frisia in Carolingian times. Maybe their existence sheds new light on two late-6th-century references to Frisians: firstly the gold coins which mention a certain *Audulfus* (a Frisian king or a Frankish victor?) together with the name *Frisia* (Bazelmans 2009, 330; Dijkstra 2011, 367), and secondly the poet Venantius Fortunatus, who in a eulogy dated 580 calls King Chilperic I 'the fear of the furthest Frisians and Suebi' (Venantius Fortunatus, *Op. Poet.* 9.1). The aforementioned evidence of royal jewellery points not only to an extension of existing elite networks, but also to socio-policital stress, whereby threats to position were strongly reflected in depositions or burial ritual. A political confrontation between Frisians and Franks would be the most likely explanation; the Frisians referred to in the second half of the 7th century would not have appeared out of the blue. The question for the period of *c.* 600 is which of the two kingdoms felt threatened by whom? Were they both part of a Frisian confederacy of kingdoms, developed to withstand growing Frankish influence? Or did the kingdom in the western Netherlands, with its long-standing cultural connection to the Frankish hinterland, feel cornered by extending Frisian power from the *terp* or the Utrecht region? For the decades around AD 700, historical sources make it clear that South and North Holland were part of the Frisian kingdom. When the Franks took control of this region they automatically labelled every coastal-dweller as Frisian, leading to the geographical use of this ethnic label, as can be seen in the *Lex Frisionum* (van Egmond, unpubl.).

Conclusions

From historical, palaeogeographical and archaeological evidence, it is clear that the Dutch western coastal area was not occupied by Anglo-Saxon groups during the 5th-century *adventus Saxonum* like the *terp* region of Friesland and Groningen. The few Anglo-Saxon-style pots and brooch present are datable to the 6th century, and are the result of growing contacts between the *terp* region, the Dutch central river area, and even England. This does not mean, as Bazelmans has already observed, that people of the Dutch coastal area did not migrate to England at all (or to other regions such as northern Gaul). But their loss of identity in the turmoil of the 3rd and 4th centuries makes them virtually impossible to trace (Bremmer 1990, 366; Bazelmans 2009, 332–3).

Why was it all quiet on the western front in the western Netherlands in the Migration Period? Because this area turned into a periphery, in terms of its geography, population numbers, land use and international politics. For people from the Anglo-Saxon homelands, *Britannia* offered better opportunities. The Dutch west coast was simply ignored (Fig. 4.5). The region regained some momentum from about AD 500 onwards, with renewed scope for settlement. Situated on the lower reaches of the major rivers of the Meuse, Old Rhine and Vecht/IJ, the Frankish hinterland played an influential part.

The Western Netherlands and the 'North Sea Culture'

Of course this did not stop the population developing contacts with the neighbouring parts of the Dutch coast or even with England. The more advantageous geographical position of South Holland made the region more 'international' than North Holland, which remained more isolated, with some more 'old fashioned' cultural traditions. Only from the 7th, or even the late 6th, century onwards, with renewed political interest from the Merovingians and subsequently the Carolingians in the Dutch west coast, does the lighting of history gradually start to appear again. It is in this period that the label Frisian was applied to the coastal region, only to be changed to Holland some five centuries later. By then, it was not so quiet at all.

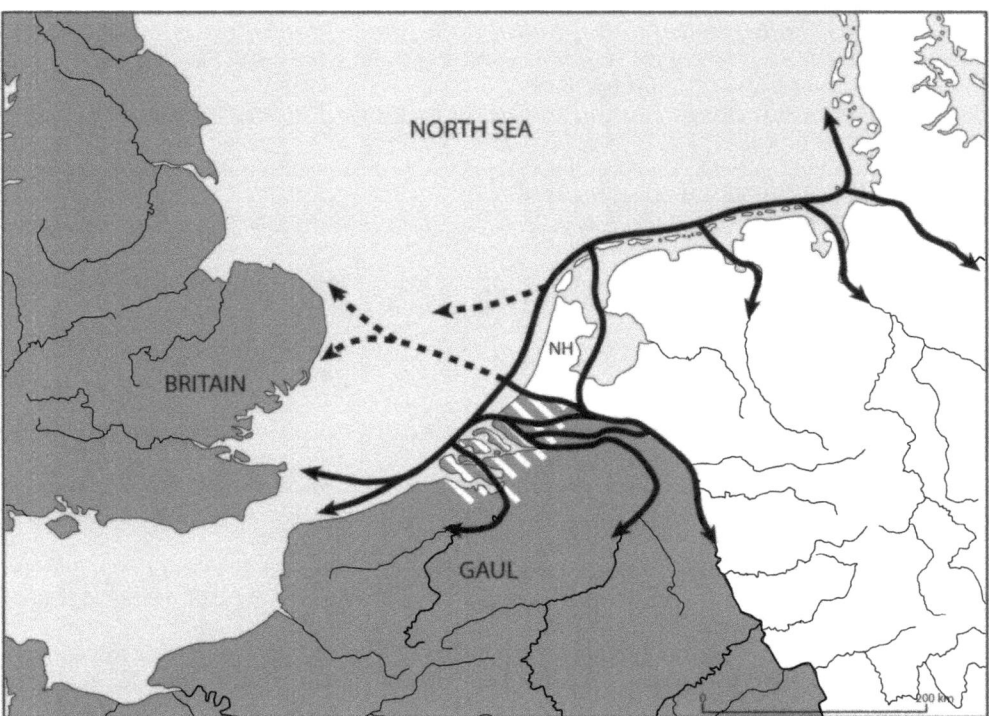

Fig. 4.5. The perifical geographical position of the western Dutch coastal area, especially North Holland (NH), in the Migration Period. Arrowed lines: main routes of water transport. Dotted lines: uncertain direct sea-crossing between the Continent and England.

References

Primary sources

Anonymous/ Melis Stoke, J. W. J. Burgers ed. 2004, *Rijmkroniek van Holland (366–1305)* (Den Haag).
Beke, Johannes de, *Croniken van den Stichte van Utrecht ende van Hollant*, Rijks Geschiedkundige Publicatiën, grote serie 180, ed. H. Bruch 1982 ('s Gravenhage).
Bede, *Ecclesiastical History of the English People with Bede's Letter to Egbert and Cuthbert's Letter on the Death of Bede*, ed. and trans. L. Sherley-Price, R. E. Latham and D. H. Farmer 1990 (London).
Gregory of Tours, *Historiae*. In *Monumenta Germaniae Historica, Scriptores rerum Merovingicarum* Vol. 1. 1, ed. B. Krusch and W. Levison, 1951, 2nd edn
Gregory of Tours, trans. F. J. A. M. Meijer 1994, *Gregorius van Tours, Historiën* (Baarn).
Geer van Jutphaas, B. J. L. de, ed. 1867 *Kronijk van Holland van een ongenoemden geestelijke* (better known as *Kronijk van den clerc uten Laghen Landen bi der see*), Werken Historisch Genootschap Utrecht, N. R. no. 6 (Utrecht).
Procopius, *De Bellis, History of the Wars* vol. 3 and 5, ed. and trans. H. B. Dewing 1961–2, The Loeb Classical Library (Cambridge Mass.).
Venantius Fortunatus, *Opera Poetica*. In *Monumenta Germaniae Historica, Auctores Antiquissimi* Vol. 4. 1, 1881 (Berlin).
Venantius Fortunatus, trans. J. George 1995, *Venantius Fortunatus: Personal and Political Poems*, Translated texts for historians 23 (Liverpool).
Vita Eligii, ed. B. Krusch 1902, *Monumenta Germaniae Historica. Scriptores Rerum Merovingicarum* Vol. 4 (Hannover), 632–742
Vita Eligii, trans. J. A. McNamara 1997, *The Life of St. Eligius, 588–660*, Internet Medieval Source Book, http://legacy. fordham. edu/Halsall/basis/eligius. asp.

Secondary sources

Bartholomew, Philip 2005, 'Continental connections: Angles, Saxons and others in Bede and in Procopius', *Anglo-Saxon Studies in Archaeology and History* 13, 19–30.
Bazelmans, Jos 2001, 'Die spätrömerzeitliche Besiedlungslücke im niederländischen Küstengebiet und das Fortbestehen des Friesennamens', *Emder Jahrbuch für historische Landeskunde Ostfrieslands* 81, 7–61.
Bazelmans, Jos 2009, 'The early-medieval use of ethnic names from classical Antiquity: the case of the Frisians'. In *Ethnic Constructs in Antiquity: The Role of Power and Tradition*, ed. T. Derks and N. Roymans (Amsterdam), 321–38.
Bazelmans, Jos, Menno Dijkstra and Jan de Koning 2004, 'Holland during the first millenium'. In *Bruc Ealles Well. Archaeological Essays Concerning the Peoples of North-West Europe in the First Millenium* AD, Acta Archaeologica Lovaniensia Monographiae 15, ed. M. Lodewijckx (Leuven), 1–36.
Bazelmans, Jos, Henny Groenendijk and Gilles de Langen 2005, 'De late prehistorie en protohistorie van Holoceen Noord-Nederland', *Nationale Onderzoeksagenda Archeologie*, Chapter 12 (version 1. 0) (www. noaa. nl).
Blok, Dirk P. 1958, 'Friese invloed aan de Rijnmond?', *Fryske Plaknammen* 11, 89–90.
Blok, Dirk P. 1959a, 'Nogmaals: Friese invloed aan de Rijnmond', *Fryske Plaknammen* 12, 17–18.
Blok, Dirk P. 1959b, 'De vestigingsgeschiedenis van Holland en Utrecht in het licht van de plaatsnamen'. In *Studies over de oudste plaatsnamen van Holland en Utrecht*, Bijdragen en Mededelingen der Naamkunde-Commissie van de Koninklijke Nederlandse Akademie van Wetenschappen 17, ed. M. Gysseling and D. P. Blok (Amsterdam), 13–34.
Blok, Dirk P. 1969, 'Holland und Westfriesland', *Frühmittelalterliche Studien* 3, 347–61.
Boeles, Pieter C. J. A. 1927, *Friesland tot de elfde eeuw; zijn oudste beschaving en geschiedenis* ('s-Gravenhage).

Boeles, Pieter C. J. A. 1951, *Friesland tot de elfde eeuw. Zijn voor- en vroege geschiedenis*, 2nd edn ('s-Gravenhage).
Boeles, Pieter C. J. A. 1958, 'De Warnen en Friesland', *Westerheem* 7, 5–12.
Boone, W. J. de 1951, 'De lage landen in de Westeuropese politiek omstreeks 500', *Tijdschrift voor geschiedenis* 64, 45–54.
Boone, W. J. de 1954, *De Franken van hun eerste optreden tot de dood van Childerik* (Amsterdam).
Boone, W. J. de 1970–1, 'An early mediaeval grave field on the Beumelerberg near Garderen, Province of Gelderland', *Berichten van de Rijksdienst voor Oudheidkundig Bodemonderzoek* 20–1, 249–492.
Bos, Jurjen M. 2001, 'Archaeological evidence pertaining to the Frisians in the Netherlands'. In *Handbuch des Friesischen*, ed. H. H. Munske, N. Århammer, V. F. Faltings, J. F. Hoekstra, O. Vries, A. G. H. Walker and O. Witts (Tübingen), 487–92.
Bree, Cor van 1997, *Een oud onderwerp opnieuw bekeken: het ingweoons* (Leiden).
Bremmer Jr, Rolf H. 1990, 'The nature of the evidence for a Frisian participation in the Adventus Saxonum'. In *Britain 400–600: Language and History*, ed. A. Bammesberger and A. Wollmann (Heidelberg), 353–71.
Brijker, J. M., and W. K. van Zijverden 2011, 'Een dynamisch landschap in de monding van de Rijn'. In *Centrale erven langs de monding van de Oude Rijn gedurende de Vroege Middeleeuwen. Archeologisch onderzoek op en rond de Zanderij-Westerbaan in Katwijk. De projecten Duinvallei fase 8 en 9 en Colligny*, ADC-rapport 2846, ed. H. M. van der Velde (Amersfoort), 17–27.
Burgers, J. W. J. 1999, *De Rijmkroniek van Holland en zijn auteurs. Historiografie in Holland door de Anonymus (1280–1282) en de grafelijke klerk Melis Stoke (begin veertiende eeuw)* (Hilversum).
Campbell, James ed. 1991, *The Anglo-Saxons* (London).
Daim, Falko 1982, 'Gedanken zum Ethnosbegriff', *Mitteilungen der Anthropologische Gesellschaft in Wien* 112, 58–71.
Dijkstra, Menno F. P. 2011, *Rondom de mondingen van Rijn & Maas. Landschap en bewoning tussen de 3e en 9e eeuw in Zuid-Holland, in het bijzonder de Oude Rijnstreek* (Leiden).
Dijkstra, Menno, and Henk van der Velde 2011, 'Plots, pots and pins. Transformations in the Rhine Estuary during the Early Middle Ages'. In *Transformations in North-Western Europe (AD 300–1000). Proceedings of the 60th Sachsensymposion 19–23 September 2009 Maastricht*, Neue Studien zur Sachsenforschung 3, ed. T. A. S. M. Panhuysen (Hannover), 9–22.
Dijkstra, Menno F. P., Arno A. Verhoeven and K. van Straten ed. in prep, *Nieuw licht op Leithon. Archeologisch onderzoek naar de vroegmiddeleeuwse bewoning in plangebied Leiderdorp-Plantage*, Themata 8 (Amsterdam).
Dinter, Marieke van 2013, 'The Roman Limes in the Netherlands: how a delta landscape determined the location of the military structures', *Netherlands Journal of Geosciences - Geologie en Mijnbouw* 92(1), 1–32.
Dirks, Jacob 1846, *Geschiedkundig onderzoek van den koophandel der Friezen van de vroegste tijden tot aan den dood van Karel den Grooten* (Utrecht).
Egmond, Wolfert S. van, 'The Frisian people at the time of Boniface: questions of ethnic identity' (unpublished).
Ellegård, Alvar 1987, 'Who were the Eruli?', *Scandia* 53, 5–34.
Es, Wim A. van 1964, 'Het rijengrafveld van Wageningen', *Palaeohistoria* 10, 181–316.
Geary, Patrick 1983, 'Ethnic identity as a situational construct in the Early Middle Ages', *Mitteilungen der Anthropologische Gesellschaft in Wien* 113, 15–26.
Gerrets, Danny A. 1999, 'Evidence of political centralization in Westergo: the excavations at Wijnaldum in a (supra-)regional perspective'. In *The Making of Kingdoms: Papers of the 47th Sachsensymposium, York, September 1996*, Anglo-Saxon Studies in Archaeology and History 10, ed. T. Dickinson and D. Griffiths (Oxford), 119–26.
Groenman-van Waateringe, Willy 1983, 'The disastrous effect of the Roman occupation'. In *Roman and Native in the Low Countries*, BAR International Series 184, ed. R. Brandt and J. Slofstra (Oxford), 147–57.

Halbertsma, Herre 2000, *Frieslands oudheid. Het rijk van de Friese koningen, opkomst en ondergang* (Utrecht).

Henderikx, P. A. 1986, 'The lower delta of the Rhine and the Maas: landscape and habitation from the Roman Period to ca 1000', *Berichten van de Rijksdienst voor Oudheidkundig Bodemonderzoek* 36, 447–599.

Hiddink, Henk A. 1999, *Germaanse samenlevingen tussen Rijn en Weser. 1ste eeuw voor - 4de eeuw na Chr.* (Amsterdam).

Hines, John 1990, 'Philology, archaeology and the adventus Saxonum vel Anglorum'. In *Britain 400–600: Language and History*, ed. A. Bammesberger and A. Wollmann (Heidelberg), 17–36.

Hines, John. 1995, 'Focus and boundary in linguistic Varieties in the North-West Germanic Continuum'. In *Friesische Studien II*. NOWELE Supplement Volume 12, ed. V. F. Faltings, A. G. H. Walker and O. Wilts (Odense), 35–62.

Holwerda, Jan H. 1914, 'Het grafveld van Rijnsburg', *Leids Jaarboekje* 11, 43–9.

Holwerda, Jan H. 1925, *Nederland's vroegste geschiedenis*, 2nd edn (Amsterdam).

Knol, Egge 2008, 'Metaal uit de Vroege-Middeleeuwen in Katwijk-Zanderij'. In *Cananefaten en Friezen aan de monding van de Rijn. Tien jaar archeologisch onderzoek op de Zanderij-Westerbaan te Katwijk*, ADC Monografie 5, ed. H. M. van der Velde (Amersfoort), 295–310.

Koning, Jan de 2003, 'Why did they leave? Why did they stay? On continuity versus discontinuity from Roman times to the Early Middle Ages in the western coastal area of the Netherlands'. In *Kontinuität und Diskontinuität. Germania inferior am Beginn und am Ende der römischen Herrschaft. Beiträge des deutsch-niederländischen Kolloquiums in der Katholieke Universiteit Nijmegen (27. bis 30. 06. 2001)*, ed. T. Grünewald and S. Seibel (Berlin), 53–82.

Koning, Jan de 2012, 'De betekenis van Noord-Holland binnen vroegmiddeleeuws Frisia', *It Baeken* 74, 3–31.

Krol, Tessa 2006, 'Angelsaksisch aardewerk in Noord-Nederland. Nieuwe perspectieven op het Noordnederlandse kustgebied na het bewoningshiaat in de vierde eeuw', *De Vrije Fries* 86, 9–32.

Kuhn, Hans 1955, 'Zur Gliederung der germanischen Sprachen', *Zeitschrift für deutsches Altertum* 86, 1–47.

Künzel, Rudi . E. , Dirk P. Blok and J. M. Verhoeff 1988, *Lexicon van Nederlandse toponiemen tot 1200* (Amsterdam).

Lanting, Jan N., and J. van der Plicht 2009–10, 'De ^{14}C-chronologie van de Nederlandse pre- en protohistorie VI: Romeinse tijd en Merovingische periode, deel A: historische bronnen en chronologische schema's', *Palaeohistoria* 51–2, 7–168.

Lanting, Jan N., and J. van der Plicht 2011–12, 'De ^{14}C-chronologie van de Nederlandse pre- en protohistorie VI: Romeinse tijd en Merovingische periode, deel B: aanvullingen, toelichtingen en ^{14}C-dateringen', *Palaeohistoria* 53–4, 283–391.

Lebecq, Stéphane 1983, *Marchands et navigateurs Frisons du haut moyen âge, Vol. 1 Essai; Vol 2. Corpus des sources ecrites* (Lille).

Martin, Toby 2015, *The Cruciform Brooch and Anglo-Saxon England*, Anglo-Saxon Studies 25 (Woodbridge).

Myres, John Nowell Linton 1989, *The English Settlements* (Oxford).

Nicolay, Johan A. W. 2014, *The Splendour of Power: Early Medieval Kingship and the Use of Gold and Silver in the Southern North Sea Area (5th to 7th century AD)*, Groningen Archaeological Studies 28 (Groningen).

Nieuwhof, Annet 2011, 'Discontinuity in the Northern-Netherlands coastal area at the end of the Roman Period'. In *Transformations in North-Western Europe (AD 300–1000). Proceedings of the 60th Sachsensymposion 19.–23. September 2009 Maastricht*, Neue Studien zur Sachsenforschung 3, ed. T. A. S. M. Panhuysen (Stuttgart), 55–66.

Pohl, Walther 1991, 'Conceptions of ethnicity in early medieval studies', *Archaeologia Polana* 29, 39–49.

Reichstein, Joachim 1975, *Die kreuzförmige Fibel. Zur Chronologie der späten römischen Kaiserzeit und er Völkerwanderungszeit in Skandinavien, auf dem Kontinent und in England*, Offa-Bücher 34 (Neumünster).
Russchen, A. 1964, 'Warns, Heruli, Thuringians', *It Baeken* 26, 301–6.
Russchen, A. 1967, *New Light on Dark-Age Frisia* (Drachten).
Russchen, A. 1979, *Bouwstenen voor een geschiedenis van "Dark-Age Frisia" Vol. 1*, s. l. (unpublished manuscript).
Schönfeld, M. 1935, 'Wiltenburg. Het ontstaan en de groei van een 'geleerdensage'', *Tijdschrift voor Nederlandse Taal en Letterkunde* 54, 1–14.
Schrijver, Peter 1999, 'The Celtic contribution to the development of the North Sea Germanic vowel system, with special reference to coastal Dutch', *NOWELE* 35, 3–47.
Schrijver, Peter 2000, 'Keltisch of niet. Twee namen en een verdacht accent'. In *Kelten in Nederland*, ed. R. Hofman, B. Smelik and L. Toorians, Utrecht, 67–87.
Springer, Matthias 2003, 'Location in Space and Time'. In *The Continental Saxons from the Migration Period to the Tenth Century: an ethnographic Perspective*, Studies in Historical Archaeoethnology 6, ed. D. H. Green and F. Siegmund (Woodbridge), 11–23.
Springer, Matthias 2006, 'Warnen', *Hoops Reallexicon der Germanischen Altertumskunde* 33, 274 –81.
Stiles, Patrick V. 1995, 'Remarks on the "Anglo-Frisian" thesis'. In *Friesische Studien II*. NOWELE Supplement Volume 12, ed. V. F. Faltings, A. G. H. Walker and O. Wilts (Odense), 177 –220.
Tilmans, Karin 1987, 'Cornelius Aurelius en het ontstaan van de Bataafse mythe in de Hollandse geschiedschrijving (tot 1517)'. In *Genoechlicke ende lustige historiën. Laatmiddeleeuwse geschiedschrijving in Nederland*, ed. B. Ebels-Hoving, C. G. Santing and C. P. H. M. Tilmans (Hilversum), 191–213.
Verwers, W. J. H., and W. J. van Tent 2015, *Merovingisch grafveld Elst-'t Woud (gemeente Rhenen, provincie Utrecht)*, Rapportages Archeologische Monumentenzorg 223 (Amersfoort).
Vos, Peter C. 2015, *Origin of the Dutch Coastal Landscape. Long-Term Landscape Evolution of the Netherlands During the Holocene, Described and Visualised in National, Regional and Local Palaeogeografical Map Series* (Groningen).
Vos, Peter C., and Robert M. van Heeringen 1997, 'Holocene geology and occupation history of the Province of Zeeland'. In *Holocene Evolution of Zeeland (SW Netherlands)*, Med. NITG TNO Nr. 59, ed. M. M. Fischer (Haarlem), 4–109.
Wagner, Annette, and Jaap Ypey 2011, *Das Gräberfeld auf dem Donderberg bei Rhenen. Katalog* (Leiden).
Wenskus, Richard 1961, *Stammesbildung und Verfassung. Das Werden der frühmittelalterichen gentes* (Köln).

5

Power and Identity in the Southern North Sea Area

The Migration and Merovingian Periods

Johan Nicolay

The southern North Sea area of the 5th to 7th centuries AD can be seen as an important 'cultural bridge' linking two power blocks: the late Roman Empire and its Frankish successor kingdom to the south, and the Scandinavian kingdoms to the north.[1] This paper discusses how such a bridge function is reflected in the material culture found along the southern North Sea coasts of the Netherlands, Germany and south-eastern England, and how this material culture relates to the rise of kingdoms and the expression of group identities. The discussion will focus on jewellery and other ornaments of gold and silver, which can be assigned to five 'cultural phases' (Nicolay 2014, 234–63). First, the cultural relations with surrounding areas, as reflected in the ornaments' shape and decoration, will be examined for each phase. Second, an attempt will be made to link the geographical distribution of ornaments that were executed in a specific style to the expression of group identity at a regional or supra-regional level – as a reflection of the extent of specific *elite networks*, which are assumed to represent the territories of early-medieval kingdoms.

The premise for this analysis is the assumption that access to gold and silver in early-medieval Europe was limited to a small group of people. It was regional or supra-regional kings who controlled the importation of these precious metals, which probably reached the North Sea world both as political gifts and through a more commercial form of long-distance exchange (for the latter, see Näsman 1991). Besides these 'horizontal' relations among leaders, networks of 'vertical' relations were established and consolidated by the distribution of valuable items as gifts between leaders (the patrons) and their followers

---

[1] This paper is the outcome of a VENI research project, funded by the Netherlands Organisation for Scientific Research (NWO). The English text was corrected by Xandra Bardet (Groningen).

(the clients) (Bazelmans 1999). As members of the royal and lower retinues would have their own groups of followers, this resulted in the well-known pyramidal structure of patron–client relations, in which a person's status was directly related to his or her 'distance from the king'.

Gold and silver were exchanged not only as gifts, but probably also as a form of currency between members of the elite and their followers – as indicated by the frequent occurrence of gold coins not transformed into jewellery. This paper, however, focuses only on the *ornaments* of gold and silver: manufactured to be worn as high-status symbols by the leading elite and to be exchanged as personal gifts among members of the royal and lower retinues, it is these items that reflect the changing cultural focus of the North Sea elite, and express group identities.

Within the research area, an interesting divide can be observed between two different 'ritual worlds': a northern world, which also includes southern Scandinavia, dominated by hoarded valuables, and a southern world, which also includes the Late Roman and Frankish areas, marked by rich burials with prestigious, partly gold and silver, grave goods (Nicolay 2014, 296–326). The two worlds are separated by the River Vlie, long since engulfed by the present-day IJsselmeer (the Netherlands). Although the different traditions of depositing valuables resulted in different archaeological datasets, the ritual investments in both worlds show a similar chronological development. This suggests that analysing socio-political developments in the southern North Sea area should be possible by studying valuable items from the area as a whole.

Phase 1 (*c.* AD 390–500):
Western Roman silver transformed into 'Saxon' ornaments

During the late 4th and 5th centuries AD, the North Sea elite was culturally focused on the Western Roman Empire to the south. The most important high-status ornaments dating from this period are silver brooches. These were made out of Late Roman silver that had reached the North Sea area especially as tribute paid to Germanic leaders in unminted form. A likely example of such payments is the famous hacksilver hoard from Großbodungen, Lkr. Eichsfeld, Thuringia, which, besides 21 *solidi*, contained over 800 g of silver vessel fragments and was probably buried in the first half of the 5th century (Berghaus 1999).

After regionally specific copper-alloy brooches had been produced in the Elbe–Weser region of northern Germany for some decades, the late 4th century saw the regional development of supporting-arm brooches into the equal-armed type (Böhme 2003, 256–7). Most of the equal-armed brooches, showing a typically Late Roman chip-carved decoration, were executed in silver, with some of the brooches of the Dösemoor and Nesse types decorated with gilding (Fig. 5.1).

The German finds of equal-armed brooches cluster in the northern part of the Elbe–Weser region (Fig. 5.2) and can be interpreted as regionally specific, 'Saxon' pieces. Less pronounced find clusters, in the northern Netherlands and south-eastern England, can be related to migrating 'Anglo-Saxons', who settled in these areas during the late 4th and 5th centuries (e.g. Böhme 1986). Probably soon after their introduction, equal-armed

Fig. 5.1. A silver-gilt equal-armed brooch from Dösemoor (Lkr. Stade). The brooch was damaged before burial. Scale 1:1 (Collection and photos: Schwedenspeider-Museum, Stade).

brooches, as well as 'Saxon' composite and cast saucer brooches, were also produced locally in south-eastern England. The initial imitations of Saxon-style ornaments evolved into several Insular forms, which, however, were no longer executed in silver, but in (gilded) copper alloy (e.g. the equal-armed brooches of the Mucking and Berinsfield types: Bruns 2003, 22–3).

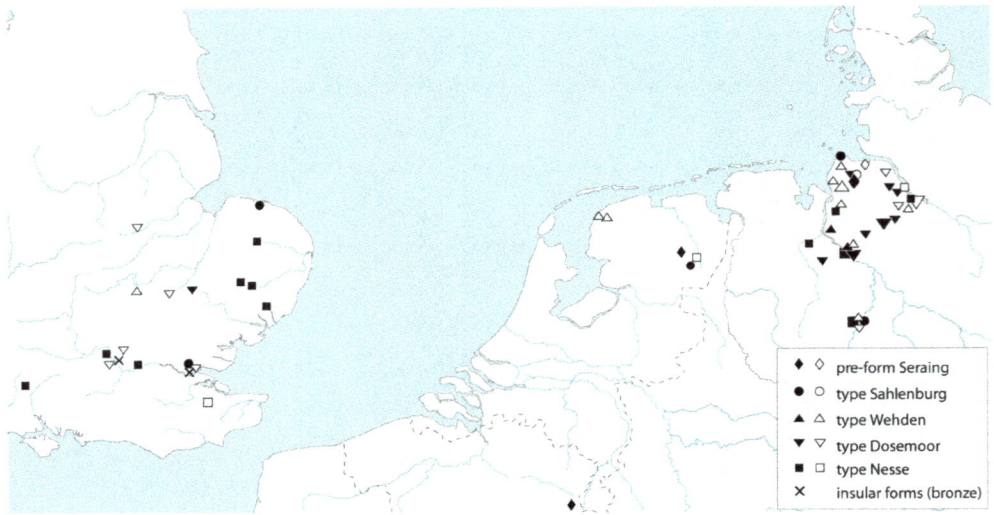

Fig. 5.2. Geographical distribution of 5th-century 'Saxon-style' equal-armed brooches, belonging to different types. Large symbol: two or more finds from the same site; white symbol: silver; black symbol: copper alloy (after Nicolay 2014, fig. 9.4).

In the southern North Sea area 'Saxon' or 'Saxon-style' brooches were worn throughout most of the 5th century. Although some of the equal-armed brooches found in south-eastern England were buried in graves dating to the late 5th or early 6th century (see Bruns 2003, 31–2), their production probably ended several decades earlier, in the third quarter of the 5th century – roughly at the same time as Nydam-style brooches in southern Scandinavia were replaced by jewellery with decoration in Salin's Animal Style I (c. AD 450–65; Rau 2010, 297–301).

Phase 2 (c. AD 475–550):
Eastern Roman gold transformed into 'Scandinavian' ornaments

In the late 5th and first half of the 6th century, a clear shift in cultural focus towards the north-east can be seen. Not only was the precious metal used for making high-status ornaments imported mainly via southern Scandinavia, as *solidi* of Eastern Roman origin; the shape and decoration of such ornaments are also typically Scandinavian. Rather than silver brooches, the find material is now dominated by gold arm- and neckrings, and above all by gold bracteates (Fig. 5.3).

The bracteates from the research area belong to the Scandinavian types A–D. On the basis of similarities in the style and execution of the central motif, the majority of these finds can be assigned to specific sub-types or *Formularfamilien*, as defined by Pesch (2007). The bracteates found in southern Scandinavia have been dated to c. AD 440/450–530/540; most pieces from the southern North Sea area were executed in 'chip-carved' relief and are relatively late, probably not being produced before c. AD 475 (Axboe 1999; 2007, 146–8).

Fig. 5.3. Type-C bracteates from the coastal areas of the northern Netherlands (Dokkum, left: IK 46) and northern Germany (Sievern, right: IK 157,2), showing close affinities in motifs and execution. Scale 2:1 (Dokkum: Nationalmuseet, Copenhagen; photo: J. Lee; Sievern: collection: Niedersächsisches Institut für historische Küstenforschung, Wilhemshaven; photo: R. Kiepe).

Burial finds from south-eastern England indicate that bracteates were still worn, and possibly also produced outside Scandinavia for some time after c. 530/540, before finally being buried up to c. 560/570 (Axboe 2007, fig. 59). The neck- and armrings are more difficult to date, but most probably were contemporary with the Scandinavian-type bracteates.

The currently known bracteates finds from the southern North Sea area show a remarkable distribution: they cluster in several small areas, separated by extensive 'empty' zones (for bracteates of type D, see Fig. 5.4). From east to west, such clusters are evident in:

1. The area around Sievern, where two bracteate hoards and a single bracteate, as well as a gold neckring buried with five gold coin pendants have been found (Hauck 1970; Aufderhaar, this vol.);
2. The north-western part of Friesland, and especially the northern part of the region called Westergo, where a bracteate hoard and single bracteates have been found (Nicolay 2005);
3. Eastern Kent, where sets of bracteates and single bracteates were buried as grave goods (Chadwick Hawkes and Pollard 1981);
4. Northern Norfolk, where a gold armring and bracteate hoard, as well as some single bracteates cluster (Behr and Pestell 2014).

Within each of these clusters, there are strong indications that these pendants are not simply imported items: die-linked pieces, execution in metals other than gold, variations in the design of the central motif and in some cases even production dies have been found. Despite their close cultural links with southern Scandinavia, most bracteates from the southern North Sea area show regional characteristics and were probably manufactured in regional workshops (see also Behr 2010, 65–71). The same is true for gold neckrings of the Mulsum type. The neckrings of this type are imitations of Scandinavian examples, and executed as hollow rather than solid pieces (Brieske 2001, 149–51).

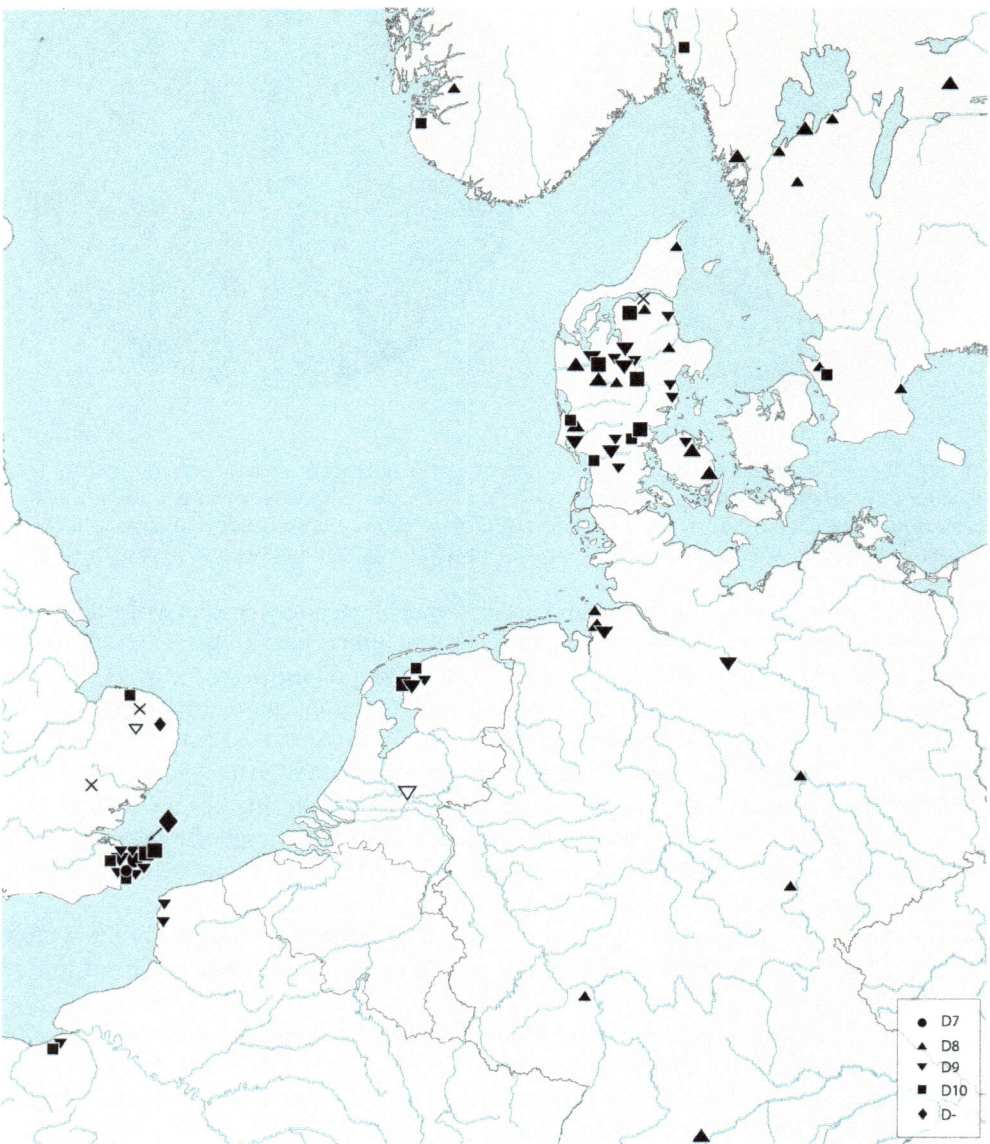

Fig. 5.4. Geographical distribution of gold and silver bracteates belonging to *Formularfamilien* D7-10, and of those that cannot be assigned to any specific *Formularfamilie* (D-). The find-spots of three copper-alloy dies for the manufacture of type-D bracteates are marked with a cross (IK 572, 589, 609). Large symbols: two or more finds from the same site; open symbols: silver or gilt silver (after Nicolay 2014, fig. 9.9).

Phase 3 (c. AD 500–600):
Frankish silver transformed into regionally specific ornaments

The 6th century saw a shift in cultural focus back to the south, where the Frankish kingdom had gradually succeeded the Western Roman Empire, together with a reversion from gold to silver ornaments. All along the southern North Sea coast, the use of Frankish-type brooches and belt-fittings is reflected in settlement and cemetery finds. Although imported Frankish ornaments were appreciated as such and worn by people living in the southern North Sea area, a substantial proportion must have been melted down and transformed into regionally specific brooches and other ornaments – as the finds from Friesland and especially Kent indicate.

In Kentish graves, the Frankish-type ornaments were often buried with Scandinavian-type bracteates on the one hand, and valuables in a typically Insular, 'Kentish' style on the other. The latter include a variety of silver or silver-gilt ornaments: large and small square-headed brooches, often decorated with garnets (c. AD 500–60), early keystone garnet disc brooches (Classes 1 and 2, c. AD 530–90), sword pommels of Bifrons–Gilton type (6th century) and silver skimmers, usually found with a ball of rock crystal (c. AD 500–60) (e.g. Brugmann 1997a, 35–40). The square-headed and related disc brooches with animal design in Style I and nielloed borders represent a further development of the Scandinavian, so-called 'Jutlandic', square-headed brooch (Haseloff 1981, 166–73; Fig. 5.5). The garnet settings were added as a new, Frankish element, the shape and decoration of the other ornaments also being inspired by Frankish pieces. As with the Scandinavian-type bracteates, a clustering of 'Kentish' ornaments in the eastern part of Kent can be seen, as the geographical distribution of early keystone garnet disc brooches illustrates (Fig. 5.6).

The cultural development in Kent is paralleled by that in the northern part of Friesland, where regionally specific brooches of the Achlum type were produced around the mid-6th century (Nicolay 2014, 87–8; Fig. 5.5). The overall shape of these silver-gilt brooches, the small disc on the bow, the hanging birds on the footplate and the decoration with niello were also modelled on the 'Jutlandic' square-headed brooches. As a regional, 'Frisian', element, the kidney-shaped knob on the footplate was added, which is known also from small-long brooches of the 'Frisian' Domburg type (Dijkstra 2011, 354–7). The finds of Achlum-type brooches show a concentration in the northern part of Westergo (Fig. 5.6), again the very area where a clustering of gold bracteates can be seen. Although no moulds have been found, the discovery of a drop of molten silver at Wijnaldum–'Tjitsma', in a stratified context dating to c. AD 500–50, may relate to the production of this silver brooch-type.

The situation in Kent and Friesland is different from that in East Anglia and Essex, where the use of silver for female ornaments during the late 5th and 6th centuries was limited to the surface decoration of brooches and to simple finger or other rings, a few bracelets, wrist-clasps of Class A and early scutiform pendants (Hines 1984). It is surprising to see that the impressive 'great square-headed brooches' (c. AD 500–70) are rarely executed in silver but in copper alloy, often with a decoration in gilding, tinning and/or sheet silver (Hines 1997). The silver or silver-decorated jewellery from East Anglia and

Fig. 5.5. Stylistic development of 'Jutlandic' square-headed brooches into 6th-century regional-style brooches. Left: a 'Jutlandic' brooch from Bifrons (A, Kent); right: a 'Kentish-style' square-headed brooch with garnet settings from Howletts (B, Kent), a keystone-garnet disc brooch from Faversham (C, Kent) and a 'Frisian-style' disc-on-bow brooch from Achlum (D, Friesland). Scale 85% (Bifrons: coll. and photo The Kent Archaeological Society/Maidstone Museum; Achlum: Fries Museum, Leeuwarden; Collectie Het Koninklijk Fries Genootschap; others: coll. British Museum, London, © The Trustees of the British Museum).

Essex is insufficiently distinctive to reveal one or more regional style groups as early as the 6th century; rather, it belongs to a broader 'eastern English' group.

In the western Netherlands and the adjacent river area of the central Netherlands, the situation was completely different. For most of the 6th century, these areas belonged to the Frankish cultural world, the famous cemetery of Rhenen–'Donderberg' (Wagner and Ypey 2011), for example, showing the full range of male and female grave goods that are typical of Frankish row-grave cemeteries.

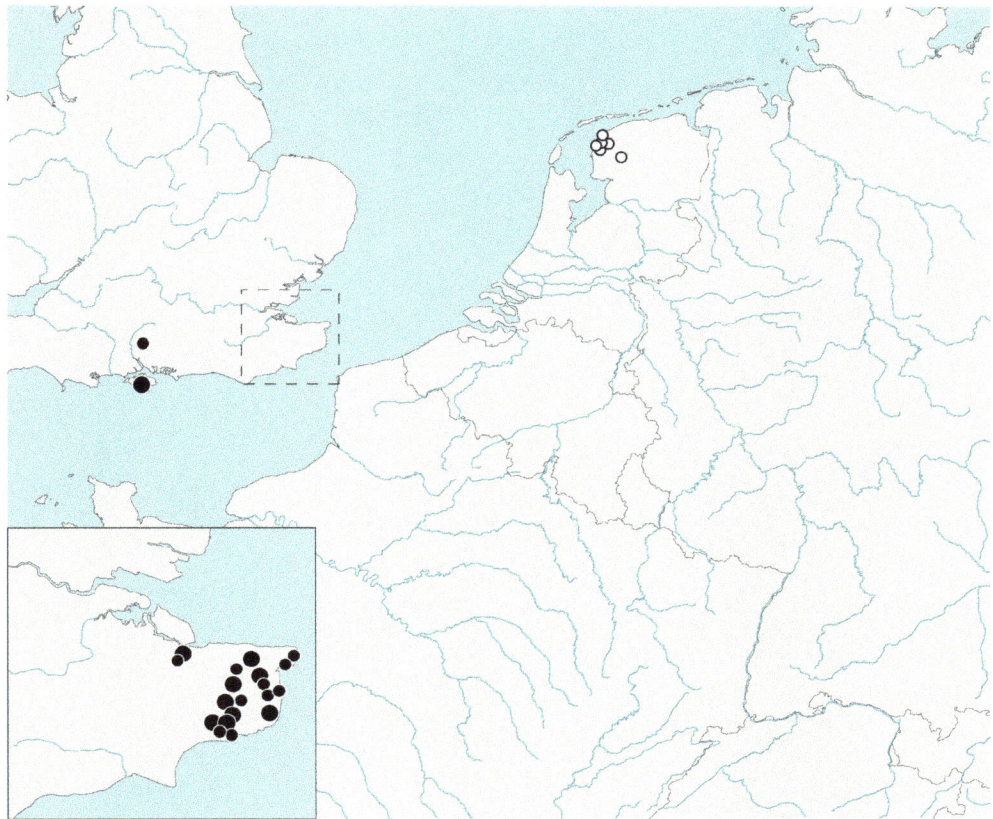

Fig. 5.6. Geographical distribution of 6th-century 'Kentish-style' keystone garnet disc brooches of Avent's Classes 1 and 2 (black symbols; not including copper-alloy imitations), and 'Frisian-style' disc-on-bow brooches of the Achlum type (white symbols). Large symbol: two or more finds from the same site (after Nicolay 2014, fig. 9.16).

Phase 4 (c. AD 590–630/640): Frankish gold transformed into regionally specific ornaments

The late 6th century and early decades of the 7th saw a further development of regionally specific ornaments, in Kent, in Friesland and now also in East Anglia. Most ornaments are jewellery and belt fittings, once more mainly executed in gold, which had reached the research area for the largest part as Frankish gold coins (*solidi* and especially *tremisses* of 'royal' and 'civic' types). Despite the wide variety of ornament-types, these are characterized by a very similar garnet and/or filigree decoration. The finds from the research area belong to a final phase of continental cloisonné art, which is characteristic of the northern periphery of the Frankish cultural world and can be dated to the late 6th century and the early decades of the 7th.

Fig. 5.7. Close cultural affinities between regional-style, filigree- and/or garnet-decorated high-status ornaments dating to the late 6th, or early decades of the 7th century: a 'Kentish-style' triangular buckle from Sarre, grave 68 (Kent, left), a 'Frisian-style' disc-on-bow brooch from Wijnaldum (Friesland, middle) and an 'East-Anglian-style' curved buckle from Sutton Hoo, mound 1 (Suffolk). Scales 2:3 (Wijnaldum) and 1:1 (others) (Sarre: coll. and photos The Kent Archaeological Society/Maidstone Museum; Wijnaldum: Fries Museum, Leeuwarden; Collectie Provincie Fryslân; Sutton Hoo: coll. British Museum, London, © The Trustees of the British Museum).

In Kent the gold ornaments comprise shield-on-tongue buckles (Fig. 5.7), composite and plated disc brooches, and pendants of various types, usually decorated with garnet and filigree work or with repoussé ornamentation. These ornaments can be seen as Kentish equivalents of contemporary Frankish pieces; at the same time, the link with Scandinavia becomes apparent in the regional 'Kentish Style II' (Høilund Nielsen 1999) and its typical execution in triple filigree – with the use of repoussé below the filigree to create extra relief.

A similar development is visible in the northern Netherlands, where garnet- and filigree-decorated disc-on-bow brooches and several types of pendants, including some with elaborate, filigree-decorated borders, can be assigned to a range of 'Frisian-style' jewellery. The most compelling examples are the disc-on-bow brooches from Wijnaldum, Wieuwerd and Hogebeintum, belonging to the Hogebeintum type (Fig. 5.7). They represent a further development of the Achlum-type brooch, showing the adoption of Frankish (garnet inlay) and Scandinavian (Style II) decoration techniques.

The gold, and also the silver, ornaments from Sutton Hoo mound 1 allow the identification of a further group of regionally specific jewellery, that was probably produced at an East Anglian workshop (Fig. 5.7). Unique to this workshop is the combination of garnet cloisonné with so-called lidded-cell and millefiori work, as can be seen on the gold shoulder clasps and purse lid. Moreover, some of the ornaments, such as the large gold buckle, are decorated with animal motifs in the regional 'East Anglian Style II' (Høilund Nielsen 1999). Fascinating about the Sutton Hoo assemblage is the mixture of 'foreign' influences, linking the ornaments to the Scandinavian area to the east (shield and helmet), the Late Roman and Frankish area to the south-east (e.g. shoulder clasps and sword pommel) and the Kentish area to the south (e.g. buckle) (e.g. Bruce-Mitford 1978). Other ornaments that were probably produced in the same workshop include some garnet-decorated pendants, such as the famous Wilton cross.

In contrast to Kent, Friesland and East Anglia, no gold jewellery or other ornaments point to the development of a regional style in Essex and the western Netherlands. The finds from Essex show a cultural relationship to East Anglia on the one hand, but especially to Kent on the other – the gold buckles from the Prittlewell chamber grave, for example, being of a typically Kentish type (Blackmore 2008). The coastal area of the western Netherlands was also culturally focused on its 'neigbouring' areas. Some gold pendants with filigree-decorated borders, found in the northern part of the western Netherlands, are typical of the northern Netherlands (Nicolay 2014, 115–16), while a gilded bronze shield-on-tongue buckle from Rijnsburg, the gilded bronze terminal mount of a drinking horn from Katwijk and the newly discovered silver hanging-bowl from Oegstgeest, found in the southern part, show a cultural link to south-eastern England (Dijkstra 2011, 232–3, 243–4; the bowl is unpublished).

The central river area of the Netherlands again occupies an exceptional position. Here, the find material is still dominated by Frankish-style ornaments, including gold filigree-decorated pendants and beads. A fragment of a Kentish keystone garnet disc brooch (class 4) from Utrecht–'Leidsche Rijn' constitutes the only evidence for any cultural relationship with south-eastern England (Nicolay 2014, 128–9).

The geographical distributions of gold ornaments that can most probably be assigned to the 'Kentish', 'Frisian' and 'East Anglian' style groups (Fig. 5.8) show the formation of larger, supra-regional elite networks in the period around the year 600, covering eastern and western Kent, the northern Netherlands and East Anglia, respectively. Within the southern North Sea area only one of the regional workshops for cloisonné jewellery can be located with certainty: at Wijnaldum. In the course of excavations and metal detection, a copper-alloy die for producing 'special boxed' gold foils, an unfinished cloisonné panel of a gold pendant and a crucible fragment with tiny gold droplets, all dating to the late 6th or 7th century, were found at this site (see also Tulp 2003, 224–5).

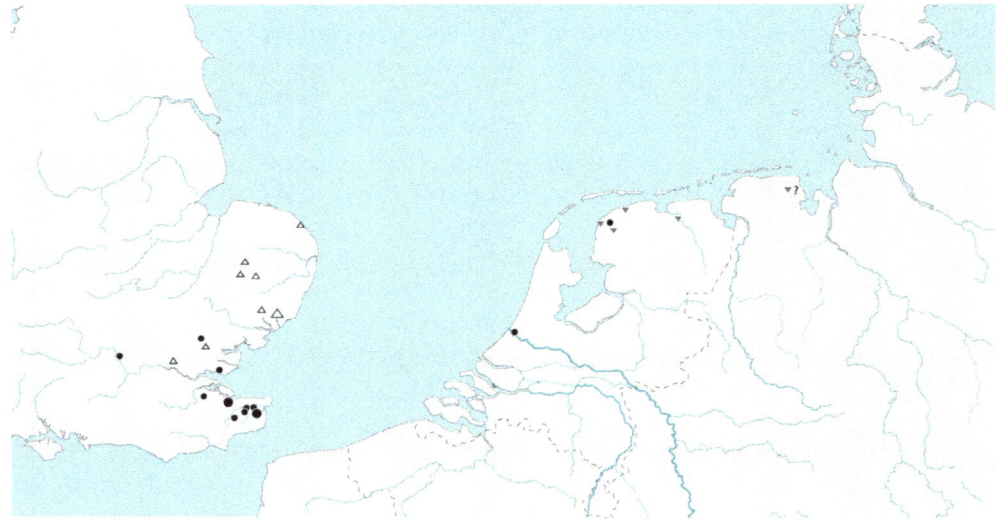

Fig. 5.8. Geographical distribution of garnet- and/or filigree-decorated ornaments with regional characteristics, dating to the late 6th and early decades of the 7th century. Black symbols: large 'Kentish-style' buckles of triangular and rectangular types; white symbols: 'East Anglian-style' ornaments with garnet decoration; grey symbols: 'Frisian-style' disc-on-bow brooches of Hogebeintum type and related jewellery (after Nicolay 2014, fig. 9.23).

Phase 5 (c. AD 600–700):
Frankish gold and silver transformed into 'Byzantine' ornaments

In the following 7th century, the regional- and supra-regionally specific ornaments, linked culturally to the Scandinavian and Frankish worlds, made way for gold and silver jewellery showing truly exotic, Byzantine influences – which, according to Geake (1997), reflect an early-medieval renaissance of the Byzantine fashion in north-western Europe. Within Kent, graves with such 'Conversion-period assemblages' are dated to c. AD 580 onwards; outside Kent, including the Dutch part of the North Sea coast, to after c. 600 (Geake 1997, 35–7). The jewellery is characterized by finger rings (silver), linked pins (gold/silver), and most notably necklaces with gold and silver pendants and beads, as well as amethyst beads. Most of these 7th-century gold and silver ornaments are known from Anglo-Saxon graves. Although once more a clustering in eastern Kent can be seen, the gold and silver ornaments show a wider distribution, also encompassing Essex and East Anglia. Moreover, continental finds show that elements of this Anglo-Saxon fashion occurred in a wider 'North Sea group'. Because of its more or less uniform character, it is no longer possible to assign these ornaments to any regional style groups.

Immigrants, power formation and the expression of group identities

The shape and decoration of the gold and silver ornaments presented above nicely demonstrate the wide and varied cultural focus of the Migration and Merovingian Period

North Sea elite: towards the Western Roman Empire in the 5th century, towards the Scandinavian and Frankish kingdoms in the 6th century, and towards the Byzantine Empire in the 7th century. An interesting question to be answered now is how this changing cultural focus relates to the political developments along the southern North Sea coasts, and, of course, to the expression of identity among members of specific elite networks.

An important event for the development of kingship in the southern North Sea area, starting in the late 4th century, is the migration of 'Saxons', 'Angles' and to a lesser extent probably also 'Scandinavians' to coasts of the northern Netherlands and south-eastern England. At this time the Dutch coastal areas were probably deserted or inhabited by no more than a small remnant of the Roman Period population (Nieuwhof 2011). Although it is generally assumed that a quite substantial part of the original population still inhabited south-eastern England, the widespread adoption of 'Anglo-Saxon' fashions is clear evidence of the arrival of new people in this area as well (e.g. Brugmann 1997b, 110–17). The situation was different in northern Germany, or at least in the northern Elbe–Weser region, where not the Late Roman but the Merovingian Period was a time of population decline and in some areas even depopulation (Nösler and Wolters 2009). Despite their different traditions and habitation histories, it was the common background of the 'Anglo-Saxon' newcomers and their relations to their homelands that tied the southern North Sea regions together in the following centuries – as is clearly reflected in the execution of high-status ornaments.

Although the size of the migrating groups and their precise origin are still heavily debated, the process of early-medieval 'power formation' in the coastal areas of south-eastern England and the Netherlands was initiated or at least accelerated by the new arrivals. Archaeologically, the first stage of this process is visible in the appearance of 'Saxon' brooches, made of silver or copper alloy. While the number of finds from England and the Netherlands is too small to reveal any regional patterning, the distribution of equal-armed and saucer brooches within northern Germany can be related to the formation of a regional kingdom. The distribution of this regionally specific, 'Saxon' jewellery probably reflects the extent of an elite network covering the area between the Lower Weser to the west, the Lower Elbe to the east and the Middle Weser to the south (Fig. 5.2). These ornaments are a direct outcome of the flow of Late Roman silver that had been paid mainly to regional leaders north of the *limes* to create alliances with Rome; after melting down, part of the silver was transformed into equal-armed brooches, giving expression to the political bond with Rome on the one hand, and fulfilling the need to express an indigenous, regional – or 'Saxon' – identity on the other.

The late 5th and 6th centuries saw the rise of a powerful elite in more westerly parts of the research areas as well; here, regional kingdoms can be reconstructed that were controlled from central places or central areas where clusters of gold bracteates have been found (Fig. 5.9): Sievern (northern Elbe–Weser region), northern Westergo, eastern Kent and northern Norfolk. In need of status symbols to give expression to their newly acquired positions, this elite chose to adopt jewellery from a new power block to the north-east: that of the Scandinavian kingdoms. The ornaments probably displayed a true or fictional ancestral link with southern Scandinavia; in this way they became an important tool in the process of legitimizing the new status positions resulting from the rise of central places along the southern North Sea coast.

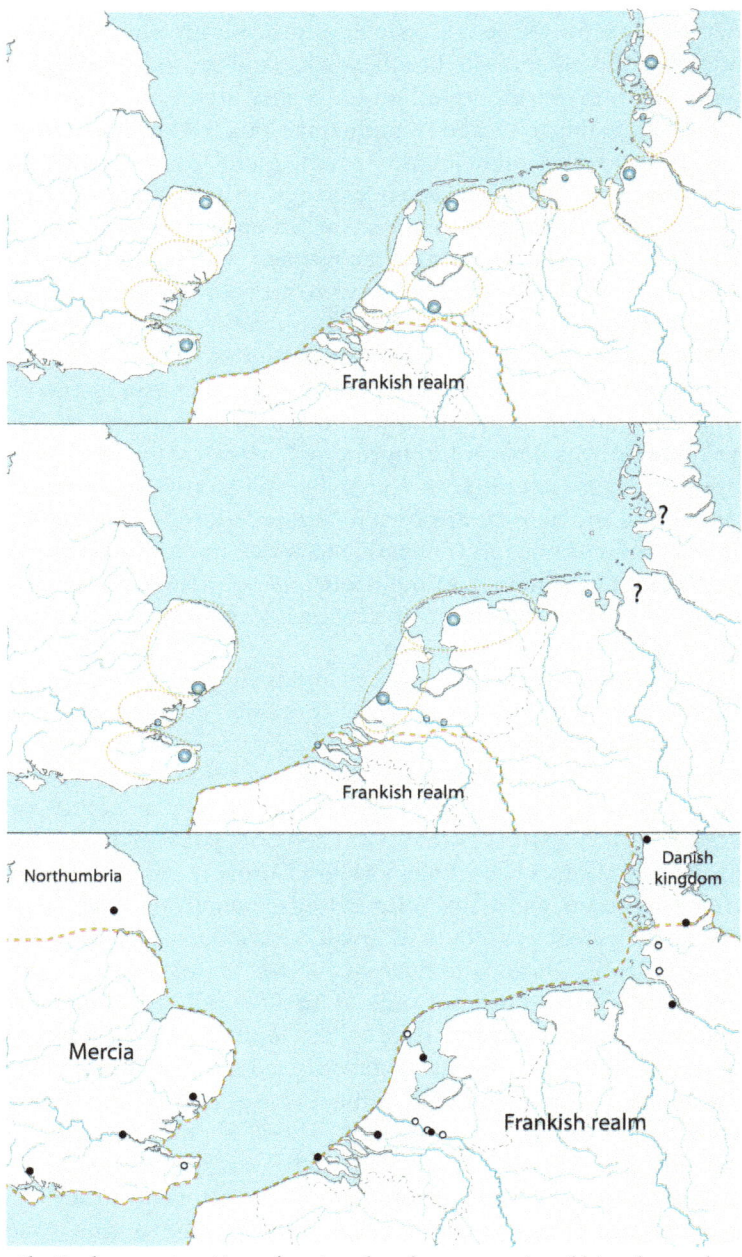

Fig. 5.9. Hypothetical reconstruction of regional and supra-regional kingdoms along the southern North Sea coast around AD 500 (top) and AD 600 (middle), and the political division of this area into territories belonging to larger political configurations around AD 804 (bottom). Large symbols: probable central-place complexes; small symbols: elite centres and trading sites (top/middle); black symbols: emporia and other specialized trading sites; white symbols: enclosures, including elite centres and missionary posts within former, Roman-period castella or city walls, in use during the early 9th century (bottom) (drawings by the author; for the individual sites, see Nicolay 2014, figs. 13.2, 13.3 and 13.5).

Instead of direct importation of a Scandinavian style by immigrants, Behr (2010, 74–6) suggests an indirect introduction via the central place at Sievern – which may have served as a 'bridgehead' linking Scandinavia to the southern North Sea world. Although the rulers of the early kingdom of Kent most probably took the Scandinavian elite as their direct example (Chadwick Hawkes and Pollard 1981; Kruse 2007), for East Anglia, Essex and also Friesland a more indirect adoption of new jewellery styles indeed seems credible. The dominant immigrant groups in these areas originated from the northern Elbe–Weser region and would have considered Sievern as the centre of their homeland. It is perfectly possible that these newcomers, as well as the indigenous elite who had adopted 'Saxon' elements in expressing their group identity, regarded the Scandinavian styles introduced into the Elbe–Weser region as elements of a new, now 'Scandinavian' or 'Saxon-Scandinavian', identity, worthy of imitation further west.

Soon after the adoption of Scandinavian-style jewellery, a development towards regionally specific status symbols can be seen – inspired by high-status ornaments from the Scandinavian north and the now powerful Frankish kingdom to the north-east and south. As no new central places seem to have sprung up in the areas where regional identities were expressed, this transition is likely to demonstrate a consolidation of established power positions. This would also explain why, after the early 6th century, Scandinavian-type bracteates and 'Jutlandic' brooches, as 'ancestral', Scandinavian, pieces, were no longer kept as valuable heirlooms. Within a few decades, these 'old' pieces were buried in Anglo-Saxon graves in association with the now more relevant, regionally specific jewellery and with imported or imitated Frankish-style ornaments.

During the late 6th century and early decades of the 7th, the rise of more extensive elite networks is not only recorded in historical sources about the Anglo-Saxon kingdoms (e.g. Yorke 2005), but also reflected in the geographical distribution of gold and silver ornaments (Fig. 5.8). Moreover, a further development of the 'regional' styles can be seen, again showing cultural affinities both with the Scandinavian and the Frankish worlds. Intriguing about this relatively short phase is the unprecedented 'investment' of valuable items, primarily made of gold, in graves and hoards. South-eastern England and the western and central Netherlands are characterized by a 'horizon' of high-status graves, including the ship burials at Sutton Hoo (e.g. Bruce-Mitford 1978) and Snape (Filmer-Sankey and Pestell 2001), while in the northern Netherlands a large number of gold status symbols were at the same time hoarded at settlement sites. The valuable items must have played a crucial role in a renewed phase of social competition, not only for supra-regional kingship (Fig. 5.9) but – as Bede (*Historia Ecclesiastica*, II.5) describes – also for overlordship. As in the preceding period, the execution of regalia and other high-status ornaments in a regional style offered the leading elite an important tool for demonstrating the extent of their elite networks to the outside world.

It is difficult to explain why the production of regionally specific ornaments came to a sudden end in the mid-7th century, when a new phase of political stabilization can be assumed. Instead of continuing to mark the range of their power by distributing regionally specific ornaments, the North Sea elite chose to distribute highly uniform ornaments, inspired by the Byzantine Empire far to the east – leaving the elite networks that were at the basis of individual kingdoms largely invisible.

Finally, the late 7th and 8th centuries saw the incorporation of these supra-regional networks into even larger political configurations (Fig. 5.9). As a result, the expression of identity through high-status ornaments took place at a completely different level, now to suit the agendas of Carolingian, Mercian and Danish kings. A renewed phase of ritual investment of valuable items is reflected in a 'horizon' of relatively rich weapon graves, found in the coastal areas of the Netherlands and German Ostfriesland (Knol and Bardet 1999). The graves, which contain Frankish-type weaponry, horse gear and glass vessels, date to the very period when large parts of the southern North Sea area were gradually conquered by Charles Martel and his successors (late 7th to early 9th century). During this phase of socio-political change and instability, both the traditional elite and their rivals saw opportunities to acquire new power positions. As part of their strategy they invested (Frankish-type) valuables in lavish funerary ritual, now on both sides of the river Vlie.

Conclusion

Valuable items of gold and silver were an essential tool of the North Sea elite, not only in the process of forming and consolidating social networks, but also for creating a sense of unity among the people they controlled. Interestingly, the cultural focus of this elite was constantly adjusted to the changing socio-political landscape – first Late Roman officers, then the Scandinavian and Frankish aristocracy being role models for the North Sea elite. While the expression of a true or fictional link with the Late Roman, 'Saxon' and 'Saxon-Scandinavian' or Scandinavian worlds was an important tool in legitimizing power positions during the 5th and first half of the 6th century, during the further 6th and early decades of the 7th century the consolidation of regional and larger elite networks was visualized by the distribution of regionally specific ornaments showing affinities with both the Scandinavian and Frankish worlds. Even before these networks were absorbed into the power structures of Frankish, Mercian and Danish rule, they had disappeared from view archaeologically when a uniform, 'Byzantine', style was adopted all along the southern North Sea coasts. The elite networks left few historical records but a particularly rich and fascinating collection of valuable items as the only tangible evidence of their past existence.

References

Primary source

Bede, *Ecclesiastical History of the English People*, ed. L. Sherley-Price, 1990 (London).

Secondary sources

Aufderhaar, Iris 2014, *Sievern, Ldkr. Cuxhaven – Analyse zur Entwicklung einer Mikroregion mit zentralörtlichen Merkmalen im westlichen Elbe–Weser-Dreieck von der ausgehenden Vorrömischen Eisenziet bis zum 6. Jh. n. Chr. Münster* (unpublished dissertation University of Münster).

Axboe, Morten 1999, 'The chronology of the Scandinavian gold bracteates'. In *The Pace of Change. Studies in Early-Medieval Chronology*, ed. J. Hines and K. Høilund Nielsen (Oxford).

Axboe, Morten 2007, *Brakteatstudier*. Nordiske Fortidsminder B-25 (Copenhagen).
Bazelmans, Jos 1999, *By Weapons Made Worthy: Lords, Retainers and their Relationship in Beowulf*, Amsterdam Archaeological Studies 5 (Amsterdam).
Behr, Charlotte 2010, 'New bracteate finds from Early Anglo-Saxon England', *Medieval Archaeology* 54, 34–88.
Behr, Charlotte, and Tim Pestell 2014, 'The bracteate hoard from Binham – an Early Anglo-Saxon central place?', *Medieval Archaeology* 58, 44–77.
Berghaus, Peter 1999, 'Großbodungen', *Reallexikon der Germanischen Altertumskunde* 13, 76–8.
Blackmore, Lyn 2008, 'Schätze eines angelsächsischen Königs von Essex. Die Funde aus einem Prunkgrab von Prittlewell und ihr Kontext'. In *Zwischen Spätantike und Frühmittelalter. Archäologie des 4. bis 7. Jahrhunderts im Westen*, ed. S. Brather (Berlin–New York), 323–40.
Böhme, Horst W. 1986, 'Das Ende der Römerherrschaft in Britannien und die angelsächsische Besiedlung Englands im 5. Jahrhundert', *Jahrbuch des Römisch-Germanischen Zentralmuseums Mainz* 33, 469–574.
Böhme, Horst W. 2003,'Das nördliche Niedersachsen zwischen Spätantike und frühem Mittelalter. Zur Ethnogenese der Sachsen aus archäologischer Sicht', *Probleme der Küstenforschung im südlichen Nordseegebiet* 28, 251–70.
Brieske, Vera 2001, *Schmuck und Trachtbestandteile des Gräberfeldes von Liebenau, Kr. Nienburg/Weser. Vergleichende Studien zur Gesellschaft der frühmittelalterlichen Sachsen im Spannungsfeld zwischen Nord und Süd*, Studien zur Sachsenforschung 5 (Oldenburg).
Bruce-Mitford, Rupert. L. S. 1978, *The Sutton Hoo Ship-burial. Volume 2: Arms, Armour and Regalia* (London).
Brugmann, Birte 1997a, 'Typology and dating'. In *The Anglo-Saxon Cemetery on Mill Hill, Deal, Kent*, The Society for Medieval Archaeology, Monograph Series 14, ed. K. Parfitt and B. Brugmann (Leeds), 31–93.
Brugmann, Birte 1997b, 'Britons, Angles, Saxons, Jutes and Franks'. In *The Anglo-Saxon Cemetery on Mill Hill, Deal, Kent*, The Society for Medieval Archaeology, Monograph Series 14, ed. K. Parfitt and B. Brugmann (Leeds), 110–8.
Bruns, Dorothee 2003, *Germanic Equal-Arm Brooches of the Migration Period. A Study of Style, Chronology and Distribution, Including a Full Catalogue of Finds and Contexts*, BAR International Series 1113 (Oxford).
Chadwick Hawkes, Sonia, and Mark Pollard 1981, 'The gold bracteates from sixth-century Anglo-Saxon graves in Kent, in the light of a new find from Finglesham', *Frühmittelalterliche Studien* 15, 316–70.
Dijkstra, Menno F. P. 2011, *Rondom de mondingen van Rijn and Maas. Landschap en bewoning tussen de 3^e en 9^e eeuw in Zuid-Holland, in het bijzonder de Oude Rijnstreek* (Leiden).
Filmer-Sankey, William, and Tim Pestell 2001, *Snape Anglo-Saxon Cemetery: Excavations and Surveys 1824–1992*, East Anglian Archaeology Report 95 (Ipswich).
Geake, Helen 1997, *The Use of Grave-Goods in Conversion-Period England, c. 600–c. 850*, BAR Britisch Series 261 (Oxford).
Haseloff, Güunther 1981, *Die germanische Tierornamentik der Völkerwanderungszeit*, Vorgeschichtliche Forschungen 17 (Berlin–New York).
Hauck, Karl 1970, *Goldbrakteaten aus Sievern. Spätantike Amulett-Bilder der 'Dania Saxonica' und die Sachsen-'origo' bei Widekund von Corvey*, Münstersche Mittelalter-Schriften 1 (München).
Hines, John 1984, *The Scandinavian Character of Anglian England in the pre-Viking Period*, BAR British Series 124 (Oxford).
Hines, John 1997, *A New Corpus of Anglo-Saxon Great Square-headed Brooches*, Reports of the Research Committee of the Society of Antiquaries of London 51 (Woodbridge).
Knol, Egge, and Xandra Bardet 1999, 'Carolingian weapons from the Cemetery of Godlinze, the Netherlands'. In *In Discussion with the Past.*, ed. H. Sarfatij, W. J. H. Verwers and P. J. Woltering (Amersfoort), 213–25.

Kruse, Pernille 2007, 'Jutes in Kent? On the Jutish nature of Kent, southern Hampshire and the Isle of Wight', *Probleme der Küstenforschung im südlichen Nordseegebiet* 31, 243–376.

Näsman, Ulf 1991, 'Sea trade during the Scandinavian Iron Age: its character, commodities, and routes'. In *Aspects of Maritime Scandinavia, AD 200–1200*, ed. O.Crumlin-Pedersen (Roskilde), 23–40.

Nicolay, Johan A. W. 2005, 'Nieuwe bewoners van het terpengebied en hun rol bij de opkomst van Fries koningschap. De betekenis van gouden bracteaten en bracteaatachtige hangers uit Friesland (vijfde-zevende eeuw na Chr.)', *De Vrije Fries* 85, 37–103.

Nicolay, Johan A. W. 2014, *The Splendour of Power: Early Medieval Kingship and the Use of Gold and Silver in the Southern North Sea Area (5th to 7th century AD)*, Groningen Archaeological Studies 28 (Groningen).

Nielsen, Karen H. 1999, 'Style II and the Anglo-Saxon elite'. In *The Making of Kingdoms*, Anglo-Saxon Studies in Archaeology and History 10, ed. T. Dickinson and D. Griffiths (Oxford), 185–202.

Nieuwhof, Annet 2011, 'Discontinuity in the northern-Netherlands coastal area at the end of the Roman Period', *Neue Studien zur Sachsenforschung* 3, 55–66.

Nösler, Daniel, and Steffen Wolters 2009, 'Kontinuität und Wandel – zur Frage der spätvölkerwanderungszeitlichen Siedlungslücke im Elbe–Weser-Dreieck'. In *Dunkle Jahrhunderte in Mitteleuropa?*, Studien zu Spätantike und Frühmittelalter 1, ed. O. Heinrich-Tamaska, N. Krohn and S. Ristow (Hamburg), 367–88.

Pesch, Alexandra 2007, *Die Goldbrakteaten der Völkerwanderungszeit – Thema und Variation* (RGA-Ergänzungsbände 36 (Berlin–New York).

Rau, Andreas 2010, *Nydam mose 1. Die personengebundenen Gegenstände. Grabungen 1989–1999* (Aarhus).

Tulp, Caroline 2003, 'Tjitsma, Wijnaldum: an early medieval production site in the Netherlands'. In *Markets in Early Medieval Europe: Trading and 'Productive' Sites, 650–850*, ed. T. Pestell and K. Ulmschneider (Trowbridge), 221–33.

Yorke, Barbara 2005, *Kings and Kingdoms of Early Anglo-Saxon England*, 2nd edn (London–New York).

Wagner, Annette, and Jaap Ypey 2011, *Das Gräberfeld auf dem Donderberg bei Rhenen. Katalog* (Leiden).

6

How 'English' is the Early Frisian Runic Corpus?

The evidence of sounds and forms

Gaby Waxenberger

In my habilitation thesis (Waxenberger 2010) I considered, amongst other things, the earliest runic inscriptions in England, from the period *c.* AD 400–650. By comparing them to the later inscriptions I found that the English runic corpus can be divided into two sub-corpora: a small Pre-Old English (Pre-OE) corpus (Fig. 6.1) and a larger Old English (OE) one (Fig. 6.2).

At the inception of runic writing in England, the Pre-OE inscriptions were written in the pre-*fuþorc*, which was based closely on the original Common Germanic (CGmc) *fuþark* (='older *fuþark*') of 24 characters with some enlargement and modifications (which are discussed in the course of this paper) during the period *c.* AD 400–610/650; that is, down to the time of the Caistor-by-Norwich brooch (*c.* AD 610–50). This inscription is of the utmost importance because it shows the new runes with their new phonemic sound-values for the first time. I regard the period of *c.* AD 610/650 as the beginning of Old English because all the relevant sound-changes were completed by then (Waxenberger, forthcoming, ch. 3). It is crucial to note that the Pre-OE inscriptions reflect early sound-changes that had otherwise only been reconstructed on linguistic principles in handbooks that did not take runic inscriptions into account.

Since the academic discussion on the question of whether or not there was ever an 'Anglo-Frisian unity' has been rekindled (see Nielsen 1994 for an overview), it seemed methodologically justified to build on the findings for the Pre-OE corpus and see to what extent the Frisian corpus shows congruence with it. Therefore I use the sound-changes of Pre-OE as a framework and examine how the Frisian runes and the sound-values they represent fit into that frame. I also look at some of the rune-forms in order to shed more light on the characteristics of the Frisian corpus. It is stressed that this is work in progress. The difficulties of such an undertaking need to be made clear from the outset.

Fig. 6.1. The distribution of the inscriptions that make up the Pre-Old English Corpus.

Fig. 6.2. The distribution of the inscriptions that make up the Old English Corpus.

The periodization of Old Frisian compared to Old English

Compared to other Germanic languages such as English and German, the attestation of a historical stage of Frisian is relatively late. What has come to be labelled Old Frisian (OFris: *c.* AD 1200–1550) is the counterpart of what is already Middle English (*c.* AD 1100–1500) whereas Old English starts in approximately AD 650 and ends *c.* 1100. The language stage prior to OE is labelled as Pre-OE and encompasses the time from approximately AD 400 to *c.* 610/650 (the date of the phonemicization of *i*-umlaut: see Waxenberger, forthcoming, ch. 3).

Table 6.1. The periodization of the English and Frisian languages in the Middle Ages

Pre-Old English	*c.* AD 400–610/650	Pre-Old Frisian	*c.* AD 400–610/650
Old English	*c.* AD 650–1100		
Early Old English	*c.* AD 650–900	Early Runic Old Frisian	*c.* AD 650–900
Middle English	*c.* AD 1100–1500	Old Frisian	*c.* AD 1200–1500

As can be inferred from Table 6.1, the historical stages of Old English and Old Frisian are not directly comparable. The manuscript documentation of Old Frisian begins *c.* 1100–25 at the earliest with 'a fragment of a Latin Psalter with interverbal Frisian glosses' whereas the 'oldest entire Frisian manuscripts to have come down on us', the Brokmer Codex (B1: 1276–1300) and the first Rüstring Codex (R1: *c.* 1300) are considerably later (Bremmer 2009, 6; Langbroek 2015; on the controversial discussion of some possible, but very little, evidence provided by the *Lex Frisionum*, *c.* AD 800, see Nielsen 1994, 122–4; cf. also Nijdam, this vol.). These texts reflect a phonological state comparable to Middle English: the inflectional endings, for example, are already levelled to /ə/ and are therefore represented by various vowel graphemes <e, i, a, o, u> in the Latin script (cf. Steller 1928, §§49–64; Bremmer 2009, 73). Additionally, root vowels do not seem to reflect the stage that they must have been in some 300 to 400 years earlier, a stage of development in which most OE inscriptions were written.

The OFris runic inscriptions appear from the first half of the 5th century and continue until the 8th/9th century. This time-span is congruent with Pre-OE and Early OE (Table 6.1). The periodization of Pre-OE and OE is primarily based on phonological features, but also on morphological developments. Since these were shared with and/or paralleled in the Frisian language/dialects of the same period, the periodization of English can also be applied to Frisian. Accordingly, I label the period from approximately AD 400–610/650 'Pre-Old Frisian'. The date of the majority of the Frisian runic inscriptions is congruent with Early OE and therefore I prefer to label the period *c.* AD 610/650–900 'Early Runic Old Frisian'.[1] There are, of course, other approaches to the periodization which use other criteria than the runes. One example may suffice to demonstrate the problems of periodization of Frisian. Bremmer (2009, xii) follows Århammar (1995, 71) according to whom the runic inscriptions would partly belong to a period of Proto- or

---

[1] For a somewhat different periodization see the homepage of the Frisian Academy (http://tdb.fryske-akademy.eu/tdb/index-en.html: accessed 9 May 2014), which proposes Proto-Old Frisian (?–AD 1200); Anglo-Frisian runes (AD 500–800); Old Frisian (AD 1200–1550); Middle Frisian (AD 1550–1800).

How 'English' is the Early Frisian Runic Corpus?

Common Frisian (*c.* AD 500–700) and partly to that of Proto-Old South-West Frisian (/Proto-Old East Frisian) (Fig. 6.3). This approach shows how difficult periodization is in general and particularly in this case. This is not the only problem we have to face when dealing with the Frisian runic corpus.

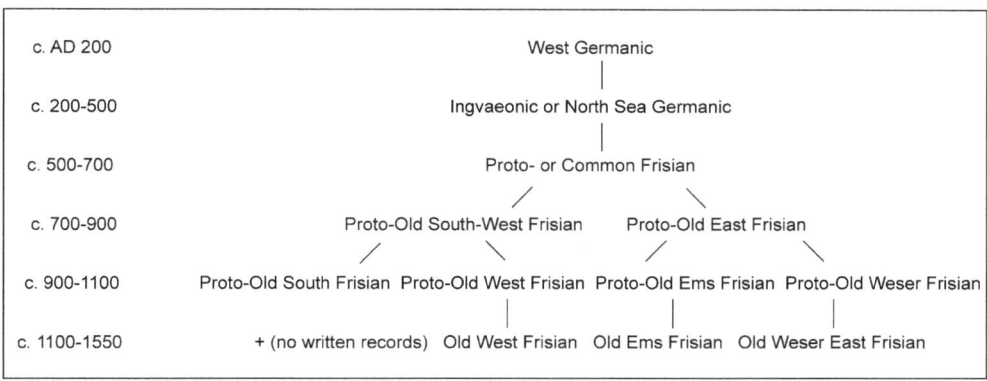

Fig. 6.3. The descent and periodization of Old Frisian according to Bremmer (2009, xii).

The Difficulties of the Frisian Corpus

The objects which are considered to belong to 'the Frisian runic tradition' were not all found in the modern-day provinces of Friesland and Groningen in the Netherlands (cf. Fig. 6.4), but also in England (the **skanomodu** *solidus*; the Southampton bone; the Glasgow/Folkstone *tremissis*), in Belgium (the Amay bone comb) and Ostfriesland, Germany (the Schweindorf *solidus*) (Looijenga 2003, 317 and 325). Conversely, Looijenga (2003, 325) also points out that, although discovered in the Netherlands, the Bergakker scabbard-mount (*c.* AD 425) and the Borgharen belt buckle (*c.* AD 600) 'do not have any Frisian connotations, but rather point to a Continental/Frankish context'. I have also excluded the Bergakker scabbard-mount from this analysis as the language of the inscription is not clear (Vennemann 1999, 152–6: Gothic; Malzahn 1998, 90: probably East Germanic; Grünzweig 2009, 160: East Germanic; Odenstedt 1999, 163–73: a macaronic Latin and Anglo-Frisian inscription; Bammesberger 1999, 180–5: possibly the WGmc forerunner of Frisian but perhaps also the WGmc forerunner of either OHG or OE; Seebold 1999, 152–62: Germanic continental dialects; Mees 2002, 23, 26: Pre-Old Low Franconian).

I shall discuss the Borgharen belt buckle later and offer some linguistic comments on the objects found in Great Britain. Moreover, I have excluded the wooden objects from Westeremden (a weaving sword/slay = Westeremden A; yew-wood stick = Westeremden B) for two reasons: first, the dates attributed to them are relatively late and in the case of Westeremden B the inscription is at least partially in a poor state, particularly regarding the critical graphemes. As these inscriptions are not unproblematic, they must be analysed separately. Furthermore, some of the Frisian inscriptions have no contribution to make in the study of either the sound-changes or the rune-forms, and these are therefore excluded as well.

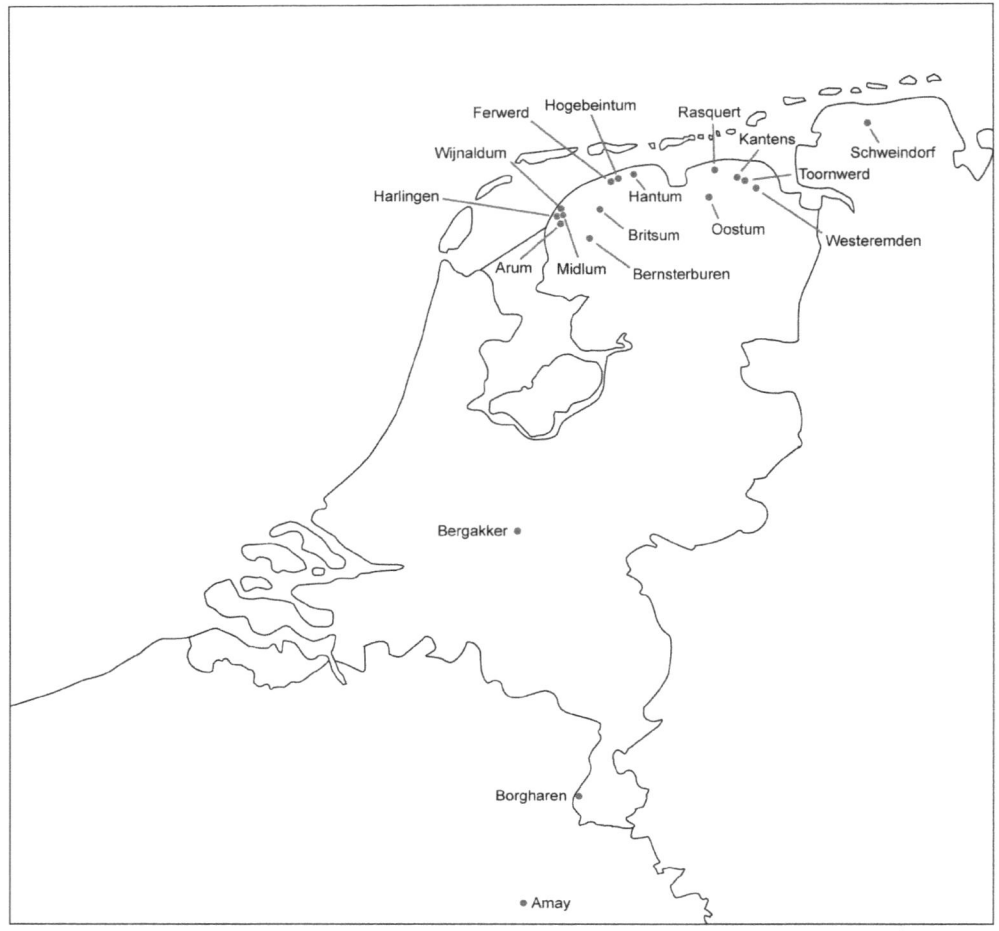

Fig. 6.4. The distributions of inscriptions considered as part of the Frisian Runic Corpus.

The Frisian inscriptions considered

For the reasons specified, I have considered the inscriptions listed in Table 6.2. On the 'Frisian Corpus' and its problems see also Düwel and Tempel (1968–70), Page (2001) and Nedoma (2014, 343–8).

The Pre-Old English Sound-changes

I have analysed the Pre-OE sound-changes reflected by the Pre-OE inscriptions elsewhere (Waxenberger, forthcoming, ch. 3) and shall here attempt to analyse the Pre-OFris corpus against the background of Pre-OE development, but will only offer comments on the complex sound-changes where necessary.

How 'English' is the Early Frisian Runic Corpus?

Table 6.2. The inscriptions considered as part of the Frisian Runic Corpus

Find	Proposed date	Artefact-type/ Material	Proposed transliteration
1. Amay (Belgium)	575–625	Comb/Bone	]eda
2. **skanomodu** coin (England?)	575–610	*Solidus*/Gold	**skanomodu**
3. Harlingen (Frisia)	575–625 (Blackburn 1991, 142: 'late 6th/early 7th century)	*Solidus*/Gold	**hada**
4. Schweindorf (Germany)	575–625 (Blackburn 1991, 142: 'late 6th/early 7th century)	*Solidus*/Gold	**weladu**
5. Ferwerd (Frisia)	6th century	Comb/Antler	*emu* r{[a]/[æ]}
6. Wijnaldum B (Frisia)	*c.* 600	Pendant/Gold	**hiwi**
7. Folkestone (England) 7a. Hunterian Museum Glasgow: coin from the same die as the lost Folkestone specimen.	*c.* 650	*Tremissis*/Gold	{æ/a}niwulufu←
8. *Hamwic* (Southampton, England)	650–9th century (see *infra,* and Waxenberger, forthcoming, ch. 2, no. 75)	Bone	**katæ**
9. Oostum (Netherlands)	8th century	Comb/Antler	*ai*b kabu deda habuku
10. Toornwerd (Netherlands)	8th century	Comb/Antler	**kobu**
11. Midlum (Frisia)	*c.* 750	*Sceatt*/Silver	**æpa**
12. Rasquert (Netherlands)	Late 8th century	Sword grip/ Whalebone	*edumæditoka*
13. Arum (Frisia)	Late 8th/9th century	Model sword/Yew	**edæ boda**
14. Bernsterburen (Frisia)	*c.* 800 (Looijenga 2003, 314)	Staff/Whalebone	**tuda** a{*w/l*}udukiusþu
15. Hantum	No date (Looijenga 2003, 316)	Plate/Bone	]?{a/æ}h{a/æ}k[

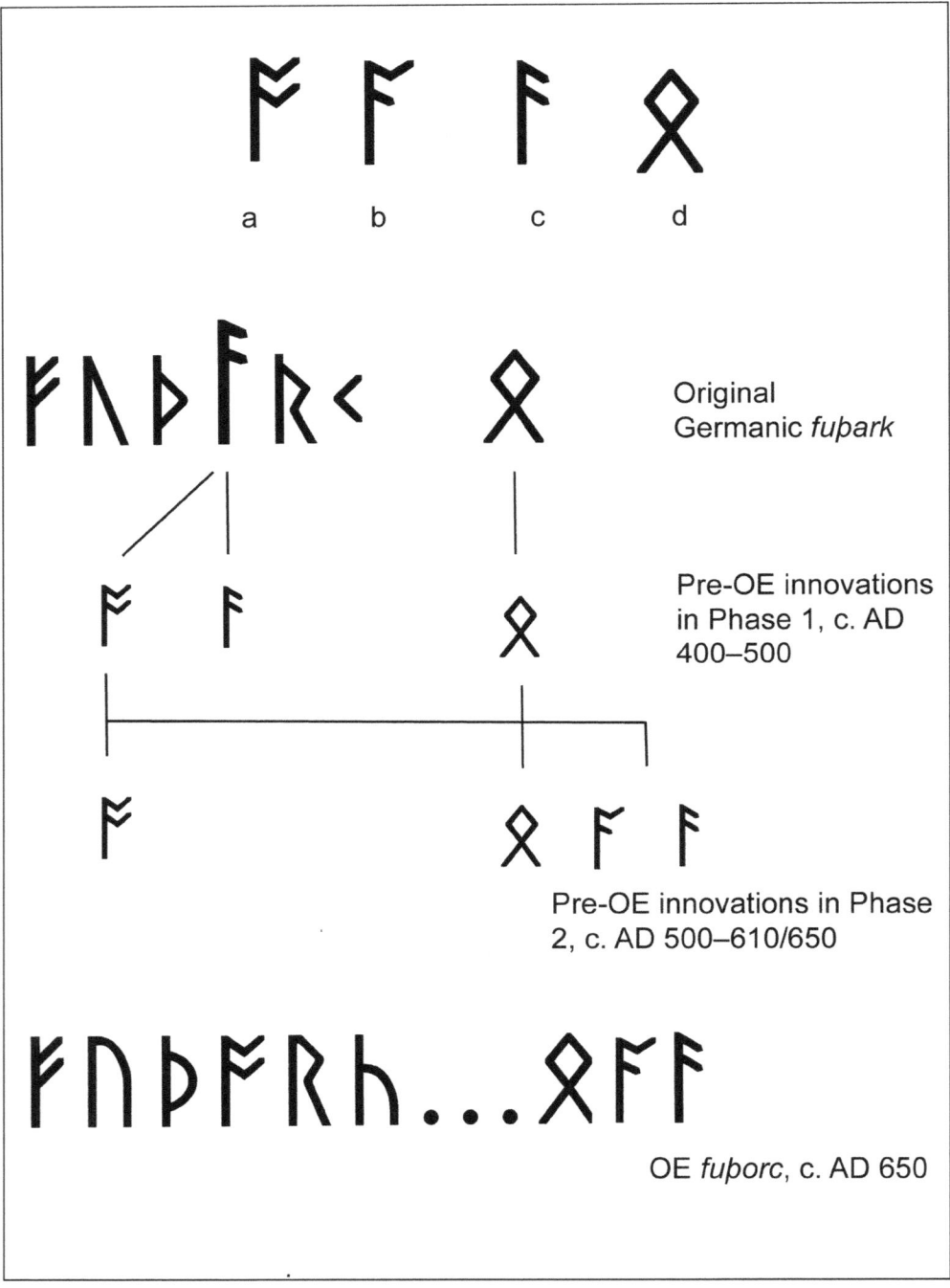

Fig. 6.5. Characteristic rune-forms of the Old English *fuþorc*: a: *ōs*; b: *āc*; c: *æsc* (formerly **ansuz*); d: the *oþil* rune. Below: diagramatic scheme of innovations in rune-form and adjustments to the order of the rune-row between the *fuþark* and the *fuþorc*.

Theoretically, the Pre-OFris period should include the decisive sound-changes that are shared by both Pre-OE and Pre-OFris but should also include the early sound-changes that are individual developments in Frisian. As I have already pointed out (above), a relatively small sub-corpus of nine early inscriptions in the Pre-OE corpus was analysed for the early sound-changes. Because of those sound-changes, the CGmc *fuþark* no longer sufficed for Pre-OE. Not only did the sound-changes require the creation of new graphemes, namely, the runes *ōs* and *āc* (Fig. 6.5a–b) but also some reshuffling of existing runes: *ansuz* /a(:)/ of the CGmc *fuþark* (where it was in position no. 4: Fig. 6.5c) adapted to the new sound-value /æ(:)/ and was shifted to the end of the row (position 26). *ōþil* (no. 24: Fig. 6.5d) experienced a shift from /o(:)/ to /œ(:)/ by *i*-umlaut. This intermediary phase marks the transition from the CGmc or older *fuþark* to the OE *fuþorc*. These four runes were established in England by the middle of the 7th century with the values /o(:)/, /a(:)/, /æ(:)/ and /œ(:)/ (summarized in Figure 6.5, lower).

Table 6.3 below gives an overview of the sound-changes and the new phonemes in Pre-OE and Pre-OFris. However, this is a simplified version of the much more complex sound-changes.

Table 6.3. Sound-changes in Pre-Old English and Pre-Old Frisian

Sound changes	Pre-OE	Pre-OFris (Nielsen 2011, 514, 517)
1. CGmc and Anglo-Frisian compensatory lengthening of *ā + nasals, together with WGmc *ā + nasal led to …	Pre-OE /ɔ̃:/	Pre-OFris /ɔ̃:/
2. The phonemic split of WGmc *ā led to…	Pre-OE /ɔ̃:/ Pre-OE /a:/	Pre-OFris /ɔ̃:/ Pre-OFris /a:/
3. Monophthongization of Gmc *ai led to …	Pre-OE /a:/	Pre-OFris /a:/ Pre-OFris /æ:/ (> OFris /e:/)
4. Monophthongization of Gmc *au led to…	OE *ēa* (< Pre-OE ?*æa*)	OFris /a:/ (< Pre-OFris ?/a:/) Pre-OFris **skanomodu**, if developed from Gmc *skaun'* (c. AD 575–610). See *infra*.

The new rune *ōs*

The sound-changes listed under 1 in Table 6.3 should have been carried through in both Pre-OE and Pre-OFris. Various sound-changes resulted in the new long nasalized Pre-OE /ɔ̃:/ which differed from the inherited long *ō* by its open quality and nasalization. Once phonemicized, this new phoneme required a new grapheme and this was the *ōs*-rune. In Early OE (at the end of 7th century/beginning of the 8th century), the long, open, nasalized Pre-OE /ɔ̃:/ and the inherited long /o:/ fell together and were denoted by the new **o**-rune *ōs* (above, Fig. 6.5 and below, Fig. 6.6b).

1. The first attestation of the *ōs*-rune (for the nasalized long vowel /ɔ̃:/) occurs on the Pre-OE Undley Bracteate (Fig. 6.7a), *c.* AD 450–500 (Hines 1990, 441; Waxenberger, forthcoming, ch.3). For the complete inscription see Waxenberger (forthcoming: ch. 2, no. 83)
2. In Pre-OFris /ɔ̃:/ is not attested. However, on the possibly OFris **skanomodu** coin

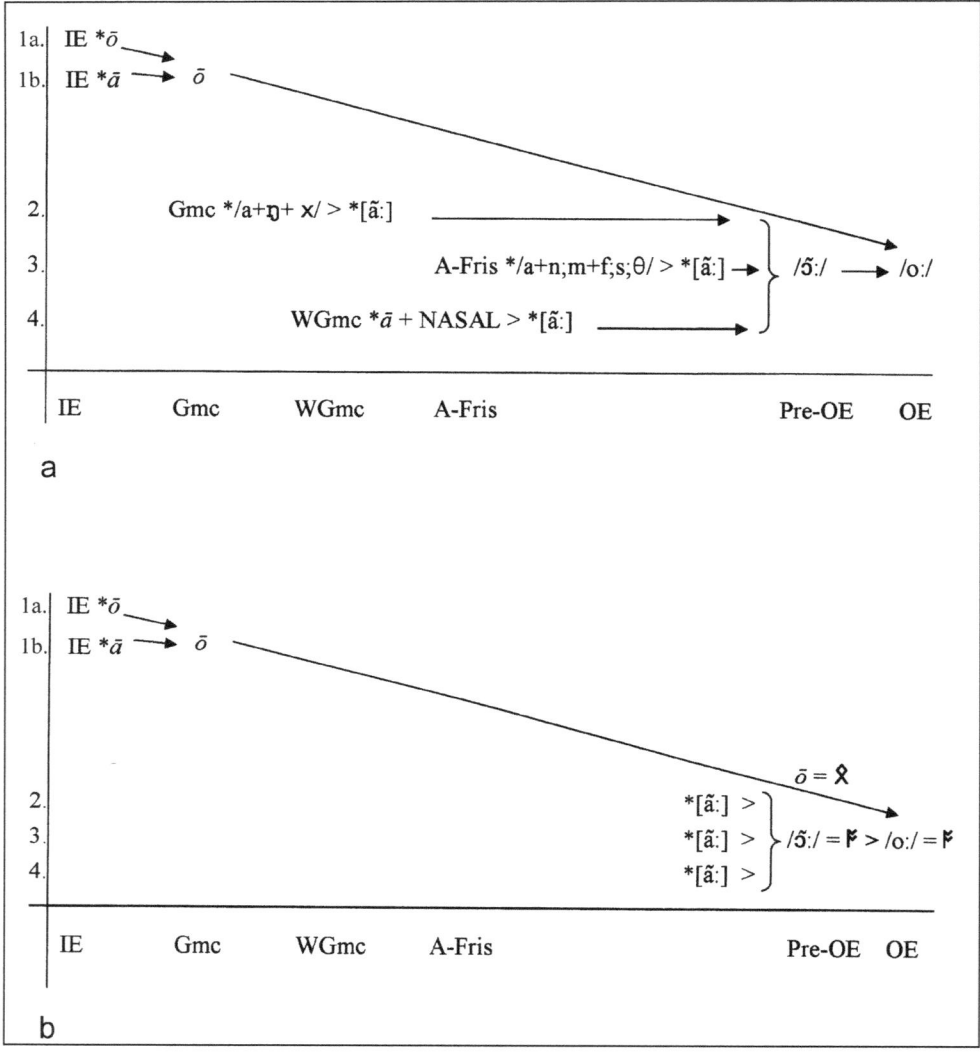

Fig. 6.6. The emergence of OE ō: a: phonology; b: runic reflexes.

(Fig. 6.7b; c. AD 575–610: Blackburn 1991, 142) the rune ōþil (Fig. 6.5d) was still used with its old sound-value, denoting the non-nasalized vowels /o/ and /o:/ in **skano-** < Gmc *skauna- (see Waxenberger, forthcoming, ch. 2, no. 71) and **modu** < Gmc *mōda-).
3. The Pre-OE Chessell Down inscription (Fig. 6.7c; c. AD 525–50: Hines 1990, 439) has both the new ōs-rune and the old ōþil-rune, with the latter being used for the allophonic vowel [œ] fronted before *i* in the next syllable. In a narrow transcription, I would give this as **ako : k̹œri**, using [k̹] for a more palatalized *k*.

If the ōs-rune **o** (as Fig. 6.5a) on the Chessell Down scabbard-mount was used to denote a masculine (masc.) name inflected according to the OE weak declension pattern, it could only be in the nominative singular (nom.sg.). The Proto-Germanic nom.sg.

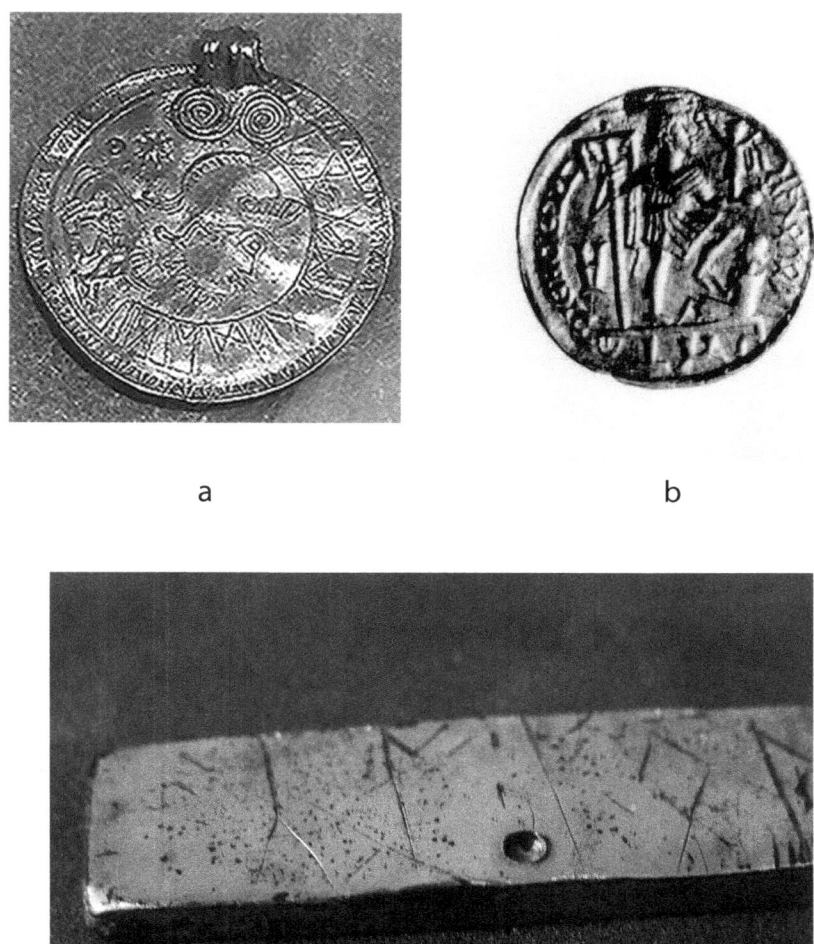

a b

c

Fig. 6.7. Key examples of the use of the ōs and oþil runes in England and Frisia. a: the Undley bracteate; b: the **skanomodu** *solidus*; c: the Chessell Down scabbard mount replica. All items © the Trustees of the British Museum.

ending *ǭ (= /ɔ̃:/) can be seen as the origin of the normal OE ending -*a* (Bammesberger 1990a, 167; Waxenberger 1996, 101). The intermediary state -ɔ (< */-ɔ:/) rather than OE -*a* for the unstressed vowels is assumed by Nielsen (2006, 211 and n.9) and he adds a comment by John Hines: 'the unaccented final vowel of **ako**' represented with ōs on the Chessell Down scabbard-mount 'might bear out this point'. Hines is absolutely right. The first evidence of **-a** (< -ɔ) in England (represented by the new āc-rune: Fig. 6.5b) in the nom.sg. ending of a weak noun (**luda**) appears only *c.* AD 610–50 on the Caistor-by-Norwich brooch.

We may compare this with **bobo** (the nom.sg. of a masculine *n*-stem noun: Nedoma 2004, 245) on the Borgharen belt buckle (*c.* AD 600), the inscription on which has been assumed to be continental by Looijenga (2003, 322) on the basis of the occurrence of the *ōþil*-rune as /o(:)/ here rather than the new *ōs*-rune, and also because the object comes from a 'small Merovingian cemetery'. Looijenga's assumption of a continental origin seems plausible from an archaeological point of view but is it also so from a runological point of view?[2]

The personal name on this object is a widespread one in the Germanic dialects according to Nedoma (2004, 245 and also 2007, 318): there are, for example, West Frankish *Bobo* (6th century: Nedoma 2004, 245) and also OE forms *Bob(b)a* (cf. Searle 1897, 109; PASE s.v. *Boba, Bobba*).

For the ending in -*o* in this name, as OFris masc. *n*-stems also regularly also end in -*a* in the nom.sg. (Steller 1928, §60) < *-ɔ (Nielsen 2006, 211) < PGmc *$\tilde{o}$ (Bammesberger 1990a, 167), the new *ōs*-rune would be expected here as well, especially since the emergence of this new rune is due to a common stock of Pre-OE and Pre-OFris sound-changes, as shown above. The ending of the OE form *Bob(b)a* would presumably have developed in Anglo-Frisian as follows: */-ɔ:/ > /-ɔ/ > Early OE/Early Runic OFris -*a*. The open vowel /ɔ/ of Pre-OE and Pre-OFris would have been rendered by the new *ōs*-rune. Instead, we have the old *ōþil*-rune here.

The etymology of the root vowel -**o**- in **bobo** is difficult (cf. Nedoma 2004, 246 and esp. 247) but it seems that -**o**- was not developed from one of the three sound-changes leading to Pre-OE /ɔ:/ (see above, Fig. 6.6). However, the rune *ōþil* used as the root vowel cannot be used as evidence for continental origin as this rune would also have been used in Pre-OE/Pre-OFris if the phoneme in question were derived from Gmc */o:/. The ending -**o**, on the other hand, represented by the *ōþil*-rune, does suggest that the Borgharen inscription is not Pre-OFris.

In the Old English Runes Corpus (OERC) proper (= post-AD 610/650), attested forms of the new *ōs*-rune appear only after the merger of the new nasal vowel /õ:/ with the old /o:/. The OERC reveals the first attestations in the late 7th or early 8th centuries, on the Brandon antler handle (late 7th–early 9th century: **wohs** < Gmc */o:/); Lindisfarne Stone I (mid-7th–8th century: **osgyþ** /o:s/ < /ɔ:/ < /õ:s-/ < */ãːs-/ < */ans-/); and the Whitby comb (7th–9th century but probably early 8th century (Waxenberger, forthcoming, ch. 3): **god** < Gmc */u/).

Here too the Old Frisian Runes Corpus is in absolute congruence with the OERC, using the new *ōs*-rune from the 8th century onwards as, for example, on the Arum yew-wood sword (late 8th century: **boda** (Looijenga 1997, 182; 2003, 309; cf. Quak 1990, 360 for an

---

[2] Looijenga (2003, 322) suggests that the runes are continental because of the *ōþil*-rune and because of the shape of the rune **b** whose pockets are far apart (cf. the S-fibula from Schwangau; the wooden stave from Neudingen; the Engers bow fibula; and the Weimar bronze belt buckle). However, in inscriptions of the Pre-OE and Early OE corpus (i.e. the Watchfield purse-mount and Caistor-by-Norwich brooch), the **b**-runes also have their pockets 'far apart'. I do not, therefore, regard this form as diagnostic of continental runes.

earlier dating)). If the analysis of **boda** (< WGmc *o* (Brunner 1965, §58)) as 'messenger' is correct, then both the forms above and this form prove the merger of the new /ɔ̄(:)/ with the old /o(:)/. The *ōs*-rune also appears on the Toornwerd bone comb (8th century: **kobu** (Looijenga 2003, 305)) and the Rasquert sword-grip (late 8th century: **oka**, a masculine *n*-stem personal name in the nom.sg. cf. OE *oca*, 'mind, intelligence' [Looijenga 2003, 317]).

In the following, I will present a synopsis of the forms and sound-value of the new *ōs*-rune in the OERC and the Pre-OFris Runes Corpus. Table 6.4 provides an overview of the rune-forms in the (Pre-)OE and Pre-OFris/Early Runic OFris runic corpora. I employ the common textbook definition of *grapheme* and *allograph* according to which a *grapheme* is 'the smallest distinctive unit in a writing system' and an *allograph* a 'variant of such a distinctive unit' (Bußmann 2002, 264. For a complete catalogue of the allograph-types in the (Pre-)OE inscriptions, see Waxenberger, forthcoming, ch. 7.2).

As can be inferred from Table 6.4, the chevron-type and the acute-angle-type of the *ōs*-rune are attested in both (Pre-)OE and (Pre-OFris)/Early Runic OFris. The new *ōs*-rune in Pre- and Early Runic OFris shows basically the same allograph-types as the Pre-OE corpus although there is not quite the same variety owing to the paucity of examples. The occurrence and distribution of the *ōs*-rune in the (Pre-OFris)/Early Runic OFris Corpus do not contradict the chronology arrived at on the basis of the Pre-OE corpus; on the contrary, the attested forms confirm it.

The phonemic split of West Germanic */a:/ and the monophthongization of Germanic */aɪ/ and */au/

The distinction between a *phoneme* and an *allophone* is essentially the same as that between a *grapheme* and an *allograph* (above). The difference between phonemes is structurally critical to the grammar of the language. Allophones are contextually governed varieties of pronunciation that are usually regular but not structurally significant. In conventional phonetic notation, allophones are represented by International Phonetic Alphabet (IPA) characters in square brackets [–] and phonemes by the same characters between forward slashes /–/.

While the phonemic split of WGmc */a:/ is a common Anglo-Frisian phenomenon, the monophthongizations of */aɪ/ and of */au/ were carried through separately in Pre-OE and Pre-OFris (Campbell 1959, §132; Nielsen 1981, nos. 54 and 58). The following section provides an overview (for more details see Waxenberger, forthcoming, ch. 3).

1. Pre-OE Phase 1 (*adventus Saxonum*–c. AD 500): Allophonic phase of WGmc */a:/ < PrGmc *$\bar{e}^1$ < IE *$\bar{e}$ (Luick 1921, 95; Campbell 1959, §255; but see Nielsen 2011, 520).

Before the monophthongization of */aɪ/, WGmc */a:/ must have had three allophones in Anglo-Frisian:

a: */a:/ + nasal resulted in the positional variant *[ɔ̄:] < *[ã:]
b: fronting of */a:/ yielded the positional variant *[æ:]
c: retraction of */a:/ led to an allophone *[ɑ:]

As allophones belong to the same phoneme, in this case */a:/, they are all represented by the same rune, in this case, the *ansuz*-rune.

2. Pre-OE Phase 2 (*c*. AD 500–610/650). The three sounds shown in Figure 6.8 are no longer positional variants (= allophones) but phonemes: /æ:/, /ɔ̄:/, /ɑ:/. New phonemes

Type 1: The chevron type	
	The side-twigs look like two chevrons. Two sub-types may be identified by the shape and alignment of the side-twigs.

Type 1A The asymmetrical chevron type	
Pre-OE corpus	**?Pre-OFris/Early Runic Frisian corpus**
 Chessell Down scabbard-mount Undley bracteate gō	Arum yew 'sword': Late 8th century (Looijenga 2003, 309); 6th–7th century (Quak 1990) 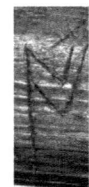 **boda**

Type 1B The pointed chevron type	
The chevrons are pointed and of approximately equal length.	
Old English corpus 7th/8th–9th(10th) century	**Early Runic Frisian corpus** Toornwerd comb: 8th century (Looijenga 2003, 305)
 Franks Casket (early 8th century)	 **kobu**

Table 6.4. An overview of the allograph types of the *ōs* rune in the Old English and Pre-Old Frisian Runic Corpora. Chessell Down and Franks Casket details, © the Trustees of the British Museum; Arum and Toornwerd details, photos: author, collection Fries Museum, Leeuwarden; Rasquert details, photos: author, collection Groninger Museum; Bramham Moor ring detail, photo: Arnold Mikkelsen, National Museum of Denmark.

How 'English' is the Early Frisian Runic Corpus?

Type 2: The acute angle type ᚾ	
Old English corpus mid-7th–9th century (and Late Anglo-Saxon Period)  Bramham Moor ring	
Type 2A Variant of the acute angle type Both ascenders end at the top of the upper line	
	Early Runic Frisian corpus Rasquert sword grip: late 8th century (Looijenga 2003, 316); 9th century (Quak 1990 363). 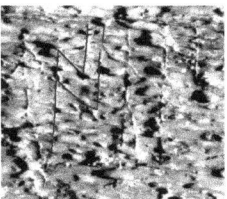

require new graphemes and therefore the new runes *ōs*, *āc* and *æsc* had to be designed and designated (Fig. 6.8b–c; cf. Fig. 6.5a–c).

The Pre-OFris development, however, was more complex than that of Pre-OE.

1. Gmc */ai/ must have become both Pre-OFris /æ:/ (> OFris *ē*; cf. Nielsen 2011, 514) and /a:/ (Fig. 6.9) under conditions that are not yet clarified (Boutkan 2011, 618).

Bremmer (2009, 27) comments that 'Gmc **ai* has monophthongization reflexes in OFris spelled <a> and <e>. The question why in some words **ai* developed to *ā* and in other words to *ē* (probably [æ:]) remains problematic and, in the end, unanswered (Hofmann 1995)'. Nielsen (1981, 58) discusses possible reasons for the development of OFris *ā* and *ē* but has no definitive answer. See also Versloot (this vol.) for his pattern of distribution.

2. Gmc */au/ was monophthongized to OFris /a:/ (Bremmer 2009, 27): **skanomodu** < ?**skauna*, if it is Frisian and if it is derived from Gmc **skauna*.

Bammesberger (1990, 459) assumes that *skanomodu* is a bahuvrihi compound with an adjectival stem *skano-* and a second element *-modu*. Since *-mod-* can be identified with the nominal stem Gmc **mōda-* (> OE neut. *mōd*; OHG *muot*), Bammersberger has proposed that *skanomodu* may have meant 'having a *skano* mind'. For *-o* (< Gmc *-a-) in **skano-** (< **skauna-*) Bammesberger (1990, 462) considers the process of 'rounding medial *-a-* in labial surroundings'.

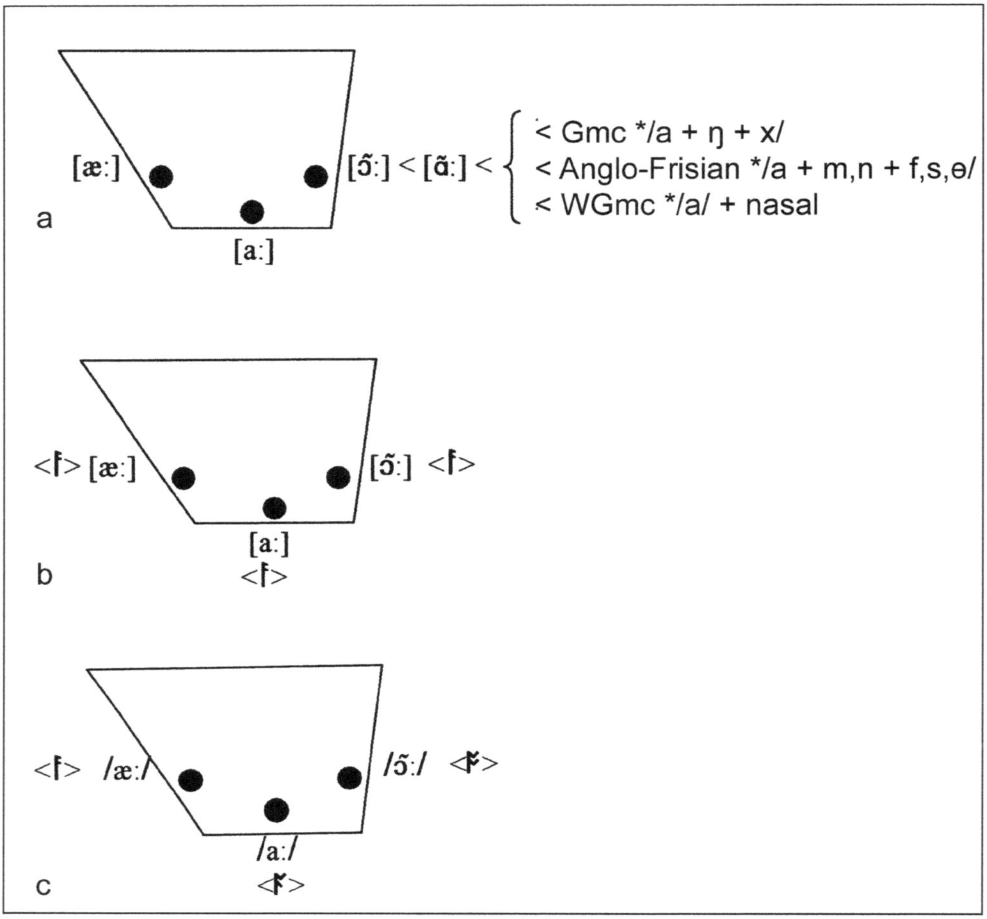

Fig. 6.8. The treatment of West Germanic */a:/. a: the allophones of West Germanic */a:/; b: runic representations of the allophones in (a); c: the new phonemes and their runic representation.

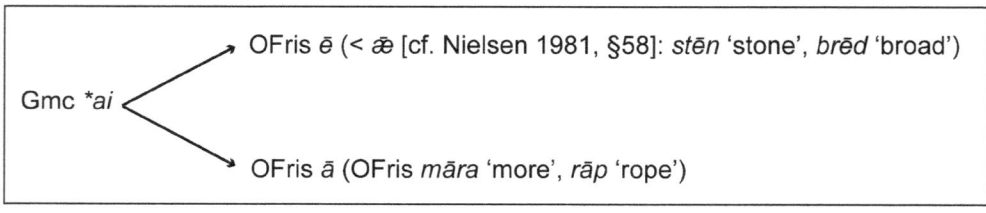

Fig. 6.9. The reflexes of Gmc *ai in Old Frisian.

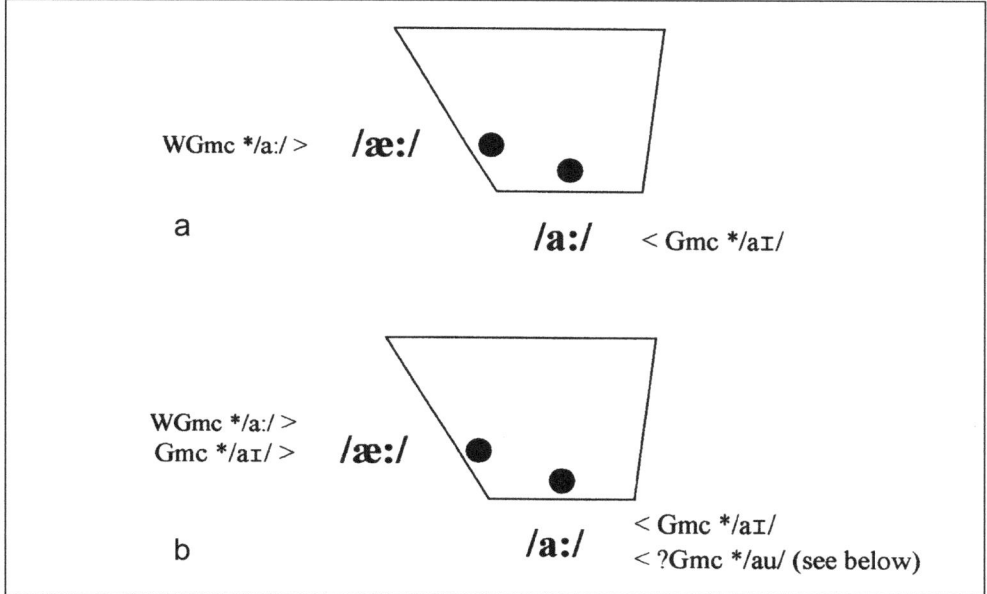

Fig. 6.10. The sources of the long vowels /æ:/ and /a:/ in (a) Pre-OE and (b) Pre-OFris.

Thus the Pre-OFris monophthongs /æ:/ and /a:/ were derived from more sources than the Pre-OE ones (Fig. 6.10).

It is commonly acknowleged that Gmc */au/ becomes OFris /a:/ (e.g. Bremmer 2009, 27: 'Gmc. *au monophthongizes without exception to OFris ā'). It is, however, of the utmost importance to stress the fact that this assumption of an exclusive development to ā is based on much later attestations: there is a gap in time between **skano-** on the **skanomodu** *solidus* (c. AD 575–610) and the beginning of OFris c. 1200; theoretically speaking, Gmc *au may not have become the monophthong ā by the beginning of the 7th century. If this were the case, -a- in **skanomodu** would not have developed from Gmc *au (cf. below). A comparison of the OE counterpart reveals the following development here: Gmc *au > OE ēa (possibly from /æ:a/). It was only in ME (from c. 1100) that ēa was monophthongized to long open /ɛ:/. These time-gaps in the evidence have at least to be kept in mind when considering the commonly proposed Frisian etymology of **skanomodu**.

The Pre-Old Frisian and Early Runic Old Frisian inscriptions with the *āc*-rune

I shall start with the two uncertain Pre-OFris objects, the **skanomodu** *solidus* and the Southampton (Hamwic) bone.

The **skanomodu** *solidus*

The two linguistic features which favour (Pre-)OFris as the language of origin of this inscription are Gmc **au* > OFris *ā* (contrasting with OE *ēa*) in the first element **skano-** (< Gmc **skaun-*) and the unstressed vowel *-u* (< Gmc **-az*) in **-modu** which is also found in other Frisian runic texts (Page 1973, 188; Looijenga 1996, 94; Hines, this vol.).

1. /a:/ in **skano-**

For Bammesberger (1990, 462) it 'would seem that *scanomodu* cannot readily be viewed as Old English. *skan-* would be fully in agreement with Frisian phonology'. Even though OE *ea* is clearly the 'end result' of Gmc **au* (above), Bammesberger points out that we do not know the intermediate stages but on 'the whole it seems preferable to accept the view that the monophthongization of Gmc **au* > *a* is a typically Frisian feature'. However, as I have already emphasized, as the monophthong /a:/ is not attested until the OFris phase (beginning *c.* AD 1200), it is at least debatable whether **-a-** in **skano-**, if derived from Gmc */*au/*, had already reached the stage /a:/ at the time of the **skanomodu** *solidus*.

Vennemann (pers. comm.) has attempted to link **skano-** (in **skanomodu**) to Gmc **skain-*, 'shine', opening up the possibility of the long /a:/, developed from Gmc */*aɪ/*, being Pre-OE in this case. And there is another possiblity: since Gmc */*aɪ/* became both OFris /e:/ (< /æ:/; OFris *stēn*, 'stone') and OFris /a:/ (*māra*, 'more'), the question arises as to whether or not **skanomodu** could not reflect a development from Gmc **skain-*, 'shine', to Pre-OFris /ska:n-/. Consequently, three phonological scenarios are theoretically imaginable for the root-vowel of the **skanomodu** *solidus*: Pre-OE /a:/ < Gmc */*aɪ/*; Pre-OFris /a:/ < Gmc */*aɪ/*; Pre-OFris /a:/ < Gmc */*au/*.

As the explanation of the root vowel is thus fraught with difficulties, it is not a reliable criterion for the provenance of the inscription. However, the root vowel is not the only criterion that has been adduced for a Pre-OFris provenance.

2. The ending **-u** in **-modu**

The 'unorganic' ending **-u** of an *a*-stem noun (Gmc **-az* (masc.); Gmc **-aⁿ* (neut.): Bammesberger 1990a, 39) is problematic, as Gmc **mōda-* is endingless in OE *mōd* (neut.) and the same would be expected in Pre-OFris (cf. OFris *mōd* masc. < **-az*: Steller 1928, 161).

For the *a*-stem nouns, e.g. **kabu** (Oostum comb: 8th/9th century; see above) and **kobu** (Toornwerd comb: 8th century) this 'might be at best a sign of instrumental case' according to Beck (1981, 74). The **-u** in **-modu** is seen as a vocative by Bammesberger (1990, 461–2) although the ending cannot be an original *a*-stem ending: IE **-e* would have been lost in Germanic and therefore **-modu** should have been ***mod**. Bammesberger considers the suggested **-u** in **weladu** (Schweindorf), which may 'etymologically [be] connected' with Norse *Vǫlundr* (*u*-stem), and it is 'therefore thinkable that a vocative in *-u* spread from some not immediately clear source, for example, from the *u*-stem *sunu*'. This word was a 'prominent *u*-stem from which a vocative ending in *-u* may have been in use at all stages of the language development' (Bammesberger 1990, 462; cf. Hines, this vol.). He thinks it 'quite possible' that *sunu* led to the further use of *-u* as a vocative marker even where it was not regularly expected.[3] He arrives at the conclusion that *-modu* can 'certainly be accounted for within the linguistic system of a West Germanic language' but 'hardly yields any direct information' as far as the underlying dialect (OE or OFris) is concerned.

Nielsen (2000, 92) is 'inclined to interpret' the ending as the nom.sg. of a feminine ō-stem noun which is compatible with the feminine ending Gmc *-ō > Pre-OFris *-u*. Although phonologically possible, this gender is confirmed neither by OE (*mōd* = neut.) nor by OS (*mōd* = masc.: Holthausen 1921, 246), or by OHG (masc. and neut.: Braune and Eggers 1987, 342). Nedoma (2004, 438; 2007, 302 and n.11) interprets the grapheme <-u> in **skanomodu** (PGmc *skauni-mōdaz*) as schwa /-ə/ < *-u < PGmc *-az*. Nedoma (2014, 348) defines this schwa as a rather close central vowel, that is, a higher schwa, [-ə̣], because, as he rightly states (see Waxenberger 2006), the regular central vowel [ə] would have been rendered by **e** in runic inscriptions.

However, the ending -**u** in **skanomodu** may represent an instrumental ending (cf. Insley 1991, 173) meaning 'by means of/with the **skanomodu** (*solidus*/coin)'. According to the case endings for the *a*-stems in Gmc, the instr.sg. ending in Pre-OE *-u* would be the only direct continuant: PGmc *-ō (Bammesberger 1990a, 39) > WGmc *-ū (Campbell 1959, §331.5) > Pre-OE/Pre-OFris *-u*.

While it is plausible to posit vocative endings for the names **skanomodu** (**skanomodu** *solidus*), **weladu** ?'Weland' (Schweindorf *solidus*), **æniwulufu** '*Æniwulf*' (Glasgow *tremissis*) and **habuku** 'hawk' (Oostum bone comb), the -**u** in the words for 'comb' (**kabu** (Oostum) and **kobu** (Toornwerd)[4] may represent the instrumental meaning 'by means of the comb' (but see also Nedoma 2014, 355–6). It can be suggested, indeed, that the ending -**u** in the Frisian corpus does not go back to one source but two: in some cases to the vocative and in others to the instrumental, and that some such cases might represent regular formulae. I see these early formulae as 'compact formulae', inasmuch as **kobu** may stand, for example, for '(I comb my hair) by means of the comb' whereas **kaba** on the Frienstedt comb (second half of the 3rd century: Schmidt and Nedoma and Düwel 2010/2011, 131) may represent, for example, the phrase '(I am called) comb'. Although denoting the same noun, **kobu** and **kaba** differ in their syntactical positions and therefore in their final vowels (but cf. Nedoma 2014, 353 who sees them as parallel attestations).

Southampton Bone I: **catæ** (Fig. 6.11)

From a linguistic point of view, **catæ** could be either (Pre-)OE or (Pre-)OFris. The interpretation of **catæ** as OFris *kate*, fem., 'finger bone', is given by Hofmann (1976, 73–4). However, Hofmann and Holthausen (1985, 55) comment that this meaning should be dismissed. Apparently, the meaning is instead 'knucklebone of a horse', as which it is also attested in Middle Low German and therefore fits Looijenga's (2003, 324) identifica-

---

[3] And also in the masculine name on the Westeremden A weaving sword, **adujislu** (Looijenga 2003, 311) and a₂dug₂islu (Nedoma 2007; 2014) which I have excluded (see above).
[4] For possible explanations of the missing nasal in **kobu** and **kabu** as well as the quantity of the vowels see Steller 1928, §4.

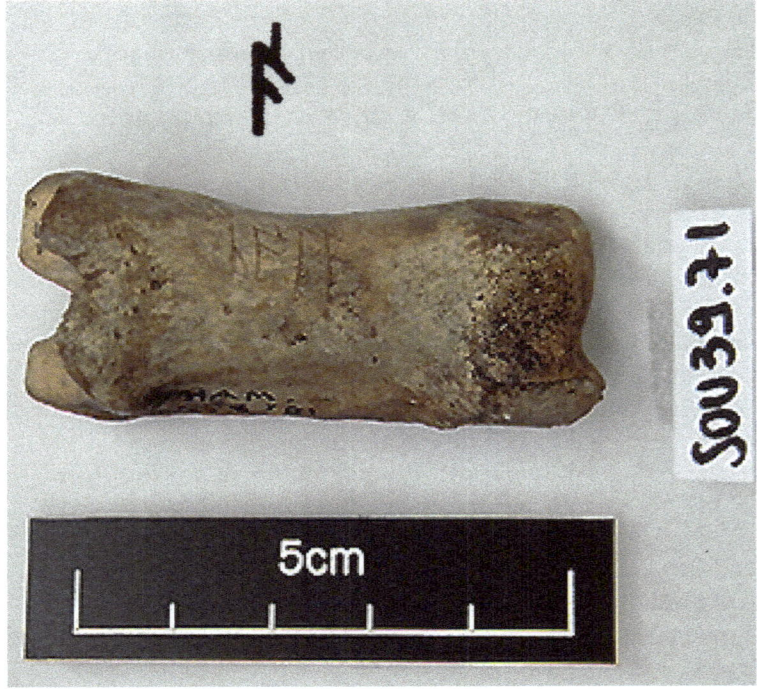

Fig. 6.11. The Southampton (Hamwic) bone: **catæ**; inset: idealized representation of the unusual *āc* rune-form.

tion of the object as the knucklebone of a horse. Page (1973, 171; 2001, 528) and Mitchell (1994, s.v. South I1), meanwhile, classify the object as a cattle bone. According to Bremmer (1981, 55) it is a 'cow's proximal phalanx'. Moreover, Quak (1990, 358) argues that the OE continuant of PGmc **kautō-* would be **cēat*, which is not attested, according to the *Dictionary of Old English*.

Besides its meaning, *katæ* has also been discussed controversially with regard to its declension class: Looijenga (2003, 324) labels it as a fem. *on*-stem; Nedoma (2007, 322) assumes an *ōn*-stem which must have been original and/or existed beside an *ō*-stem. The inscription would therefore name the object/material (Nedoma 2004, 425; 2007, 322).

Nielsen (1991, 299; 2000, 92) sees **katæ** '(-æ < Gmc **-ōm* < IE **-ām*)' as an acc.sg. of a fem. *ō*-stem. According to Nielsen (1991, 301) -æ(-) represents a 'reduction' (< Gmc **-a(-)*), derived 'from IE **-a/-o* + nasal' and he argues (2000, 92) that -æ, if seen in the 'runic Frisian phonological context, is best interpreted as an acc.sg fem. *o*-stem ending with a fronted reflex of **-a* (< Gmc **-on*)'. Nedoma (2004, 425), however, points out that the acc.sg. in -æ seems logically and syntactically incongruent. In his glossary, Bremmer (2009, 201) lists OFris *kāte*, 'knuckle-bone' as a feminine noun but assigns no class to it. If, however, the noun is a fem. *n*-stem, the ending must have undergone an innovation, according to Bammesberger (1990a, 167): the nom.sg. ending of the weak feminine does not go back to PGmc **-ō̃* but to PGmc **-ó* which must have developed to Pre-OE -æ (> OE -*e*).

The same development may be assumed for the Pre-OFris. fem. *n*-stem nouns and for this reason the ending -æ does not give any hints as to the inscription's provenance but leaves both possibilities open: formally, -æ (> OE -*e*) could be Early OE, but the ending -æ may also be Pre-OFris.

Page (1973, 171; 1999, 168), on the other hand, sees **catæ** as representing OE *cat(t)*, 'cat', or *catte*, 'she-cat', as a personal name, 'parallel to other animal personal names (e.g., *Wulf*, *Culfre*, *Duva* and allied to ON *kǫttr* which was used as a nickname)'. In the second edition of his *Introduction to Old English Runes*, Page (1999, 169) also takes the possibility of an OFris provenance into account, a theory which he sees as supported by the facts that Hamwic was a port with trading links to Frisia, and the unusual form of the *āc*-rune (see Fig. 6.11). From an exclusively linguistic viewpoint, both OFris *kāte* and OE *catte* are possible, as runic writing does not typically double consonants (cf. Waxenberger, forthcoming, ch. 9), and as OE *cat*, masc. or neut., also existed as a wk. fem. *catte* (*Dictionary of Old English*, s.v. *cat*, *catte*). OE *cat(e)*; *catte*, 'cat' (< Medieval Latin *cattus*; *catta*: Holthausen 1934, 44) occurs only eight times and both class and gender cannot be clearly analysed ('m. or n., also wk., f. or n.': *Dictionary of Old English* 2003: s.v. *cat*, *catte*; see also Kluge and Seebold 2002, 479).

From the runological point of view, the side-twig of the **a**-rune in **katæ** is unique in the OERC (see Waxenberger, forthcoming, ch. 7.5: rune **a**); it has been categorized as the characteristically Frisian rune-form (Nedoma 2004, 425). Nedoma (1991–3, 120) sees a connection with some of the Frisian inscriptions (Arum, Westeremden A, Oostum), 'die den Widerhaken nicht am Rand, sondern in der Mitte des oberen Seitenzweiges aufweisen' ('which display the reverse turn not at the edge, but in the middle, of the upper by-stave'). He considers the possibility that these variants may be specifically Frisian. As for the attested rune-forms and allograph-types, Table 6.5 shows that both the chevron and the acute angle type exist in the Frisian corpus. It is important to note that the allegedly 'typical Frisian type' is attested only twice in my corpus. To sum up, the Frisian *āc*-rune **a** and its allograph-types are congruent with the Pre-OE and OE allographs.

Attested forms of the allograph-types in the English and Frisian corpora

Allograph-types 1B and 2B, commonly labelled 'Frisian', are relatively rare (Table 6.5): Type 1B, sub-type of Type 1 (chevron type), occurs on the Oostum bone comb (x1) and Type 2B, a sub-type of Type 2 (acute angle type), is attested on the Arum yew sword (x1) and on the possibly Frisian Southampton bone (Fig. 6.11) (x1). In total, these are three attested examples of sub-types 1B and 2B out of a total of 11 attested examples (including the two possibly Frisian inscriptions) in the collected corpus. As can be inferred from Table 6.5, Type 1 was used in the Frisian corpus: the usage of the sub-types listed was probably not dependent on a particular school, especially not since Type 1 and sub-type 1B appear on the same object, the Oostum bone comb. Nedoma (2014, 345) sees the **o**-rune on the Toornwerd comb as a type in its own right; in my opinion, however, the carver could not link the ascender of the upper chevron to the very end of the upper descender of this chevron as, in this case, the ascender would have been too close to the ascender of the lower chevron (Table 6.4).

Type 1: The chevron type

 The two (approximately) parallel side-twigs descend at an acute angle to the stave.
The upper side-twig begins at the top of the main stave.
The ascender of the upper side-twig is at an acute angle to the upper side-twig.
The upper side-twig occurs in the form of a chevron.

Old English runic corpus **Type 1**: mid 7th-9th(/10th) century	Early Runic Old Frisian corpus **Type 1** The direction of writing is from left to right: the side-twigs descend to the right. Oostum bone comb (Tab. 2.9: Quak 1990, 363; Looijenga 2003, 304) 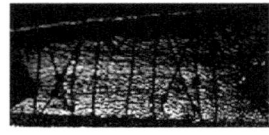 **deda**  **habuku**
Frisian forms **Type 1A** (direction of writing L>R) Upper side-twig stops in the middle compared with the lower side-twig. Bernsterburen staff (Tab. 2.14: Looijenga 2003, 314). 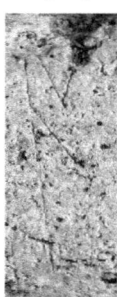 *from* **tuda**	**Type 1B** (direction of writing L<R) Upper side-twig has approximately the same length as the lower side-twig. The ascender starts in the middle of the upper side-twig. Oostum bone comb (see above)  **kabu**

Type 2: The acute angle type

In contradistinction to Type 1, the ascender of Type 2 is approximately parallel to the main stave. The ascender starts from the end of the upper side-twig.

Type 2A: The acute angle type with final position ascender

Pre-Old Frisian or Pre-Old English?

The **skanomodu** *solidus*

Old English runic corpus 7th-9th centuries	Pre-Old Frisian and Early Runic Frisian Corpus
 Caistor-by-Norwich brooch, c. AD 610-650 (Hines 1991a, 6-7)	Amay comb-fragment, c. AD 575-625 (Looijenga 2003, 303)
 Brandon tweezers	
Ruthwell cross	Harlingen *solidus* (Looijenga 2003, 306) 
Shropham lead plate	

Type 2B: The acute angle type with central ascender

The ascender does not acend from the end of the upper side-twig but from approximately its first third.

?Early Old Frisian Corpus-?Early Old English
  Southampton bone (7th-9th century): see Fig. 6.11

Early Old Frisian Corpus

 Arum yew sword, 6th-7th century (Quak 1990, 360)/late 8th century (Looijenga 2003, 309)

Table 6.5. An overview of the allograph types of the *āc* rune in the Old English Runic Corpus and the Pre Old-Frisian and Early Runic Frisian Corpora. **skanomodu** *solidus*, © the Trustees of the British Museum; Caistor-by-Norwich and Shropham details: photos, author, reproduced by kind permission of Norfolk Museums Service; Brandon detail, photo, author, reproduced by kind permission of Suffolk Archaeology; Amay; Arum, Bernsterburen, Harlingen and Oostum details, photos: author, collection Fries Museum, Leeuwarden.

The Harlingen solidus *(c. AD 575–625)*

The inscription reads **hada**: a nom.sg. masc. *n*-stem noun *Had(d)a*. This has been seen as a personal name; however, the quantity of the root vowel is not clear: both long /a:/ (< Gmc */aɪ/) and short /a/ have been considered. Beck (1981, 75) proposed identifying the word with Gmc **haþaz*, 'restraint, confinement', involving Gmc */a/ > Pre-OFris /a/; Looijenga (2003, 307) has proposed either Gmc **haiþ-*, cf. Gothic *haidus*, 'way, manner', from **haiþi*, 'clear' (Kaufmann 1965, 17, 200), reflecting Gmc */aɪ/ > Pre-OFris /a:/; she points out that this would be the 'only instance of monophthongization of Gmc **ai* […] represented by the *ac* rune'. Alternatively, she suggests (2003, 307) a reflex of Gmc **haþu-*, 'battle' (nom.sg. masc. *n*-stem) involving Gmc */a/ > Pre-OFris /a/.

Despite the unclear etymology of the word, the following conclusion may be drawn: according to the dating of the object to *c.* AD 575–625 and because the new *āc*-rune was used in both the root (?/a:/ - ?/a/) and the ending (/a/), and on the premise that the word is Frisian and not English (OE *Had(d)a*; *Head(d)a*: cf. Searle 1898, 275, 281–2), the Harlingen *solidus* is further evidence that the new *āc*-rune was (well) established (in Frisia) in approximately *c.* AD 575–625. This is in congruence with the only slightly later English material. In the English corpus proper (not counting the **skanomodu** *solidus*) this rune is only attested at *c.* AD 610–50 on the Caistor-by-Norwich inscription, which marks the beginning of the OE period. The name **luda** on the Caistor-by-Norwich brooch bears witness to the use of the new rune *āc* as a word-final vowel (the nom.sg. ending). Nielsen (2000, 117 n.52) regards the Selsey gold fragments as 'the first runic item in England' showing the *āc*-rune. However, I do not take this inscription into account here since neither its reading nor its date ('late 6th to 8th centuries': Hines 1990, 448) is certain (see Waxenberger, forthcoming, ch. 2, no. 74).

The Glasgow/(Folkstone) tremissis *(mid-7th century)*: **æniwulufu**

For different reasons, the inscription on the Glasgow (Hunterian Collection) *tremissis* is one of the most problematic ones in the corpus. Besides the problematic -**u** at the end of the second element, the first element, transcribed as **æni**- here, confronts us with various problems.

The first of these problems is the date of the object and the language stage of the inscription. Although it came to light as part of the Hunterian Collection in Scotland, Blackburn (1991, 143–4) notes that 'William Hunter (d. 1783) bought extensively on the Continent, including many continental *tremisses*, so that a British find-spot is not necessarily implied by its presence in this collection.' Blackburn (*loc. cit.*) dates the Glasgow *tremissis* to the mid-7th century. He comments that the coin 'appears to be an authentic struck coin from the same dies as the Folkestone find, but it is a different specimen.' According to Blackburn, the designs and legends copy those of a Merovingian *tremissis* from south-western France, with the insertion into the obverse legend of runes, and he revises the coin's previous dating, to *c.* AD 600 or a little later, on the grounds of 'a specific gravity that implies a fineness of around 50 per cent gold'. The question for the linguist, however, is the stage of the language on the object. Does that reflect the language of the prototype, possibly as early as AD 580, or does it mirror the language of *c.* 650? Thus two scenarios are imaginable.

The second problem is the etymology of the root vowel of the first element: there are two conceivable possibilities. One involves Gmc */aɪ/, with Gmc *aini- > Pre-OE/?Pre-OFris *āni- (by monophthongization of Gmc */aɪ/ > /a:/) > i-umlauted Pre-OE/?Pre-OFris *ǣni-. The other involves Gmc */au/, with Gmc *aun-i- (cf. Insley 1991, 173) > Pre-OFris *āni- > Pre-OFris *ǣni- by i-umlaut.

The well-attested OE masc. name Ēanwulf (cf. Searle 1897, 211; Sweet 1885, 555; *PASE*: s.v. EANWULF), derived from Gmc *au-, may support an attribution to Gmc *au. Another reason for preferring Gmc *au is Nielsen's (2011, 514) comment on the phonemic split of Pre-OFris */æ:/. According to him the allophones of */æ:/ (< Gmc */aɪ/) coalesced with Pre-OFris /a:/ only in 'grave' environments (= back vowels, labial and velar consonants: defined by Crystal (1997, 177) as 'articulatorily and acoustically ... those involving a peripheral articulation in the vocal tract, and a concentration of acoustic energy in the lower frequencies'). Since -n- is not a grave consonant, a stage */æ:/ is ruled out and leaves us with Gmc */au/ as a forerunner.

It has been suggested by Looijenga (2003, 306) that the *ansuz*-rune (cf. Fig. 6.5c) reflects i-umlaut and so should be read as æ (see above). If the earlier date of c. AD 580 is assumed, i-umlaut may still have been in its allophonic phase (see Waxenberger, forthcoming, ch. 3 for more details) as was the case in Pre-OE at the same time. However, the new āc-rune may have already been established (see Waxenberger, forthcoming, ch. 3.11.7 at least for Gmc */aɪ/ of scenario 1 and for Pre-OE /a:/ from all sources of scenario 2). I assume that the new āc-rune would most likely have been used for the i-umlaut allophone [æ:] of monophthongized /a:/ of scenario 1 and of /a:/ of all sources for scenario 2.

If, however, the later date, c. AD 650, is taken into account, i-umlaut must already have been phonemicized and hence would be represented by the new æsc-rune. For this reason, the later date suggested by Blackburn is also feasible from a linguistic point of view whereas the earlier date is fraught with uncertainties, especially since the source of the vowel represented by the *ansuz*-rune, Gmc */aɪ/ or Gmc */au/, is not clear.

The allographs of the runes *ċen* and *hægel*:

I shall finally analyse the allograph-types of the runes **k**/*cēn* and *hægel*, which developed variant forms in the different phases of Pre-OE and Pre-OFris.

The **k**-rune

In the transition period of the 5th and 6th centuries, the **k**-rune of the Older *fuþark* (Table 6.6, types 1–3) was still used. Type 3 appears only once, on the Chessell Down scabbard-mount. As the next step in the development, the old **k**-rune of Type 2 was put on a main-stave as type 4. By simplification the type 5a was developed from type 4.

Comparing the Pre-OE corpus with the corpus of the Pre-OFris and Early Runic OFris inscriptions, only the Pre-OE types (Table 6.6, types 1–3) are unattested in the Frisian corpus (Table 6.7); type 4 occurs on the **skanomodu** *solidus* and type 5a is well attested in the 8th century. This, however, is not a complete catalogue as this is work in progress.

Table 6.6. Variants and developments of rune no. 6 in the rune-row: the **k** rune, or **c** (*ćēn*), in the Pre-Old English and Old English Runic Corpora.

Shape of rune	Name of rune	Date-range	TYPE NUMBER	Number of attested examples
ᚲ	?*kaunan	5th–6th centuries	TYPE 1	1
ᴧ	?*kaunan	6th century (c. AD 500–550)	TYPE 2	1
ᚴ	?	c. AD 525–550 Chessell Down scabbard-mount	TYPE 3	1
ᚴ	?	6th(–early 7th) century	TYPE 4	6
ᚴ ᚴ	ćēn	(Late 7th–)8th–9th(–11th) centuries	TYPE 5a	6
h	ćēn	Late 7th–9th centuries	TYPE 5b	8
h	ćēn	8th–10th or 11th centuries	TYPE 5c	10

The single-barred **h**-rune

As can be inferred from the table below, the single-barred **h**-rune was definitely used down to c. AD 560 in England. If the Wijnaldum gold pendant (c. AD 600; Fig. 6.12a) does show a single-barred **h**-rune, the Frisian material would not contradict the English evidence. Additionally, the English corpus has two more, albeit uncertain attestations of the single-barred **h** in a 6th-/7th-century date-bracket: the Cleatham hanging bowl (6th or 7th century: Hines and Bayliss eds 2013, 475): [..]edih; the Sandwich stone (possibly 6th/7th century): the date of this inscription and the identification of the runes are uncertain, especially the **h** as its shape is unusual (Fig. 6.12b; see Waxenberger, forthcoming, ch. 2 no.70).

On the premise that the Harlingen inscription is Frisian, the double-barred rune **h** seems to be attested considerably earlier in the Frisian corpus (c. AD 575–625: see below, Table 6.8) than in the English one. The first attestations of the double-barred **h** in the English Corpus stem from approximately 700.

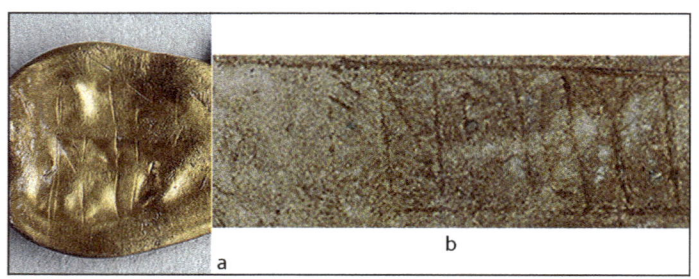

Fig. 6.12. Examples of the single-barred **h** rune. a: the Wijnaldum B gold pendant (photo: the Fries Museum, Leeuwarden); b: the Sandwich stone (Canterbury Museums and Galleries).

Table 6.7. The distribution of variant types of the runes in Table 6.6 in Pre-Old English and Pre-Old Frisian inscriptions.

	ᚲ ᚴ Types 1 and 2	ᚨ Type 4	ᚼ ᚩ Type 5a	ᚠ Type 3
England	c. 450–550 Loveden Hill urn: **þi{c/u}w** c. 500–50 Watchfield purse-mount: **hariboki**	c. 525–50 Chessell Down scabbard mount: **ako** c. 520–70 Chessell Down pail: **…kkkaaa**		c. 525–50 Chessell Down scabbard mount: **cœri**
?Pre-OFris		c. 575–610: **skanomodu**	7th–9th century Southampton bone: **katæ**	
Early Runic Frisian		Undated, Hantum bone plate: **]?{a/æ}h{a/æ}:k[**	8th century Oostum comb: **kabu habuku** 8th century Toornweerd comb: **kobu** Late 8th/9th century Rasquert bone handle: **oka**	

Table 6.8. The distribution of the single- and double-barred **h** rune in early English and Frisian inscriptions.

	Single-barred **h** ᚺ	Double-barred **h** ᚻ
England	c. 425–550	Earliest attestations, c. 700
	c. 425–75 (Hines 1990, 442): Caistor-by-Norwich astragalus	'698 or thereabouts' (Derolez 1981, 21): St Cuthbert's coffin
	c. 500–50 (Scull 1986, 127): Watchfied purse-mount	Early 8th century: Whitby comb, dated on linguistic grounds and by the rune-forms
	c. 525–60 (Hines 1990, 440): Wakerley brooch	Early 8th century (Waxenberger, forthcoming): Auzon/Franks Casket
Frisia	c. 600 Wijnaldum gold pendant	Earliest attestation c. 575–625
		c. 575–625: Harlingen *solidus*
		8th century: Oostum comb
		undated: Hantum bone plate

Conclusions

From the inscriptions I have looked at, the following can be concluded.

1. For the long vowels /a:/ and /o:/, the Frisian material is in line with the results gained from the (Pre-)OE corpus. As can be inferred from Table 6.9 below, by the end of the 6th century/mid-7th century (the latest date for Caistor-by-Norwich brooch), the *āc*-rune must have been well established as it was used for both /a:/ and also already for the short /a/.

Table 6.9. The use of the *āc* rune for both /a:/ and /a/ in early Frisian and English inscriptions.

The *āc* rune ᚫ		
?Frisian inscription	Frisian inscription	Old English inscription
skanomodu *solidus* c. AD 575–610	Harlingen *solidus* c. AD 575–625	Caistor-by-Norwich brooch, c. AD 610–650
skanomodu /a:/	**hada** /a(:)/-/a/	**luda** /a/

2. The allograph-types of the new *āc*-rune are – with two exceptions – congruent. These exceptions, however, are only sub-types: the first is the sub-type 1B of the chevron type (type 1) which occurs just once, on the Oostum comb. The second is sub-type 2B of the acute angle type on the Arum yew-wood sword and on the possibly Frisian Southampton bone (see above, Table 6.5). However, the small number of these sub-types does not allow for any conclusion with regard to a certain school, especially since the Oostum bone comb shows both Type 1 (x2) alongside sub-type 1B (x1) (Table 6.5).

3. The new *ōs*-rune is well integrated in the Frisian corpus both as a representative of the sound-value and in the form of allograph-types.

4. After analysing the distribution of the old *ōþil*-rune and the new *ōs*-rune, the Borgharen belt buckle can plausibly be assigned to the inscriptions written in the Common Germanic *fuþark*.

5. For linguistic reasons, the **skanomodu** *solidus* can reliably be assigned neither to the Frisian nor to the English inscriptions. Likewise, the categorization of the Southampton bone as Frisian or English is possible neither on runological nor linguistic criteria.

6. The only obvious deviation of some of the Frisian inscriptions is the ending -**u** in *a*-stems but this 'deviation' may be due to the use of special grammatical cases in what are mostly one-word inscriptions: the vocative for the names on coins and the instrumental on combs. The question as to whether or not -**u** is a characteristic of Pre-OFris/Early Runic OFris cannot be solved here (cf. Düwel and Tempel 1968–70 and Nielsen 1994, 120, with refs.): more research needs to be carried out on this complex question especially as some of the early objects exhibiting this feature may not be Frisian (e.g. the **skanomodu** *solidus*).

7. The Frisian allographs of the **k/c**-rune considered are also in line with the OE material. The fact that *cēn* is still used for a velar /k/ in **catæ** makes a narrow dating to between AD 650 and the earlier 9th century possible in light of the English material and also the rune-forms.

8. The Frisian corpus, defective as it may be, provides valuable information on, for example, the beginning of the use of the double-barred **h**. On the premise that the Harlingen inscription is Frisian, the double-barred rune **h** seems to be attested considerably earlier in the Frisian Corpus (on the Harlingen *solidus* c. AD 575–625: see above, Table 6.8; cf. also Hines, this vol., for a slightly later dating to the first half of the 7th century). The first attestations of the double-barred **h** in the English Corpus stem from around the year 700.

In this paper, I have made an attempt to demonstrate the problems of the so-called Frisian corpus. More research needs to be carried out on the Pre-OFris subcorpus with respect to dating of the early objects and their provenances.[5] Although this is work in progress, I feel confident that the Pre-OFris sub-corpus is closely aligned with the Pre-OE sub-corpus. The obvious deviation, the final -**u** in some inscriptions, may also turn out not to be an exclusively Pre-OFris characteristic, should the possible Pre-OE provenance

---

[5] Prof. John Hines, Dr Nelleke IJssennagger and Dr Tineke Looijenga are carrying out research regarding the reliability of the dating method on the basis of the percentage of gold in the *solidi*. Typologically, Professor Dr Bernd Päffgen (LMU Munich) dates the **skanomodu** *solidus* to the first half of the 6th century, the Schweindorf *solidus* to *c*. 600 and Harlingen even earlier than 600 (pers. comm., 18 November 2015).

be corroborated for the **skanomodu** *solidus* in the future. Only an interdisciplinary approach combining archaeology, numismatics, linguistics and runology can shed more light on this complex problem.

References

Århammar, Nils 1995:71, 'Zur Vor- und Frühgeschichte der Nordfriesen und des Nordfriesischen'. In *Friesische Studien II*. NOWELE Supplement Volume 12, ed. V. F. Faltings, A. G. H. Walker and O. Wilts (Odense), 63–96.

Bammesberger, Alfred 1990, 'SKANOMODU: Linguistic Issues''. In *Britain 400–600: Language and History*, Anglistische Forschungen 205, ed. A. Bammesberger, A. Wollmann (Heidelberg), 457–66.

Bammesberger, Alfred 1990a, *Die Morphologie des urgermanischen Nomens*, Indogermanische Bibliothek, Untersuchungen zur vergleichenden Grammatik der germanischen Sprachen 2 (Heidelberg).

Bammesberger, Alfred 1999, 'Die Runeninschrift von Bergakker: Versuch einer Deutung'. In *Pforzen und Bergakker: Neues zu Runeninschriften*, Beiheft zu Historische Sprachforschung (Historical Linguistics), Ergänzungsheft 41, ed. A. Bammesberger and G. Waxenberger (Göttingen), 180–5.

Bammesberger, Alfred 2003, 'The *Harford Farm* brooch runic inscription', *Neophilologus* 87, 133–5.

Beck, H. 1981, 'A runological and iconographical interpretation of North-Sea-Germanic rune-solidi', *Michigan Studies* 7(1), 69–87.

Blackburn, Mark 1991, 'A survey of Anglo-Saxon and Frisian Coins with runic inscriptions'. In *Old English Runes and their Continental Background*, Anglistische Forschungen 217, ed. A. Bammesberger (Heidelberg), 137–89.

Boutkan, Dirk 2011, 'Phonology and orthographic system of Old Frisian'. In *Handbuch des Friesischen*, ed. H. H. Munske, N. Århammer, V. F. Faltings, J. F. Hoekstra, O. Vries, A. G. H. Walker and O. Witts (Tübingen), 613–20.

Braune, W. 1987, *Althochdeutsche Grammatik*, bearbeitet von H. Eggers, 14th edn, Sammlung kurzer Grammatiken germanischer Dialekte, Hauptreihe 5 (Tübingen).

Bremmer, Rolf H. 1981, 'Frisians in Anglo-Saxon England: a historical and toponymical investigation', *Fryske Nammen* 3Århammar *et al.* Beetstra, W. T. Breuker, Ph. H. Spahr van der Hoek, Johan Jacob [Bearb.].: Fryske Akademy, 45–94.

Bremmer, Rolf H. 2009, *An Introduction to Old Frisian: History, Grammar, Reader, Glossary* (Amsterdam): John Benjamins.

Brunner, Karl 1965, *Altenglische Grammatik: Nach der angelsächsischen Grammatik von Eduard Sievers*, Sammlung kurzer Grammatiken germanischer Dialekte, Hauptreihe 3 (Tübingen).

Campbell, Alistair 1959, *Old English Grammar* (Oxford).

Crystal, Davis 1997, *A Dictionary of Linguistics and Phonetics*, 4th edn (Oxford): Blackwell.

Derolez, René 1981, 'The runic system and its cultural context', *Michigan Germanic Studies* 7, 19–26.

Dictionary of Old English in Electronic Form A–F: see Healey diPaolo, A. *et al.* ed. 2003.

Düwel, Klaus, and W. D. Tempel 1968–70, 'Knochenkämme und Runeninschriften aus Friesland. Mit einer Zusammenstellung aller bekannten Runenkämme und einem Beitrag zu den friesischen Runeninschriften', *Palaeohistoria* 14, 353–91.

Integrated Frisian Language Database, Fryske Akademy. Accessed via http://tdb. fryske-akademy. eu/tdb/index-en. html on 9 May 2014.

Healey DiPaolo, A. *et al.* ed. 2003, *Dictionary of Old English in Electronic Form A-F* (Toronto).

Hines, John 1990, 'The runic inscriptions of Early Anglo-Saxon England'. In *Britain 400–600: Language and History*, Anglistische Forschungen 205, ed. A. Bammesberger; A. Wollmann (Heidelberg), 437–55.

Hines, John 1991, 'A new runic inscription from Norfolk', *Nytt om Runer* 6, 6–7.
Hines, John and Alex Bayliss ed. 2013, *Anglo-Saxon Graves and Grave Goods of the 6th and 7th Centuries AD: A Chronological Framework* (Leeds).
Hofmann, Dietrich 1976, 'Eine friesische Runeninschrift in England', *Us Wurk* 25, 73–6.
Hofmann, Dietrich, and Anne T. Popkema 2008, *Altfriesisches Handwörterbuch* (Heidelberg): Winter.
Hofmann, Dietrich 1995, 'Zur Monophthongierung von germanisch *ai* und *au* im Altfriesischen und in seinen Nachbarsprachen'. In *Lingua Theodisca*, Beiträge zur Sprach- und Literaturwissenschaft, ed. J. Cajot, L. Kremer and H. Niebaum (Münster), 23–36.
Holthausen, Ferdinand 1921, *Altsächsisches Elementarbuch*, Germanische Bibliothek 5, 2nd edn (Heidelberg): Winter.
Holthausen, Ferdinand 1934, *Altfriesisches Wörterbuch* (Heidelberg).
Holthausen, Ferdinand 1985, *Altfriesisches Wörterbuch*, 2nd edn by D. Hofmann (Heidelberg).
Insley, John 1991, 'Appendix 2: The personal name *Āniwulf/*Æniwulf'. In *Old English Runes and their Continental Background*, Anglistische Forschungen 217, ed. A. Bammesberger (Heidelberg), 172–4.
Kluge, Friedrich 2002, *Etymologisches Wörterbuch der deutschen Sprache*, 24th edn by E. Seebold (Berlin).
Kluge, Friedrich 2004, *Etymologisches Wörterbuch der deutschen Sprache*, 25th edn by E. Seebold (Berlin).
Looijenga, Tineke 1996, 'Checklist Frisian runic inscriptions'' In *Frisian Runes and Neighbouring Traditions*, Amsterdamer Beiträge zur älteren Germanistik 45, ed. A. Quak and T. Looijenga, 91–108.
Looijenga, Tineke 1997, *Runes: Around the North Sea and On the Continent AD 150–700, Texts and Contexts* (Groningen).
Looijenga, Tineke 2003, *Texts & Contexts of the Oldest Runic Inscriptions*, The Northern World 4, North Europe and the Baltic c. 400–1700 AD, Peoples, Economics and Cultures (Leiden – Boston).
Luick, Karl 1921, *Historische Grammatik der englischen Sprache*, Band 1., 1. Abteilung (Leipzig).
Mees, Bernard 2002, 'The Bergakker inscription and the beginnings of Dutch', *Amsterdamer Beitrage Zur Alteren Germanistik* 56, 23–6.
Malzahn, Melani 1998, 'Die Runeninschrift von Bergakker: Zur Beziehung von Runenmetaphorik und Skaldenpoesie', *Die Sprache* 40, 85–101.
Mitchell, M. (1994), *Corpus of English Runes* (Basel).
Nedoma, Robert 1991–3, 'Zur Runeninschrift auf der Urne A. 11/251 von Loveden Hill', *Die Sprache* 35, 115–24.
Nedoma, Robert 2004, *Personennamen in südgermanischen Runeninschriften*, Studien zur altgermanischen Namenkunde I,1,1, Indogermanische Bibliothek, 3. Reihe (Heidelberg).
Nedoma, Robert 2007, 'Die voraltfriesischen Personennamen der Runeninschriften auf dem Webschwert von Westeremden, dem Schwertchen von Arum und anderen Denkmälern', *Advances in Old Frisian Philology*, Amsterdamer Beiträge zur älteren Germanistik 64, ed. R. H. Bremmer, S. Laker and O. Fries, 299–324.
Nedoma, Robert 2014, 'Voraltfriesisch -u im Nominativ und Akkusativ Singular der maskulinen a-Stämme', *Directions for Old Frisian Philology*, Amsterdamer Beiträge zur älteren Germanistik 73, ed. R. H. Bremmer, S. Laker and O. Vries, 343–68.
Nielsen, Hans Frede 1981, *Old English and The Continental Germanic Languages: A Survey of Morphological and Phonological Interrelations*, Innsbrucker Beiträge zur Sprachwissenschaft 33 (Innsbruck).
Nielsen, Hans Frede 1991, 'Unaccented vowels in Runic Frisian and Ingveonic', *Old English Runes and their Continental Background*, Anglistische Forschungen 217, ed. A. Bammesberger (Heidelberg), 299–303.
Nielsen, Hans Frede 1994, 'Ante-Old Frisian: a review', *NOWELE* 24, 91–136.

Nielsen, Hans Frede 2000, *The Early Runic Language of Scandinavia, Studies in Germanic Dialect Geography*, Indogermanische Bibliothek, Erste Reihe (Heidelberg).
Nielsen, Hans Frede 2001, 'Frisian and the grouping of the older Germanic languages'. In *Handbuch des Friesischen*, ed. H. H. Munske, N. Århammer, V. F. Faltings, J. F. Hoekstra, O. Vries, A. G. H. Walker and O. Witts (Tübingen), 512–23.
Nielsen, Hans Frede 2006, 'The vocalism of the Undley runes viewed from a North-Sea Germanic perspective'. In *Das fuþark und seine einzelsprachliche Weiterentwicklung*, Ergänzungsbände zum Reallexikon der Germanischen Altertumskunde 51,ed. A. Bammesberger and G. Waxenberger (Berlin –New York) 209–15.
Odenstedt, Bengt 1999, 'The Bergakker inscription. Transliteration, interpretation, message: some suggestions'. In *Pforzen und Bergakker: Neues zu Runeninschriften*, Beiheft zu Historische Sprachforschung (Historical Linguistics), Ergänzungsheft 41, ed. A. Bammesberger and G. Waxenberger (Göttingen), 163–73.
Page, Raymond I. 1973, *An Introduction to English Runes* (London).
Page, Raymond I. 1999, *An Introduction to English Runes*, 2nd edn (Woodbridge). The Boydell Press
Page, Raymond I. 2001, 'Frisian Runic inscriptions'. In *Handbuch des Friesischen*, ed. H. H. Munske, N. Århammer, V. F. Faltings, J. F. Hoekstra, O. Vries, A. G. H. Walker and O. Witts (Tübingen), 523–30.
PASE = Prosopography of Anglo-Saxon England <http:www. pase. ac. uk>.
Quak, Arend 1990, 'Runica Frisica'. In *Aspects of Old Frisian Philology*. Amsterdamer Beiträge zur älteren Germanistik 31–2, ed. R. H. Bremmer, G. van der Meer and O. Vries (Amsterdam), 357–70.
Schmidt, Christoph, Robert Nedoma and Klaus Düwel 2010/2011, 'Die Runeninschrift auf dem Kamm von Frienstedt, Stadt Erfurt' *Die Sprache* 49, 123–86.
Scull, Chris 1986, 'A sixth-century grave containing a balance and weights from Watchfield, Oxfordshire, England', with contributions by D. Nash, B. Odenstedt and R. I. Page, and a Technical Appendix by S. Pollard, *Germania* 64, 105–38.
Searle, William G. 1897, *Onomasticon Anglo-Saxonicum, A List of Anglo-Saxon Proper Names from the Time of Beda to that of King John* (Cambridge).
Seebold, Elmar 1999, 'Die Runeninschrift von Bergakker'. In *Pforzen und Bergakker: Neues zu Runeninschriften*, Beiheft zu Historische Sprachforschung (Historical Linguistics), Ergänzungsheft 41, ed. A. Bammesberger and G. Waxenberger (Göttingen), 157–62.
Steller, Walther 1928, *Abriss der Altfriesischen Grammatik* (Halle).
Sweet, Henry ed. 1966, *The Oldest English Texts, Edited with Introduction and a Glossary*, EETS os 83 (Oxford).
Vennemann, Theo 1999, 'Note on the runic inscription of the Bergakker scabbard mount'. In *Pforzen und Bergakker: Neues zu Runeninschriften*, Beiheft zu Historische Sprachforschung (Historical Linguistics), Ergänzungsheft 41, ed. A. Bammesberger and G. Waxenberger,152–6.
Voyles, Joseph 1992, *Early Germanic Grammar, Pre-, Proto-, and Post-Germanic Languages* (Academic Press Inc. Harcourt Brace Jovanovich. San Diego).
Waxenberger, Gaby 1996, *Die Zuordnung der altenglischen Substantive zu den Flexionstypen untersucht am Buchstaben D* (Munich).
Waxenberger, Gaby 2006, 'The representation of vowels in unstressed syllables in the Old English Runic Corpus'. In *Das ältere Fuþark und seine einzelsprachlichen Weiterentwicklungen*, Ergänzungsbände zum Reallexikon der Germanischen Altertumskunde 51, ed. A. Bammesberger and G. Waxenberger (Berlin; New York), 272–314.
Waxenberger, Gaby 2010, *Towards a Phonology of the Old English Runic Inscriptions and an Analysis of the Graphemes* (Munich).
Waxenberger, Gaby (forthcoming), *A Phonology of Old English Runic Inscriptions* (with a Concise Edition), RGA-E (Berlin).

7

The Geography and Dialects of Old Saxon

River-basin communication networks and the distributional patterns of North Sea Germanic features in Old Saxon

Arjen Versloot and Elżbieta Adamczyk

North-West and North Sea Germanic: fluid perceptions

The Germanic languages witnessed a rapid series of changes between the 4th century and the 7th: from the fairly homogeneous North-West Germanic 'Gallehus' idiom of the 4th century, the language split into a number of dialects, which had developed fairly well recognizable linguistic identities by the time of their first attestations, dated approximately to the late 7th century (Nielsen 2000, 288–93). An important focal point of linguistic innovations (phonological and morphological) lies in the region around the North Sea, and their spread affected the adjacent dialects of Old English, Old Frisian and, to some extent, Old Saxon, which are, therefore, commonly referred to as the North Sea Germanic languages.[1] In particular, the similarities between Old English and Old Frisian are so striking that they led earlier researchers to assume a common Anglo-Frisian unity on the Continent, which later, after the migration of the Angles and some of the Saxons to Britain, split into two languages (e.g. Siebs 1889). The perception of the affinity between North Sea Germanic languages changed entirely with Kuhn's (1955) ground-breaking paper, in which a new grouping of Germanic dialects was postulated and the concept of North-West Germanic linguistic unity – lasting approximately until the Migration Period – was introduced. A few years later, in line with Kuhn's hypothesis, DeCamp (1958) revised the understanding of the emergence of Old English dialects, showing that the bulk of the dialectal variants in Old English post-date the colonization of Britain and therefore do not reflect earlier continental dialect or tribal configurations (see also Nielsen 1998). Consequently, the new interpretation of the mutual relations

---

[1] For an extensive catalogue of these linguistic features see Nielsen (1985, 103–54).

between these dialects evolved into the modern perception of North Sea Germanic as a group of language varieties, participating to a lesser or greater extent in a series of linguistic innovations that have their geographical origin in the North Sea area (cf. Stiles 1995). These innovations can be dated to the period during and after the migration of the Germanic tribes to Britain.[2] The familiar division into English, Frisian and Saxon is the result of a gradual geographical reorganization of linguistic features, which led to the enhancement of linguistic boundaries and eventually to the emergence of distinct linguistic identities (Århammar 1990; Versloot 2014a).

While Old English and Old Frisian are clearly in the centre of these North Sea Germanic innovations, Old Saxon is often characterized as a West Germanic hybrid, a mixed language, which combines influences from North Sea Germanic and Continental West Germanic, more specifically Franconian. Nielsen (1985, 255) concludes that Old Saxon 'has basically no specific features of its own'. This issue has been the subject of extensive dispute between Krogh (1996; 2002; 2013) and Klein (2000; 2004), undertaken in a series of publications. While Klein conceives of Old Saxon as a *Mischsprache* ('mixed language'), Krogh postulates a prehistoric *Alleingang* ('separate path') of Saxon, dating it long before the Migration Period (Krogh 2002, 12). Krogh's point of view was strongly contested in Klein's papers, who postulates a much later chronology for the emergence of Old Saxon, with the decisive stages of the development dated not earlier than the 4th/5th century AD (Klein 2004, 21). In our view, however, the term 'mixed language' does not seem entirely adequate either, as it implies a mixture of two originally discrete units, presupposing their independent existence, which goes against the idea of a North West Germanic dialect continuum. Likewise, Nielsen's (1985, 255) observation that Old Saxon shows very few independent innovations runs counter to the definition of Old Saxon as a discrete member of the Germanic language family. This matches Stiles's (2013, 20) description of Old Saxon as showing 'no early unique innovations' and being 'most easily defined negatively as that continental West Germanic that is not High German, nor Frisian, nor Dutch'. The lack of early unique innovations implies inherent linguistic stability. In general, linguistic stability is expected to correlate with demographic stability. The Old Saxon region was demographically the most stable part of the West Germanic language territory: Old Saxon was spoken in a region with continuous Germanic settlement. High German, Dutch and English are largely founded on a Celtic-Romance substratum, and Frisian is the result of a renewed settlement of an earlier (largely) abandoned region. This linguistic archaism is manifested in a range of phonological and morphological features of Old Saxon, including the limited reduction of unstressed vowels (when compared to Old Norse, Old Low Franconian, Old Frisian and Old English), limited application of *i*-mutation and no post-Proto-Germanic *a*- or *u*-mutations or breaking processes (cf. Old Norse, Old Frisian, Old English), no large-scale consonant shifts (cf. Old High German), and very limited analogical levelling of endings from major (productive) to minor noun-classes (see also Klein 1977, 537).

---

[2] Despite the abundant evidence from studies following Kuhn's hypothesis, which has established itself as a majority view, the idea of a pre-migration Ingvaeonic 'Sprachgemeinschaft' on the Continent still occasionally reemerges (e.g. Stiles 1995, 207; Van Bree 1997, 11–15; and Kortlandt 2008).

The Geography and Dialects of Old Saxon

The phonological and morphological shape of Old Saxon reflects very well the intermediate position it occupies among the West Germanic languages. With respect to morphology, Old Saxon appears to share many features with Old High German and Old Low Franconian (Klein 2004, 14). In terms of phonology, in particular when it comes to the developments in unaccented syllables, Old Saxon goes together with Old English and Old Frisian (Nielsen 2001, 79–84, 93). Such a distribution of shared and similar features, i.e. with the inclination towards Franconian (Low and Middle) on the one hand, and towards Old Frisian and Old English on the other, is exactly what can be expected from a group of dialects that are geographically situated between the North Sea and the Middle Rhine region (Stiles 1995, 201–5): geographical proximity is in general the best predictor of linguistic nearness (Nerbonne 2010).

A fact that so far has not been explicitly addressed in the existing literature on Old Saxon and seems to be taken for granted is the distribution of the individual linguistic features ascribable to the influence of the mentioned languages. The Old Saxon sources with the highest density of North Sea Germanic features are found in a region which geographically cannot exactly be referred to as 'coastal', concentrating in Eastphalia, including places such as Merseburg and Magdeburg. Such a geographical distribution remains inconsistent with the observation, quoted earlier, that geographical vicinity is the best predictor of linguistic similarity. This apparent anomaly becomes even more conspicuous when Old Dutch is included in the comparison. While some North Sea Germanic developments (such as the uniform verbal indicative present plural ending -að) indisputably covered the entire Old Saxon linguistic area, the Dutch linguistic territory shows (historical traces of) North Sea Germanic developments only in a narrow strip along the coast (Van Bree 1997; De Vaan 2012). This is remarkable given the fact that the distance from, for instance, 's-Hertogenbosch to the coast (c. 100 km) is very much shorter than that from, say, Osnabrück (c. 200 km) (belonging to the Saxon area). In fact, the North Sea Germanic linguistic traces in the coastal regions of Belgium and Holland do not extend more than 50 km inland. The extension of the coastal North Sea Germanic innovations in Old Saxon, therefore, forms a bulge, protruding deep into the Continent and reaching as far as Merseburg.

In order to gain more insight into the distribution of linguistic features in the Saxon territory, the concept of North Sea Germanic, and in particular, how it is interpreted in the present study, needs to be more precisely specified. Following the views of Stiles (1995, 211) and Århammar (1990, 13), we consider North Sea Germanic to be a *Sprachbund* of language varieties, whose boundaries are the result of a combination of expansion and partial retreat of linguistic innovations. The typical North Sea Germanic features are innovations that had once been expansive, but were later pushed back – a process that for many features stopped at a line that became the Frisian language boundary. Other innovations from the south, such as the High German Consonant Shift, did not expand further north than the line that was later interpreted as the southern limit of Low German and Dutch. When examining the dissemination of North Sea Germanic features, one should realize that the attested distribution is the result of both developments: the expansion and partial rollback of northern features, and the expansion of southern features. Significantly, the concepts of 'southern' and 'northern', relevant on a macro-scale, turn out to denote rather 'west' and 'east' on a regional scale: the North

Sea Germanic features are more abundantly represented in (eastern) Old Saxon than in (western) Old Dutch (apart from the narrow littoral zone), and within the Old Saxon territory they turn out to be more common in Eastphalia than in Westphalia.

The present paper offers a tentative mapping of the spread of a range of North Sea Germanic features in Old Saxon. The patterns resulting from the mapping confirm the assumed dialectal contrasts in Old Saxon. The aim of the paper is to account for the attested distribution of linguistic features by recourse to the geo-morphological substratum of the linguistic area of present-day Low German, Frisian and Dutch. In the discussion of the geographical dissemination of the North Sea Germanic features, the question of the (reconstructed) diachronic order of their emergence will also be addressed.

The dialectal distribution of North Sea Germanic features in Old Saxon

Given the existing textual evidence for Old Saxon, the conditions for a fruitful dialect geography of this language are not very auspicious. The bulk of the textual material comes from two sources: *Heliand* and *Genesis*, both dated to the 9th century. The former text is preserved in three manuscripts (M, C and S), originating in different scriptoria and characterized by fairly diversified linguistic profiles. They seem to form a continuum with respect to the Ingvaeonic nature of the text, with MS C being the least Ingvaeonic, MS S showing the Ingvaeonic features most extensively, and MS M occupying an intermediate position in this respect. A clear correlation with the dating of the manuscripts emerges, since both M and S, which attest to a more Ingvaeonic character, are dated earlier (9th century) than C (10th century) (Nielsen 1994, 201). While codex M may have originated in the centre of the Old Saxon territory (Corvey) (Krogh 1996, 115), it is still a copy of an earlier version that was probably written outside the Old Saxon area. Two other monasteries, Fulda and Werden, which are also considered to be potential places of origin of this manuscript, are respectively located in the High German-speaking area (Fulda) and close to the Low Franconian-speaking area (Werden) (Cordes and Holthausen 1973, 15–17). The origin of the Straubing fragment (*Heliand*-S), which is characterized by the most explicit North Sea Germanic features, testifying potentially to a large scale dialectal adaptation of the original, is unknown (see Klein 1990). Equally problematic is the origin of the other text, *Genesis*, which cannot be precisely located (the surviving manuscript is dated to the second half of the 9th century). Of the minor sources (including tithing lists, blessings, church calendars, a confession of faith, a renunciation of the devil, tax rolls, glosses, place-names and personal names), a large part comes from Essen and Werden, and clearly there is no textual material that could with certainty be located in the area north of Osnabrück.

In order to obtain a detailed picture of the geographical spread of North Sea Germanic features in Old Saxon, the inventory of relevant features was compiled, based on the detailed information found in Krogh (1996, 141–288) and Klein (1990, 202). Tiefenbach's comprehensive dictionary (2010) served as the basis for checking the attestations of words explicitly mentioned in these studies as exhibiting the relevant features. The study focused on the attestations from the minor documents, leaving out the data from *Heliand* and *Genesis*, as the manuscripts of these texts cannot be unambiguously located. Table 7.1 presents the inventory of investigated phonological and morphological features, with commentaries and a set of examples, as well as the number of lemmas and tokens found in the analysed material. The material presented in Table 7.1 served as the basis for mapping the North Sea Germanic linguistic developments (see also Fig. 7.1). A more extensive historical-linguistic account of these phenomena is provided in Appendix 1.

Table 7.1. The inventory of North Sea Germanic features and their attestations in the Old Saxon material

Feature	Lemmas #	Tokens #	Comments
1a. aN ~ oN	7	68	The velarization of PGmc *a to <o> before a nasal in *fram* > *from*, *mann* > *monn*, *gang* > *gong*, *namo* > *noma*.
1b. aNþ ~ ōþ	1	9	The velarization of PGmc *a before a nasal in *ōthar* 'other', with an early loss of the nasal before a voiceless fricative.
2. a > e	3	11	The spontaneous fronting of PGmc *a, attested in *deg, gles, therf*.
3. *ai > ǣ, ā	1	1	The vowels ǣ, ā, resulting from the monophthongization of PGmc *ai, are considered to be a NSGmc feature, in contrast to ē found elsewhere in the OS material.
4. *au > ō ~ ā	3	18	The vowel ā which is a result of the monophthongization of PGmc *au is considered to be a NSGmc feature, in contrast to ō found elsewhere in the OS material.
5. chronology of primary *i*-mutation and apocope	1	5	The nom./acc. pl. form *menn* 'men' shows an early application of *i*-mutation < PGmc *manni(z), prior to the loss of -*i* after a heavy syllable. The more common nom./acc. pl. form *mann* shows the reverse order.
6. scope of primary *i*-mutation	2	10	The *i*-mutation of short *a* ('primary *i*-mutation') is consistently reflected in the spelling as <e>.
7. os ~ as	36	40	PGmc ōC appears as *o* in Old High German but as *a* in Old English and Old Frisian; OS attests to both forms.
8. metathesis in 'horse'	1	3	Forms with metathesis, such as *hers* for *hross* (cf. Old Frisian *hors*), are considered to be NSGmc.
9. a + *i*-mutation > i	2	10	Further raising of the root vowel through vowel harmony with the following vowel: PGmc *stadi- > *stid-*, once also *biki* for *beki*, cf. Riustring Old Frisian *stidi*.
Total	57	175	

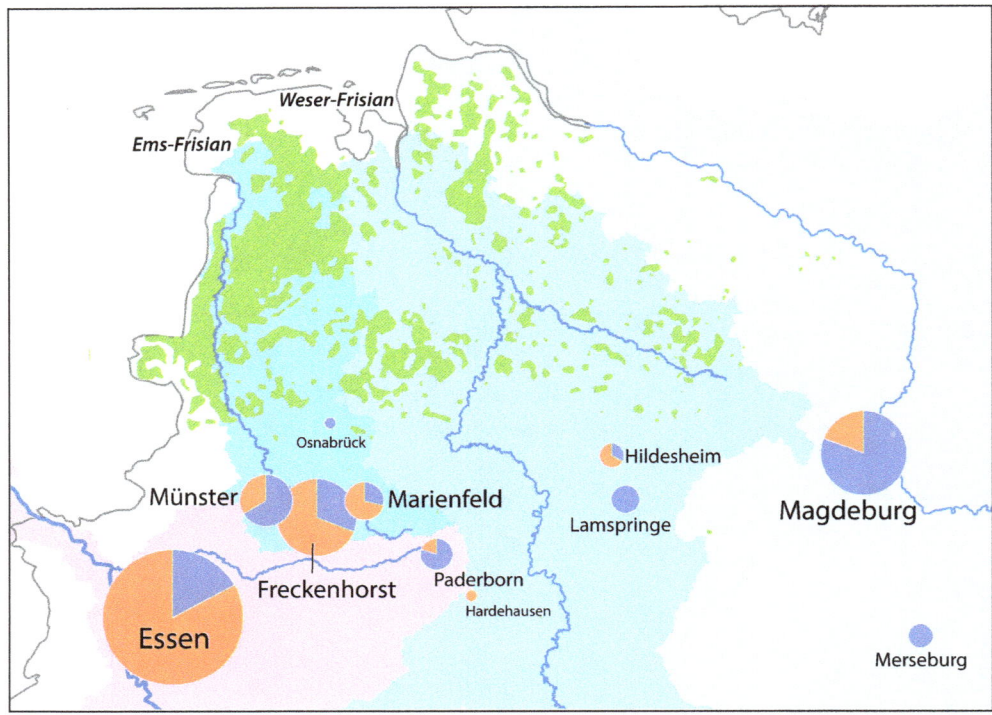

Fig. 7.1. The distribution of North Sea Germanic features in the Old Saxon material (presented in Table 7.1) against the background of the main river basins and peat bog areas. River Elbe basin, pale blue; River Weser basin, mid-blue; River Ems basin, dark blue; River Rhine basin, pink. Green: peat bog areas. The pie-charts show the proportion of North Sea Germanic (deep blue) to Continental Germanic (deep pink) tokens, and the size of the pie-charts associated with the named centres represents the overall number of tokens, from 1 at Hardehausen and Osnabrück to 80 at Essen.

The 175 tokens come from 42 sources that are localized in the traditionally Old Saxon linguistic area, which means that glosses from places beyond this territory, e.g. from Cologne, or Fulda, were not included. On the basis of the information found in Tiefenbach (2010, xiii–xxxviii), Klein (1990, 201) and Krogh (1996, 111–38), the sources were assigned to 12 locations. The assignment of individual texts to these locations was fairly unambiguous, except the 'Strassburg glosses to Isidore' which, despite Tiefenbach's reservations, were assigned to Hildesheim (Tiefenbach 2010, xxx). Werden was merged with Essen on purely technical grounds, namely, to avoid symbol overlap on the map. The psalm fragments known as the Lublin (*PsLub*) and Wittenberg (*PsWit*) Psalm Fragments, which show various North Sea Germanic features, were assigned to a cultural centre in the east, Magdeburg, combining linguistic evidence with physical attestation of the fragments in the east. This assignment of the sources to Magdeburg is largely arbitrary, and theoretically other cultural centres, such as Halberstadt or Halle, would have been just as good guesses. What matters here is, however, not the exact location, but the fact that the text must have been affiliated with some cultural centre in the east and not in any other part of the region.

An important aspect of the analysis which must be made explicit on account of its potential bearing on the interpretation of the data is the interference of diachrony and geography. In particular, what has to be excluded is the possibility that geographical contrasts reflect only diachronic contrasts. The investigated material covers the period from the early 9th century until the early 13th century, but approximately two-thirds of the data come from *c.* AD 1000 or earlier. Overall, the linguistic profile of the available texts correlates with their attestation dates and accordingly, the material tends to show less of the North Sea Germanic character at a later date. This tendency can be positively confirmed for the Westphalian locations, but for Eastphalia, sources younger than AD 1100 are missing. The overall geographical and diachronic trends are summarized in Table 7.2, which provides a detailed percentage distribution of North Sea Germanic features in the examined material with respect to their date of attestation and location.

Table 7.2. Geographical and diachronic distribution of North Sea Germanic features in Old Saxon. The notation '<=1000' means that the source is estimated to have originated around the year 1000 or earlier, '>1000' means that the origin is later than the year 1000. 'n' refers to the absolute number of tokens.

	<=1000	n	> 1000	n
Essen/Werden	18%	74	13%	8
Westphalia	73%	15	32%	37
Eastphalia	74%	31	100%	10

The fluctuations in percentages for Essen/Werden and Eastphalia fall within the bounds of chance; only for Westphalia is the contrast between the two periods statistically significant, which means that the texts from this region show a tendency to abandon North Sea Germanic features with time. Overall, it can be concluded that the diachronic bias as attested in the investigated material is limited and therefore all the relevant data could be combined and presented in one map as in Figure 7.1. The map is based on the absolute number of tokens for all features, despite the fact that some features are represented with many more tokens than others.[3]

The pattern emerging from the distribution of North Sea Germanic features is very transparent and informative. The map shows a clear east-west division of linguistic features: the southwest area with Essen and Werden is predominantly Franconian, the middle zone in north-east Westphalia is mixed, while the east is dominated by North Sea Germanic features. The relevance of the geographical shape of the landscape for the attested distribution of linguistic features, in particular, of the river basins and the peat bogs in the northern coastal region, will be addressed below.

---

[3] An alternative counting where every feature was assigned an equal weight was also performed. The correlation between the proportions based on crude token counting and the weighted counting is 0.98, which means that both results are entirely compatible. We therefore opted for basing the map on token counting, because it more adequately reflects the amount of the attested material from each locality.

The geo-linguistic nature of the dialectal distribution

Theodor Siebs (1901, 1157, 1166) believed that the North Sea Germanic traces in the Merseburg Glosses were the result of extralinguistic circumstances, namely the Frisian immigration: 'Aus den weserfries. Gegenden scheinen [...] diejenigen Friesen gekommen zu sein, denen wir die fries. Sprachformen der Merseburger Quellen verdanken' ('those Frisians to whom we are indebted for the Frisian linguistic elements of the Merseburg sources appear to have come from the Weser Frisian districts'). His views were underpinned by a somewhat naïve conviction that language change and specific linguistic features could only come with the actual mobility of people: the more features of Language A a given language displayed, the more speakers of Language A were believed to be involved in the language community. Such an approach has long been abandoned and replaced by models of language change, where change is conceived of in terms of expansive waves that result from social events, such as contact between speakers of different dialects and varieties enjoying different prestige.

With reference to the interaction between the early Frisian and Saxon linguistic communities, Klein (1990, 220) describes a dynamic situation where Old Frisian had developed away from Old Saxon through its own innovations already before the 9th century, while Old Saxon lost various North Sea Germanic features after the subjugation of the Saxon territory by Charlemagne. If this assumption is correct, one may expect that the North Sea Germanic features in Old Saxon antedate the 9th century. In this context, it can also be claimed, although not as an imperative, that the oldest features had reached farthest into the Saxon territory by the 9th century, i.e. when North Sea Germanic innovations, according to the development outlined above, no longer streched beyond the Frisian region on the Continent. The implication of this interpretation is that the oldest North Sea Germanic features covered the entire Old Saxon region, and with time their scope was more and more restricted (namely to Eastphalia).

We have evaluated this hypothesis by identifying the spatial and temporal fluctuations in the spread of North Sea Germanic features in Old Saxon (the details can be found in Appendix I). A synopsis of dating and distribution of the North Sea Germanic features, which are ordered chronologically, is provided in Table 7.3. The geographical and diachronic spread of these features in the Old Saxon area is compared to their distribution (and dating) in the Old Frisian material.

The material presented in Table 7.3 shows that there is no link between the geographical extension of the examined North Sea Germanic features and their chronology, i.e. the dating of individual features does not provide any prediction about their geographical scope. North Sea Germanic features are most consistently applied in the east. Westphalia goes mostly with the south-west, but shows a few instances where a North Sea Germanic innovation was introduced but later reversed (as shown in the figures in Table 7.2). Importantly, it is above all a few later innovations that are fairly prominent also in Westphalia, including the rising of i-mutated $a > i$, a development that has only limited application in Old Frisian. It means that the scope of the North Sea Germanic innovations was not per definition shrinking with time. The data in Table 7.3 indicate that the North Sea region was the centre of innovations, at least until the 9th century. The massive 'de-Ingvaeonization' of Low German took place only after AD 1100: none of the North Sea Germanic features enumerated in Table 7.3 can be identified in Modern Low German equivalents of lemmata (vocabulary items) which originally contained them. Table 7.4 presents a selection of lemmata which could potentially reflect North Sea Germanic features from two varieties of Old Saxon as compared to the material from 20th-century Low German (Westphalian and Holstein) (Gehle 1977), as well as corresponding examples from Old Frisian and their modern cognates.

Table 7.3. Synopsis of dating and spread of North Sea Germanic (NSGmc) features in Old Saxon compared to Old Frisian. White cells are used to mark the absence of a NSGmc feature, light grey cells to mark partial implementation of a feature, dark grey cells denote full implementation of a NSGmc feature; cells marked by dash lines show changes which occurred during the OS period.

Feature	Dating	South-West (Essen/Werden)	West-phalian	Eastphalian	Old Frisian
1. aN ~ oN (N = nasal)	One of the oldest NSGmc features; in English and Frisian before AD 500	allophonic	allophonic	phonemicized (after 800)	phonemicized (after 800)
2. a > e	One of the oldest NSGmc features; in English and Frisian before AD 600	no	no	limited	general
3. *ai > æ, ā	7th-century innovation from the north	no	no	widespread	widespread
4. au > ō ~ ā	7th-century innovation (Frisian 6th century, Old High German 8th century)	[oː]	[ɔː] > [oː]	[ɑː]	[ɑː]
5. i-mutation older than i-apocope	7th-/8th-century innovation from the north (including North Germanic)	no	no	yes	yes
6. primary i-mutation	7th-/8th-century innovation from the north (including North Germanic)	restricted	restricted, partly reversed	general	general (plus secondary i-mutation)
7. Nom./acc. pl. a-stem ending -as < -os	7th-/8th-century NSGmc innovation	limited	yes	yes	yes (-ar)
8. metathesis in 'hors'	after AD 800	(lacking attestation)	varied; reversed (?)	yes	yes
9. a + i-mutation > i	Further development of i-mutated PGmc short *a in light syllable stems, which postdates primary i-mutation	no	yes	yes	only Riustringen Old Frisian

The material examined and its interpretation allows one to conclude that the introduction of North Sea Germanic innovations in Old Saxon was anything but a monolithic event. The developments examined in our survey cover more than three centuries, and include the earliest phonological features, such as the allophonic split of Proto-Germanic *a, down to late phenomena such as vowel harmony in *stidi, biki*, with only limited parallels in Old Frisian. Eastphalian is (almost) always involved in the phenomena investigated and mostly concurs with Old Frisian, but this should not be interpreted as indicative of the fact that Eastphalian was nearly identical with Old Frisian (Klein 1990). The substantial overlap between Eastphalian Old Saxon and Old Frisian in Table 7.3 is a result of the selection of the linguistic features. The selection criterion for the investigation was the presence of North Sea Germanic-like variants in Old Saxon. A random selection of linguistic features would show many differences between Eastphalian Old Saxon and Old Frisian. The fact that any of the variants in Table 7.3 shows a strong similarity to the corresponding Old Frisian forms is thus a result of an *a priori* selection of linguistic features. The fact that it is almost always Eastphalian and to a much lesser extent the other dialects that show such a correspondence, however, cannot be ascribed to a bias in the data selection. It is rather indicative of the fact that *if* a North Sea Germanic feature was present in Old Saxon at all, it would most likely be present in Eastphalia.

Table 7.4. A selection of lemmas potentially containing the NSGmc features in two varieties of Old Saxon, Old Frisian, and their equivalents in modern Low German and Frisian. The forms marked in bold are non-NSGmc.

Feature	OS Essen/ Werden	OS East- phalian	Modern Low German	Old Frisian	Modern West Frisian
aN ~ oN	óthar, **fan**/fon	óđer, fon	**anner(e), van**	ōther, fon	oar, **fan**
a > e	glas	gles	**Glas**	gles	glês
*au > ō ~ ā	**brod**	brad	**Braut/Brot**	brād	brea
primary *i*-mutation	stedi/**stadi**	stidi	**Stadt**	stede/stidi	stêd
metathesis in 'hors'	**hros**	hars	**Ross**	hors	hoars

The geographical rationale for the Old Saxon dialectal distribution

The North Sea Germanic character of West Germanic dialects, most clearly applying to Old English and Old Frisian, but just as much to some of the varieties of Old Saxon, is a result of both selective expansion and partial rollback of linguistic features. Of primary interest to the present study is the ways along which these linguistic features and thus the networks of communication could spread.

Given the high density of road networks in the 21st century, especially in the Low Countries and northern Germany, it may be hard to imagine the overland travelling conditions in earlier days. The lowland regions in particular were characterized by poor drainage conditions, including large swamps, peat bogs and muddy roads until relatively recently. The spread of peat bogs in the 18th century in the present-day Lower Saxony region is visible on the map in Figure 7.1. It must be observed that the marked area is only a fraction of the peat bog area reconstructed for the earlier times (Vos and Knol 2014). Such a shape of the landscape, with extensive areas of land hardly accessible to people, was a major factor hindering the communication between neighbouring linguistic communities. Consequently, for transportation of people and goods over larger distances, one had to rely on waterways, i.e. mainly rivers (Siegmüller and Jöns 2011). This significance of waterways is also reflected in the fact that the major inland cities of the region were located likewise on the banks of (small) rivers, e.g. Münster on the Aa,

Osnabrück on the Hase and Hannover on the Leine (the basin areas of the main rivers are marked in the background on Figure 7.1 as well). It can be inferred that the drainage network of a river basin, with the major river in the centre, constituted a natural traffic network along which people travelled in the past.

The Saxon region is dominated by four major rivers: the Rhine, Ems, Weser and Elbe. The Rhine constitutes the western extension of the Old Saxon region, the Elbe formed from a point somewhat to the east of Hamburg a boundary to the territory inhabited by the Slavic peoples. The division into river basins corresponds by and large to the major linguistic divisions of the Old Saxon area: Westphalia (Rhine and Ems), Engria (Weser) and Eastphalia (Elbe). Through the Rhine river, the south-western region was closely connected to the Rhineland and Meuse region, which constituted the core of the Frankish realm. This geographical affinity is well manifested in the linguistic nature of the texts originating in the south-west which exhibit the smallest proportion of North Sea Germanic features and the profound influence from Franconian dialects.

The Ems is a relatively minor river and its importance as an axis of transport is impeded by two other geo-morphological features: the Teutoburger Wald (Fig. 7.2), being the northern enclosure of the Westphalian Basin, and the extensive peat bog area that stretched from the northern fringe of the Teutoburger Wald to the coast. The watershed between the Rhine and the Ems does not constitute a major landscape boundary, and hence the Westphalian Basin (*Münsterland*) rather unites than divides the linguistic landscape, with an orientation predominantly towards the south-west. All of these geographical units, relevant from the linguistic point of view, are presented in Figure 7.2.

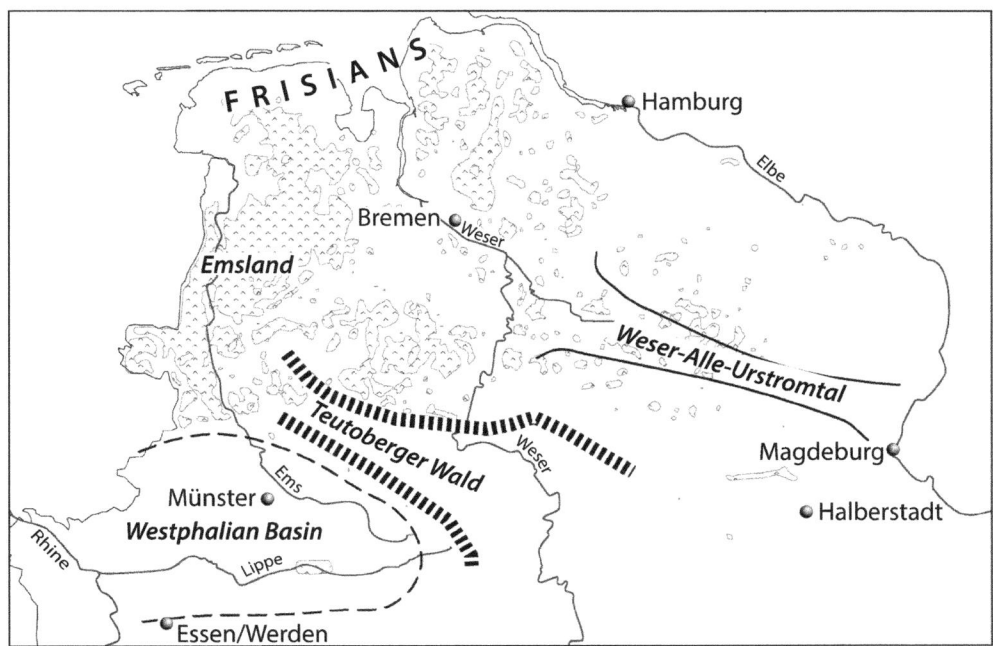

Fig. 7.2. Northern Germany, with *Münsterland* in the Westphalian Basin, the Teutoburger Wald, and the valley of the Weser-Aller *Urstromtal*.

The Weser river forms the major axis of the remaining part of the Saxon region. The Weser-Aller *Urstromtal*, in fact, continues towards Magdeburg into the upper course of the Elbe (Fig. 7.2). In contrast to the Lippe and Rhine basins, and the *Münsterland* region, the Weser and Elbe basins are oriented towards the north and end exactly in the Frisian-speaking area, which forms the core of North Sea Germanic on the Continent.

The coastal regions of the North Sea, directly draining towards the sea and not to any of the main rivers, i.e. Ems, Weser or Elbe, are shown in white in Figure 7.1. They overlap entirely with the medieval extension of the Frisian-speaking area in the coastal territories of present-day Germany. This geographical correlation reflects the importance of natural habitats for the formation of socio-economical, and consequently, speech communities (cf. Århammar 1990, 6). Just as much as the river basins are important for the travel networks on the Continent, the river estuaries constitute the main organising units of travel, contact and (speech) communities in the coastal areas. It can be very well observed in the Frisian region, with the main dialects grouped around the estuaries of (former) Boorne/Middelsee (Old West Frisian), Ems (Old Ems Frisian) and Weser (Old Weser Frisian).

To summarize, even if the distance from Essen to the North Sea coast (as the crow flies) is much shorter than from Merseburg to the North Sea coast (Essen–Rhine estuary *c.* 220 km, Merseburg–Bremerhaven *c.* 370 km), these two regions differ profoundly in their cultural and thus linguistic orientation as determined by geographical circumstances: for the south-west, it is the Franconian Rhine Valley that serves as the orientation point, for the Eastphalian towns such as Merseburg, Halberstadt and Magdeburg, it is the Weser delta, with its Frisian-speaking population. This linguistic orientation of Eastphalia towards the north-west was enhanced by the fact that both towards the south and the east there were barriers of a different nature, i.e. linguistic and geographical. Namely, the region to the east was inhabited by the Slavic peoples, while the area to the south was a zone of hills and medium high mountains which form the southern enclosure of the North German Plain (*Mittelgebirgsschwelle*) (Hänsgen, Lentz and Tzschaschel 2010, 146).

Additional evidence from place-names

Some additional support for the assumption about the significance of the river basins in the spread of linguistic features in the Old Saxon territory comes from present-day place-names. For the purpose of the present study, we analysed place-names containing the element *-stad(t)*, which, depending on whether the form was affected by *i*-mutation or not (Proto-Germanic **stadi-*, 'place, city'), are attested as *-stad(t)/-statt* or *-stedt/-stede*. A clear east–west division, following very much the boundaries of river networks, arises when mapping this particular case of *i*-mutation in present-day place-names. Given the distribution of *i*-mutation in West Germanic languages, the forms with *-e-* could be expected in the North Sea Germanic-oriented varieties, while the forms in *-a-*, lacking *i*-mutation, could be expected in the south-west. Figure 7.3 shows the distribution of present-day place-names ending in *-stad(t)/-statt* versus the names in *-stedt/-stede* in the formerly Old Saxon area. The map includes also place-names attested in the Old Saxon material (based on Tiefenbach 2010).

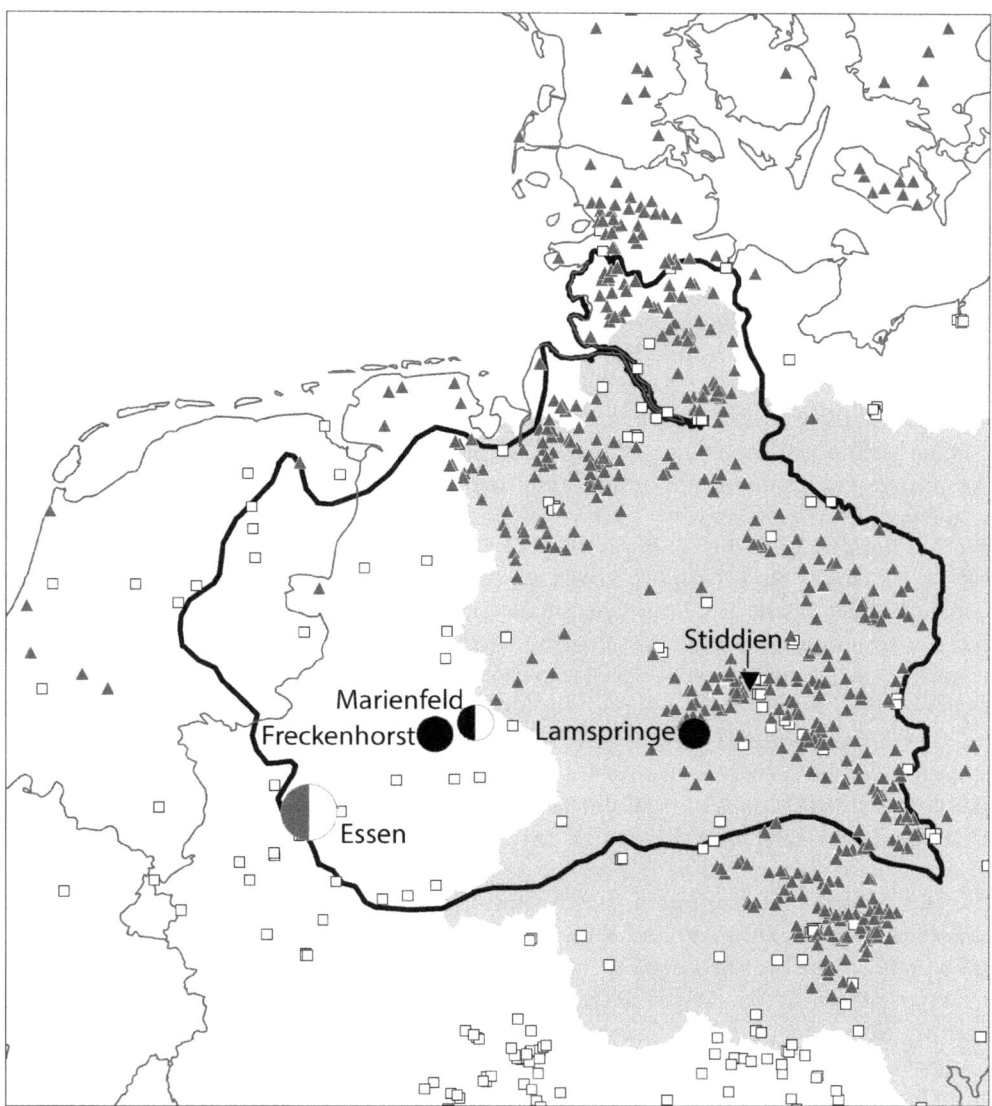

Fig. 7.3. The distribution of *i*-mutated forms in the word *stad-/sted-* in present-day place-names and in Old Saxon onomastic material. White squares: *stad-*; grey triangles: *sted-*; black: *stid-*. The bounded zone is the Old Saxon language area and the area shaded grey the Weser and Elbe river basins.

The forms in *-sted(e)* are confined to the territory of the present-day western Netherlands, East Friesland and (former) Oldenburg, and to the east and south-east of the (Old) Saxon region. Such a distribution of forms confirms again a south-eastward extension of the North Sea Germanic feature, i.e. the *i*-mutated vowel in *-sted*, which clearly overlaps with the river basins of Weser and Elbe. The form showing the result of *i*-mutation is otherwise (and expectedly) found in the (formerly) Frisian coastal regions, in North

Albingia and further north into the (formerly) Danish-speaking area. The distribution of *sted(e)* vs. *stadt* in present-day place-names makes a perfect match with the reconstructed early spread of *i*-mutation in Germanic in the 7th/8th century (cf. feature 6 in the Appendix). This distribution corresponds largely to that found in the Old Saxon material, although it is, at the same time, not entirely consistent with it.

The circles on the map refer to the evidence from Old Saxon texts, glosses and place-names. The Old Saxon forms with *-stad* come mostly from the younger sources and are found in the west, i.e. the present-day *-stad* area. The instances with *-stid-*, which show the effects of vowel harmony in *i*-mutated forms, are attested predominantly in the centre and east of the Old Saxon region, which corresponds to the pattern of spread of *i*-mutation therein. Despite this general overlap between the modern and old data, some discrepancies are evident. Apart from a single form *Stiddien* (which is believed to originate from **Stedi-hēm*), modern place-name material does not attest to forms in *-stid(e)*, with vowel harmony. At the same time, isolated traces of *i*-mutation and additional vowel harmony are found quite unexpectedly in the old material in the area to the west, in the present-day *-stad(t)*-region (*-stedi* in Essen/Werden area, and *-stidi* in Freckenhorst). Given this evidence of *i*-mutation in the western Old Saxon material, it can be concluded that the sharp geographical division in the modern place-name map is possibly the result of a Franconian-based expansion of the forms with *-stad*, which did not spread further than the Rhine and Ems river basin regions.[4] In the light of the discrepancy between the evidence from modern place-names and from the Old Saxon material, the present-day place-name evidence should not be too readily interpreted as a direct reflex of the early-medieval spread of linguistic features across West Germanic.

Another phonological feature for which place-names can provide evidence and which can be informative about the extent of the North Sea Germanic influence in the Old Saxon area is the palatalization of Proto-Germanic **k*. Figure 7.4 presents the spread of forms with palatalized *-k-* in present-day place-names, which is supposed to reflect the Old Saxon palatalization of *-k-*. The map shows that all instances of palatalized **k* are found within the Weser and Elbe river basin areas. This distribution indicates that the spread of North Sea Germanic features in Old Saxon was largely determined by the river networks. As far as the Old Saxon material is concerned, this feature is very scantily attested in the Old Saxon place-names. The only two forms which could be identified are *Ekanscetha*, 'Essen-Steele' and *(H)ékholta*, 'Eckholt', attested in sources from Essen and Freckenhorst (Westphalia) (Tiefenbach 2010, 492). Both testify to a lack of palatalization of **k*, confirming thus the distribution of non-palatalized/palatalized forms based on modern evidence.

---

[4] It must be observed that light syllable *i*-stems, such as *stedi*, retained the final vowel *-i* in all cases in the singular, where it triggered primary *i*-mutation. The noun is indeed consistently attested as *stedi* in the nom./acc.sg. in *Heliand*. In Old High German, where the final consonant was geminated as a result of the High German Consonant Shift, one expects the form *stat(t)* in the nom./acc.sg., but *stetti* in the genitive and dative singular. Old Saxon and Old Frisian show also occasionally the variant *stid-*, attesting to vowel harmony. The Old Saxon nom./acc.sg. *stad* seems to be a newer form, which probably emerged under the influence of Franconian. Regrettably, the oldest Old Low Franconian source, the *Wachtendonk Psalms*, does not contain any attestation of the nom./acc.sg. of the noun. In *Leidse Willeram* nom.sg. *stad* and dat.sg. *stede* are attested, which stays in line with the Old High German data.

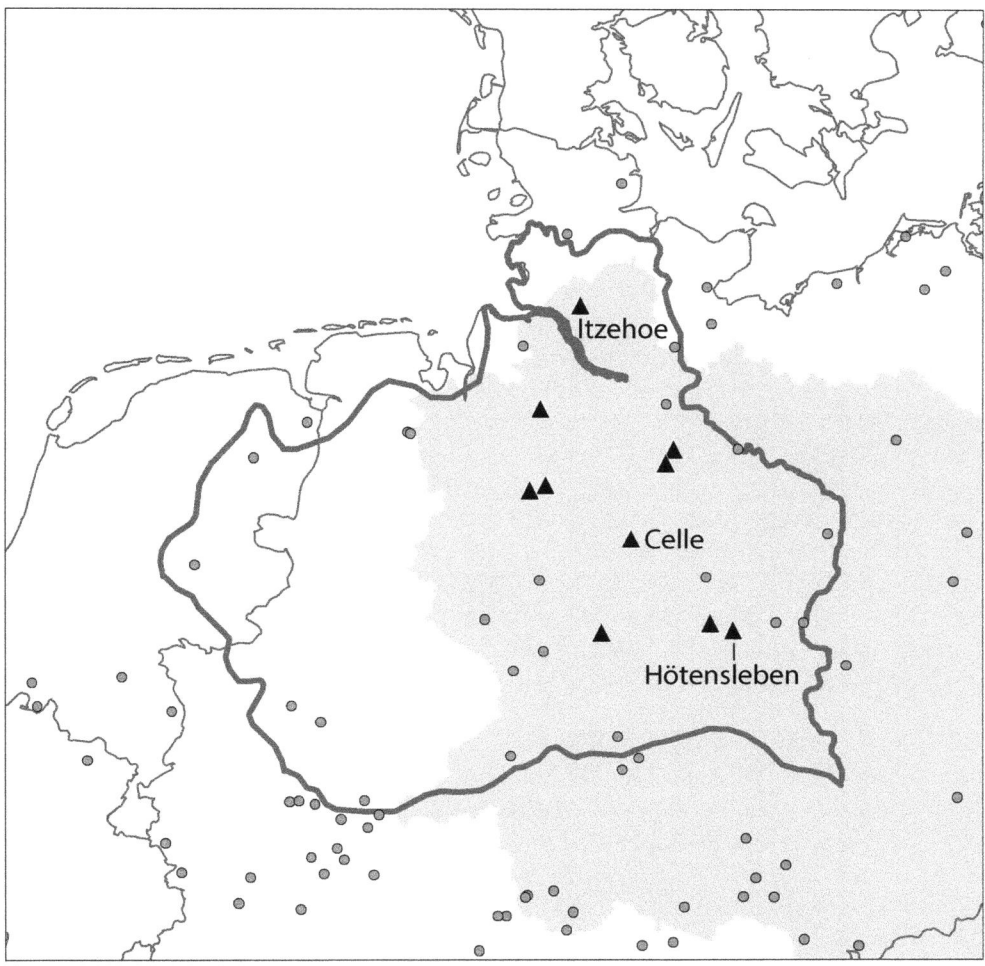

Fig. 7.4. The distribution of forms with palatalized -k- in present-day place-names. The black triangles denote names with palatalization of k > tz. The triangles without names refer to names starting with *eitz-* (< *ēk-* < PGmc **aik-* 'oak'). The small grey circles denote place-names with *E(e)k-, Eik-, Eich-* without palatalization.

Conclusions

The present paper has addressed the issue of the anomalous distribution of innovative linguistic North Sea Germanic features on the Continent, which shows a clear southward bulge into the Old Saxon region. Such a deep inland expansion was absent in the (present-day) Dutch area, where historical sources attest only to a limited spread of North Sea Germanic features in a maximally 50 km wide zone along the coast. We reconstructed the geographical configuration of North Sea Germanic features in the Old Saxon linguistic area, as far as they could be deduced from the scarcely attested textual material.

The distribution of features presented in Figure 7.1 parallels the patterns known from the earlier studies, with North Sea Germanic features ascribed to the textual material from Eastphalia. In the present study, however, special attention was paid to the fact that the areas which are farthest away from the North Sea – on the foothills of Harz and Thüringer Wald – show more North Sea Germanic features than the dialects staying in closer geographical vicinity to the North Sea.

An evaluation of a range of distinct linguistic features indicates that the observed dialect contrast in Old Saxon should not be interpreted uniquely in terms of a regionally confined implementation of North Sea Germanic features, neither should Eastphalian be viewed as representing a relic of what was once a uniform, North Sea Germanic Old Saxon. The dialectal contrasts should instead be conceived of as a result of various waves of the spread of areal features, each with their own maximal extension and potential later rollback. It seems therefore neither correct to refer to Old Saxon as 'originally North Sea Germanic' (Sanders 2000, 1290–1), nor to consider North Sea Germanic as one coherent linguistic phenomenon with a fixed extension in space or time.

It can be concluded that the factor which determined the pattern of distribution of linguistic features is of a non-linguistic nature and involves travel and communication networks, where river basins and natural corridors play a major role. The network of the Weser, its present-day branches and the corridor of the Weser–Aller *Urstromtal*, ending at the River Elbe near Magdeburg, formed a natural sphere of contact with the Frisian language area along the North Sea. The south-western regions of Münsterland, cut off from the north by the Teutoburger Wald and the Emsland peat bogs, and even more so the region around Essen and Werden, were geographically oriented towards the Rhine Valley, which was dominated by the Franks. The Frankish political dominance in the Rhine and Maas river basins stretched all the way to the north-west, up to the peat belt in Holland, separating the Frankish influence from the seaward oriented populations along the narrow inhabitable coastal zone.

The inland extension of the North Sea Germanic linguistic features should therefore be interpreted as a reflection of communication networks which developed along the lines of economic and political contacts, and were guided by the travel networks of those days. The various natural barriers of that time (which are entirely invisible on modern maps), however, did not allow a regular and gradual inland extension of North Sea Germanic features, but resulted in a concentration of these features along the river networks. The inhabitants of the Rhine and Maas basins, politically dominated by the Frankish kings with their inland orientation, and in contrast to the (so far) independent Frisian nation with its maritime connections and trading interests, turned out to be largely insensitive to the linguistic innovations from the coastal linguistic communities.

Appendix 1

A detailed discussion of the North Sea Germanic features examined

All the abbreviations used in the present study are based on the list of abbreviations found in Tiefenbach's dictionary (2010).

1. aN ~ oN: Velarization of PGmc *a before nasals

This is one of the oldest North Sea Germanic features in English and Frisian. It is manifested in the development of an additional rune, known as ōs (Fig. 7.5a). This particular rune is already found in the Undley bracteate (East Anglia), which is commonly dated to the late 5th century (Waxenberger 2013, 45–6 and this vol.), a date which can be accordingly considered a *datum ante quem* for the velarization.

The form of OS *ōthar*, 'other' implies that the velarization of *a* before nasals antedated the loss of nasals before voiceless fricatives: **anþar > *onþar > *ōⁿþar > ōthar*. Even if the phonetic colouring of the vowel is an early development, the phonemicization of the velarized realization of *a* took place only at a much later date (Boutkan 1997; Versloot 2014b).[5] The data from Essen and Werden testify to a strong lexical division of this feature. It is common in the word *ōthar*, but in words with a short vowel before a retained nasal, such as *fan*, 'of', *man*, 'man', *namo*, 'name', the spellings with <o> are nearly absent. In Eastphalian the velarized forms such as *from*, 'from', *noman*, 'name (acc.sg.)' and *gongas*, 'walk (acc.pl.)', are commonly found.

In *Heliand*, a few instances of *ōthar* are attested without a velarized *a*, i.e. *athr-/adr-*. These instances with <ath/d> spelling are only found in paradigm forms which regularly show syncope (e.g. gen.sg. *athres*). Apparently, the vowel was shortened before the cluster /ðr/ and subsequently treated as any other short [ɔ] in closed syllables, which appears as <a> in the western sources.

a   b

Fig. 7.5. The new runes ōs (a) and āc (b).

2. Spontaneous fronting of PGmc *a: a > e (when not hampered by blocking environments)

This is another early North Sea Germanic phonological feature in English and Frisian, and must be older than the year 600. The introduction of a rune known as *āc* (Fig. 7.5b) to represent [a] attests to the spontaneous fronting of *a > e*. This new rune is already

---

[5] For a discussion of the phonemic or allophonic interpretation of velarized *a* see Waxenberger (2013, 20–1 and this vol.). Waxenberger adheres to the principle that only phonemic contrasts were rendered in writing.

found on the **skanomodu** *solidus* (probably Frisian), which is commonly dated to the late 6th century (Waxenberger 2013, 30 and this vol.; Hines, this vol.).

As the spellings <e> for PGmc *a are not very common in OS, it can be questioned whether the realization of PGmc *a as [æ] or [ɛ] was ever as widespread in OS as the verlarized pronunciation of PGmc *a before nasals. Even in the Eastphalian sources, forms with <e> are an exception, e.g. *dage* (PsWit) alongside *dege* (GlMers) 'day (dat.sg.)'. The Merseburg Glosses seem to be the most consistent in applying the fronting, but they provide very little material. In *Heliand*-S, which in general linguistically concurs with the Eastphalian sources, instances with fronted PGmc *a are rare (Klein 1990, 205). It seems that this development was never widespread in OS and was confined to Eastphalia.

3. Monophthongization of *ai > ǣ, ā

The monophthongization of PGmc *ai is almost exceptionless in OS. The regular development of *ai in OS is ē, but some sources, especially the eastern ones, exhibit an incidental development to <a> or <æ> instead of ē. The dataset used in the present study contains only one instance; however, Gallée (1993, 73–4) mentions many more examples from the onomastic material, especially from Corvey and Merseburg. It must be observed that the development to /a:/ or /æ:/ was common in specific phonological environments in Frisian, and the OS instances with <a> or <æ> are found in similar phonological contexts (Versloot 2017). The data do not testify to a large scale shift from ē to ā, and therefore we conclude that the outcome with <a> or <æ> was confined to the east from the very beginning of the monophthongization process, which can be dated to the 7th century in OS.

4. Monophthongization of *au > ō ~ ā

The monophthongization of PGmc *au is limited to Frisian, Low German and Dutch, affecting High German only partly. The spelling <a> is the default form in OFris, while <o> is common in OHG and OLF. OS witnesses an alternation between <a> and <o>, with the latter form being dominant in *Heliand* and *Genesis*, and the former in *Heliand-S*. Likewise, considerable vacillation between the two alternative forms is attested in the material from Westphalia, whereas the sources from Essen/Werden attest predominantly to <o> spellings, which matches the common practice in *Heliand*. The spellings may reflect a gradual phonetic realization, ranging from [ɑ:] in the north to [o:] in the south. No extensive geographical or diachronic shifts were detectable in the investigated material. The monophthongization can be dated to the 7th century (in Frisian to the 6th century, in OHG to the 8th century).

5. The dating of *i*-mutation

i-mutation was an innovation that spread into OS from the north in the 7th and 8th centuries and was confined here only to short *a* (primary *i*-mutation).[6] One of the triggers

---

[6] The subsequent developments in Middle Low and High German show that *i*-mutation was still an active process that could affect many more vowels until a relatively late date. The fact that the

of *i*-mutation was PGmc short *-*i*, which disappeared after heavy syllables prior to the earliest attestations of OS. In the intersecting waves of (primary) *i*-mutation and apocope of word-final short PGmc *-*i*, the North Sea Germanic dialects developed morphological *i*-mutation (among others) in the plural of root nouns, while most OS dialects, OLF and OHG had lost the final -*i* before the application of *i*-mutation, and hence they show an identical form in the nom./acc.sg. and nom./acc.pl. in this group of nouns. The presence of this feature is most consistently attested in the OS root noun *mann* (cf. E. *man* ~ *men*). The *i*-mutated forms of *mann* are found in Eastphalian (one positive example and no counterexamples) and in *Heliand-S* (9 times). These OS dialects take an intermediate position between Continental and North Sea Germanic: with OE and OFris they share the chronology of the application of *i*-mutation and apocope of short *-*i* after heavy syllables, while with OHG and OLF they share the limited scope of *i*-mutation which applies only to short *a*. *Heliand-S* contains some more examples of the application of primary *i*-mutation before *i*-apocope, as illustrated by the acc.sg. *creht* against *craft* found in the other sources (for a further discussion of incidental traces of *i*-mutation triggered by short *-*i*, see Klein 1990, 206–8; Krogh 1996, 175–82).

6. The scope of primary *i*-mutation

Another trigger for *i*-mutation in OS was the synchronic presence of -*i* that escaped apocope in pre-OS (when derived from PGmc long *-*ī* or when following a light syllable). The effect of the presence of -*i* was also confined to *i*-mutation of the root vowel *a* (primary *i*-mutation). The light syllable noun *stedi*, 'city' (< PGmc *stadiz) shows consistent application of *i*-mutation in *Heliand* and *Genesis*. In south-western sources, however, *i*-mutation is not always attested in *stedi/stad*. The scarce data suggest that the form *stad* spread from the south-west, ultimately even from the Franconian linguistic area. However, the attestation of -*stadi* in the nom./acc.pl. in late-9th-century sources from Werden suggests that the application of primary *i*-mutation was more limited in the south-west, irrespective of any potential Franconian impact (cf. feature 9 and section 5).

7. -*os* ~ -*as*

The development of -*os* > -*as* was a North Sea Germanic innovation, implemented in Frisian in the 6th century (Versloot 2016b; cf. Boutkan 1995, 436). While the south-west dialects of OS attest to -*os* with continental vowel quality, the other OS sources (after 900), including the material from Eastphalia, show predominantly -*as*. In *Heliand* (including *Heliand-S*) the form -*as* is only a minority form (Boutkan 1995, 190). On account of many similarities

---

triggers of *i*-mutation are still present in most contexts in OS and OHG fuels theories about an early pan-Germanic application of *phonetic i*-mutation and a later date of *phonemicization* in the south (for a discussion with further references see Buccini 1995, 34). However, this theory cannot explain the lack of *i*-mutation in forms such as nom./acc.pl. *man*, which can only be reasonably explained if we assume that *i*-mutation (also as an allophonic feature) occurred later than the apocope of short word-final -*i*. Also the fact that particularly farther to the south, in various High German dialects, *i*-mutation does not apply at all in quite a few environments (Salmons 2012, 125–7) attests to a diminishing impact of the process in the south.

between *Heliand-S* and Eastphalian sources with respect to other features, the contrast in the distribution of *-as* and *-os* in these sources may be interpreted as a chronological one. This implies that the transition of *-os* > *-as* was on its way in the east not earlier than in the 9th century. The only fact which runs counter to this interpretation is the form *bergas* from Werden (*GlWerdC*), dated to the early 9th century.[7]

A case where the south-western form is an innovation, and the northern and eastern dialects attest to the retention of an original OS form is the alternation of *-os/-as* with *-a*. The latter ending is interpreted here as a Franconian borrowing from the south-west contact zone, which can be dated to the 9th century, and which subsequently spread through the rest of Low Saxon in the later centuries (Quak 1989).

8. Metathesis in 'hors'

This development is not particularly restricted to the North Sea Germanic region, as evinced by the place-names in *-born*, 'source' in the Middle German region which is linguistically Franconian (cf. German *Brunen*, Dutch *bron*). Metathesis is frequently found in OFris in words such as *hors, berna, gers* (cf. High German *Roß, brennen, Gras*, English *horse, burn* but *grass*). In Frisian, the process must post-date the apocope of *-u* after heavy syllables, which had not been implemented there before the year 800 (Versloot 2016b).[8]

9. PGmc **a* + *i*-mutation > *i*

A number of OS light syllable nouns affiliated with *i*-stem declension, with PGmc root vowel **a* and *i*-mutation, seem to show the effects of vowel harmony, e.g. *biki*, 'brook', *stidiu*, 'place, spot'.[9] Evidence from *Heliand-S* is missing, whereas the other *Heliand* manuscripts attest only to *sted-*. The development of PGmc **stadi-* and **baki-* > *stid-* and *bik-*, respectively, has parallels in Old Weser Frisian, but is not a common North Sea Germanic phenomenon. The Weser Frisian dialect shows alternating pairs with vowel harmony, such as *stede ~ stidi*. The effect of mutual assimilation of vowels across syllables (through vowel harmony and various mutations) is in general more common in North Germanic and North Sea Germanic than in Continental West Germanic varieties. The development must be younger than the primary *i*-mutation (cf. feature 6). Figure 7.6 presents the geographical distribution of the vowels found in the OS light syllable *i*-stems with PGmc root vowel **a*.

---

[7] Three forms in *-as*, found in the source labelled *Indic*, are dated to the late 8th century by Krogh (1996, 126), but to the 12th century by Tiefenbach (2010, xxxiii). The forms in *-as* in the late 8th century in *AbrPal* may have been influenced by OE (just as the forms *halogan gast*, 'Holy Spirit').
[8] Weser OFris attests to a plural form *gerso*, 'grasses', with retention of the *-o* < *-u* occuring only after a light syllable. This implies that at the time of the operation of apocope, the form was still **græsu*, with a single coda consonant (cf. Boutkan 1996, 67).
[9] The dat.sg. form *stida*, attested in *RegFrek*, evinces an intraparadigmatic levelling of *-i-*.

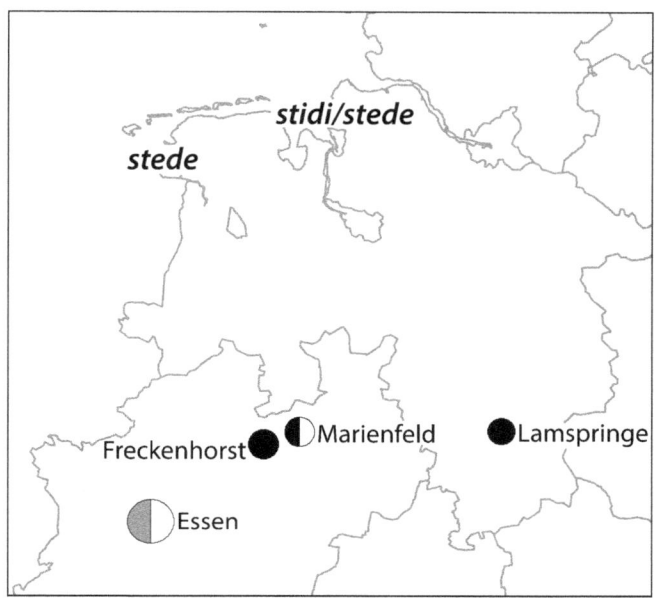

Fig. 7.6. The geographical distribution of forms with different root vowels in *stedi*, 'town' and *beki*, 'creek'. The map includes also Old Saxon place-names containing these two nouns (Tiefenbach 2010, 490–7) (these were not included in the aggregate Figure 7.1). Some nom./acc. sg. forms were excluded because of the lack of the *i*-mutation-triggering vowel (**stedi* > *stad*). White: *stad*-; grey: *sted*-; black: *stid*-.

10. North Sea Germanic features which were not included in the mapping

A few further features which were not included in the mapping deserve closer attention, including two additional characteristics frequently referred to as North Sea Germanic phenomena and two OS-OE innovations which are not shared by OFris.

One of the North Sea Germanic features which were not included in the map is the loss of nasals before unvoiced fricatives. The process is difficult to date, as the time span between its phonetic emergence and the final stage of denasalization of the vowel is considerable (cf. Versloot 2014b, 31–2). The feature is well attested across Germanic languages and has a different scope depending on the type of the fricative. Accordingly, the loss of /n/ before /f/ is found in Dutch (*vijf*, 'five' vs. High German *fünf*); the loss of /n/ before /s/ is common in North Germanic (Danish *gås*, 'goose') and is also attested in Low Rhine Franconian (Old Limburgian) already in the late 9th century (INL, s.v. *unsa*). The loss of /n/ before /þ/ is characteristic only of North Sea Germanic: OE, OFris and OS. Before /s/ and /þ/, the loss of /n/ is widespread in OS, even in the south-west, but 6 out of the 9 tokens from Eastphalia show <n>, as in *uns*, 'us' and *munde*, 'mouth' (PsLub, PsWit). At the same time, all 9 relevant tokens in the Straubing fragment testify to a lack of /n/. If the assumption that the Straubing fragment reflects the oldest (attested) stage of the Eastphalian dialect is correct, the presence of /n/ in the modern Eastphalian variety can be interpreted as a case of a later restoration of the nasal (König 2001, 160).

A morphological feature frequently considered to be a North Sea Germanic innovation is the extension of the dative singular form of the first and second person pronouns, *mi* and *thi*, to the accusative (e.g. Nielsen 1985: 113). While commonly found in OLF and OFris, its distribution in OE and OS is diversified, depending largely on the dialect. In both languages the picture is biased by the state of affairs attested in the dominant varieties: West Saxon for OE and the *Heliand* idiom, representing the language from the southwest, for OS. It is precisely the dominant dialect of West Saxon and the south-western OS dialects that are most advanced with respect to the loss of the historical accusative form. In Anglian and in OS from the area beyond the south-western region, the old accusative forms are pretty much alive (as confirmed by the material from Paderborn and Eastphalia). In Eastphalian these forms survived even into the modern dialects (König 2001, 160). This feature therefore shows a North Sea Germanic spread in a literal way, i.e. it is most prominent in the varieties geographically closest to the North Sea, including Kentish and West Saxon, OFris, OLF and south-western OS.

Finally, Nielsen (1985, 125,126) discusses two morpho-phonological phenomena which are exclusively shared by OE and OS. The first one is a shared archaism: OS *bium, biun* and OE *beom, biom* (< PIE *b^hеuн-* (or *b^huен-*)) (Philippa *et al.* 2003, s.v. *zijn, bouwen*) in contrast to *bim, bin* in OFris, OLF and OHG. The other phenomenon involves a common innovation, found in the plural paradigm of the verb *to be*, where *sind* can be extended with *-on*, *-un* in OE and OS. This latter feature can also be found in adjacent Franconian dialects (not in Low Franconian though). The forms *biun* and *sindon* are found predominantly in the region Essen and Westphalia (Freckenhorst), while Eastphalia and the Straubing fragment attest to *bin/bim* and *sind*, corresponding thus to the OFris forms.

References

Århammar, Nils R. 1990, 'Friesisch und Sächsisch. Zur Problematik ihrer gegenseitigen Abgrenzung im Früh- und Hochmittelalter'. In *Aspects of Old Frisian Philology*, Amsterdamer Beiträge zur älteren Germanistik 31–2, ed. O. Vries, R. H. Bremmer Jr. and G. van der Meer (Groningen–Amsterdam–Atlanta), 1–25.

Boutkan, Dirk 1995, *The Germanic "Auslautgesetze"* (Amsterdam–Atlanta).

Boutkan, Dirk 1996, *A Concise Grammar of the Old Frisian Dialect of the first Riustring Manuscript* (Odense).

Boutkan, Dirk 1997, 'The origin of *mon*. The representation of Proto-Germanic a before nasals in the Old Frisian Codex Unia', *It Beaken* 1, 1–13.

Bree, Cor van 1997, *Een oud onderwerp opnieuw bekeken: het Ingweoons* (Leiden).

Buccini, Anthony F. 1995, 'Ontstaan en vroegste ontwikkeling van het Nederlandse taallandschap', *Taal en tongval* 8, 8–66.

Cordes, Gerhard, and Ferdinand Holthausen 1973, *Altniederdeutsches Elementarbuch: Wort- u. Lautlehre* (Heidelberg).

DeCamp, David 1958, 'The genesis of the Old English dialects: a new hypothesis', *Language* 34/2, 232–44.

Gallée, Johan Hendrik 1993, *Altsächsische Grammatik*. 3rd edn (Tübingen).

Gehle, Heinrich 1977, *Wörterbuch westfälischer Mundarten: Hochdeutsch-Plattdeutsch* (Münster).

Hänsgen, Dirk, Sebastian Lentz and Sabine Tzschaschel 2010, *Deutschlandatlas: unser Land in 200 thematischen Karten* (Darmstadt).

INL. Geïntegreerde Taalbank. *Historische woordenboeken op internet*. www. gtb. inl. nl last accessed 15 February 2016.
Klein, Thomas 1990, 'Die Straubinger Heliand-Fragemente: Altfriesisch oder Altsächsisch?' In *Aspects of Old Frisian Philology*, Amsterdamer Beiträge zur älteren Germanistik 31–2, ed. O. Vries, R. H. Bremmer Jr. and G. van der Meer (Groningen–Amsterdam–Atlanta), 197–225.
Klein, Thomas 2000, 'Zur Stellung des Altsächsischen', *Jahrbuch des Vereins für Niederdeutsche Sprachforschung* 123, 7–32.
Klein, Thomas 2004, 'Wann entstand das Altsächsische?', *Jahrbuch des Vereins für Niederdeutsche Sprachforschung* 127, 7–22.
König, Werner 2001, *Dtv-Atlas Deutsche Sprache* (München).
Kortlandt, Frederik 2008, 'Anglo-Frisian', *NOWELE* 54/55, 265–78.
Krogh, Steffen 1996, *Die Stellung des Altsächsischen im Rahmen der germanischen Sprachen* (Göttingen).
Krogh, Steffen 2002, 'Noch einmal zur Stellung des Altsächsischen: Eine Antwort auf Thomas Klein', *Jahrbuch des Vereins für Niederdeutsche Sprachforschung* 125, 7–25.
Krogh, Steffen 2013, 'Die Anfänge des Altsächsischen' *NOWELE: North-Western European language evolution* 66/2, 141–68.
Kuhn, Hans 1955, 'Zur Gliederung der germanischen Sprachen', *Zeitschrift für deutsches Altertum und deutsche Literatur* 86, 1–47.
Nerbonne, John 2010, 'Measuring the diffusion of linguistic change', *Philosophical Transactions of the Royal Society of London. Series B, Biological sciences* 365/1559, 3821–8.
Nielsen, Hans Frede 1985, *Old English and the Continental GermanicLlanguages: A Survey of Morphological and Phonological Iinterrelations*, Innsbrucker Beiträge Zur Sprachwissenschaft 33, 2nd edn (Innsbruck).
Nielsen, Hans Frede 1998, *The Continental Backgrounds of English and its Insular Development until 1154* (Odense and Portland)
Nielsen, Hans Frede 2000, *The Early Runic Language of Scandinavia: Studies in Germanic Dialect Geography* (Heidelberg).
Nielsen, Hans Frede 2001, 'Frisian and the grouping of the older Germanic languages'. In *Handbuch des Friesischen*, ed. H. H. Munske, N. Århammer, V. F. Faltings, J. F. Hoekstra, O. Vries, A. G. H. Walker and O. Witts (Tübingen), 512–23.
Philippa, Marlies, F. Debrabandere, Arend Quak, Tanneke Schoonheim and Nicoline van der Sijs 2003, *Etymologisch woordenboek van het Nederlands* (Amsterdam) via http://www. etymologiebank. nl/ last accessed 6 February 2016.
Quak, Arend 1989, 'Meervoudvorming in Oudsaksisch en Middelnederduits', *Amsterdamer Beiträge zur älteren Germanistik* 28, 43–54.
Salmons, Joseph C. 2012, *A History of German: What the Past Reveals about Today's Language* (Oxford).
Sanders, Willy 2000, 'Reflexe gesprochener Sprache im Altniederdeutschen (Altsächsischen)'. In *Sprachgeschichte: Ein Handbuch zur Geschichte der deutschen Sprache und ihrer Erforschung. 2. Teilband*, 2nd edn, ed. W. Besch, A. Betten, O. Reichmann and S. Sonderegger (New York), 1288–93.
Siebs, Theodor 1889, *Zur Geschichte der Englisch-friesischen Sprache* (Halle a/d Saale).
Siebs, Theodor 1901, 'Geschichte der friesischen Sprache'. In *Grundriss Der Germanischen Philologie* vol. 1, 2nd edn, ed. H. Paul (Strassburg), 1152–464.
Siegmüller, Annette, and Hauke Jöns 2011, 'Aktuelle Forschungen zu Weser und Hunte als Wege der Kommunikation und des Austauschs während des 1. Jahrtausends nach Chr.', *Nachrichten aus Niedersachsens Urgeschichte* 80, 97–115.
Stiles, Patrick V. 1995, 'Remarks on the "Anglo-Frisian" thesis'. In *Friesische Studien II*. NOWELE Supplement Volume 12, ed. V. F. Faltings, A. G. H. Walker and O. Wilts (Odense), 177–220.
Stiles, Patrick V. 2013, 'The Pan-West Germanic Isoglosses and the Subrelationships of West Germanic to Other Branches', *NOWELE: Unity and Diversity in West Germanic I* 66 (1), 5–38.

Tiefenbach, Heinrich 2010, *Altsächsisches Handwörterbuch = A Concise Old Saxon Dictionary* (Berlin).
Vaan, Michiel de 2012, 'Taalcontact in Noord-Holland: een inleiding', *It Beaken* 74:1/2, 77–84.
Versloot, Arjen Pieter 2014a, 'Methodological reflections on the emergence of Old Frisian', *NOWELE: Unity and Diversity in West Germanic III* 67/1, 23–49.
Versloot, Arjen Pieter 2014b, 'The Runic Frisian vowel system: the earliest history of Frisian and Proto-Insular North Frisian', *Amsterdamer Beiträge zur älteren Germanistik* 72, 35–62.
Versloot, Arjen Pieter 2016a, 'Proto-Germanic *ai in North and West Germanic', *Folia Linguistica Historica* (Berlijn).
Versloot, Arjen Pieter 2016b, 'Unstressed vowels in Runic Frisian: the history of Frisian and the Germanic "Auslautgesetze."' *Us Wurk* 65, 1–39.
Vos, Peter C. and Egge Knol 2014, *Paleogeografische kaarten van het Waddengebied tussen Marsdiep en Weser. 500 v. Chr. - heden* (Groningen).
Waxenberger, Gabriele 2013, 'The reflection of pre-Old English sound changes in pre-Old English runic inscriptions'. In *Recording English, Researching English, Transforming English*, ed. H. Sauer and G. Waxenberger (Frankfurt am Main), 17–64.

8

Between Sievern and Gudendorf

Enclosed sites in the north-western Elbe–Weser triangle and their significance in respect of society, communication and migration during the Roman Iron Age and Migration Period

Iris Aufderhaar

Even today, the waterways of the seas and rivers provide important signposts to the infrastructure of world-wide trade, transport and communication. Likewise in the 1st millennium AD, the maritime routes along the coasts, together with the rivers and streams and the almost undefined land routes (Bischop 2000, 27) that marked the landscapes of northern Europe through bogs and wet valley bottoms provided the practical foundations for regional and trans-regional communication and the transportation of goods (Jöns 2009, 390–1; Nørgaard Jørgensen 2003, 195; for an overview, Siegmüller 2011; Siegmüller and Jöns 2012, 575–6; 2011, 98). Together with the land routes and the inland waters that connected these to areas lying further inland, they formed a regular network of communication routes (Ellmers 2005, 74–5; 1999, 597; Jöns 2009, 389).

Archaeologically, the importance of the waterways in goods exchange can be demonstrated through the distribution of foreign goods (cf. Brather 1996, 46). For the first half of the 1st millennium AD this can be seen particularly through objects of provincial Roman origin in the areas located north of the *limes* (e.g. Eggers 1951; Lund Hansen 1987; Erdrich 2001; 2002). The mapping of these objects reveals the greatest concentrations in the vicinity of major watercourses and by the coasts (most recently Siegmüller and Jöns 2011, 98; Jöns 2009, 389–91).

Research into the archaeologically tangible basic structure of regional and trans-regional communication, which has been pursued particularly vigorously around the Baltic area during the past twenty years, has been able to show that, during the whole of the 1st millennium, control of the land routes and waterways can be seen to have had great social significance. In this light, attention has been paid in many places to the establishment of landing places (Ulriksen 1998; 2004), trans-shipment sites and beach

Fig. 8.1. The location of the enclosed sites Heidenschanze and Heidenstadt at Sievern, Stadt Geestland, Cuxhaven-Gudendorf, and of the site of Spieka-Knill in the north-western Elbe–Weser triangle. Reconstruction of the overland routes according to Hans Aust (1956, 124) and course of the coastline during the Roman Iron Age according to Karl-Ernst Behre (1999, Abb. 1). Graphics: Iris Aufderhaar, NIhK. Base map: NIBIS *Kartenserver* [2013], Geological Map 1:50,000 – Landesamt für Bergbau, Energie und Geologie [LBEG], Hannover.

markets (Thomsen *et al.* 1993), which served as portals between long-distance and internal transport. The significance of the communication and transport routes and of control of these links can also be recognized in the relatively frequently discovered construction of ramparts, canals, sea-barriers and blockades in rivers and lakes in southern Scandinavia (see Nørgaard Jørgensen 2001; 2003).

The north-western Elbe–Weser triangle

Many authors have already drawn attention to the connectivity between the area of north-western Germany and trans-regional communication and goods exchange, as well as to the importance of this area's river systems as transport routes in the first half of the 1st millennium AD (esp. Herke 1990; Erdrich 2001; Bischop 2001). Alongside written sources, their arguments have drawn especially on the distribution of Roman imports

Fig. 8.2. Bracteates from Sievern, Stadt Geestland. Finds from 1999. Photo: Rolf Kiepe, NIhK. From Aufderhaar 2015, Abb. 9.

(as an overview, Siegmüller and Jöns 2011, 100). In the case of the Elbe–Weser triangle, the clear concentration of foreign items of Roman origin (collected by Erdrich 2002), and the distribution of gold bracteates with similar designs (*Formularfamilien*: Pesch 2007), along the North Sea coast allows us also to assume that the coastal zone between the mouths of the rivers Weser and Elbe constituted an important link in a transport route between southern Scandinavia and the Rhine, as well to the area of Anglo-Saxon settlement in the south and east of England, as, for instance, it has been modelled by Martin Segschneider (2002) for the 6th century AD (cf. also Aust 1980, 1; Siegmüller and Jöns 2011, 100). Furthermore, the distribution of particular forms of dress-accessory (for an overview, Böhme 1986), or the evidence of 5th-century pottery (Capelle 1995, 14–16), which are found both in the Elbe–Weser triangle and in southern and eastern England, allows us to conclude that the established connections also played a crucial role in the population movement of the Migration Period (see Capelle 1995, 7–18).

Through research undertaken by the *Niedersächsisches Institut für historische Küstenforschung* in recent years, it has also been possible to gain concrete evidence of the forms of organization of communication in the case of the coastal zone of north-western Germany and its immediately adjacent rivers. It has thus been possible to uncover traces of the landing sites of boats and ships, and of beach markets and craft-production sites (most recently Siegmüller 2015).

Sievern/Land Wursten: a microregion with central-place features

The above is particularly clearly visible in the area of the mouth of the Weser. Here, a settlement complex can be traced in the region of Sievern (Fig. 8.1) from the 1st century AD to 5th century, integral components of which are both numerous remains located on the sandy gravels (*Geest*) of the Hohe Lieth and the chain of settlement mounds (*Wurten*) in the Wurster Marsh stretching out alongside the *Geest* including Feddersen Wierde (Haarnagel 1979) and Fallward (Schön 1999a). Altogether this complex meets all of the criteria in terms of features and functions of a central place (Aufderhaar 2015; 2016).

On the function of the settlements in the marsh and on the edge of the *Geest*

Of particular importance to this region as a central place of the late pre-Roman Iron Age and the first half of the 1st millennium AD (Aufderhaar 2015; Zimmermann 2005, 371) was a distinct intensification in foreign objects of (provincial) Roman and Scandinavian provenance. It is more than anything else finds of precious-metal artefacts of the 5th and 6th centuries AD from the vicinity of Sievern that emphasize the special character of this area. In quantity alone – as well as five looped gold *solidi* they include a punch-decorated neckring with overlapping terminals of Scandinavian type (Häßler 2003, 106–14, 124–8; Hauck 1970, 23) and a total of fourteen Migration-period gold bracteates (Fig. 8.2) – these form a unique assemblage in the context of Germany (Aufderhaar 2015, 137–9; Hauck 1970). They also testify to the wide-reaching connections of the population of the Sievern region with the elites of southern Scandinavia and Anglo-Saxon England, and to a recognized and shared pictorial language within this region (Pesch 2011; 2005, 8–9).

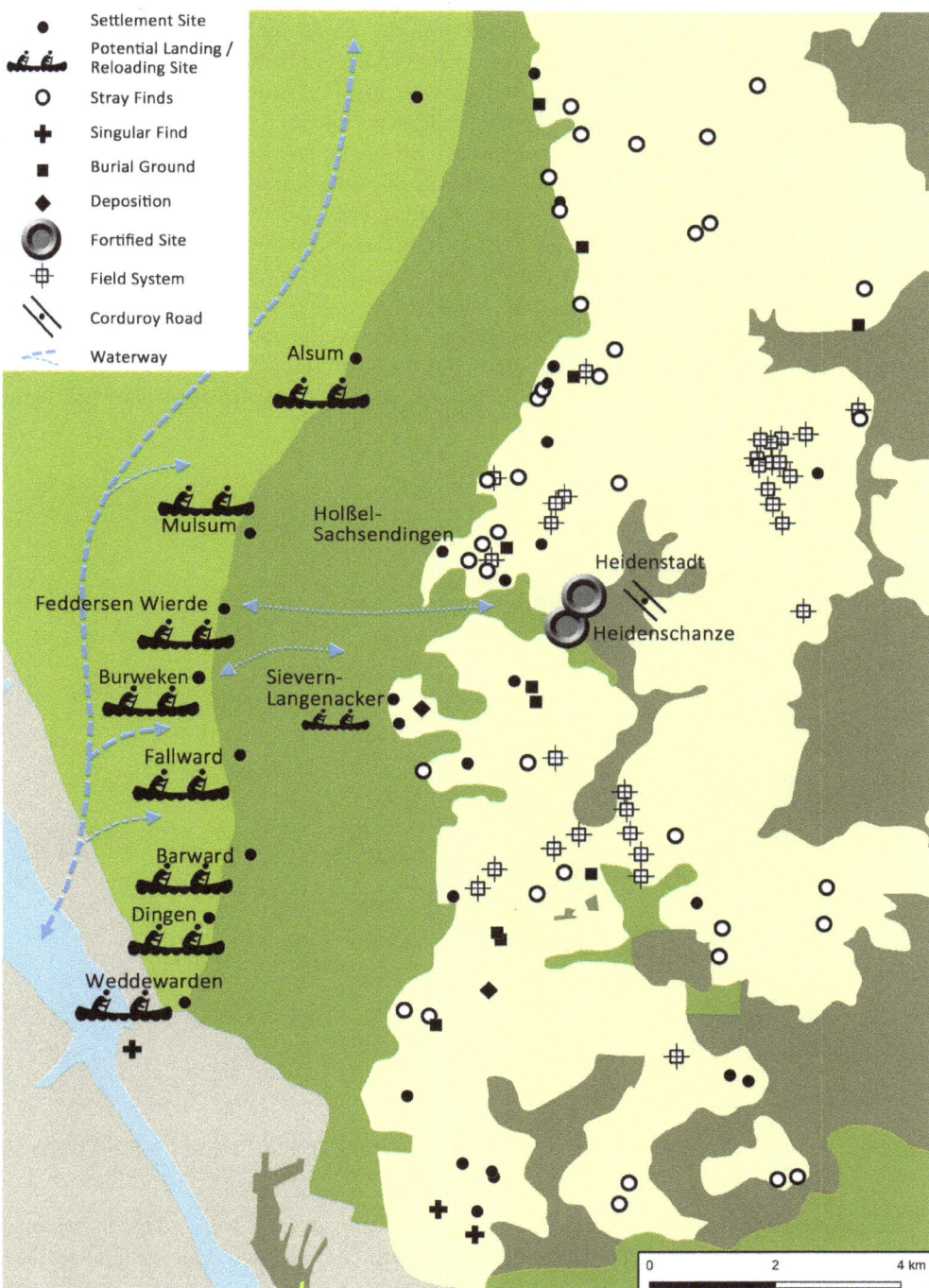

Fig. 8.3. The Sievern/Land Wursten region. Model of the function of the marsh and *Geest*-edge settlements as landing and trans-shipment sites. Base map: NIBIS *Kartenserver* [2013], Geological Map 1:50,000 – Landesamt für Bergbau, Energie und Geologie [LBEG], Hannover.

In addition to this, through the inclusion of items of provincial Roman origin (summarized by Erdrich 2002) which have been retrieved from the cemeteries, settlements and hoards as well as from detector surveys of the topsoil (Aufderhaar *et al.* 2011, 186–7; Aufderhaar 2016, 39–59), it is also possible to identify clear concentrations in the area of the marsh settlements, and to some extent also in the area of the edge of the *Geest*. These show that the population settled in this zone had greater access to such items.

In the marsh of Land Wursten, a series of settlements was founded in the course of the 1st century BC (Fig. 8.3). They lay in the shelter of a fossil shore bank right beside the coastline of the day, at distances of 1.3 to 3.2 km apart, and thus within immediate reach of the coastal shipping routes (Haarnagel 1979, 15–22). At the same time, regular contact with the *Geest* lying up to 3 km further east was of even greater importance to the occupants of these settlements, as many daily essentials such as wood for building, as well as for craft activities or the production of charcoal, and also stone and bog iron, were unavailable in the marsh itself.

Fig. 8.4. Feddersen Wierde (Ldkr. Cuxhaven). Jetty and waterfront revetment from Settlement Horizon 1c (first half of the 1st century AD). From Siegmüller and Jöns 2012, Abb. 5.

How much importance the connection with the various waterways had for the marsh-dwellers may be shown by the discovery of a carefully constructed landing place that was uncovered in Settlement Horizon 1c of Feddersen Wierde, from the first half of the 1st century AD (Fig. 8.4). This was constructed in a bay in a minor branch of a channel, surrounded by the settlement on the south-western side (Scheschkewitz 2010, 296, fig. 9; Haarnagel 1979, 176, Tafn. 157,1–158,3, Beilage 23) and provided a sheltered area with relatively calm navigable water. Amongst the components of this landing place was a jetty which ran from the bank to the deepest part of the bay some three to four metres out. This bay probably never ebbed fully out at low water. The vulnerable bank of the land area was reinforced with wattled panels and a row of closely spaced posts. Since the posts in the immediate vicinity of the jetty were markedly stronger, Haarnagel (1979, 176) suggested that they served as mooring posts.

Altogether, the mound settlements and their features thus lay in an ideal position to serve as landing places (cf. Siegmüller and Jöns 2011, 98–100). A markedly higher number of intrusive objects of Roman origin such as can be ascertained in the assemblages of finds from Feddersen Wierde and Barward but also in the cemetery of the mound settlement of Dingen (summarized by Erdrich 2002, 120–9) provide clear evidence that at least some of these settlements were able to exploit their favourable topographical position in respect of transport, and that at some of these places sites developed at which boats could land and goods for transportation further using smaller methods of carriage could be unloaded (Aufderhaar and Brandt 2011, 54). In this respect, the mound settlements certainly did not constitute specialized landing places or beach markets, such as have been identified in southern Scandinavia in the Late Roman Iron Age and Migration Period in light of Lundeborg (Thomsen *et al.* 1993); rather, they were permanently established settlements whose hinterlands provided the natural necessities for agricultural exploitation as their economic basis, and which adopted a role as landing places as an additional and secondary function (cf. Scheschkewitz 2010, 296).

Not until the Late Roman Iron Age was a site established between the mounds of Feddersen Wierde and Fallward in the Burweken meadowland (Schmid 1990, 363–4, Abb. 1,4, 2 and 3). In contrast to the settlement mounds that were protected from the tide by the fossil sea bank, the Burweken site was situated in part of the newly formed marshland stretching between that fossil sea bank and coastline of the day. Furthermore, the entire structure of this site differed clearly from the mound settlements of Land Wursten (Fig. 8.3). The settlement-related features here lay in an area vulnerable to flooding, and were presumably adapted for purely seasonal use (pers. comm. A. Siegmüller). The topographical position in front of marshland that was beginning to silt up, and a regular structure revealed by magnetometry, along with a large number of potsherds, encourage the idea that this site played some special role within the wider settlement pattern. One possibility is that it served as a seasonal landing and trans-shipment site (Aufderhaar 2015, 136; 2016, 203–7).

The fact that, alongside the many agriculturally directed settlements of the Roman Iron Age in the immediate boundary zone between the edge of the *Geest* and the marsh, there were also settlements which fulfilled a role as trans-shipment sites, is suggested by a discovery in the meadowland of Langenacker in Sievern (Fig. 8.3). In the three excavated trenches, no signs of agrarian character could be found in the deposits. Rather, various pit furnaces and the find material itself provide evidence of a primary craft use of this area that, in light of the heavy influence of the groundwater on the land here may only have been possible on a seasonal basis.

The favourable position of this find spot in respect of transport routes, on a tongue of the *Geest* which extended into the surrounding marsh, also encourages one to interpret a number of base-metal objects of Roman origin found in the Langenacker area in terms of the features being closely linked to the settlements of Land Wursten, and with the transport routes from the marsh to the interior. In support of the case that contact between the marsh area of Land Wursten and these settlements was of particular importance for the settlement of the area, attention may be drawn to a wooden structure which was uncovered through prospecting in the marsh area that extends into the Langenacker meadowland, and which is assigned to the Early Roman Iron Age by AMS radiocarbon dating. This was composed of logs laid in a chequer pattern and anchored to the ground with stakes; it may have served as a revetment for the bank or to stabilize a track.

The whole find-complex leads one to believe that this settlement was also a component of the system as a trans-shipment site, forming the interface between the transportation and communication routes of the marsh and the *Geest* at this location (Aufderhaar 2015, 129, 133; 2016, 150–92 and 207; Aufderhaar *et al.* 2011, 206–11).

On the significance and function of the enclosed sites of Heidenschanze and Heidenstadt in the *Geest* region

Around the time of the establishment of settlement in the marsh zone, the *Geest* region behind it had an enclosed site of 12.5 ha constructed in it, which became known as the *Heidenschanze* ('Heathen Fort') in the literature (Fig. 8.5). The strongly defended and, during the period of the 2nd and 1st centuries BC and 1st century AD, repeatedly enhanced system of ramparts of the Heidenschanze, including reinforcement with a palisade set in front of it, came eventually to have a total length of 2,000 m and a height of some 2 m. Together with the basic plan involving inner and outer ramparts, plus a few well-constructed entrances, this testifies to a clear defensive character for the structure (Schön 2000a; 2000b; Haarnagel 1965; 1971). This is also reflected in the choice of settlement location, in a naturally protected site on a *Geest* knoll surrounded by lower land (Aufderhaar *et al.* 2011, 203).

The system of ramparts and the position of the Heidenschanze, however, are not solely evidence of a purely defensive role; in particular, in addition, they reflect a community or communal group's need for self-representation (Aufderhaar 2015, 130). Inside the central area, indeed, signs of building were found (Haarnagel 1965, 168–70), although because of the only small area excavated nothing could be discovered concerning the construction or function of this building. In the area of the outer defensive bank, by contrast, no evidence of contemporary buildings could be identified (Aufderhaar *et al.* 2011, 204–5), although this does not exclude use of the area, for some periodical events for instance (Haarnagel 1971, 14; 1965, 177–8). Furthermore, the Heidenschanze was located appropriately in terms of transport topography on the meeting point of a land route running south–north (cf. Aust 1956, 124; Haarnagel 1961, 77, 85, Abb. 2) and the Sievern Beck, which in the late pre-Roman Iron Age and the first half of the 1st millennium AD was a navigable link between the coastline of the day and the maritime routes along it and the marsh of Land Wursten and its settlements (Brandt 2015, 293; Aufderhaar and Brandt 2011).

The position of the Heidenschanze in the hinterland of the landing and trans-shipment sites, contemporary with and also on the nodal point of both transport routes, allows us to infer that the land routes of the *Geest* but above all the waterways along the mouth

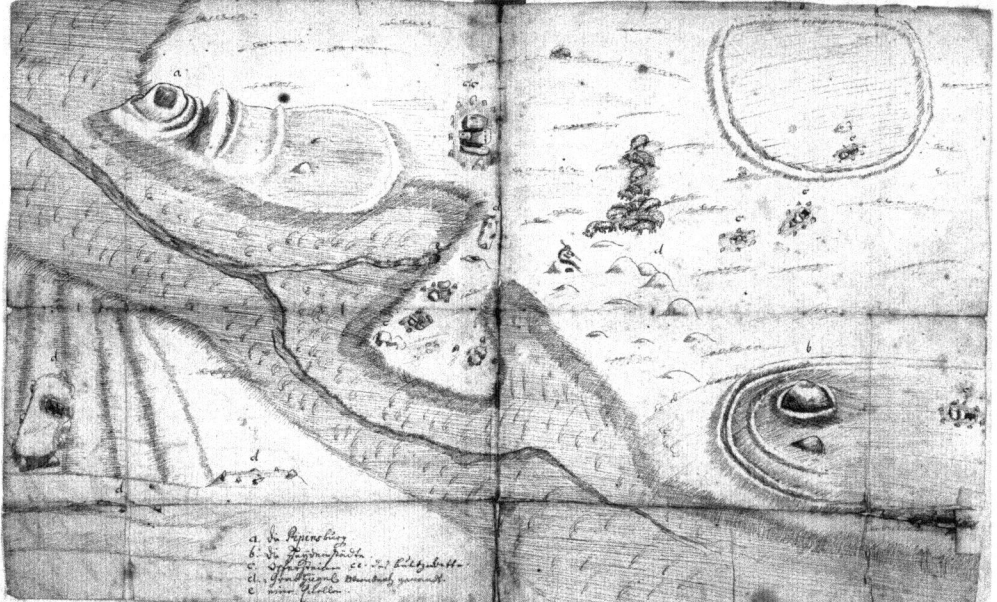

Fig. 8.5. Drawing of the landscape and monumental features at Sievern, Ldkr. Cuxhaven, around the year 1750 in MS *Palaeogentilismus Bremensis* of Martin Mushard. Left: Early-medieval Pipinsburg. Right, upper: Heidenstadt. Right, lower: Heidenschanze. Original in the Landesbibliothek Oldenburg. From Aufderhaar *et al.* 2011, Abb. 2.

of the Weser and the Weser estuary were controlled and possibly also defended from here, and that thus the system was completed by the coastal landing sites in the marsh (Aufderhaar 2016, 260–70).

However, Haarnagel's hypothesis (1961, 84–5) can hardly be confirmed by archaeological means: that behind the methodically executed resettlement of whole households in the marsh area, for which the new settlers had not only to bring in to the new settlement site their full households and livestock but also, above all, every bit of material for their buildings, could be inferred the driving power of the social elite to whom he attributed the construction of the Heidenschanze.

Following the abandonment of the Heidenschanze towards the end of the 1st century AD, the established system of settlements with various functions appears to have continued and indeed to have consolidated itself through to the Migration Period. In the course of the 4th and 5th centuries AD, however, with the abandonment of the mound settlements and of the settlement in Langenacker, this system evidently came to an end (Aufderhaar 2015, 132–6; 2016, 247–59).

Precisely at this juncture the construction of another enclosed site took place in the *Geest* region, which is now known by the name of *Heidenstadt* ('Heathen Site') (Fig. 8.5). Both the inner structure and the selection of location for this site show clear differences from the Heidenschanze. The 4.3 ha Heidenstadt was thus simply protected by a single ditch-and-bank system, in relation to which only partial remains of a wall in front or any internal revetment of the rampart that was piled up upon the rising sandy ground have been preserved. In the course of the archaeological excavations which the Archäologische Denkmalpflege des Landkreises Cuxhaven has conducted on three occasions so far since 2006 on the enclosure little, if any, evidence of a structure resembling a gateway has been found (Aufderhaar *et al.* 2011, 194–202).

The use of the Heidenstadt as a defensive site or refuge thus seems implausible, while the Heidenschanze was only 800 m away and less effort would have been required for the refortification of the system of ramparts of its central enclosure; these still stand up to 2 m high today.

The whole find-complex, and the lack of evidence of any contemporary building in the interior, clearly argue against any function of the Heidenstadt as a defensive fortification. Rather the rampart appears to express the enclosure of an interior space whose role should rather be ascribed to that of an assembly site in a ritual-cultic or social context (Aufderhaar 2015, 136–7; Aufderhaar *et al.* 2011, 201) – as is indicated for the Sievern region and Land Wursten for the Middle Ages and the Early Modern Period (Aufderhaar 2016, 267). The region has a few place- or field-names which contain the term *dingen*: the dwelling mound Dingen, part of the modern village of Imsum, and the land areas of Sachsendingen and Dingerweden situated immediately north of the Sievern Beck at the transition between the *Geest* and the clay area (Seghorn *et al.* 1995, 113, 171, 224). According to the analysis of Jürgen Udolph (1994; 2006; 2010, 57–8) such place-names may indicate sites where assemblies took place on a regular basis.

Among them, the area of Sachsendingen is of special interest. References to a farm at this site can be traced in the records of the Abbey of Neuenwalde as far back as 1383 (Rüther 1905). They document the donation of the farm as well as the parcel of land *thu den Sassegen Dynghen / thu den Sassegen Dinghen* (Rüther 1905, 143–5, Nos. 113–14) to the abbey. According to Udolph (pers. comm.), this may be translated as 'at the Saxon thing place / assembly site'. If such institutions were long lived, the interpretation of Sievern as an assembly site may also be revealed by historical documents. During his research into the medieval and post-medieval jurisdiction of the Land Wursten, Erich von Lehe (1973, 158; 1926, 80–1) also found references to a thing place of the public rural assembly (*allgemeine Landversammlung*) which was held in the immediate vicinity of the Feddersen Wierde (see also van Lengen 2003, 58, Abb. 1, 85).

Support for the interpretation of the role of the Heidenstadt, and possibly also of the Heidenschanze, in this way may also be found in the fact that both enclosed sites were embedded in a landscape which was characterized both by the interface with the moorlands that were difficult to cross and hostile to settlement and also especially by a high number of monuments to human activity such as megalithic graves and Bronze-age barrows. Some of these monuments in the landscape were incorporated into the ramparts of both enclosures (Aufderhaar *et al.* 2011, 179–80, Abb. 2).

Ethnographic studies have been able to show that such assertion of genealogical derivation can contribute to the process of communal or social generation (Parker Pearson 1999, 139–41), while it may also be exploited to legitimize claims of power or possession for the community (Abegg 2006, 271–3; Bernbeck 1997, 258–9).

The significance that the moorlands of the Sievern region had for its population in ritual terms is reflected in the numerous items which have been found deliberately deposited in a kettle bog (Aufderhaar 2015, 130; Schön 1987, 7; Aust 1982, 575–7) and in the marginal areas of the larger moorlike areas. Likewise the many gold hoards of the 6th century AD from Sievern have been found in the surroundings of the enclosed sites and the adjacent moorlands, and again demonstrate the importance of this area (Aufderhaar 2015, 137–8; 2016, 222–46). At the same time, the clear concentration of gold items in the Sievern area demonstrates that, despite the breaking up of the coastal settlements in the course of the 5th century AD, this region was still connected to transregional communication routes (Aufderhaar and Brandt 2011, 52), and that it certainly also had some special significance in social, political or religious terms.

The idea that the construction of the Heidenstadt and the deposition of the bracteates in the vicinity of Sievern could be connected to the progressive abandonment of several settlements in the marsh zone and in the *Geest* area, and also with the emigration of some of the population to England, is an attractive one, but in the final analysis it is simply unprovable.

Gudendorf-Köstersweg, Stadt Cuxhaven

In contrast to the enclosed sites of Sievern, there was a system of ramparts that is now lost, and has only been investigated to a minor extent, at Köstersweg in Gudendorf, Stadt Cuxhaven (Fig. 8.1); this has received little scholarly attention. The first investigations of the segment of rampart known as 'Oller Heiddiek' in the south-west of the Cuxhaven municipality were undertaken as early as 1928–9 by the later town archaeologist Karl Waller (1959, 23–4) because the earthwork was due to be removed to prepare the ground for agrarian use. According to the description of Bolko von Richthofen (1936, 37) and the plan of Karl Waller (1959, Kartentafel, Karte C) this section of the rampart extended approximately north-west–south-east across an outlier of *Geest* on the eastern slope of the Hohe Lieth. The surviving section-drawing shows a smoothly arched rampart heaped up upon sand, which revealed no signs of any structure of turves or any internal timber bracing. Despite the massive damage from the 1920s, the course of this barrier is still recognizable in some aerial photographs as a clear vegetational-growth anomaly.

During the subsequent demolition, some twenty fragments of millstone and sherds of pottery were retrieved. The material is now lost, but it was attributed to the 1st century AD by von Richthofen (1936, 37).

South of the rampart, according to the records of Karl Waller (*Ortsakte der Stadtarchäologie Cuxhaven*), when the heathland was ploughed in the 1920s, evidence of settlement was found in the form of wells, fire pits, granite millstones, whetstones and polishing stones, together with many sherds of pottery. The idea that there had been an extensive settlement site within the area bounded by the rampart was confirmed by several trial trenches, the discoveries in which were also assigned by Waller (1959, 23–4) to the Early Roman Iron Age.

In the course of archaeological excavations in the 1970s under the direction of Wolf Dieter Tempel (1980, 448 Abb. 1 no. 10, 449 Abb. 2, top) in the cemetery located immediately to the south of Köstersweg (cf. also Schön 2002; Schmid 1965; Waller 1959), a segment of rampart and remains of settlement were also found. The excavator interpreted this discovery as the western segment of an enclosing wall, 'in the interior of which, settlement remains of the Early Roman Iron Age through to the Migration Period were discovered' (Tempel 1980, 450, translated).

The association with settlement and transport topography

The topographical and practical communicational position of the system of ramparts at Gudendorf-Köstersweg is comparable with those of the Heidenschanze at Sievern. It is located in the eastern edge of the *Geest* ridge of Hohe Lieth, projections of which protrude into the marsh zone of Land Hadeln (Fig. 8.1).

The line of the land route reconstructed by Hans Aust (1956, 124; Haarnagel 1961, 77 84, Abb. 2) ran – depending upon how it crossed the floodplain of the Sieverner Bach around the Heidenschanze – on the uplands of the present district of Holßel diagonally across the *Geest* ridge of the Hohen Lieth and thence along its eastern side up to the hills of Cuxhaven (Fig. 8.1). It thus provided the settlement area of Gudendorf-Köstersweg with a valuable connexion to the regional and transregional land routes and a link to the enclosed sites of Sievern. The transport routes also formed a key target for the excavations of 1966 directed by Peter Schmid. He thus investigated approximately northeast–south-west aligned ridges in the ground and slight rises in the cemetery area 'which clearly [represent] the boundaries of ancient trackways' (Schmid 1965, 401, translated) that had been in use during the period of burial (Aust 1966).

To the east, the *Geest* ridge of the Hohen Lieth is bounded by the marsh of Land Hadeln, which runs from the southern bank of the mouth of the Elbe north of the

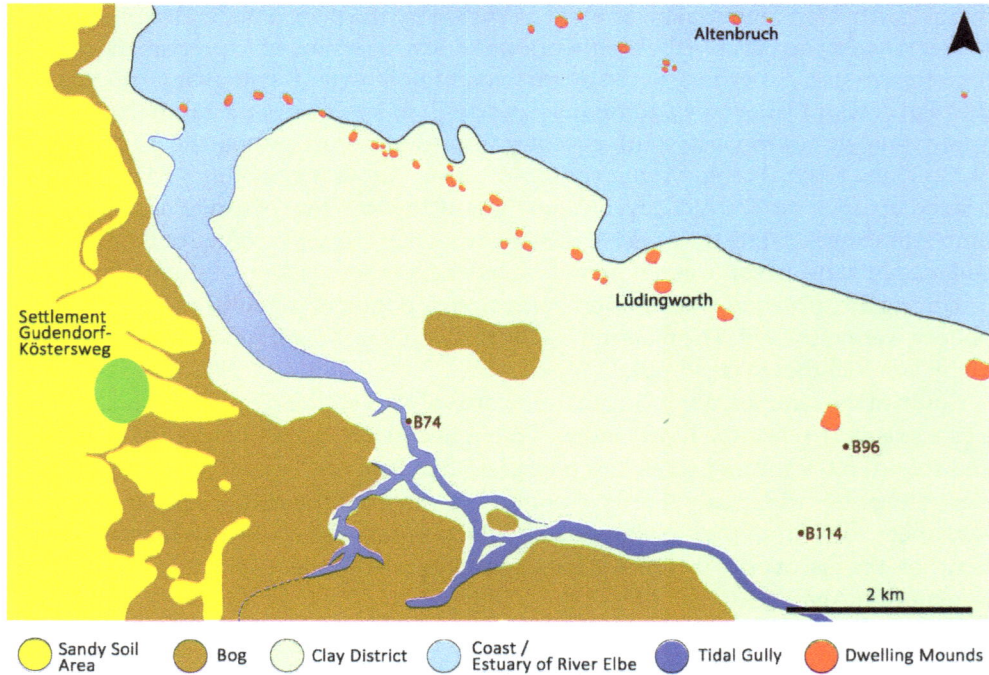

Fig. 8.6. Reconstruction of the palaeotopography of the *Geest* and marsh zones around Gudendorf-Köstersweg, Stadt Cuxhaven, in the first half of the 1st millennium AD. Graphics: Annette Siegmüller, NIhK, on the basis of data from the geological/soil-type maps of the marshes of Niedersachsen 1:5000 and the soil maps of the marsh region 1:25,000. From Aufderhaar and Siegmüller 2015, Abb. 5.

Hadeln Bay down to the raised ridges of the Bederkeser *Geest* in the south. The evaluation of information that geoscientific and geological mapping and coring have provided shows that the shoreline of the then still young marsh must have lain around 3–5 km further south than the present southern shore of the Elbe estuary in the Roman Iron Age.

Furthermore, the data enable us to reconstruct a major tidal waterway that ran through the western edge of the Hadelner marsh in the Roman Iron Age and probably also further on into the 1st millennium AD, which thus ran more or less parallel to the eastern edge of the *Geest* (Fig. 8.6). The creation of fine-grained sand banks and the erosion of the lower moor peat even within minor branches situated well inland testifies, for this period, to relatively high rates of flow. The force of the water which resulted probably hindered any silting of the waterway for a long time. North-east of the settlement site of Gudendorf the channel was relatively broad and had few side-branches. As, in this area, a depth of 1–2 m can be determined, even deeper water can be inferred for the broad main arm, so that it was undoubtedly navigable by small boats up to close to the edge of the *Geest*. While a chain of sunken and raised bogs ran between the course of the channel and the *Geest* region to the south and south-east of settlement site of Gudendorf, the channel was separated from the hills of Gudendorf only by a relatively narrow and thus clearly easily bridged band of sunken bog some 100–200 metres wide. Consequently, the settlement zone at Köstersweg was located in a protected but at the same time also a favourable position for natural communications (Aufderhaar and Siegmüller 2015, 157–9, Abb. 5).

This has left its mark also in the find material from the settlements and cemeteries in the wider area around Gudendorf. Here too it is possible to see a clear concentration of foreign items of Roman origin. Both the Roman Iron Age and Migration Period cemetery of Altenwalde, Stadt Cuxhaven, some 4 km from Gudendorf (Busch 1995, 242, 268, 280, 286), and likewise the cemetery of Gudendorf, which lay immediately alongside the ramparted structure and is as yet only partially published (most recently, Schön 2002), have produced various finds of provincial Roman provenance. These include *terra sigillata* vessels, coins, bronze and silver vessels, and metal dress-accessories and equipment such as brooches, chain mail and military belt-fittings (summarized in Erdrich 2002, 102–10; Schön 1989).

In the same way, in the case of at least eight of the Roman Iron Age settlement sites in the marshlands of Land Hadeln, it is documented that those who lived in these marsh settlements also had access to foreign goods. The find material here includes above all fragments of Roman pottery, glass and glass beads, as well as Roman coins (Erdrich 2002, 102, 110, 130–2; Schön 1999a, 36; 1999b).

The topographical situation of these settlements on the shoreline of the Elbe mouth and on the smaller watercourses (Schmid 1995, 226–7; Haarnagel 1976, 11–14, 16–17) encourages one to conclude that the marsh settlements – like the settlements in the marsh area of Land Wursten – provided well-suited landing places for ships which travelled along the Elbe. The reconstruction of the palaeo-landscape of the marsh of the western side of Land Hadeln with is waterways leads to the view that here, too, a water network of channels and streams provided convenient paths for smaller boats and thus contact with the *Geest* areas (Aufderhaar and Siegmüller 2015, 153).

Fig. 8.7. Greyscale plot of the magnetometer survey of Gudendorf-Köstersweg. Graphics: Dirk Dallaserra and Iris Aufderhaar, NIhK. Base map drawn from the *Geobasisdaten* of the Niedersächsiche Vermessungs- und Katasterverwaltung, German base map 1:5000, sheets 22801 and 22807, © LGLN 1996. From Aufderhaar and Siegmüller 2015, Abb. 7.

Between Sievern and Gudendorf

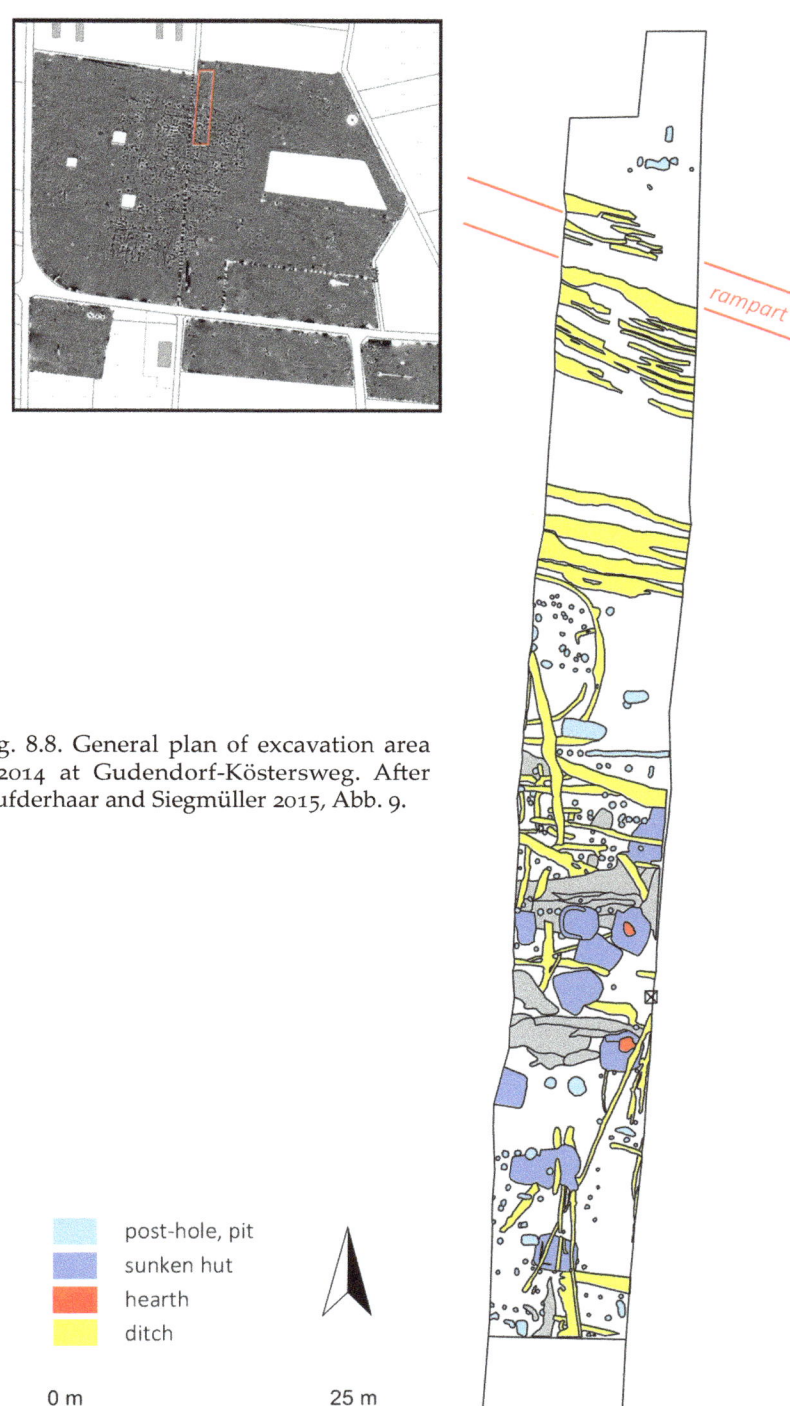

Fig. 8.8. General plan of excavation area 1/2014 at Gudendorf-Köstersweg. After Aufderhaar and Siegmüller 2015, Abb. 9.

The results of geomagnetic surveying and archaeological sondages

In Gudendorf, an area of 25 ha in total was surveyed by magnetometer, incorporating the entire settlement area, the rampart and parts of the cemetery. In the greyscale plot (Fig. 8.7) a strong concentration of round to rectangular, distinct and sharply defined anomalies can be seen within a fairly clearly bounded area some 300 m long and 200 m wide, in addition to elongated to bow-shaped, less clearly visible structures. The northern limit of this area is formed by the rampart area, which appears in the greyscale plot as a weak, rather streaky looking anomaly, which adjoins the settlement with a narrow boundary line (Aufderhaar and Siegmüller 2015, 161–2).

In the summer of 2014, what was indicated by the geophysics was tested by means of an archaeological sondage. The area excavated, a north–south strip around 110 m long and 12 m wide (Fig. 8.8), was selected so that an area would be exposed which not only appeared in the greyscale magnetometry plot as one with potential settlement structures but also cut across the line of the rampart. The archaeological discoveries were able to confirm the results of the geophysics thoroughly. In the area opened, a dense concentration of partially intercutting archaeological features appeared, which agreed closely with the anomalies visible in the greyscale magnetometric plot. In addition, a clear division into two was evident within the area of excavation.

This involved the southern part of the whole north–south trial trench being marked by a clear density of overlying settlement traces which, in the course of the excavation, proved to be as the remains of post-pits – often in clear rows – trenches, pits and *Grubenhäuser*. On the evidence of the stratigraphical relationships, the construction of *Grubenhäuser* in the settlement area was one of the latest phases of use of the Köstersweg site. It was possible to collect pottery from the features which enable us to date the structures uncovered in the area excavated to the period between the 2nd and the 4th/5th centuries AD. The finds from the area excavated also suggest that the settlement area was associated with craft-production.

The northern part of the trench, by contrast, was dominated by three groups of ditches lying parallel to one another. These crossed the area excavation site in a north-west–south-east direction and thus respected the line of the rampart, insofar as it can be reconstructed through cartography and cropmarks. The position of the rampart itself is not really detectable in the area, but in the long section along the edge of the trench the remains of the base of the rampart appeared clearly. In the sand of the rampart-fill it was possible to find remains of pottery and flecks of charcoal. In order to exclude any erroneous date from the preserved material from the settlement finds immediately to the south of the rampart, samples were taken for dating by means of the Optically Stimulated Luminescence (OSL) technique from the remaining soil of the Iron-age moraine and from three separate areas of the rampart-fill (Aufderhaar and Siegmüller 2015, 164–6, Abb. 9). The examination in the Geographical Institute of the Justus-Liebig-Universität of Gießen gave the samples taken from the rampart fill (sample nos. GI138–GI140) an age of 2.1±0.2 ka, indicating a construction date for the system of ramparts at Gudendorf similar to that for the enclosure of Heidenschanze at Sievern, within the last two centuries BC and the 1st century AD.

Spieka-Knill

Considerably less is known about a ditched site which was first discovered together with other settlement traces, in the context of a rescue excavation, in the year 2000 in the district of Spieka-Knill, Gemeinde Wurster Nordseeküste (Fig. 8.1). As evidence of a possible defensive enclosure one may note segments of two ditches up to 4.2 m wide which, on the evidence of the stratigraphy recorded, represent separate settlement phases. From the fill of the older of the two ditches pottery was retrieved which can be assigned to the Roman Iron Age (*Ortsakte Spieka, Archäologische Denkmalpflege Ldkr. Cuxhaven*). No set of ramparts associated with the ditches has yet been identified.

The alignment of the north–south ditches, running parallel to the edge of the *Geest*, does, however, suggest that the naturally protected site of a settlement was additionally guarded by means of the ditches here. This conforms to the observation that, to the east of the ditches, on the side of the *Geest*, the surface finds recorded by the *Archäologische Landesaufnahme des Landkreises Cuxhaven* independently point to the presence of a widespread settlement area of the Roman Iron Age and the Migration Period. Furthermore, in the course of other rescue excavations, many additional settlement features including two buildings, *Grubenhäuser* and wells have been recorded, with pottery of the Roman Iron Age in their fills (Schön 2001; Aust 1982, 706 No. 81; 1980, 1–2).

The association with settlement and transport topography

Spieka-Knill lies on the northern end of the Roman-period marsh in Land Wursten, as it can be reconstructed from the results of the historical-geographical researches of Werner Haarnagel (1979), Peter Schmid (1988) and most recently Karl Ernst Behre (1994). According to these studies, the marsh ran in a broad sweep closer to the *Geest* zone here, and at the hills of Spieka-Knill was probably only about 700 m across (Fig. 8.1). The find spot itself is located in an exposed position on the western slope of the Hohe Lieth on a distinct spur of land which is bounded to the west by the marsh of Land Wursten and to the south by the 400 m wide valley of the Scharnsteder Bach, across which the settlement would have had access to the coast (Aufderhaar and Siegmüller 2015, 159–61).

Of especial importance for the find spot of Spieka-Knill and its connection with the coastal maritime links along the North Sea coast is the discovery of a D-bracteate (Axboe *et al.* 1989, IK 472) which was retrieved from ploughsoil only about 100 m from the settlement site in 1977. It strongly suggests that in the 6th century the settlement had a special place in the western Elbe–Weser region, and in links with the area of southern Scandinavia (Aust 1982, 708 No. 102; 1980). It is in fact, up to now, the only bracteate find in the north-western Elbe–Weser triangle that does not lie within Sievern's immediate area of influence (for an overview Häßler 2003, 128–9; Hauck 1970).

The Spieka bracteates are classified by Alexandra Pesch (2007, 268–75) as an associated form (D8,a) of her *Formularfamilie* D8, the pictorial design of which displays a short, straight link between the end of the shoulder loop and the upper leg. This then runs parallel with the edge of the pictorial field and bends as the lower leg towards the centre of the design, so that the three sections form a bracket-like shape.

The principal area of distribution of *Formularfamilie* D8 is in Jutland and southern central Sweden; it is markedly less frequent on the Continent. In Niedersachsen the only other specimen so far know is from Sievern, about 10 km south of Spieka (Axboe *et al.* 1989, IK 506; cf. Pesch 2007, 270, 413–15). With the strongly jagged outer edge of the D-shaped eye-frame, the design of the piece from Spieka appears to stand close to that from Sievern (cf. Fig. 8.2, upper), which is assigned to *Formularfamilie* D9 (Pesch 2007, 276–85; Axboe *et al.* 1989, IK 505 and IK 507).

According to the model of Hans Aust (1956, 124; cf. also Haarnagel 1961, 77, 84, Abb. 2) the find spot of Spieka lay on one side of the main line of the overland route that linked the enclosed sites of Sievern and Gudendorf. On the basis of the distribution of burial mounds in the *Geest* regions of the north-western Elbe–Weser triangle, Annette Siegmüller (2015, 176–7, Abb. 2) has reconstructed side-roads by which the settlements on the western side of the Hohe Lieth – including the settlement at Spieka-Knill – may have been connected to the main routeway and thus to the areas of Sievern and Gudendorf.

The results of geomagnetic surveying and archaeological sondages

At Spieka-Knill, an area of 10.8 ha has been surveyed by magnetometer (Fig. 8.9). As at Gudendorf (above), the greyscale plot revealed numerous clear structures, dominated by sharply defined, large oval to rectangular anomalies. The occasional elongated structures lying in between these may be of natural origin, although an interpretation as enclosed tracks or ditches is not impossible. There is also a series of anomalies including many small dipoles scattered across the entire area which are probably to be attributed to metal fragments, burnt clay and stone within the activity layer (Aufderhaar and Siegmüller 2015, 162–4).

Also in the case of the site of Spieka-Knill, the results of magnetometric survey were tested by an archaeological sondage, in the summer of 2015. The preliminary results of the excavations are briefly presented here.

In the area of 65 × 11 m opened, and in a trial trench some 70 m long and 3 m wide north of the main area of excavation, a dense concentration of archeologically recognizable structures was uncovered. In the process of excavation, these could be identified as the remains of pits and fence-trenches, and particularly rows of posts and wall-trenches of houses as well as *Grubenhäuser*. In keeping with the results of the geophysics, as expected, close agreement between the anomalies mapped and the positions of *Grubenhäuser* was established. In contrast to Gudendorf, however, the remains of the ordinary buildings and the ditch-lines were not strongly reflected in the magnetometry.

In the edge-section of the excavated trench, a 25 cm thick humic layer was observed between the ploughsoil and the sandy natural ground. In contrast to the relatively find-poor topsoil, this layer was characterized by many flecks of charcoal and fragments of pottery, so that it could be considered the remains of a culture layer, which was probably the source of the dipoles scattered over the entire area surveyed.

As well as pottery of the Roman Iron Age and Migration Period, the finds from Spieka-Knill comprised remains of craft-production such as slag and metallurgical ceramics, including heavily burnt sherds, fragments of tuyère and half of an ingot-mould. There were also some imported goods, including fragments of various *terra sigillata* vessels

Fig. 8.9. Greyscale plot of the magnetometer survey of Spieka-Knill, Ldkr. Cuxhaven. Graphics: Dirk Dallaserra and Iris Aufderhaar, NIhK. Base map drawn from the *Geobasisdaten* of the Niedersächsiche Vermessungs- und Katasterverwaltung, German base map 1:5000, sheet 22171, © LGLN 1996. From Aufderhaar and Siegmüller 2015, Abb. 8.

and three coins, probably also of Roman origin.

Up to the area that is affected by modern building, the magnetometric prospection appears to have investigated the site of a widespread settlement of the Roman Iron Age and the Migration Period relatively fully, which must then have covered an area of more than 4 ha. Alongside evidence for the use of the excavated area for craftwork, there are also remains of imported goods, which, together with the bracteate find of 1970 (Aust 1980), corroborate the close connection of this settlement with the system of communication routes of the Roman Iron Age and Migration Period.

Structural models and prospects

The state of research presented here makes it clear that a comprehensive assessment of the settlement structure within the north-western part of the Elbe–Weser triangle is required, in order to reconstruct the settlement structure and social organization of the first half of the 1st millennium AD in the area between the mouths of the Weser and Elbe. Only then can it be possible to understand how social, economic and religious life was organized in this area, which was extremely favourable for transport and highly significant for transregional communications. With it, the two enclosed sites at Sievern and Gudendorf played a central role, and the communities settled around them had access to transregional exchange of goods. We can therefore infer that they profited from the transport routes along the North Sea and within the estuaries of the Elbe and the Weser.

The construction, maintenance and preservation of the enclosure system at Gudendorf, just like that at Heidenschanze and later Heidenstadt at Sievern, is evidence of a huge communal investment from a population that would presumably have been drawn from the wider hinterland of the enclosed sites. It is a plausible suggestion that these works were initiated and organized by members of a socially recognized upper class, whose influence was sufficient to mobilize an appropriate level of manpower.

The range of finds renders it clear that this circle of people not only had access to appropriate goods but also, at least in part, had some knowledge of the Roman-influenced customs of representation. In the case of the Migration Period, the bracteate finds from the area of Spieka-Knill and the Sievern region, and the neckring found there, suggest contact with the elites of southern Scandinavia and south-eastern England (Aufderhaar and Brandt 2011, 51–2).

The interim assessment of the excavation results also reveals that to some extent the enclosed sites and the settlement structures in their hinterlands followed individual courses of development after their foundation in the final centuries BC or the 1st century AD. It is in any event to be assumed that, although the enclosed sites of Sievern and Gudendorf were set back from the coastline on the edge of the *Geest* ridge of the Hohe Lieth, they had access to the transport routes along the Outer Weser and the area of the mouth of the Elbe through the mound settlements in the adjacent marshland. The find spot of Spieka-Knill, by contrast, enjoyed direct access to the coast and to the Scharnsteder Bach which flowed down from the *Geest*. The land route reconstructed by Aust (1956), at least, also ran in the immediate vicinity of the enclosed site of Gudendorf-Köstersweg. This shows that the enclosed sites were probably also connected to land routes and that these were also under the supervision and protection of those sites.

The pattern of settlements around the enclosed sites thus occupied key points in the network of water- and land-based communication routes. With this, a role in the management and maintenance of the land routes – but particularly the maritime routes – in the western Elbe–Weser triangle can also be assumed for the settlement pattern around the enclosed sites of Sievern and Gudendorf-Köstersweg, as well as for the region around Spieka-Knill. They not only had control over the routes along the coast but also over ships which travelled or crossed the estuaries of the great river-systems.

Also noteworthy is the distribution of the settlement areas with enclosed sites along the coast line of the north-western Elbe–Weser triangle (Fig. 8.1). If one agrees with the inferences of Torsten Capelle (1995, 7), who proposed that the maritime routes of the first half of the 1st millennium AD kept within sight of the coast and that journeys involved nightly landfalls or anchoring in shallow waters, the individual landing points may be associated with single days' stages.

Altogether there is much to suggest that the early enclosed sites in the *Geest* region of the western Elbe–Weser triangle, along with the settlement pattern that surrounded them, constituted a structural foundation for communication and trade routes in the hinterland of the coastal landing places in the period between the birth of Christ and the Migration Period, or at least for certain phases within this period.

References

Abegg, Angelika 2006, 'Orte der Toten. Nachbestattungen der Römischen Kaiserzeit in eisenzeitlichen Grabhügeln'. In *Studien zur Lebenswelt der Eisenzeit*, Reallexikon der germanischen Altertumskunde, Ergänzungsband 53, ed. W. R. Teegen *et al.* (Berlin–New York), 265–78.

Aufderhaar, Iris 2015, 'Der Raum Sievern und das Land Wursten – Zur Entwicklung und Bedeutung einer Region mit zentralörtlichen Merkmalen im westlichen Elbe–Weser-Dreieck'. In *Mensch – Landschaft – Meer: 75 Jahre Niedersächsisches Institut für historische Küstenforschung*, Siedlungs- und Küstenforschung im südlichen Nordseegebiet 38, ed. E. Strahl, A. Siegmüller, M. Karle and U. M. Meier (Rahden–Westf.) 123–44.

Aufderhaar, Iris 2016, 'Sievern, Ldkr. Cuxhaven. Analyse zur Entwicklung einer Mikroregion mit zentralörtlichen Merkmalen im westlichen Elbe–Weser-Dreieck von der ausgehenden Vorrömischen Eisenzeit bis zum 6. Jh. n. Chr.', *Studien zur Landschafts- und Siedlungsgeschichte im südlichen Nordseegebiet* 8 (Rahden–Westf.).

Aufderhaar, Iris, and Annette Siegmüller 2015, 'Befestigungen und Siedlungen im nordwestlichen Elbe–Weser-Dreieck – Erste Ergebnisse der Untersuchungen in Gudendorf und Spieka-Knill'. In *Mensch – Landschaft – Meer: 75 Jahre Niedersächsisches Institut für historische Küstenforschung*, Siedlungs- und Küstenforschung im südlichen Nordseegebiet 38, ed. E. Strahl, A. Siegmüller, M. Karle and U. M. Meier (Rahden–Westf.), 145–71.

Aufderhaar, Iris, Felix Bittmann, Imke Brandt, Hauke Jöns, Christina Klein, Matthias D. Schön, Harald Stümpel, Steffen Wolters and Wolf Hajo Zimmermann 2009, 'Neue Forschungen am Zentralplatz von Sievern, Ldkr. Cuxhaven', *Germania* 87, 173–220.

Aufderhaar, Iris, and Imke Brandt 2011, 'Herrschaft am Knotenpunkt. Die Verkehrsanbindungen der Region Sievern, Ldkr. Cuxhaven, während des frühen 1. Jahrtausends n. Chr', *Archäologie in Niedersachsen* 14, 50–4.

Aust, Hans 1956, 'Studien zur Urgeschichte der südlichen Hohen Lieth. Übersicht der Funde und Versuch ihrer zeitlichen Einordnung', Unveröffentlichte Mittelschullehrer-Prüfungsarbeit, Pädagogische Hochschule Oldenburg.

Aust, Hans 1966, 'Gudendorf (Kösters Weg), Kr. Land Hadeln', *Nachrichten des Marschenrates zur Förderung der Forschung im Küstengebiet der Nordsee* 7, 15–16.

Aust, Hans 1980, 'Ein neuer D-Brakteat aus Nordholz, Ldkr. Cuxhaven, Niedersachsen', *Studien zur Sachsenforschung* 2, 1–4.

Aust, Hans 1982, 'Die Vor- und Frühgeschichte des Landkreises Cuxhaven 1. Altkreis Wesermünde', Unveröffentlichte Dissertation, Universität Hamburg.

Axboe, Morten, Klaus Düwel, Karl Hauck, Lutz von Padberg and Heike Rulffs 1989, *Die Goldbrakteaten der Völkerwanderungszeit 3:1. Ikonographischer Katalog (IK3, Text)*, Münstersche Mittelalter-Schriften 24/3:1 (München).

Behre, Karl-Ernst 1994, *Kleine historische Landeskunde des Elbe–Weser-Raumes* (Stade).

Berke, Stefan 1990, *Römische Bronzegefäße und Terra Sigillata in der Germania libera*, Boreas – Münstersche Beiträge zur Archäologie, Beiheft 7 (Münster).

Bernbeck, Reinhard 1997, *Theorien in der Archäologie.* Uni-Taschenbücher 1964 (Tübingen–Basel).
Bischop, Dieter 2000, *Siedler, Söldner und Piraten. Chauken und Sachsen im Bremer Raum. Begleitpublikation zur Ausstellung im Focke-Museum/Bremer Landesmuseum vom 08.03. bis 14.05.2000,* Bremer Archäologische Blätter, Beiheft 2 (Bremen).
Bischop, Dieter 2001, *Die römische Kaiserzeit und frühe Völkerwanderungszeit zwischen Weser und Hunte* (Oldenburg).
Böhme, Horst Wolfgang 1986, 'Das Ende der Römerherrschaft in Britannien und die angelsächsische Besiedlung Englands im 5. Jahrhundert', *Jahrbuch des Römisch-Germanischen Zentralmuseums Mainz* 33, 469–574.
Brandt, Imke 2015, Sievern, Ldkr. Cuxhaven, und sein Umland – Paläotopographie des ersten nachchristlichen Jahrtausends. In *Mensch – Landschaft – Meer: 75 Jahre Niedersächsisches Institut für historische Küstenforschung,* Siedlungs- und Küstenforschung im südlichen Nordseegebiet 38, ed. E. Strahl, A. Siegmüller, M. Karle and U. M. Meier (Rahden/Westf.), 287–96.
Brather, Sebastian 1996, 'Merowinger- und karolingerzeitliches „Fremdgut" bei den Nordslawen. Gebrauchsgut und Elitenkultur im südwestlichen Ostseeraum', *Prähistorische Zeitschrift* 71, 46–84.
Busch, Ralf 1995, *Rom an der Niederelbe,* Veröffentlichungen des Hamburger Museums für Archäologie und die Geschichte Harburgs (Helms-Museum) 74 (Neumünster).
Capelle, Torsten 1990, *Archäologie der Angelsachsen* (Darmstadt).
Eggers, Hans Jürgen 1951, *Der römische Import im freien Germanien,* Atlas der Urgeschichte 1 (Hamburg).
Ellmers, Detlev 2005, 'Seewege'. In *Reallexikon der germanischen Altertumskunde* 28 (Berlin, New York), 74–84.
Erdrich, Michael 2001, *Rom und die Barbaren. Das Verhältnis zwischen dem Imperium Romanum und den germanischen Stämmen vor seiner Nordwestgrenze von der späten römischen Republik bis zum gallischen Sonderreich,* Römisch-Germanische Forschungen 58 (Mainz).
Erdrich, Michael 2002, *Corpus der römischen Funde im europäischen Barbaricum 4. Hansestadt Bremen und Bundesland Niedersachsen* (Bonn).
Haarnagel, Werner 1961, 'Probleme der Siedlungsforschung im Küstengebiet zwischen Weser und Elbe in der Spätlatènezeit', *Jahrbuch der Männer vom Morgenstern* 42, 74–85.
Haarnagel, Werner 1965, 'Die Grabung auf der Heidenschanze bei Wesermünde im Jahr 1958'. In *Studien aus Alteuropa. Festschrift für K. Tackenberg 2,* Bonner Jahrbücher, Beiheft 10:2, ed. R. von Uslar and K. J. Narr (Köln–Graz), 142–78.
Haarnagel, Werner 1971, 'Die Ringwallanlagen Heidenschanze und Pipinsburg im Kreis Wesermünde, Gemarkung Sievern'. In *Ringwall und Burg in der Archäologie West-Niedersachsens. Ausstellung in der „Burg" Arkenstede des Museumsdorfes Cloppenburg, Juni bis Oktober 1971,* ed. H. Ottenjann (Cloppenburg), 11–18.
Haarnagel, Werner 1976, 'Die Marschen- und Wurtenentwicklungen im Elbe–Weser-Winkel'. In *Das Elb-Weser-Dreieck 2. Forschungsprobleme – Exkursionen: Stade, Zeven, Bremervörde, Buxtehude,* Führer zu ur- und frühgeschichtlichen Denkmälern 30 (Mainz), 1–22.
Haarnagel, Werner 1979, *Die Grabung Feddersen Wierde. Methode, Hausbau, Siedlungs- und Wirtschaftsformen sowie Sozialstruktur,* Feddersen Wierde 2 (Wiesbaden).
Häßler, Hans-Jürgen 2003, *Frühes Gold. Ur- und frühgeschichtliche Goldfunde aus Niedersachsen. Fundgeschichte und kulturhistorische Impressionen.* Begleitheft zu Ausstellungen der Urgeschichts-Abteilung des Niedersächsischen Landesmuseums Hannover 10 (Hannover).
Hauck, Karl 1970, *Die Goldbrakteaten aus Sievern. Spätantike Amulett-Bilder der „Dania Saxonica" und die Sachsen-„Origo" bei Widukind von Corvey.* Münstersche Mittelalter-Schriften 1 (München).
Jöns, Hauke 2009, 'Überlegungen zu Transport- und Kommunikationswegen des 1. Jahrtausends im nordwestdeutschen Küstengebiet'. In *Historia Archaeologica. Frühes Mittelalter im nördlichen Europa. Festschrift Für Heiko Steuer,* Reallexikon der germanischen Altertumskunde, Ergänzungsband 70, ed. S. Brather (Berlin), 389–413.
Lehe, Erich von 1926, *Grenzen und Ämter im Herzogtum Bremen – Altes Amt und Zentralverwaltung*

Bremervörde, Land Wursten und Gogericht Achim, Studien und Vorarbeiten zum Historischen Atlas von Niedersachsen 8 (Göttingen).

Lehe, Erich von 1973, *Geschichte des Landes Wursten* (Bremerhaven).

Lengen, Hajo van 2003, 'Tota Frisia: Sieben Seeland und mehr. Die territoriale Gliederung des freien Frieslands im Mittelalter: ein Überblick mit einer Karte'. In *Die friesische Freiheit des Mittelalters: Leben und Legende. Begleitband zur Sonderausstellung der Ostfriesischen Landschaft, 15. Juni bis 14. September 2003*, ed. H. van Lengen (Aurich), 56–89.

Lund Hansen, Ulla 1987, *Römischer Import im Norden. Warenaustausch zwischen dem Römischen Reich und dem freien Germanien während der Kaiserzeit unter besonderer Berücksichtigung Nordeuropas*, Nordiske Fortidsminder B:10 (Kopenhagen).

Nørgård Jørgensen, Anne 2001, 'Sea defence in the Roman Iron Age'. In *Military aspects of the aristocracy in Barbaricum in the Roman and Early Migration Periods. Papers from an International Research Seminar at the Danish National Museum, Copenhagen, 10–11 December 1999*, Publications from the National Museum, Studies in Archaeology and History 5, ed. B. Storgaard (Copenhagen), 67–82.

Nørgård Jørgensen, Anne 2003, 'Befestigungsanlagen und Verkehrskontrolle auf dem Land- und Wasserweg in der vorrömischen Eisenzeit und der römischen Kaiserzeit'. In *Sieg und Triumpf. Der Norden im Schatten des Römischen Reiches*, ed. L. Jørgensen, B. Storgaard u. L. Gebauer Thomsen (Copenhagen), 194–209.

Parker Pearson, Mike 1999, *The Archaeology of Death and Burial* (Stroud).

Pesch, Alexandra 2005: 'Und die Götter sind überall', *Archäologie in Deutschland* 4, 6–9.

Pesch, Alexandra 2007, *Die Goldbrakteaten der Völkerwanderungszeit. Thema und Variation*, Reallexikon der germanischen Altertumskunde, Ergänzungsband 36 (Berlin–New York).

Pesch, Alexandra 2011, 'Netzwerk der Zentralplätze. Elitenkontakte und Zusammenarbeit frühmittelalterlicher Reichtumszentren im Spiegel der Goldbrakteaten'. In *Die Goldbrakteaten der Völkerwanderungszeit. Auswertungen und Neufunde*, Reallexikon der germanischen Altertumskunde, Ergänzungsband 40, ed. W. Heizmann and M. Axboe (Berlin–New York), 231–77.

Richthofen, B. von 1936, 'Burgwallforschung in Hamburg', *Nordelbingen* 12, 35–8.

Rüther, Heinrich, 1905, *Urkundenbuch des Klosters Neuenwalde* (Hannover–Leipzig).

Scheschkewitz, Jonathan 2009, 'Die Ringwallanlagen in Nordwestniedersachsen'. In *Ringwälle und verwandte Strukturen des ersten Jahrtausends n. Chr. an Nord- und Ostsee*, Schriften des Archäologischen Landesmuseums 5, ed. M. Segschneider (Neumünster), 185–99.

Schmid, Peter 1965, 'Neufunde aus dem kaiser- bis völkerwanderungszeitlichen Gräberfeld von Gudendorf, Kr. Land Hadeln', *Germania* 43, 401–4.

Schmid, Peter 1988, 'Die mittelalterliche Neubesiedlung der niedersächsischen Marsch'. In *Archeologie en landschap*, ed. M. Bierma, O. H. Harsema and W. van Zeist (Groningen), 133–64.

Schmid, Peter 1990, 'Siedlungsarchäologische Ergebnisse zum mittelalterlichen Landesausbau im Land Wursten', *Jahrbuch der Männer vom Morgenstern* 69, 355–66.

Schmid, Peter 1995, Archäologische Ergebnisse zur Siedlungs- und Wirtschaftsweise in der Marsch. In *Geschichte des Landes zwischen Elbe und Weser 1. Vor- und Frühgeschichte*, Schriftenreihe des Landschaftsverbandes der ehemaligen Herzogtümer Bremen und Verden 7, ed. H.-E. Dannenberg and H.-J. Schulze (Stade), 221–50.

Schön, Matthias D. 1987, *Opfer der Vorzeit. Moorfunde, Depotfunde aus dem Landkreis Cuxhaven. Führer zu Ausstellungen und Geländedenkmalen* 3 (Bad Bederkesa).

Schön, Matthias D. 1989, 'Zum Import römischer Metallgefäße in das nordwestliche Elbe–Weser-Dreieck während der jüngeren Römischen Kaiserzeit'. In *Landschaft und regionale Identität. Beiträge zur Geschichte der ehemaligen Herzogtümer Bremen und Verden und des Landes Hadeln*, Schriftenreihe des Landschaftsverbandes der ehemaligen Herzogtümer Bremen und Verden 3, ed. H.-J. Schulze and H.-E. Dannenberg (Stade), 38–51.

Schön, Matthias D. 1999a, *Feddersen Wierde, Fallward, Flögeln. Archäologie im Museum Burg Bederkesa, Landkreis Cuxhaven* (Bad Bederkesa).

Schön, M. D. 1999b, 'Gräber und Siedlungen bei Otterndorf-Westernwörden, Landkreis Cuxhaven', *Probleme der Küstenforschung im südlichen Nordseegebiet* 26 (Oldenburg), 123–208.

Schön, Matthias D. 2000a, 'Die Heidenschanze bei Sievern. Eine fast 2000 Jahre alte Befestigung', *Archäologie in Niedersachsen* 3, 57–9.

Schön, Matthias D. 2000b, 'Eindrucksvolle Befestigung an der Nordseeküste', *Archäologie in Deutschland* 2/2000, 43.

Schön, Matthias D. 2001, 'EG Nordholz, Spieka FStNr. 81', *Nachrichten des Marschenrates zur Förderung der Forschung im Küstengebiet der Nordsee* 38, 28.

Schön, Matthias D., 2002, 'Ein Körpergrab von dem gemischt belegten Gräberfeld von Gudendorf bei Cuxhaven'. In *Forschungen zur Archäologie und Geschichte in Norddeutschland. Festschrift für Wolf-Dieter Tempel*, ed. U. Masemann (Rotenburg–Wümme), 299–315.

Seghorn, Irmgard, Else Syassen, Fritz Hörmann, Ude Meyer, Christian Morisse, Eberhardt Nehring and Egon Stuve 1995, *Flurnamensammlung Wesermünde. Die Flurnamen des Grundsteuerkatasters von 1876*, Sonderveröffentlichungen des Heimatbundes der Männer vom Morgenstern 27 (Bremerhaven).

Segschneider, Martin 2002, 'Trade and centrality between the Rhine and the Limfjord around 500 AD. The beachmarket on the Northfrisian island Amrum and its context'. In *Central Places in the Migration and Merovingian Periods. Papers from the 52nd Sachsensymposium 2001*, Uppåkrastudier 6, ed. B. Hårdh and L. Larsson (Lund), 247–56.

Siegmüller, Annette 2015, 'Siedlung – Verkehrsweg – Landschaft. Römisch-kaiserzeitliche Landeplatzstrukturen im Unterweserraum'. In *Mensch – Landschaft – Meer: 75 Jahre Niedersächsisches Institut für historische Küstenforschung*, Siedlungs- und Küstenforschung im südlichen Nordseegebiet 38, ed. E. Strahl, A. Siegmüller, M. Karle and U. M. Meier (Rahden–Westf.), 173–90.

Siegmüller, Annette 2011, 'Vom Umschlagplatz zum Ufermarkt', *Archäologie in Niedersachsen* 14, 63–6.

Siegmüller, Annette, and Hauke Jöns 2011, 'Aktuelle Forschungen zu Weser und Hunte als Wege der Kommunikation und des Austauschs während des 1. Jahrtausends n. Chr.' *Nachrichten aus Niedersachsens Urgeschichte* 80, 97–115.

Siegmüller, Annette and Hauke Jöns 2012, 'Ufermärkte, Wurten, Geestrandburgen. Herausbildung differenter Siedlungstypen im Küstengebiet in Abhängigkeit von der Paläotopographie im 1. Jahrtausend', *Archäologisches Korrespondenzblatt* 42, 573–93.

Tempel, Wolf-Dieter 1980, 'Ein völkerwanderungszeitlicher Grabhügel beim sächsischen Gräberfeld von Gudendorf, Stadt Cuxhaven, Niedersachsen', *Studien zur Sachsenforschung* 2 (Oldenburg), 447–55.

Thomsen, Per O., Benno Blæsild, Nis Hardt and Karsten Kjer Michaelsen 1993, *Lundeborg – en handelsplads fra jernalderen*, Skrifter fra Svendborg og Omegns Museum 32 (Ringe).

Udolph, Jürgen 1994, *Namenskundliche Studien zum Germanenproblem*, Ergänzungsbände zum Reallexikon der Germanischen Altertumskunde 9 (Berlin, New York).

Udolph, Jürgen 2006, 'Thing und Thie in Ortsnamen', *Namenskundliche Informationen*, Beiheft 23, 37–53.

Udolph, Jürgen 2010, 'The Evidence of Central Places in Place Names'. In *Trade and Communication Networks of the First Millennium AD in the Northern Part of Central Europe: Central Places, Beach Markets, Landing Places and Trading Centres*, Neue Studien zur Sachsenforschung 1, ed. B. Ludowici, H. Jöns, S. Kleingärtner, J. Scheschkewitz and M. Hardt. (Hannover), 49–68.

Ulriksen, Jens 1998, *Anløbspladser: Besejling og bebyggelse i Danmark mellem 200 og 1100 e. Kr.* (Roskilde).

Ulriksen, Jens 2004, 'Danish coastal landing places and their relation to navigation and trade'. In *Land, Sea and Home. Proceedings of a Conference on Viking-Period Settlement at Cardiff, July 2001*, Society for Medieval Archaeology, Monograph Series 20, ed. J. Hines, A. Lane and M. Redknap (Leeds), 7–26.

Waller, Karl 1959, *Die Gräberfelder von Hemmoor, Quelkhorn, Gudendorf und Duhnen-Wehrberg in Niedersachsen*, Beiheft zum Atlas der Urgeschichte 8 (Hamburg).

Zimmermann, Wolf Hajo 2005, 'Sievern §1 Archäologisch', *Reallexikon der germanischen Altertumskunde* 28 (Berlin–New York), 368–74.

9

Cultural Convergence in a Maritime Context

Language and material culture as parallel phenomena in the early-medieval southern North Sea region

Pieterjan Deckers

There is little doubt that close links existed between communities on both sides of the southern North Sea in the centuries following the Migration Period. From an archaeological perspective, the numerous *sceattas* produced in the Low Countries in the late 7th and 8th centuries AD and found in considerable quantities in England are undeniable evidence of this (Metcalf and Op den Velde 2010), as are the technical and stylistic correspondences between high-status dress items such as the 'royal' disc-on-bow brooches found in the northern Netherlands and England (e.g. Olsen 2006; Nicolay 2014 and this vol.). These frequent contacts are corroborated by historical evidence, for instance confirming the central position of the 'Frisians' in long-distance trade (Lebecq 1983) or the diplomatic interaction between the Warni, an aristocratic group living in the Rhine estuary, and Anglian royalty in the 6th century (Dijkstra 2004, 397; Dijkstra and de Koning, this vol.; Pestell, this vol.).

However, overseas interaction amounted to more than lively diplomatic and economic exchanges; moreover, the archaeological evidence for such interaction is not limited to the core areas of social, economic and political development around the southern North Sea, most notably Friesland, East Anglia and Kent. The present paper approaches this 'North Sea Culture' from another perspective. It takes as its main area of study a more peripheral region, coastal Flanders, and considers its relations with both the North Sea region and the hinterland. Furthermore, it focuses on 'lowly' categories of material culture belonging to the domestic sphere, far away from the halls of kings and warlords.

Coastal Flanders in the Merovingian Period

Generally speaking, most of the archaeological evidence from the Merovingian Period (AD 500–750) is found in the eastern part of coastal Flanders, an area broadly corresponding to the Carolingian administrative unit of the *pagus Flandrensis*. Two major landscape-types can be discerned in this region. Along the coast lies the present-day polder area, which prior to the 10th–11th century consisted of an unembanked coastal wetland crossed by tidal channels. By the 7th–8th century, large parts of it were naturally silting up to supra-tidal levels, forming extensive saltmarshes and salt meadows. On its landward side, this area is bounded the Pleistocene cover-sand region.

The latter area is probably the most extensively excavated early-medieval settlement landscape of Flanders. Merovingian settlement appears to have been centred on the 'Zandstraat', the Roman road following the sandy ridge forming the edge of the coastal plain, from the Late Roman fort of Oudenburg to the location of present-day Bruges (Hollevoet 2011). In the coastal plain proper, archaeological evidence for dispersed permanent settlement dates back to at least the mid-7th century (e.g. Ervynck *et al.* 2012, 155).

Based on a chapter from the author's doctoral dissertation (Deckers 2014, 447–540) presented at the conference 'Across the North Sea' in the Fries Museum in Leeuwarden in June 2014, the present paper focuses on two categories of material culture from coastal Flanders that shed light on the nature of the overseas connection between coastal communities along the North Sea littoral: the main type of pottery produced by these people, and the houses in which they lived. For brevity's sake, bibliographic references in these case studies have been limited to those strictly necessary.

Case study 1: Organic-tempered pottery

So-called organic-tempered pottery dominates the assemblages from the early-medieval settlements along the Zandstraat and in the coastal plain (Hamerow *et al.* 1994; Hollevoet 2006) (Fig. 9.1). This hand-made, mostly undecorated pottery is tempered by organic material, a technique which after firing results in numerous voids in a blackened fabric. Despite the presently ill-understood variability in the fabric (including the exact nature of the tempering agent), it is an easily recognizable pottery-type that is very distinct from the contemporary techniques of tempering with grog in the Scheldt basin (cf. De Groote and De Clercq 2015) or grit-tempering in the Campine region (Verstappen 2015).

Across the North Sea, organic-tempered pottery appears in the 5th century in southeastern England up to the Thames Valley. It rises sharply in prominence in the later 6th century, especially on settlements in coastal and agriculturally marginal landscapes (Hamerow *et al.* 1994, 14; Jervis 2012). The pottery type is also attested along the coast of the Netherlands from the Rhine area up to the province of Friesland, where it is called 'Tritsum ware' (e.g. van Es 1969, 132; Taayke and Knol 1992, 85–6; Dijkstra 2011, 352–3). Its counterpart in the interior is so-called Hessens-Schortens ware, tempered with stone grit (e.g. Taayke and Knol 1992, 86–7).

Based on the ready availability of the raw materials in the local landscape, the suitability of the fabric for firing in open fires or simple ovens, the low degree of standardization and the prevalence of simple, hand-made form-types, it is assumed that organic-tempered

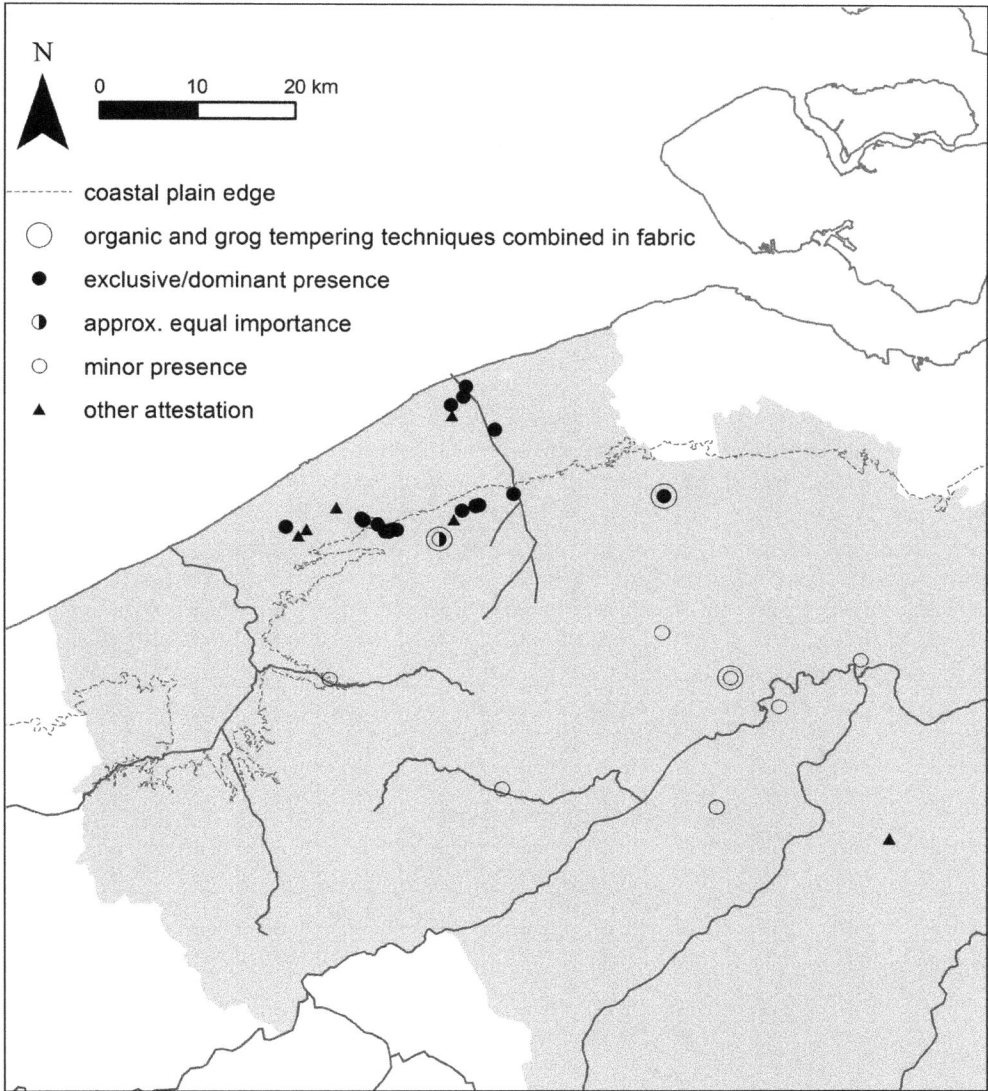

Fig. 9.1. Distribution of organic-tempered pottery in assemblages of Merovingian-period date in western Flanders. The indications of relative importance reflect the proportion of organic- to grog-tempered pottery.

pottery was produced at the household level (Hollevoet 2006). Whereas the choice of temper may have been a response to what the landscape afforded in terms of pottery production and ways of life (Jervis 2012; Deckers 2014, 506–7), this does not suffice to explain the coherence and endurance of the tradition across its entire distribution area and lifetime.

Anthropology offers a plausible explanatory mechanism for the dispersal and reproduction of this pottery tradition. Ethnographic research has shown that household-level pottery production is, almost without exception, a female activity (e.g. Arnold 1991, 28–9; Sassaman and Rudolphi 2001, 420). The transmission of pottery techniques typically occurred along the matriline, as part of the skill-set acquired before a woman moved away to live with her new husband. As such, the continued exchange of marriage partners between coastal communities, over the course of eight to ten generations, emerges as a reasonable explanation to account for the establishment and reproduction of the organic-tempered pottery tradition around the southern North Sea from the 6th century to the mid-8th.

Case study 2: Domestic architecture

Like organic-tempered pottery, aspects of domestic architecture have long been used as evidence for the close links between coastal communities from the continental seaboard from Flanders to north-western Germany and eastern England (e.g. Theuws 1996, 755–9; Hamerow 1999; Dijkstra 2004, 399–401; 2011, 191–222; van der Velde and Dijkstra 2008, 435–40). However, in contrast to the pottery, 6th- to 8th-century domestic architecture in the southern North Sea area is characterized, above all, by a diversity of architectural templates and concepts, often distinct from those circulating in regions further inland.

Houses from this period in coastal Flanders are typically single-aisled and rectangular, and feature wall-trenches. They thus differ significantly from the post-built structures that are the rule further inland, not only in the Scheldt basin (Fig. 9.2), but also in the eastern Netherlands (Heidinga 1987; Huijts 1992; Waterbolk 2009; Theuws 2014).

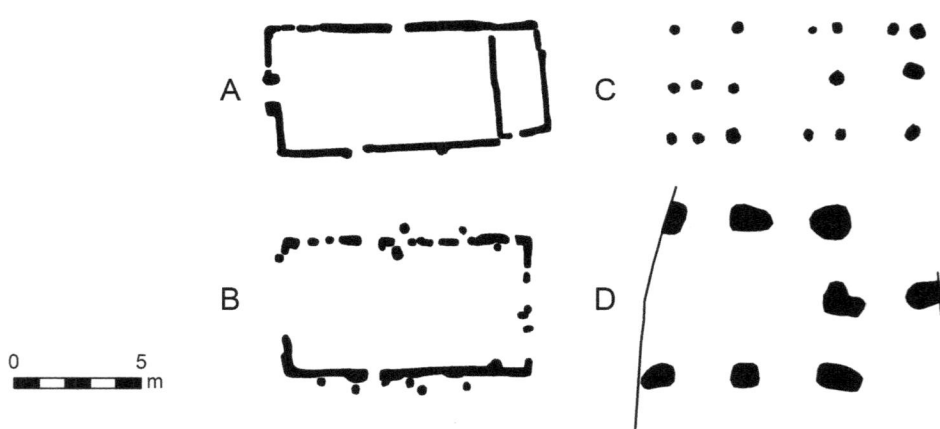

Fig. 9.2. A comparison of typical structures from the Flemish coastal region and the Scheldt valley. A: Sint-Andries-Kosterijstraat building 1; B: Sint-Andries-Kosterijstraat building 7; C: Kerkhove; D: Nevele-Merendreestraat building 2. After Hillewaert and Hollevoet 2006, fig. 10 (A–B) © Flanders Heritage Agency; Rogge 1981, fig. 4 courtesy of V. O. B.o.W.; (C) © De Logi and Van Cauwenbergh 2010, fig. 18; (D) © Ename Expertisecentrum voor Erfgoedontsluiting vzw / Kale - LeieArcheologische Dienst.

A particular sub-group, possibly the dominant house-type in coastal Flanders in the 7th–8th centuries, appears to largely lack external or internal supports, rendering the remains of these houses relatively ephemeral and hard to recognize, in particular on the deeply ploughed, less easily legible clay soils of the coastal plain (see Fig. 9.2a). Nonetheless, good parallels can be found along the coast further north (Fig. 9.3).

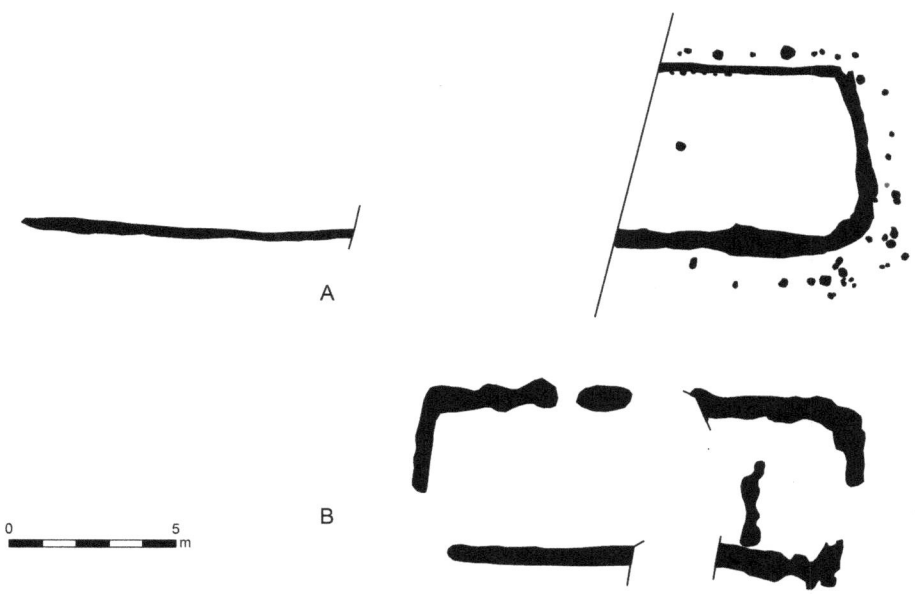

Fig. 9.3. Houses from the Dutch coastland supported by wall posts rather than internal or external supports (cf. Fig. 2A). A: Serooskerke-Gapingse Watergang building 7.2; B: Den Haag Frankenslag building 3. According to the excavators, the posts depicted in A are of limited depth and may belong to later phases of the house. After Dijkstra and Zuidhoff 2011, fig. 2.5.9 (A): © ADC ArchaeoProjecten; Magendans and Waasdorp 1989, fig. 8 (B).

More broadly speaking, coastal domestic architecture of the Low Countries is also characterized by diversity, which arguably contrasts with the more coherent regional traditions inland. Within this range of architectural forms, numerous architectural and technical connections can be found between coastal Flanders and the continental seaboard up to north-western Germany. A conspicuous and oft-cited example of such connections (e.g. Theuws 1996, 755–6) is the very similar layout of buildings at Roksem in coastal Flanders, Uitgeest on the coast of North Holland and Flögeln-Dalem in north-western Germany (Haarnagel 1984, 186; Besteman 1990; Hollevoet 1991, fig. 7). Other houses in Flanders and the western Dutch coastal region show similar features not often found in the interior, such as a single, unpaired entrance near the end of one of the long sides. Such correspondences reveal a shared conception and use of space, both in and around the house.

In other respects, the southern North Sea littoral is characterized by the non-adoption of architectural developments which are typical of regions further inland. This is evident, for instance, in the persistence of often turf-built three-aisled buildings or byre sections in Friesland in particular, but also further west along the Dutch coast and eastwards into north-western Germany (e.g. Hinz 1964, 9; van Es 1973, 343–4; Waterbolk 2009, 90; Woltering 1975). A similar form of rejection may be found in the delayed adoption of bow-shaped walls, probably introduced in the 7th century in the Rhine-mouth area (Dijkstra 2011, 219–20) but only appearing in the adjoining coastal areas of Flanders and North Holland in the 9th century (see Deckers 2014, 492).

Generally speaking, many of the houses from coastal Flanders and the Dutch littoral fit well into Anglo-Saxon architectural traditions, with their widespread use of wall trenches (cf. Marshall and Marshall 1993, 376–80), certain wall-building techniques (Dijkstra and van der Velde 2008, 437–8), the prevalence of short houses without byre section, and the continued use of straight rather than bowed walls (Dijkstra 2011, 216–17; Hamerow 1999, 120; cf. James *et al.* 1984, 198–9). Annexes on the long end of buildings, a typical Anglo-Saxon feature of the 7th–8th centuries (James *et al.* 1984, 190, table 2; Marshall and Marshall 1993, 379), were found at several of the Flemish houses (e.g. Hillewaert and Hollevoet 2006, fig. 10 no. 5; also see Hollevoet 2002, 173 n.19), but also further north (e.g. Bult *et al.* 1990, 156).

The availability of resources or the greater ecological variability and resulting social and economic variation of the coastal landscape have been invoked as explanations for the distinctiveness of early-medieval architecture in the coastal region of the Low Countries (Besteman 1990, 103; Bult and Hallewas 1990, 83; Theuws 1996, 759). Thus short houses without byre sections may reflect different practices or attitudes towards livestock (Hamerow 2002, 47–8), or perhaps indicate a more specialized lifestyle (e.g. Bult *et al.* 1990, 155–61).

However plausible, such explanations fail to account for the nature of the diversity observed. Inland, regional traditions arguably more often tend to follow their own, internal developmental dynamic through time (allowing for the construction of coherent chronotypologies). In the coastal region, however, external, long-distance influences appear to have been a much more important source of architectural variation. Clearly, throughout the entire period under consideration, inspiration for architectural responses to the coastal environment's requirements posed by the coastal environment was found in the wider southern North Sea region, sometimes over considerable distances.

North Sea Germanic: the linguistic background

The chronology of these developments in pottery and housebuilding precludes an explanation limited to the 'great migrations' of the 3rd–5th centuries. Rather, the appearance in the 6th century and endurance of these features over the course of more than two centuries highlights the continuity of overseas interaction of coastal communities in the southern North Sea region. However, the question remains why the cultural pattern appears as it does. I propose that this pattern conforms to a plausible scenario for contemporary linguistic developments around the North Sea.

The North Sea Germanic or Ingvaeonic sub-family of the West Germanic languages has long been recognized. Its existence is most evident in the strong similarities between Old English, Old Frisian and, to a lesser extent, Old Saxon (e.g. Nielsen 2001; Bremmer 2009; Hines, this vol.), but the coastal dialects of Dutch also fell under its influence (van Bree 1997, 30–9). It is furthermore generally assumed that by the 8th century several distinct languages arose from this North Sea Germanic grouping (see below). However, the process leading up to that episode of divergence remains open to debate. Many authors believe that Ingvaeonic features emerged in the north-west German homelands, before their dispersal during the Migration Period (e.g. Samuels 1971, 5–8; Voss 1995; Quak 2002, 568). Some even see the presence of ingvaeonisms as historical coincidences caused by the decreasing influence of Franconian on the North Sea periphery (Heeroma 1965; Stiles 1995, 211–12).

Many others, however, have argued for overseas diffusion of at least some Ingvaeonic innovations within the southern North Sea region, after the Migration Period (Kuhn 1955, 23–44; DeCamp 1958; van Bree 1997, 16–20; Nielsen 2001, 520–1; Trousdale 2005). Most relevant for the present discussion is John Hines's hypothesis that Ingvaeonic innovations spread from west (Old English) to east (Old Saxon) across the North Sea between the 5th and 8th century within a dialect continuum (Hines 1995). This continuum resulted from continuous contact between the dispersed, linguistically diverse communities established around the southern North Sea in the wake of the Migration Period. The emergence of common features is therefore not the result of a common origin, but the outcome of continued interaction.

Hines formulated these ideas at a time when linguists were becoming increasingly aware of the shortcomings of the phylogenetic model in conceptualizing language change, some even postulating that such simple divergence may be a rather rare occurrence, and that change is in the majority of cases driven by contact, rather than isolation, between linguistic communities (e.g. Mufwene 2000, 14; Heggarty 2007, 320–1; Luraghi 2010, 339). Very recently, Heggarty (2015, 603) used the case of North Sea Germanic as his illustration of choice of the limited applicability of divergence models and the underestimated prevalence of dialect continua in the past.

Interesting, also, is the 'social network' approach to language change advocated by Malcolm Ross (1997; following Milroy 1987). Here, Hines's hypothesis is presented as an example of language convergence, more particularly koineization (Fig. 9.4). In the post-migration context of the 5th to 6th centuries, the geographic coherence of speech communities collapsed, and new, but relatively weak, social relationships were formed throughout the southern North Sea area. Linguistic features that previously allowed identification with particular groups lost their emblematic value and were more freely exchanged ('dialect levelling') (Ross 1997, 236–8). In this case, the koineization process remained incomplete: there most probably never existed a common 'North Sea Germanic' language (such as the 19th-century construct of Anglo-Frisian).

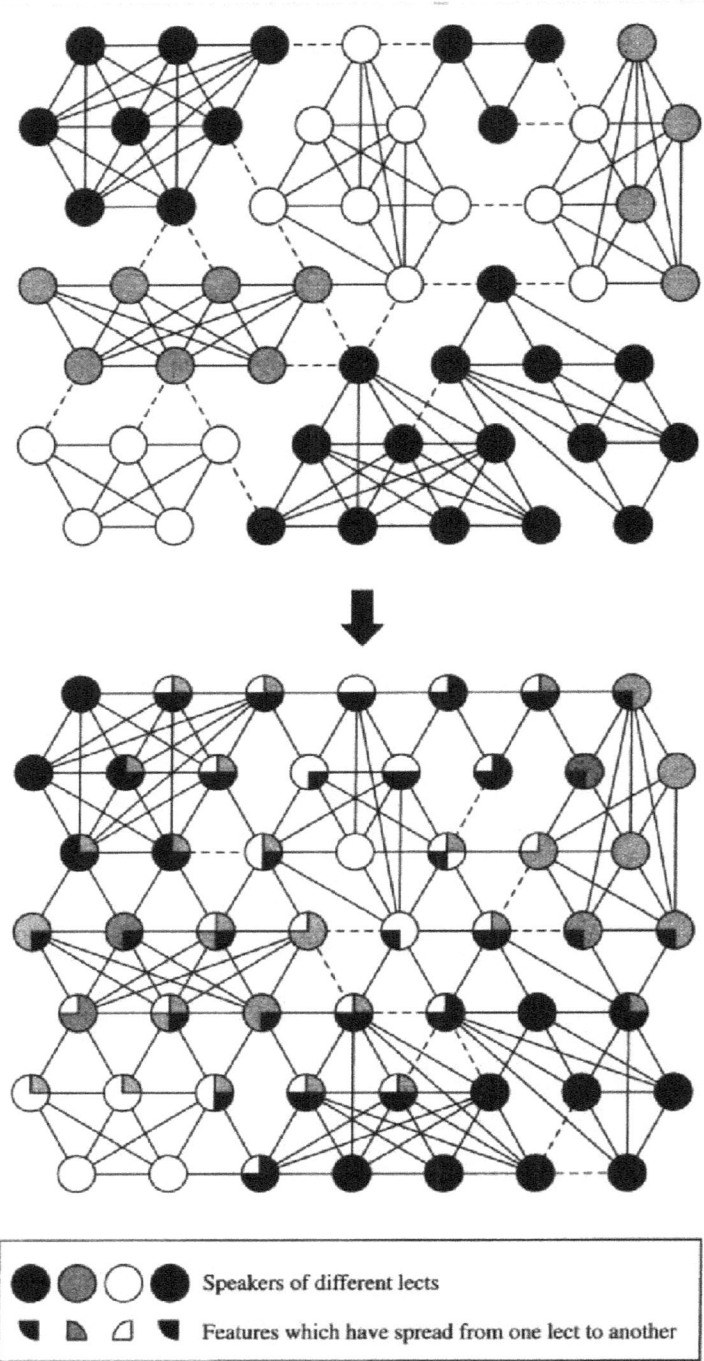

Fig. 9.4. The linguistic koineization process from a social network perspective, showing the preceding stage of disorder and the formation of a new social and linguistic configuration (Ross 1997, fig. 13.16).

Cultural Convergence in a Maritime Context

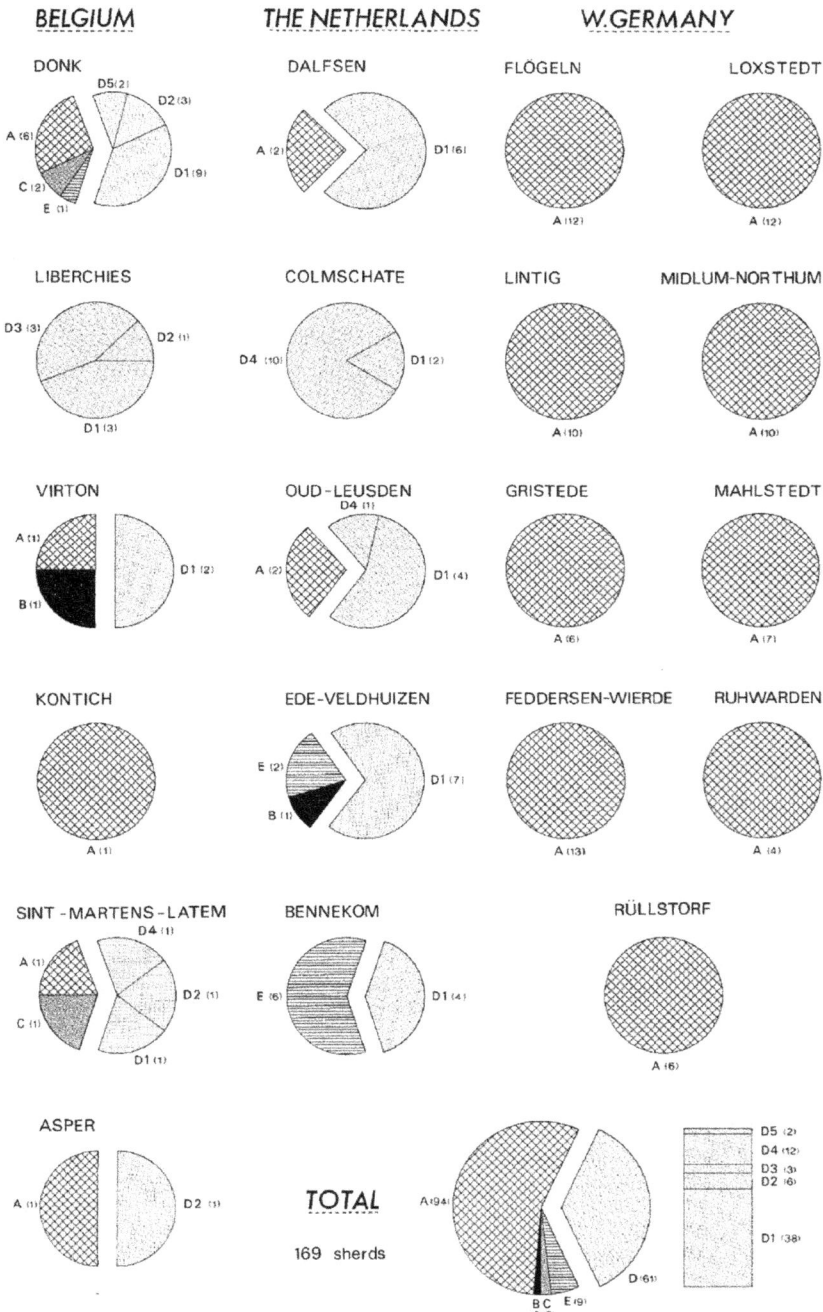

Fig. 9.5. Petrographic analysis of 3rd- to 5th-century pottery demonstrates the great variability of tempering traditions in the Low Countries, corresponding to the linguistic 'patchwork' stage in the koineization process (cf. Fig. 4) (De Paepe and Van Impe 1991, fig. 10): © Flanders Heritage Agency.

Similar developments in material culture?

Whereas koine-formation depends on many factors (Garrett 2004, 49), conspicuously it often occurs within a context of maritime interaction, even without particularly intensive forms of interaction (e.g. Mühlhäusler *et al.* 1996; Waddell and Conroy 1999). Linguistically, the early-medieval southern North Sea region is thus no exception. However, could we find evidence for this in archaeological observations? As far as 6th- to 8th-century domestic architecture is concerned, the diversity and fluidity of expressions arguably conform to a stage of 'dialect continuum' as envisaged by Hines. In this view, eastern England and Friesland can be envisioned as cores from which innovations respectively spread (e.g. annexes) or were rejected (e.g. the single-aisled template).

The regional pottery traditions in this period provide a less easy fit, seemingly conforming more to a pattern of divergence. However, at the origins of these regional traditions lies exactly the pattern that would be expected: in the 3rd to 5th centuries, a great diversity of pottery production techniques can be observed in western Flanders and beyond (Fig. 9.5). These include tempering with organic materials – which may have its origins in the northern Dutch wares of Late Roman date (Taayke and Knol 1992, 85) – but also with stone grit of various types, bone, grog and sand (De Paepe and van Impe 1991; Rogge 1996, 131–2; De Clercq *et al.* 2006, 63; for England and northern France see Vince 2005, 225–6; Soulat *et al.* 2012). By the 6th century, this initial diversity had crystallized into distinct regional traditions, including a koine-like dominance of organic tempering amongst many coastal communities in the southern North Sea area. At the site level, this process is perhaps most easily traced at Mucking (Hamerow 1993, 27–31).

Discussion: a linguistic analogue and parallel for archaeological observations

The similarity between the converging tendencies in language and material culture around the southern North Sea during this period is more than coincidental. The pertinence of the linguistic model is situated at two levels. Firstly, as archaeologists have realized in the past (Robb 1993; Renfrew 2000), linguistic hypotheses may serve as a model of and analytical tool for cultural change that helps us to make sense of the archaeological record. Here, language as well as the technological acts involved in the making of pottery and houses are expressions of 'communities of practice' (e.g. Gosselain 2000; Sassaman and Rudolphi 2001; Bucholtz and Hall 2004; Memmott and Davidson 2008; Jordan and O'Neill 2010). The same social processes underlie these cultural developments, regardless of the fact that they now fall under the remit of distinct academic spheres.

However, Hines's linguistic hypothesis, viewed through the lens of Ross's social-network conceptualization, is more than an analogue model for archaeological developments in a general sense. As a hypothesis explaining the correspondences between North Sea Germanic languages, it also provides a historical parallel for the particular time and place under consideration. The material-cultural developments correspond, in space and time, to what might be expected on the basis of the linguistic hypothesis, namely a period of convergence in areas with Ingvaeonic influence starting in the

5th/6th centuries and ending in the 8th. As such, the linguistic hypothesis, plausible but difficult to confirm, finds independent support in archaeological evidence for cultural convergence (cf. Drinka 2010, 329–30 on the necessity of external evidence in historical linguistics). Indeed, previous discussions of the archaeological evidence for overseas contact in the period and area under question have used similar terminology (albeit purely in a descriptive, analogous sense); most notable are Russchen's 'North Sea koine' (1967, 62) and Reichstein's 'kulturelle Ausgleichzone' (1984).

One question that remains untouched is why the proposed process of koineization occurred at different rates for different cultural expressions – language, domestic architecture and pottery. In the case of the former two, convergence was incomplete by the 8th century. On the other hand, pottery traditions in the southern North Sea region developed from a post-migration cultural patchwork to a koine-like state already in the course of the 6th century.

One reason for these differing convergence rates might be that pottery may have attained significance as an emblematic expression of regional identity. At least in Flanders, it would be a mistake to infer a lack of interaction from the relatively strict boundaries between the coastal and Scheldt-basin traditions. The few sites where both tempering techniques co-occur, sporadically even in the same vessel (e.g. Hollevoet 1992, 229–30), show that these communities must have been well aware of these different practices – all the more so because of the visual differences (in form spectrum and surface colour) between both pottery types. More likely, therefore, is that the rapid emergence of distinct, bounded regional traditions can be explained by an instrumentalization of this difference as an active element in the formation of distinct group identities.

More broadly speaking, the differences in the speed of the convergence process may relate to the transmission of these cultural traits within communities of practice. Cultural Transmission (CT) theory sets out to understand the reproduction and adaptation of cultural features through an examination of the content, context and nature of the transferral of information between individuals (Eerkens and Lipo 2007). The differing rates of koineization may thus result from the different characteristics of this transmission.

Table 9.1. A simplified overview of some of the different characteristics of the transmission of pottery production and house-building in early-medieval coastal Flanders.

	Pottery production	*House-building*
Technological content	simple	complex
Frequency of transmission	yearly	generational (at the household level)
Presumed context and mode of transmission	Close relations, one-to-one/few (matriline)	many-to-many, household/community-based

According to the principles of CT, the different characteristics of traditions of pottery production and house-building would result in an accurate transmission of the former, allowing for little deviation, whereas the transmission of practices associated with the latter offers greater scope for experimentation and the dispersal of new elements (Table 9.1). In short, if identity theory helps to explain how pottery technology in coastal Flanders might have crystallized so quickly into distinct regional traditions, CT theory accounts for its largely unchanged reproduction over eight to ten generations and the much more diverse practices in domestic architecture in the same time-frame.

Divergence: the end of North Sea Culture?

Most linguists agree that distinct languages emerged from the North Sea Germanic continuum in the course of the 8th century. Divergence took over from convergence as the predominant linguistic process, resulting in the appearance of several Old English dialects as well as Old Frisian. As Hines notes, this is obviously not the result of isolation, but more likely of political centralization and a concomitant shift of emphasis from 'centripetal foci' of innovation to linguistic boundaries (Hines 1995, 54–6).

Important changes can also be observed in this period in the categories of material culture under consideration. Generally speaking, in coastal Flanders as well as in the interior, 'Merovingian' architectural traditions were replaced by the 10th century by a more homogeneous tradition of single- or three-aisled, heavy post-built constructions (e.g. Huijbers 2014). House plans from the Carolingian period are relatively rare in Flanders. Only at one coastal site is the new, heavy, post-built house type attested in the 9th century (Hollevoet and Hillewaert 2002), confirming the introduction in the coastal region of new architectural templates and constructional techniques at this time. The already mentioned relatively late introduction of the bowed wall in this area, also in the 9th century, is a further symptom of the growing impact of the broad cultural developments of the interior in the coastal region. These changes represent divergence from England (although here too, 8th/9th-century buildings are scarce). Here, the continental innovation of bow-sided houses was never introduced (Hamerow 1999, 135–6) and architectural development during the Middle and Late Anglo-Saxon Periods continued at a more gradual pace (Hamerow 2011, 130–1).

The development in pottery production at this juncture is easier to trace. Organic-tempered pottery is completely replaced by sand-tempered pottery in the middle decades of the 8th century in southern and eastern England (e.g. Timby 1988, 44; Blackmore 2003, 229–34). Across the North Sea, its disappearance is less accurately dated, but it probably ranges from the 7th century in the Rhine estuary (Dijkstra 2008, 273–4) to the late 7th/early 8th century elsewhere in the northern and western Netherlands (Lanting and van der Plicht 2010, 150) and around or shortly after the middle of the 8th century in coastal Flanders (Deckers 2014, 185). At about the same time, the regional pottery traditions of the interior were similarly replaced by sand-tempered pottery, as the new form-type of the globular pot was gradually adopted across the Low Countries (Verhoeven 1998, 32–3).

It is obvious from historical as well as archaeological evidence that intensive contact across the North Sea continued. If anything, commercial activity peaked in the late 7th and 8th century, and other evidence as well points to the continuity of overseas social interaction throughout the Carolingian Period (e.g. Thomas 2012). Hence, an explanation should be sought in an adjustment of the social connections of coastal communities around the southern North Sea, rather than increasing isolation.

The disappearance of distinct tempering traditions in the Low Countries could signify a decreased need for identitary differentiation within the Carolingian realm. It is striking, however, that the new technique and form-type chosen for this, sand-tempered globular pots, appears to originate in the Dutch river area (Verhoeven 1998, 251). This does not reflect a straightforward imposition of the cultural norms of the political core, the Carolingian Empire, on the coastal periphery ('carolingization') – a simple realignment of coastal communities from predominantly maritime to more terrestrial affiliations reflected in the adoption of the traditions of the interior. Rather, it represents a cultural homogenization of coast and interior alike. Furthermore, it seems improbable that these innovations in material culture served as salient markers of newly emerging identities according to political fault lines, as is supposed for language. Therefore, the linguistic explanation of political centralization as the direct driver for cultural change does not entirely satisfy. The link between the two phenomena is likely to be indirect, as the changes in material culture might well be related to economic reorganization in turn effected by the growing emphasis on landed property, associated with the emergence of the Carolingian and Anglo-Saxon state in the 'long 8th century' (see, e.g., Wickham 2005, 339–79). Comparable 'political' explanations have been offered in the past in relation to the end of the organic-tempered pottery (Blinkhorn 1997, 120; Deckers and Tys 2012; Jervis 2012).

Conclusions

It has been argued in this paper that the archaeological developments in the southern North Sea area during the centuries following the Migration Period may be cast as a parallel for contemporary linguistic developments. In particular, the linguistic hypothesis of North Sea Germanic as a developing but ultimately incomplete maritime koine was identified as a helpful analytical model for the study of material culture. The developments in pottery and domestic architecture in this period support the view of cultural convergence in this maritime space between the 6th century and the 8th.

With a common process of convergence affecting multiple cultural expressions, the old concept of 'North Sea Culture' (e.g. Hallewas *et al.* 1975) makes more sense than ever. Far from abiding by the traditional 'Childean' archaeological culture concept (e.g. Childe 1956, 16), marked by boundedness and exclusivity, this idea refers to the mesh of connections and commonalities evident in the early-medieval archaeology of the southern North Sea region. It is to be understood not as a 'hybrid' of different cultural influences, but as a dynamic cultural system that makes sense in its own right and operated largely outside the homogenizing tendencies of major political centres of power (Deckers and Tys 2012). It forms the cultural correlate to the economic freedom experienced by coastal communities, as evident from their easy access to imported goods (Loveluck and Tys 2006).

Whereas commercial and diplomatic contact continued unabated, a shift towards a greater alignment with developments in the interior occurred in pottery production and house building in the 8th century. Linguists hold that at this time, distinct languages emerged from the North Sea Germanic continuum as a result of the growing centralization of regional kingdoms. Whereas the observed changes in material culture do not similarly reflect the establishment of new and strengthened cultural boundaries, they may well attest to the growing impact of these political developments on socio-economic structures and daily life.

Language, like material culture, is a product of communities of practice – groups that share certain ways of 'doing things'. On this basis of shared underlying social processes, there is much to be gained, for both linguists and archaeologists, by crossing disciplinary boundaries. As this study has demonstrated once more, linguistic models may provide a framework for understanding archaeological phenomena, while the latter may help corroborate the former's validity.

This approach comes with certain difficulties and dangers. How do we establish whether cultural phenomena have a common cause (for example, overseas contact between low-ranking coastal communities)? The historical linguist Heggarty (2015, 602) recently argued that indicators for the relation between cultural phenomena include coincidence in space and time, and commensurateness in scale. However, such guidelines are far from easy to implement in any but the most broad-brush scenarios. What margin of error do we allow in considering the coincidence of cultural phenomena? How do we measure and compare 'scale' in such disparate phenomena as speech, pot-making and house-building?

One way to take this forward will be to take into account the particular dynamics of different cultural practices. Even disregarding the different resolutions of space and time inherent in various sources of evidence, aspects of practice and culture may be differently affected by the same external factor, and the effects may occur in different locations and at different rates. As demonstrated here, archaeological and anthropological theorizing (e.g. on cultural transmission and identity) may be of help in understanding such variation.

Nonetheless, what was presented here remains a simplification in various respects. With domestic pottery and houses, this study has considered only two categories within a much wider range of material culture available for study. Furthermore, representing these as 'low-status' material culture – evidence for the contact between coastal communities of no special social standing – arguably introduces an unnecessary dichotomy in relation to the more often-discussed archaeological and historical evidence for commercial and high-ranking diplomatic contact, as well as a false impression of uniformity and equality amongst these communities.

The linguistic concept of the koine as the outcome of multilateral language contact is also often framed within such egalitarian assumptions (e.g. Siegel 2001, 175), perhaps to distinguish it from contact languages emerging from the strongly asymmetric power relationships of the colonial era. However, this need not imply an absence of hierarchies of power within the North Sea Culture as depicted here. Cultural convergence was probably not an undifferentiated, organic, bottom-up process driven by interaction between coastal communities on equal footing. Rather, the dialect continuum must have formed a patchwork of cultural contact situations between self-identified communities at multiple levels. Factors of significant if variable impact on the dispersive success of cultural features must have been emerging economic and political dominance of some groups as well as continued, if small-scale population movement (cf. the range of scenarios proposed by Renfrew 1989; Heggarty 2015, 616–19). Indeed, it seems likely that the success of the cores of innovation or resistance was determined at least partly by the power and prestige associated with these (speech) communities. Further detailed studies of cultural variation, incorporating multiple types of evidence and informed by an interdisciplinary theoretical framework, will no doubt help us to come to grips with the complexity of overseas interaction in the post-migration southern North Sea region and to understand these processes in a more fine-grained, multi-faceted way.

References

Arnold, Philip J. 1991, *Domestic Ceramic Production and Spatial Organization: A Mexican Case Study in Ethnoarchaeology* (Cambridge–New York).

Besteman, Jan C. 1990, 'North Holland AD 400–1200: turning tide or tide turned?'. In *Medieval Archaeology in the Netherlands Studies Presented to H. H. van Regteren Altena*, Studies in Prae- En Protohistorie 4, ed. J. C. Besteman, J. M. Bos and H. A. Heidinga (Assen en Maastricht), 91–120.

Blackmore, Lynn 2003, 'The pottery'. In *Middle Saxon London: Excavations at the Royal Opera House 1989–99*, MoLAS Monograph 15, ed. G. Malcolm and D. Bowsher (London), 225–41.

Blinkhorn, Paul 1997, 'Habitus, social identity and Anglo-Saxon pottery'. In *Not so Much a Pot, More a Way of Life. Current Approaches to Artefact Analysis in Archaeology*, ed. C. Cumberpatch and P. W. Blinkhorn (Oxford), 113–24.

Bree, Cor van 1997, *Een oud onderwerp opnieuw bekeken: het Ingweoons. Tekst op basis waarvan op 25 september 1997 een afscheidscollege is gegeven bij het afscheid als hoogleraar historische taalkunde en taalvariatie in de Vakgroep Nederlands te Leiden* (s.l).

Bremmer, Rolf 2009. *An Introduction to Old Frisian: History, Grammar, Reader, Glossary* (Amsterdam–Philadelphia).

Bucholtz, Mary, and Kira Hall 2004, 'Language and identity'. In *A Companion to Linguistic Anthropology*, ed. A. Duranti (Malden–Oxford), 369–94.

Bult, Epko J., and Daan P. Hallewas 1990, 'Archaeological evidence for the early-medieval settlement around the Meuse and Rhine deltas up to ca AD 1000'. In *Medieval Archaeology in the Netherlands Studies Presented to H. H. van Regteren Altena*, Studies in Prae- En Protohistorie 4, ed. J. C. Besteman, J. M. Bos and H. A. Heidinga (Assen en Maastricht), 71–90.

Bult, Epko J., Jan van Doesburg and Daan P. Hallewas 1990, 'De opgravingscampagne in de vroegmiddeleeuwse nederzetting bij Valkenburg (Z. H.) in 1987 en 1988'. In *Graven bij Valkenburg III. Het archeologisch onderzoek in 1987 en 1988*, ed. E. J. Bult and D. P. Hallewas (Delft), 147–66.

Childe, Gordon V. 1956, *Piecing Together the Past : The Interpretation of Archaeological Data* (London).

Clercq, Wim De, Hadewijck Van Rechem, Vanessa Gelorini, Marc Meganck, Ernst Taayke and Heidi Tency 2006, 'Een meerperioden-vindplaats langs de Schelde te Zele Kammershoek. Een grafheuvel uit de bronstijd, een erf uit de Gallo-Romeinse periode en sporen van Germaanse inwijkelingen'. In *Een Lijn Door Het Landschap. Archeologie en Het VTN-Project 1997–1998*, Archeologie in Vlaanderen Monografie 5(2), ed. I. In 't Ven and W. De Clercq (Zellik), 177–229.

DeCamp, David 1958, 'The genesis of Old English dialects: a new hypothesis', *Language* 34, 232–44.

Deckers, Pieterjan 2014, 'Between Land and Sea: Landscape, Power and Identity in the Coastal Plain of Flanders, Zeeland and Northern France in the Early Middle Ages (AD 500–1000)'. Unpublished Ph.D. dissertation, Vrije Universiteit Brussel (Brussels).

Deckers, Pieterjan, and Dries Tys 2012, 'Early medieval communities around the North Sea: a "maritime culture"?'. In *The Very Beginning of Europe? Cultural and Social Dimensions of Early-Medieval Migration and Colonisation*, Relicta Monografieën 7, ed. R. Annaert, K. De Groote, Y. Hollevoet, F. Theuws, D. Tys and L. Verslype (Brussels), 81–8.

Dijkstra, Juke, and Frieda S. Zuidhoff 2011, 'Vindplaats 7 "Gapingse Watergang"'. In *Kansen op de kwelder. Archeologisch onderzoek op en rond negen vindplaatsen in het nieuwe tracé van de Rijksweg 57 en de Nieuwe Ringweg ter hoogte van Serooskerke (Walcheren)*, ADC Monografie 10, ed. J. Dijkstra and F. S. Zuidhoff (Amersfoort), 337–90.

Dijkstra, Menno F. P. 2004, 'Between Britannia and Francia. The nature of external socio-economic exchange at the Rhine and Meuse estuaries in the Early Middle Ages', *Bodendenkmalpflege in Mecklenburg-Vorpommern* 51 (Jahrbuch 2003), 397–408.

Dijkstra, Menno F. P. 2008, 'Aardewerk uit de Vroege Middeleeuwen'. In *Cananefaten en Friezen aan de monding van de Rijn. Tien jaar archeologisch onderzoek op de Zanderij-Westerbaan te Katwijk (1996–2006)*, ADC Monografie 5, ed. H. M. van der Velde (Amersfoort), 269–93.

Dijkstra, Menno F. P. 2011, *Rondom de mondingen van Rijn en Maas. Landschape en bewoning tussen de 3e en de 9e eeuw in Zuid-Holland, in het bijzonder de Oude Rijnstreek* (Leiden).

Dijkstra, Menno F. P., and Henk M. van der Velde 2008, 'Sporen en structuren behorend tot de vroeg-middeleeuwse bewoning in het noordelijke deel'. In *Cananefaten en Friezen aan de monding van de Rijn. Tien jaar archeologisch onderzoek op de Zanderij-Westerbaan te Katwijk (1996–2006)*, ADC Monografie 5, ed. H. M. van der Velde (Amersfoort), 127–66.

Drinka, Bridget 2010, 'Language contact'. In *The Continuum Companion to Historical Linguistics*, ed. S. Luraghi and V. Bubenik (London–New York), 325–45.

Eerkens, Jelmer W., and Carl P. Lipo 2007, 'Cultural transmission theory and the archaeological record: providing context to understanding variation and temporal changes in material culture', *Journal of Archaeological Research* 15, 239–74.

Ervynck, Anton, Pieterjan Deckers, An Lentacker, Dries Tys and Wim Van Neer 2012, '"Leffinge - Oude Werf": the first archaeozoological collection from a terp settlement in coastal Flanders'. In *A Bouquet of Archaeozoological Studies. Essays in Honour of Wietske Prummel*, Groningen Archaeological Studies 21, ed. D. C. M. Raemaekers, K. Esser, R. C. G. M. Lauwerier and J. T. Zeiler (Groningen), 153–64.

Es, Willem A. van 1969, 'Early medieval hand-made pottery from Den Burg, Texel, Prov. North Holland', *Berichten van de Rijksdienst voor het Oudheidkundig Bodemonderzoek* 19, 129–34.

Es, Willem A van. 1973, 'Terp research; with particular reference to a medieval terp at Den Helder', *Berichten van de Rijksdienst voor het Oudheidkundig Bodemonderzoek* 23, 337–45.

Garrett, Paul B. 2004, 'Language contact and contact languages'. In *A Companion to Linguistic Anthropology*, ed. A. Duranti (Malden–Oxford), 46–72.

Gosselain, Olivier P. 2000, 'Materializing identities: an African perspective', *Journal of Archaeological Method and Theory* 7, 187–217.

Groote, Koen De, and Wim De Clercq 2015, 'La production de céramique du Haut Moyen Âge en Flandre (Belgique). Bilan et perspectives'. In *Tourner autour du pot ... les ateliers de potiers médiévaux du Ve au XIIe siècle dans l'espace Européen*, Publications du CRAHAM: Série Antique et Médiévale, ed. F. Thuillier and E. Louis (Caen), 361–71.

Haarnagel, Werner 1984, 'Hausbau'. In *Archäologische und naturwissenschaftliche Untersuchungen an ländlichen und frühstädtischen Siedlungen, Band 1. Ländliche Siedlungen*, ed. G. Kossack, K. Behre and P. Schmid (Weinheim), 167–93.

Hallewas, Daan P., Hendrik A. Heidinga, Herman H. van Regteren Altena and Gerard IJzereef ed. 1975, *De "Noordzeecultuur". Een onderzoek naar de culturele relaties van de landen rond de Noordzee in de vroege middeleeuwen. Project middeleeuwse archeologie, 1972–1974*, I. P. P. Working Paper (Amsterdam).

Hamerow, Helena 1993, *Excavations at Mucking. Volume 2: The Anglo-Saxon Settlement*, English Heritage Archaeological Report 21 (London).

Hamerow, Helena 1999, 'Anglo-Saxon timber buildings: the continental connection'. In *In Discussion with the Past. Archaeological Studies Presented to W. A. van Es*, ed. H. Sarfatij, W. J. H. Verwers and P. J. Woltering (Zwolle–Amersfoort), 119–28.

Hamerow, Helena 2002, *Early Medieval Settlements: The Archaeology of Rural Communities in North-West Europe, 400–900* (Oxford–New York).

Hamerow, Helena 2011, 'Anglo-Saxon timber buildings and their social context'. In *The Oxford Handbook of Anglo-Saxon Archaeology*, ed. H. Hamerow, D. A. Hinton and S. Crawford (Oxford–New York), 128–55.

Hamerow, Helena, Yann Hollevoet and Alan Vince 1994, 'Migration Period settlements and "Anglo-Saxon" pottery from Flanders', *Medieval Archaeology* 38, 1–18.

Heeroma, Klaas 1965, 'Wat is Ingweoons?', *Tijdschrift voor Nederlandse Taal- en Letterkunde* 81, 1–15.

Heggarty, Paul 2007, 'Linguistics for archaeologists: principles, methods and the case of the

Incas', *Cambridge Archaeological Journal* 17, 311–40.

Heggarty, Paul 2015, 'Prehistory through language and archaeology'. In *The Routledge Handbook of Historical Linguistics*, ed. C. Bowern and B. Evans (Oxford–New York), 598–626.

Heidinga, Hendrik A. 1987, *Medieval Settlement and Economy North of the Lower Rhine: Archaeology and History of Kootwijk and the Veluwe (the Netherlands)* (Assen–Maastricht).

Hillewaert, Bieke, and Yann Hollevoet 2006, 'Andermaal Romeins en vroegmiddeleeuws langs de Zandstraat te Sint-Andries/Brugge (prov. West-Vlaanderen)', *Relicta* 1, 121–40.

Hines, John 1995, 'Focus and boundary in linguistic varieties in the North-West Germanic continuum'. In *Friesische Studien II*. NOWELE Supplement Volume 12, ed. V. F. Faltings, A. G. H. Walker and O. Wilts (Odense), 35–62.

Hinz, Hermann 1964, 'Zur Vorgeschichte der Niederdeutschen Halle', *Zeitschrift für Volkskunde* 60, 1–22.

Hollevoet, Yann 1991, 'Een vroeg-middeleeuwse nederzetting aan de Hoge Dijken te Roksem (gem. Oudenburg)', *Archeologie in Vlaanderen* 1, 181–96.

Hollevoet, Yann 1992, 'Een luchtfoto opgegraven. Middeleeuwse landelijke bewoning langs de Meersbeekstraat te Snellegem (gem. Jabbeke, prov. West-Vlaanderen)', *Archeologie in Vlaanderen* 2, 227–35.

Hollevoet, Yann 2002, 'd'Hooghe Noene van midden Bronstijd tot volle Middeleeuwen. Archeologisch onderzoek in een verkaveling langs de Zandstraat te Varsenare (gem. Jabbeke, prov. West-Vlaanderen)', *Archeologie in Vlaanderen* 6 (1997–8), 161–89.

Hollevoet, Yann 2006, 'Céramiques domestiques du Haut Moyen Âge en Flandre'. In *La céramique du Haut Moyen Âge dans le Nord-Ouest de l'Europe, Ve-Xe Siècles. Actes du Colloque de Caen 2004. Bilan et perspectives dix ans après le Colloque d'Outreau*, ed. V. Hincker and P. Husi (Condé-sur-Noireau), 243–7.

Hollevoet, Yann 2011, 'Vondsten en vindplaatsen uit de vroege middeleeuwen'. In *Op het raakvlak van twee landschappen. De vroegste geschiedenis van Brugge*, ed. B. Hillewaert, Y. Hollevoet and M. Ryckaert (Brugge), 80–95.

Hollevoet, Yann, and Bieke Hillewaert 2002, 'Het archeologisch onderzoek achter de voormalige vrouwengevangenis Refuge te Sint-Andries/Brugge (prov. West-Vlaanderen). Nederzettingssporen uit de Romeinse tijd en de Middeleeuwen', *Archeologie in Vlaanderen* 6 (1997–8), 191–207.

Huijbers, Antoinette 2014, 'Huisplattegronden van agrarische nederzettingen uit de Volle Middeleeuwen in het Maas-Demer-Scheldegebied'. In *Huisplattegronden in Nederland. Archeologische sporen van het huis*, ed. A. G. Lange, E. M. Theunissen, J. H. C. Deeben, J. van Doesburg, J, Bouwmeester and T, de Groot (Amersfoort–Eelde), 367–419.

Huijts, Carl 1992, *De voor-historische boerderijbouw in Drenthe : reconstructiemodellen van 1300 vóór tot 1300 na Chr.* (Arnhem).

James, Simon, Anne Marshall and Martin Millett 1984, 'An early medieval building tradition', *Archaeological Journal* 141, 182–215.

Jervis, Ben 2012, 'Making-do or making the world? Tempering choices in Anglo-Saxon pottery manufacture'. In *Make-Do and Mend: Archaeologies of Compromise, Repair and Reuse*, ed. B. Jervis and A. Kyle (Oxford), 67–80.

Jordan, Peter, and Sean O'Neill 2010, 'Untangling cultural inheritance: language diversity and long-house architecture on the Pacific northwest coast', *Philosophical Transactions of the Royal Society B* 365, 3875–88.

Kuhn, Hans 1955, 'Friesisch und Nordseegermanisch', *Us Wurk* 4, 37–46.

Lanting, Jan N., and Johannes van der Plicht 2010, 'De 14C-chronologie van de Nederlandse pre- en protohistorie VI: Romeinse tijd en Merovingische periode, deel A: historische bronnen en chronologische thema's', *Palaeohistoria* 52 (2009–10), 27–168.

Lebecq, Stéphane 1983, *Marchands et navigateurs frisons du haut moyen âge* (Lille).

Logi, Adelheid De, and Stijn Van Cauwenbergh 2010, *Archeologisch onderzoek Nevele-Merendreedorp. 4 mei tot 25 juni 2010*, KLAD-Rapport 20 (Aalter).

Loveluck, Chris, and Dries Tys 2006, 'Coastal societies, exchange and identity along the Channel and southern North Sea shores of Europe, AD 600–1000', *Journal of Maritime Archaeology* 1, 140–69.
Luraghi, Silvia 2010, 'Causes of language change'. In *The Continuum Companion to Historical Linguistics*, ed. S. Luraghi and V.Bubenik (London–New York), 358–70.
Magendans, J. Renée, and J. A. Waasdorp 1989, *Franken aan de Frankenslag. Een vroeg-middeleeuwse nederzetting in 's-Gravenhage*, VOM-reeks ('s-Gravenhage).
Marshall, Anne, and Garry Marshall 1993, 'Differentiation, change and continuity in Anglo-Saxon buildings', *Archaeological Journal* 150, 366–402.
Memmott, Paul, and James Davidson 2008, 'Exploring a cross-cultural theory of architecture', *Traditional Dwellings and Settlements Review* 19, 51–68.
Metcalf, Michael, and Wybrand Op den Velde 2010, *The Monetary Economy of the Netherlands, c. 690 – c. 760 and the Trade with England: A Study of the "Porcupine" Sceattas of Series E*, Jaarboek voor Munt- en Penningkunde (Amsterdam).
Milroy, Lesley 1987, *Language and Social Networks*, 2nd edn (Oxford).
Mufwene, Salikoko S. 2000, 'Population contacts and the evolution of English', *The European English Messenger* 9, 9–15.
Mühlhäusler, Peter, Tom Dutton, Darrell T. Tryon and Stephen A. Wurm 1996, 'Post-contact pidgins, creoles and lingue franche, based on non-European and indigenous languages'. In *Atlas of Languages of Intercultural Communication in the Pacific, Asia and the Americas*, ed. S. A. Wurm, P. Mühlhäusler and D. T. Tryon (Berlin–New York), 439–70.
Nicolay, Johan A. W. 2014, *The Splendour of Power: Early Medieval Kingship and the Use of Gold and Silver in the Southern North Sea Area (5th to 7th Century AD)*, Groningen Archaeological Studies 28 (Groningen).
Nielsen, Hans F. 2001, 'Frisian and the grouping of the older Germanic languages'. In *Handbuch des Friesischen*, ed. H. H. Munske, N.Århammer, V. F. Faltings, J. F. Hoekstra, O. Vries, A. G. H. Walker and O. Witts (Tübingen), 512–23.
Olsen, Vibeke S. 2006, 'The development of (proto-)disc-on-bow brooches in England, Frisia and Scandinavia', *Palaeohistoria* 47–8 (2005–6), 479–528.
Paepe, Paul De, and Luc van Impe 1991, 'Historical context and provenancing of Late Roman hand-made pottery from Belgium, the Netherlands and Germany. First Report', *Archeologie in Vlaanderen* 1, 145–80.
Quak, Arend 2002, 'Nordic and North Sea Germanic relations'. In *The Nordic Languages*, ed. O. Bandle *et al.* (Berlin–New York), 568–72.
Reichstein, Joachim 1984, 'Der Nordseeraum als kulturelle Ausgleichzone'. In *Archäologische und naturwissenschaftliche Untersuchungen an ländlichen und frühstädtischen Siedlungen, Band 1. Ländliche Siedlungen*, ed. G. Kossack, K. Behre and P. Schmid (Weinheim), 386–94.
Renfrew, Colin 1989, 'Models of change in language and archaeology', *Transactions of the Philological Society* 87, 103–55.
Renfrew, Colin 2000, 'At the edge of knowability: towards a prehistory of languages', *Cambridge Archaeological Journal* 10, 7–34.
Robb, John 1993, 'A social prehistory of European languages', *Antiquity* 67, 747–60.
Rogge, Marc 1981, 'Een Merovingische nederzetting te Avelgem-Kerkhove (West-Vlaanderen)'. In *De Merovingische Beschaving in de Scheldevallei. Handelingen van Het Internationaal Colloquium Kortrijk, 28–30 Oktober 1980*, West-Vlaamse Archaeologica Monografieën 2, ed. A. Van Doorselaer (Kortrijk), 67–102.
Rogge, Marc 1996, 'Van tijdelijk herstel tot desintegratie (van Diocletianus tot Honorius, 284–423)'. In *De Taalgrens: Van de Oude tot de Nieuwe Belgen*, ed. D. Lamarcq and M. Rogge (Leuven), 99–137.
Ross, Malcolm 1997, 'Social networks and kinds of speech-community event'. In *Archaeology and Language I. Theoretical and Methodological Orientations*, One World Archaeology 27, ed. R. Blench and M. Spriggs (London–New York), 209–61.

Russchen, Albertus 1967, *New Light on Dark-Age Frisia* (Drachten).
Samuels, Michael L. 1971, 'Kent and the Low Countries: some linguistic evidence'. In *Edinburgh Studies in English and Scots*, ed. A. J. Aitken, A. McIntosh and H. Pálsson (London), 3–19.
Sassaman, Kenneth, and Wictoria Rudolphi 2001, 'Communities of practice in the early pottery traditions of the American Southeast', *Journal of Anthropological Research* 57, 407–25.
Siegel, Jeff 2001, 'Koine formation and creole genesis'. In *Creolization and Contact*, Creole Language Library 23, ed. N. Smith and T. Veenstra (Amsterdam–Philadelphia), 175–97.
Soulat, Jean, Anne Bocquet-Liénard, Xavier Savary and Vincent Hincker 2012, 'Hand-made pottery along the Channel coast and parallels with the Scheldt valley'. In *The Very Beginning of Europe? Cultural and Social Dimensions of Early-Medieval Migration and Colonisation*, Relicta Monografieën, ed. R. Annaert, K. De Groote, Y. Hollevoet, F. Theuws, D. Tys and L. Verslype (Brussels), 215–24.
Stiles, Patrick V. 1995, 'Remarks on the "Anglo-Frisian" thesis'. In *Friesische Studien II. Beiträge Des Föhrer Symposiums Zur Friesischen Philologie Vom 7.-8. April 1994*, North-Western European Language Evolution Supplement, ed. V. F. Faltings, A. G. H. Walker and O. Wilts (Odense), 177–220.
Taayke, Ernst and Egge Knol 1992, 'Het vroeg-middeleeuwse aardewerk van Tritsum, gem. Franekeradeel (Fr.)', *Paleo-Aktueel* 3, 84–8.
Theuws, Frans 1996, 'Haus, Hof und Siedlung im nördlichen Frankenreich (6.-8. Jahrhundert)'. In *Die Franken. Wegbereiter Europas. Vor 1500 Jahren: König Chlodwig Und Seine Erben, Vol. 2: Alltagskultur Im Frankenreich*, ed. A. Wieczorek, P. Périn, K. von Welck and W. Menghin (Mainz), 754–68.
Theuws, Frans 2014, 'Vroegmiddeleeuwse huisplattegronden uit Zuid-Nederland en hun weergave'. In *Huisplattegronden in Nederland. Archeologische sporen van het huis*, ed. A. G. Lange, E. M. Theunissen, J. H. C. Deeben, J. van Doesburg, J. Bouwmeester and T. de Groot (Amersfoort–Eelde), 314–39.
Thomas, Gabor 2012, 'Carolingian culture in the North Sea world: rethinking the cultural dynamics of personal adornment in Viking-Age England', *European Journal of Archaeology* 15, 486–518.
Timby, Jane 1988, 'The Middle Saxon pottery'. In *Southampton Finds, Volume 1: The Coins and Pottery from Hamwic*, Southampton Archaeology Monographs 4, ed. P. Andrews (Southampton–Gloucester), 73–124.
Trousdale, Graeme 2005, 'The social context of Kentish raising: issues in Old English sociolinguistics', *International Journal of English Studies* 5, 59–76.
Velde, Henk M. van der, and Menno F. P. Dijkstra 2008, 'The Rhine estuary in the Roman Period and the Early Middle Ages'. In *Cananefaten en Friezen aan de monding van de Rijn. Tien jaar archeologisch onderzoek op de Zanderij-Westerbaan te Katwijk (1996–2006)*, ADC Monografie, ed. H. M. van der Velde (Amersfoort), 413–46.
Verhoeven, Arno A. A. 1998, *Middeleeuws gebruiksaardewerk in Nederland (8ste–13de eeuw)*, Amsterdam Archaeological Studies 3 (Amsterdam).
Verstappen, Peter 2015, 'Vroegmiddeleeuws handgevormd aardewerk in de provincie Antwerpen', *Terra Incognita* 7, 93–106.
Vince, Alan 2005, 'Ceramic petrology and the study of Anglo-Saxon and later medieval ceramics', *Medieval Archaeology* 49, 219–45.
Voss, Manfred 1995, 'Kent and the Low Countries revisited'. In *Linguistic Change under Contact Conditions*, Trends in Linguistics Studies and Monographs 81, ed. J. Fisiak (Berlin–New York), 325–63.
Waddell, John, and Jane Conroy 1999, 'Celts and others: maritime contacts and linguistic change'. In *Archaeology and Language IV. Language Change and Cultural Transformation*, One World Archaeology 35, ed. R. Blench and M. Spriggs (London–New York), 127–38.
Waterbolk, Harm Tjalling, 2009, *Getimmerd Verleden. Sporen van voor- en vroeghistorische houtbouw op de zand- en kleigronden tussen Eems en IJssel*, Groningen Archaeological Studies 10 (Groningen).

Wickham, Chris 2005, *Framing the Early Middle Ages : Europe and the Mediterranean 400–800* (Oxford–New York).
Woltering, Philippus J. 1975, 'Occupation history of Texel I: The excavations at Den Burg: Preliminary Report', *Berichten van de Rijksdienst voor het Oudheidkundig Bodemonderzoek* 25, 7–36.

10

The Kingdom of East Anglia, Frisia and Continental Connections, c. AD 600–900

Tim Pestell

East Anglia has long been appreciated as sharing links with the Continent, and the Netherlands in particular, through its geographical position on the North Sea littoral. While the sea has always acted as a conduit between the two areas, the extent and duration of particular phases of contact has been more difficult to assess. The question is particularly interesting in the case of Frisia, as linguistic similarities have suggested a close relationship with England. Likewise, the Netherlands coastal regions appear to have had limited settlement, suggesting the movement of peoples from the Anglo-Saxon west (Bremmer 1990; Knol 2009; Nieuwhof 2013). In this paper I examine the nature of these contacts following the Migration Period of the 5th and 6th centuries and before the opening of the Viking Age.

I use the kingdom of East Anglia as the basis of study for two reasons. First, as a defined political, geographical and possibly cultural entity in the Anglo-Saxon period, it provides us with a unit that maintained its integrity at a number of levels throughout this period. Second, and perhaps most pertinent, it is the obvious place to look for evidence of cultural interaction, being the political and topographical land unit within England geographically closest to early-medieval Frisia (Fig. 10.1). In its Anglo-Saxon sense, East Anglia may broadly be defined as the modern English counties of Norfolk and Suffolk, although as Bede makes clear, the Isle of Ely was certainly included within it in the late 7th century at least (*Historia Ecclesiastica* IV.19). Surrounded by sea to the north and east, and partially isolated by the extensive marshlands of the Fens to the west, only to the south, and the border with the kingdom of the East Saxons, was there more traversable countryside. With its long coastline and rivers draining into the North Sea, East Anglia was a kingdom particularly suited to maritime communication, and an almost island-like territory itself on England's east coast.

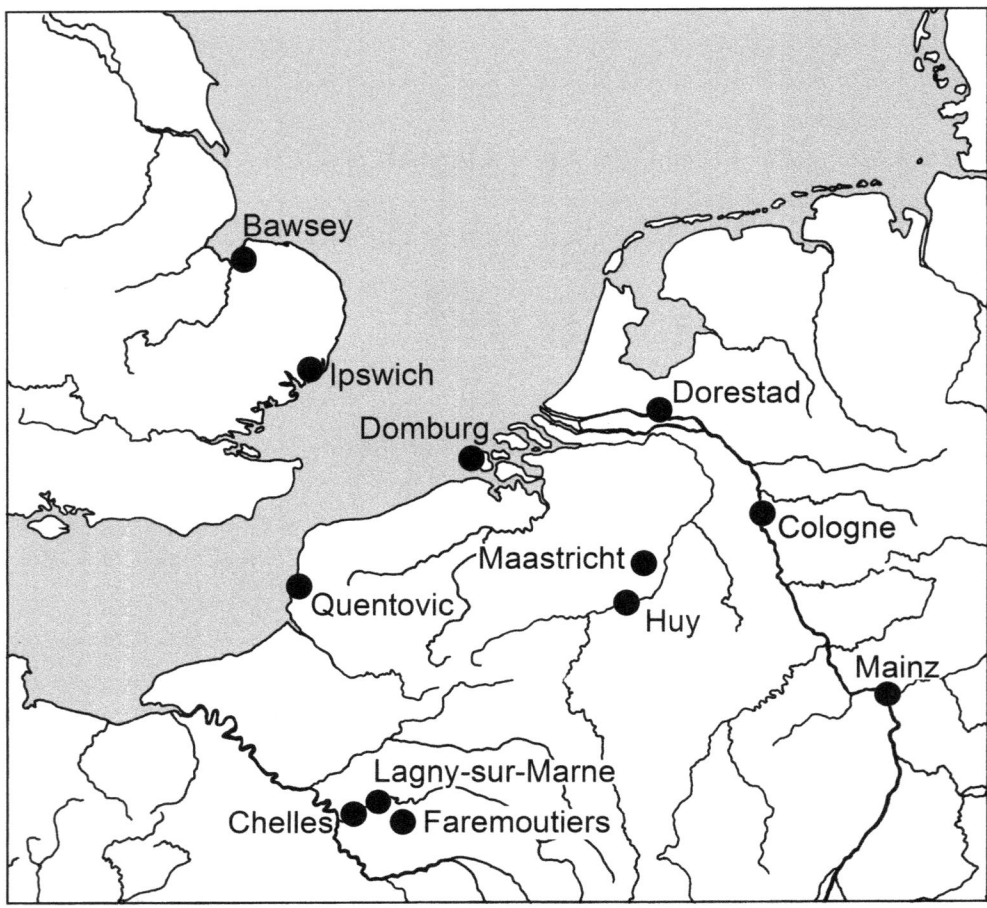

Fig. 10.1. The East Anglian kingdom and the Continent, showing the principal sites referred to in the text.

Historical background

It seems right to discuss the sources that chronicle the historical kingdom's relations with the Continent first. Sadly, these are limited, reflecting the paucity of documentation for East Anglia more generally. They begin with the mid-6th-century account by Procopius of the proposed marriage between Radigis, son of Hermegisl who ruled the continental Warni, to 'a maiden born in Brittia, whose brother was then king of the nation of the Anglii' (Procopius, *History of the Wars*, VIII, 20). The story is of uncertain veracity, as the characters and their tribes are otherwise unknown or difficult to locate accurately, but the focus is on the Rhine area, as Procopius makes it clear that he understood the Warni to live on the shore of the North Sea, east of the Rhine – in the area later called Frisia. On his father's death, Radigis attempted to break his engagement and become betrothed instead to his step-mother, who was sister of Theudebert, king of the Warni's powerful neighbours, the Franks. On arriving with an army of 100,000 men, the spurned

Anglian bride obliged Radigis to reconsider and marry her after all. If nothing else, the tale illustrates the diplomatic alliances being woven by rulers around the North Sea littoral during the Migration Period.

From Bede, we learn that Christianity was brought to the East Anglian kingdom by Felix, a Burgundian, sent by Archbishop Honorius of Canterbury, *c.* 630, with the co-operation of the new king, Sigeberht (*Historia Ecclesiastica*, II.15). The latter had formerly fled into exile in Gaul to shelter from his dynastic rival Rædwald, and was there baptised.[1] It may be that new Merovingian king Dagobert I (629–39) saw Sigeberht as a potentially useful ally or pawn to help promote to the East Anglian throne, and thus garner some future political influence in the kingdom. Sigeberht's name has been seen as a possible indication of a Merovingian dynastic connection, being the same as three Merovingian rulers, perhaps notably King Sigibert II of Austrasia and Burgundy (d. 613). Indeed, Wood has suggested Rædwald may have been married to a Frankish royal, some familial dispute leading Sigeberht to flee to the Continent (Wood 1991, 9–10).

This use of the name Sigibert or Sigeberht is also of interest given recent numismatic discoveries in East Anglia. The use of pseudo-Imperial gold continental *solidi* as pendant jewellery is well known, and at the date these coins were struck and used, it is clear that in England they were considered essentially non-numismatically, perhaps as stores of wealth or 'special-purpose' money. Thus, while having a value attached to their manufacture in precious metal, they were not in common circulation for commercial transactions (Williams 2013, 135–6). While a range of coin-types is known, two discoveries of 7th-century high-status burials provide an interesting perspective on their use. The first is that of a female excavated in grave 93 at Boss Hall, Ipswich. The burial was particularly notable for its fine composite disc brooch inlaid with a carpet of cloisonné garnets. On a necklace from the grave was a gold solidus of Sigibert III (639–56), minted at Marseilles (Scull 2009, 16–18 and figs. 2.20–2.21). The coin had been mounted with a suspension loop riveted through the coin. The second burial was discovered in January 2015 near Diss in South Norfolk.[2] This female had been buried with a magnificent gold and garnet pendant, and a necklace string including a pair of die-identical *solidi* of Sigibert III. Again, the coins had been mounted with suspension loops that were riveted on (Fig. 10.2).

How should we view these finds? Both burials were of significant women, quite probably aristocrats within East Anglian society. At one level it may simply be coincidence that both burials include coin-pendants of Sigibert III. Stray-finds of other pierced and mounted coins show that various coin-types were once worn and lost (Naylor 2015). However, in both burials the piercings gave primacy to the obverse bust of Sigibert, for it to be orientated head upright rather than the cross on the reverse. Equally interesting, John Naylor (2016) has observed that other English examples of this coin-type of Sigibert III feature loops attached with rivets, implying that all were imported and modified together. So, do these coin-pendants signify more than simply the reuse of convenient *solidi*

---

[1] Bede records Sigeberht as King Eorpwald's brother, the latter being Rædwald's son. However, William of Malmesbury and Florence of Worcester record this relationship as being through their mother. If Rædwald's stepson, Sigeberht could have been the representative of a rival line (Yorke 1990, 67–8).
[2] The site is still being investigated, hence its location is still being withheld. From the evidence of metal-detected finds, it seems possible that there may be other, 7th-century, graves on the site.

Fig. 10.2. *Solidi* of Sigibert. A: Boss Hall, Ipswich, Suffolk (copyright Ipswich Museum); B: 'Near Diss', Norfolk (copyright Norwich Castle Museum and Art Gallery).

by these aristocratic women? That the burial near Diss had two die-identical coins shows that both had been kept together since their arrival in England; in the case of the Boss Hall burial, originally dated *c*. 690–700 (Scull 2009, 101 and 114, but cf. Hines and Bayliss eds 2013, 505–9), the Sigibert III coin may have been curated for some time before being used as a grave-good. As Williams has pointed out (2006, 166), coins at this period had a symbolic function, making them desirable to wear, and it must be a strong possibility at least that there was a deliberate rather than random choice behind their incorporation in these grave assemblages.[3] The Rhine-mouth focus to the northern part of Sigibert's Austrasian kingdom may additionally have led to stronger contacts with the East Angles.[4]

[3] Is it significant that another Suffolk female burial with a coin-pendant, grave 30 at Coddenham (Penn 2011, 26–70), was of Dagobert I (629–39), Sigibert III's father, thus maintaining the dynastic connection?
[4] For instance Wood (2016) has suggested East Anglia may have been the perfect staging post for the young Dagobert II to be exiled to Ireland.

It is in the nature of the narrative Bede provides us with that we see East Anglia's continental connections focused upon the Christian, Merovingian, realms. He thus describes Fursa, the Irish missionary who had come to East Anglia *c.* AD 633–4 and founded a monastery at *Cnobheresburg*,[5] moving on in about 644 (*Historia Ecclesiastica*, III.19), possibly on Sigeberht's death (Whitelock 1972, 6). Handing over care of the monastery to his brother Foillán who had come to England with him, Fursa journeyed to the court of Clovis II of Neustria (reigned 638–56) and his mayor of the palace, Eorconwald or Erchinoald (640–57), an appearance suggesting some connection with East Anglia (Wood 1991, 7). Given land at Lagny-sur-Marne, about sixteen miles east of the centre of Paris, he founded a monastery there *c.* AD 645.

Perhaps as important as Clovis and his *maior* Erchinoald was the king's wife Balthild. As queen, she patronized the nunnery at Faremoutiers-en-Brie, to which Sæthryth and Æthilberg, daughters of King Anna of East Anglia (reigned early 640s; d. 654) subsequently both became abbesses. For both to have succeeded to the position suggests some close familial role or connection with the monastery.[6] Another East Anglian royal to become a nun abroad was Hereswith, who married Anna's brother, Æthelric, and who was mother of the East Anglian king Aldwulf (*c.* 663/4–713); she joined the convent of Chelles refounded by Balthild (*Historia Ecclesiastica*, IV.23). Their presence on the Continent surely also raises questions about Balthild's own origins. Described as 'from lands across the sea ... from the race of the Saxons' (*Vita Domnae Balthildis*, ii), this convention is generally taken to indicate her Anglo-Saxon origins. That her *vita* describes her as sold to Erchinoald as a slave may be true but equally the presence of these East Anglian princesses in Neustrian nunneries might reflect political as well as spiritual influence, 'although it would be going too far to see them as hostages' (Wood 1991, 12). If there were a later political relationship between the two areas and Balthild's origins were of any relevance, it may help explain why three royal East Anglian women came to Neustria, two becoming abbesses, the other, a queen mother, retiring *c.* 657 to Chelles like Balthild had.

Given these tantalizing hints at contact, a find from Norfolk raises intriguing questions. In March 1998, a gold seal matrix was found at Postwick, about four miles outside Norwich. On one side is the legend 'Baldehildis', around a face with long hair beneath a cross, while on the other is a naked couple in an intimate embrace, beneath a cross (Fig. 10.3; Norwish Castle Museum 2000.42). The matrix clearly finds its closest parallels in continental signet rings, such as that of Childeric (d. 481/2) which also showed a full-face portrait with centrally parted hair around which was a reversed inscription (Pestell 2012). A more relevant parallel is a gold seal-ring with swivelling matrix mentioned by Bishop Avitus of Vienne in his letter to Bishop Apollinaris of Valence which clearly worked just as the Postwick matrix once did (Shanzer and Wood 2002, 251–7). The name *Baldehildis* reiterates the continental nature of the object, the *-is* ending being consistent with Germanic documentary sources for the nominative of female personal names.

---

[5] The site has traditionally been associated with the Roman Saxon Shore fort at Burgh Castle in Norfolk on little good evidence. It could as easily have been at the similar forts of Brancaster or Caister, or indeed at another, smaller, Roman site (Pestell 2004, 56–7).

[6] Whitelock proposes that their retirement to Frankia 'suggests that there were at that time no nunneries in or near East Anglia' (1972, 8) although they of all people would have been in a position to found nunneries themselves.

Fig. 10.3. The Balthild matrix found in Postwick, Norfolk. (a) obverse; (b) reverse. Copyright Norwich Castle Museum and Art Gallery.

Of course, it might be that the gold matrix from Postwick does not belong to the historical Balthild, and it will be impossible to ever prove that it was (Fouracre 2015). If so, the find reveals the loss of a seal matrix belonging to another woman called Balthild, again from the Continent and – based on style – at this same date. Likewise, it would have been for a woman of the highest status, thus needing to seal documents, and able to afford one made of 98% pure gold. With only one historically attested Balthild, whose life and connections fit the use of such a matrix, it seems easier to accept that this is one of those rare occasions where archaeology and a documented individual coincide.[7] We cannot guess how or why the matrix should have made its way to Norfolk, but Postwick is only a few miles from an important early centre at Caistor St Edmund. Its discovery in East Anglia perhaps reiterates a link between this Merovingian queen and her original homeland.

Beyond the Bedan narrative, an absence of source material makes it harder to see links between the kingdom and the wider Continent. A brief glimpse is given in the reign of King Ælfwald (713–49). His sister, it seems, may have been Eadburgh who was to become abbess of Thanet and who corresponded with Boniface, missionary to the German peoples (Boniface, *Letters* II, XXII, XXVI and LIII). Some familial interest may be represented as Ælfwald also wrote to Boniface; a surviving letter from *c*. 747–9 promised that the seven canonical hours would be kept in the monasteries of East Anglia (*Boniface*, Letter LXV; Hoggett 2014). Churchmen clearly maintained contacts with their opposite numbers on the Continent, as Cuthwine, bishop of the East Anglian see of *Dommoc*

---

[7] We must of course bear in mind such claims would be natural for an author also responsible for curating this object! However, the double-sided nature of the matrix with 'personal' and 'public' sides suggests it was made for the actual person Balthild, rather than to represent this person by an official. Of course, this does not preclude the possibility the ring was subsequently given as a gift.

some time between 716 and 731, is recorded as visiting Rome by Bede, while William of Malmesbury records King Aldwulf (663/4–713) being addressed in a letter along with other Anglo-Saxon kings, by Pope Sergius c. 693 (Whitelock 1972, 15). Similarly, Abbot Lull of East Anglia apparently visited Alcuin on the Continent, as he is said by Alcuin to have described Alhheard and Tidfrith – bishops of the two East Anglian sees – as leading good lives (Whitelock 1972, 17).

The evidence of material culture

If there is a frustration at the lack of documentary evidence for East Anglia, the region has been blessed with a rich archaeological resource that provides some compensation. I shall look at three principal forms of evidence. First, metalwork, largely comprising items of jewellery and other decorative fittings; second, coinage, which like the other metalwork has largely been recovered by metal-detectorists; and finally pottery, discovered both in excavations and fieldwalking surveys.

Underpinning any analysis of the material culture is an appreciation that it can be difficult to use finds as evidence for migration, settlement or trade, as a multiplicity of readings are possible to explain the presence and use of specific finds. These issues of agency in the structuring and use of material culture do, however, also tacitly rely upon a recognition that some sense of shared values must have existed in the use of objects in which a prism of distinctiveness can be created by different objects (Pader 1982; Lucy 1998; Stoodley 1999; Martin 2015). These differences make East Anglia, with its abundant metal finds, such a fruitful place for analysis. It is also a feature that carries a health warning for analysis. Norfolk and Suffolk led in the movement to record finds made by metal-detecting from the early 1980s and this long relationship means that East Anglia has a much larger corpus of material than most other areas of England.[8] As such, statistically alone, it is likely to have more examples of unusual metalwork, for instance the particularly impressive Hispano-Visigothic belt buckle plate from Caistor St Edmund (Fig. 10.4A), of late 6th- to early 8th-century date (Rogerson and Ashley 2011, 256). Less exotic but still unusual are the Frankish-style belt counter-plates and sword-chapes shown in Figure 10.4B–E of late 6th or early 7th-century date from Paston and Scole. While such metalwork provides us with alternative geographies of contact to the written sources, it is nevertheless difficult evidence to deploy. In standing out against the more usual native assemblages of metalwork they may indicate the possessions of foreigners in the region; equally, they were possibly owned by Anglo-Saxons trying to say something about their own status, identity or continental cultural contacts.

Nevertheless, the discovery of a number of distinctive continental object-assemblages in excavations at the Buttermarket site in Ipswich do suggest that here we might well be looking at individuals buried with grave-goods signalling their distinctive origins and ethnic identity. The most conspicuous of these accompanied a male burial, grave 1306, in which only the palm cups, knife and one spearhead might be considered normal in the

---

[8] This continues today, Norfolk regularly recording more metalwork finds than other English counties – about 15,000 items per annum – and has consistently yielded more cases of Treasure (historical items of gold and silver) than anywhere else in the UK.

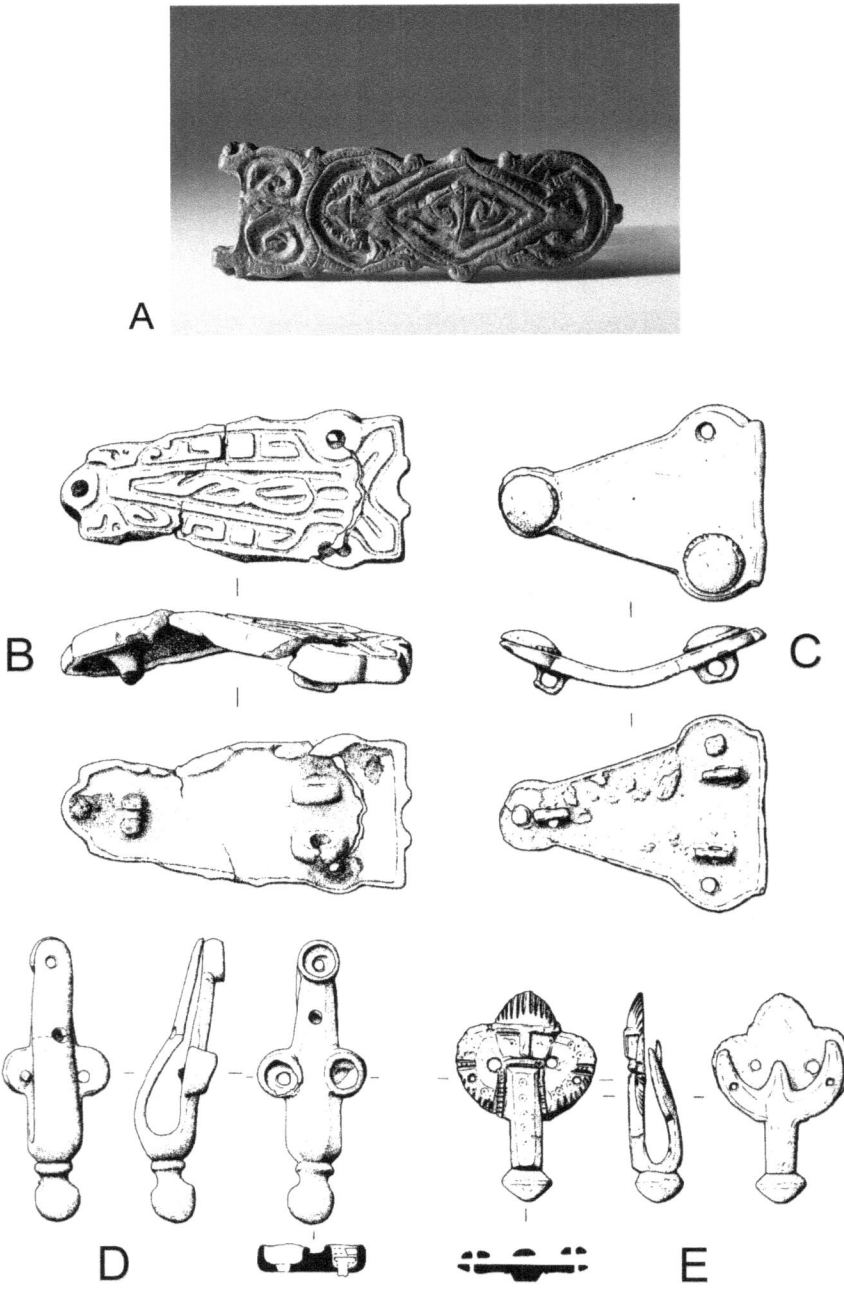

Fig. 10.4. (A) Visigothic belt counter-plate from Caistor St Edmund, Norfolk (copyright Norwich Castle Museum and Art Gallery); Frankish belt counter-plates from (B) Paston and (C) Scole. Sword-chapes from (D) Burnham Market and (E) Diss. All drawings by Jason Gibbons, copyright Norfolk Historic Environment Service.

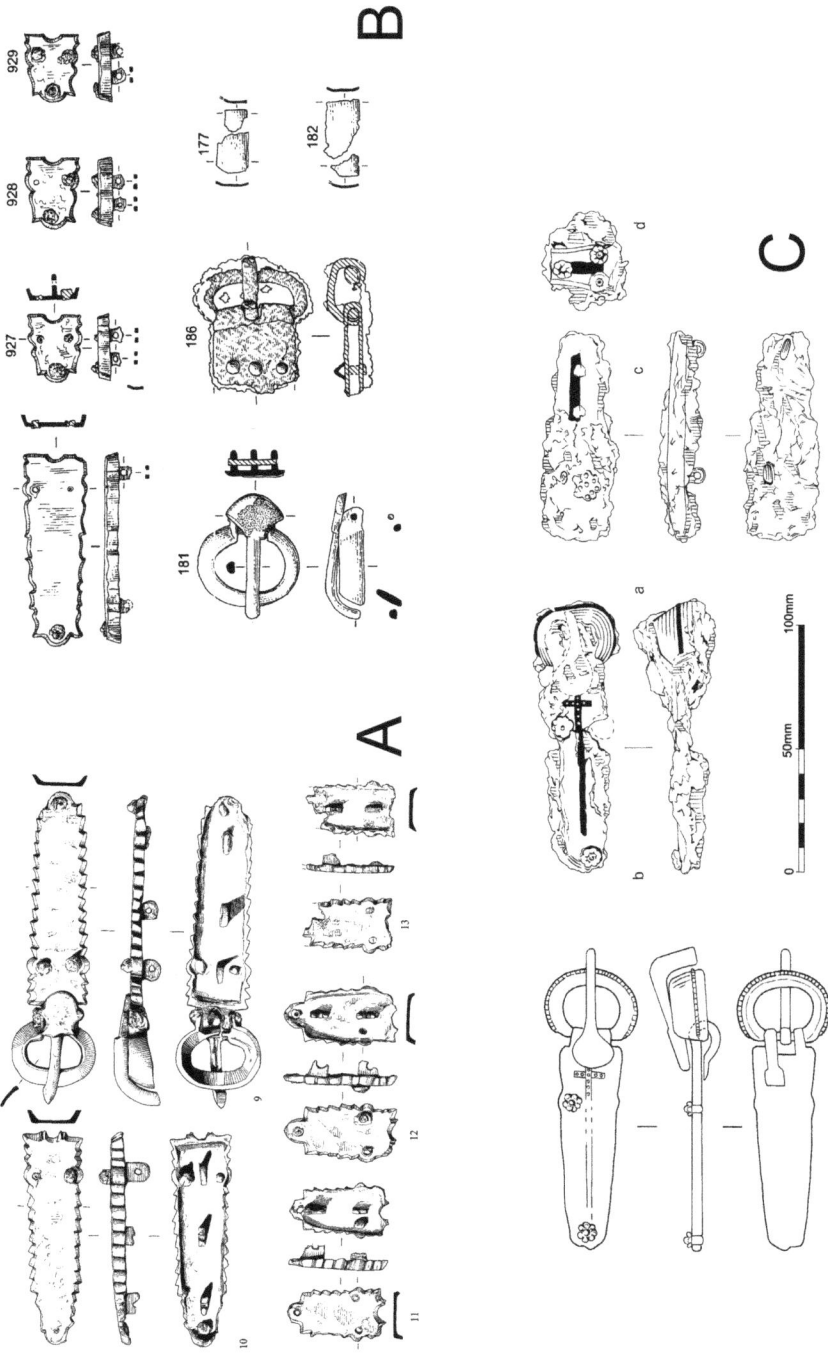

Fig. 10.5. Frankish belt-suites. (A) Ipswich Buttermarket, grave 1306 (copyright Suffolk County Council); (B) St Mary's Stadium, Southampton, grave 3520 (copyright Wessex Archaeology); (C) Long Acre, London, Grave J (copyright Museum of London Archaeology).

context of an English burial, although equally at home in continental ones. However, the *seax* and fittings, belt suite, shield boss and large spearhead are all best paralleled on the Merovingian Continent and are virtually unknown in England (Fig. 10.5A). Given the comprehensive nature of the assemblage, rather than comprising one or two individual items of foreign character, the implication is that the person was a foreigner and buried with his possessions that point to an origin in the Lower Rhineland, Netherlands or northern France (Scull 2009, 138–40 and 247–8, figs. 3.38–3.43; 2011). Nor is this grave alone in containing such continental objects; grave 2297 contained a *seax* and belt suite, of *Typ Tauberbischofsheim*, while the man in grave 3871 was likewise provisioned with such a belt-suite (Scull 2009, 293).

The use of continental-style objects as grave-goods suggesting the burial of at least three foreigners, and by extension the presence of a foreign community, is given weight by the cemetery being contained within a known trading site or *emporium* – exactly the sort of place where one might expect to see foreign merchants arriving, living, working and occasionally dying. Such a picture is reiterated by the discovery of such grave-goods in cemeteries from two other English *emporia*, those of *Hamwic*, modern Southampton, and *Lundenwic* or London. In Southampton, a very similar *seax* and belt suite of Frankish style was found in grave 3520, likewise of *c.* AD 540/50–670/80, while a distinctive crescentic gold pendant accompanying a female in grave 4202 has a direct parallel from the *terp* at Wijnaldum (Birbeck *et al.* 2005). From London, an iron belt-suite, S361, was recovered in grave J [588], deposited *c.* 680–710 AD (Scull 2012, 285), from a dispersed cemetery in the Long Acre/Floral Street area. While we should be wary that such continental grave-goods would only have been used in the burial of foreigners, their use by locals would have provided a pointed expression of difference from the prevailing material culture. As such, they would have inevitably made some statement of identity and contact with the Continent, not least by English merchants who made regular trips abroad.

Just as continental trade continued after the end of burial with grave goods, so there was no diminution in the appearance of continental material in the archaeological record. Various brooch-types are now being recognized in England that are clearly of continental origin, dating from the end of the 7th century, through to the 10th and 11th centuries (Thomas 2012). A number stand out in an English context by their general rarity, for instance examples of enamelled 'saint' brooches or *Heiligenfibeln* of *c.* AD 825–900. They have a general Frankish-continental distribution, but examples have been found in West Acre and Elsing in Norfolk (Fig. 10.6A).[9]

Among other continental types are the brooches of 9th- or even 10th-century date from Kelling, set with a central glass pellet, which finds parallels from near Paderborn and Friesland, and an altogether more ornate brooch of composite construction from Martham, set with glass pellets and filigree, again with similar examples from Frisia (Fig. 10.6B–C) (Rogerson and Ashley 2011, 257–8, figs. 6.42 and 6.43; Eggenstein *et al.* 2008, 290–1 Kat Nr. 147.8; Bos 2007/8, 712, fig. 4a 2.3.1–9). Perhaps most exceptional is a fragment of a hinged bracelet from Bracon Ash in Norfolk, dating to the second half of the 8th century (Fig. 10.6D). In the early Carolingian Tassilo Chalice Style, it depicts seven fields of back-turned zoomorphic interlace and is one of very few British-found

---

[9] That from West Acre is now Norwich Castle Museum (hereafter NCM) 1994.163.

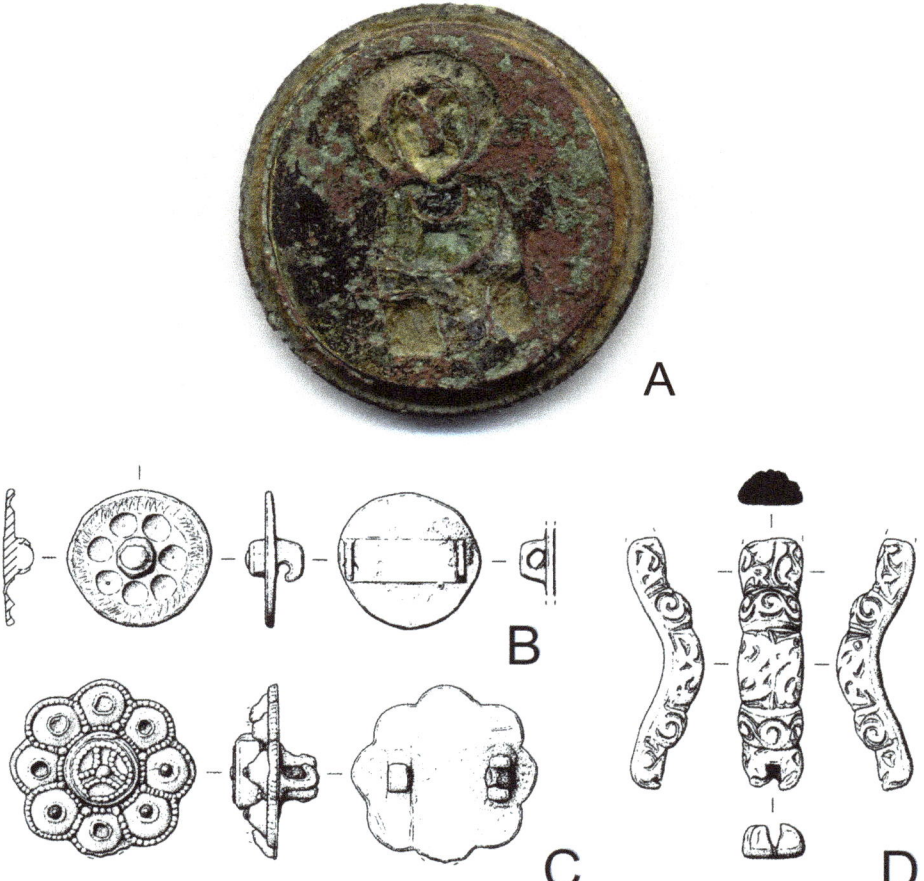

Fig. 10.6. (A) 'Saint' brooch from West Acre, Norfolk (copyright Norwich Castle Museum and Art Gallery); continental disc brooches from Kelling (B) and Martham (C); bracelet fragment from Bracon Ash (D). Drawings B–D by Jason Gibbons, copyright Norfolk Historic Environment Service.

items in this style. A complete example is known from Truchtlaching, Bavaria (Rogerson and Ashley 2010, 131; Eggenstein *et al.* 2008, 200, Kat. Nr. 44). These finds all attest to an ongoing mechanism for the importation and use of foreign goods, if not of foreigners themselves. However, if we are choosing to examine evidence for close cultural contact, arguably it is those forms of material culture that are shared which are most useful. Perhaps the most obvious sign of this is in the use of small equal-armed brooches known as 'ansates'. Indeed, their continental origins in the 7th century have become almost lost as their use was adopted so widely across Anglo-Saxon England and especially, it seems, in East Anglia.

Ansate brooches have been considered by various scholars, and catalogued with typologies developed by Hübener (1972) and Thörle (2001). The most important recent discussion is by Weetch (2014) and the following observations are highly dependent upon her unpublished work, the use of which is gratefully acknowledged.

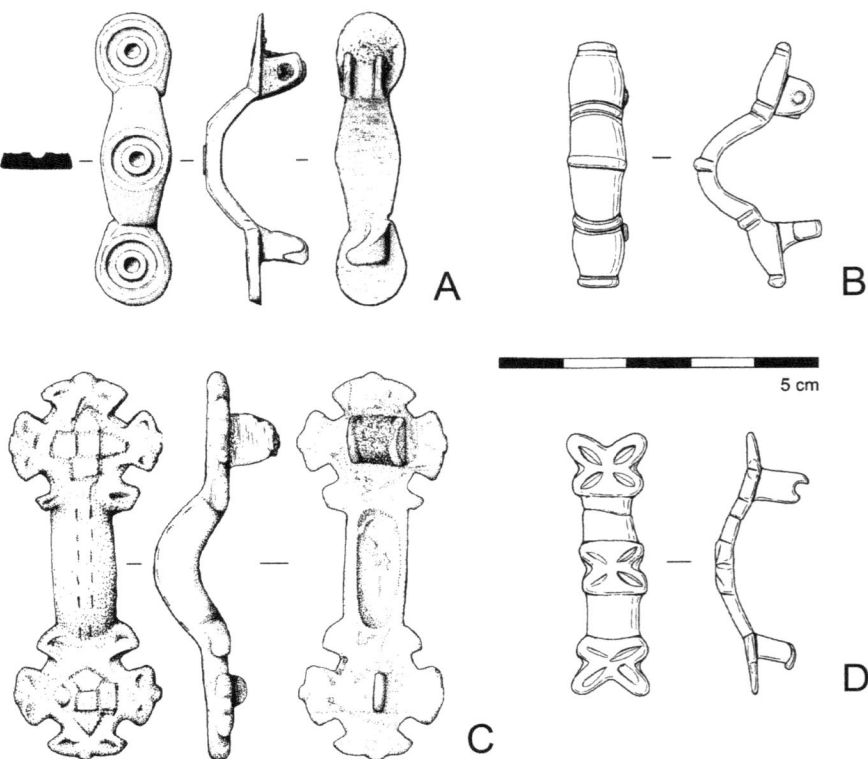

Fig. 10.7. Examples of ansate brooches. (A) Beachamwell, Norfolk; (B) Great Barton, Suffolk; (C) Little Barningham, Norfolk; (D) Great Barton, Suffolk. Drawings A and C by Jason Gibbons, copyright Norfolk Historic Environment Service; B and D by Donna Wreathall, copyright Suffolk Archaeological Service.

The fashion for ansate brooches in England had its *floruit* in the 9th–10th centuries, compared to the 8th–9th centuries on the Continent, which is probably why some types, for instance Thörle's earlier Gruppe I variant, are almost completely absent in England, yet plentiful on the Continent (Weetch 2014, 230). Despite this, the widespread use of the general ansate form shows that a continental fashion became adopted and then adapted so that some types were almost absent from England while common on the Continent and vice versa. Such conditions can only have occurred as a result of local production as well as importation. Thus, Thörle's *Gruppen* I and III–VI seem to be imports into England, while II.Aiii, VII.B, VIII.B and XI.D (for example) were probably made locally.

The adoption of ansate brooches is important for showing the sharing of a common form of dress accessory yet at the same time the subtle nuances that could be projected through its variations. For instance Gruppe XII have variants Ai of 'Domburg' type, where they were found in significant quantities, while Aii of 'East Harling' type, with a distribution concentrated upon the East of England 'may be products of Frisian craftsmen working within East Anglia' (Weetch 2014, 260) (Fig. 10.7A–B). They might thus reflect chronological, geographical or social differentiation, while yet being part of a shared dress tradition.

What might this tell us about the nature of contact or exchanges with Frisia? Despite appearing in the 6th century in northern Merovingian graves their adoption in England from the 8th century reflects for Weetch 'new trade networks that facilitated the import of a wide variety of non-prestige goods' (2014, 248). Trade is therefore seen as the motor helping to drive the adoption of fashion, both with northern France and Frisia, with East Anglia sharing specific brooch forms particularly strongly with Frisia from the 9th century, for instance those of Types VIII.B and Type XII (Fig. 10.8: Weetch 2014, 258–60). Perhaps most interesting is that Weetch sees the 9th century as a period of change, with a decline in the contacts between southern England and the north French and Frisian coast – coincident with the decline of *Hamwic* – not being matched on the east coast. Instead, the shared use of new ansate brooch-types, seems to show new or modified social networks occurring 'borne out of contact with maritime traders and distant places' (ibid., 268).

Coins and trade

The role of *emporia* and *wic* sites in general thus provides an interesting element in this debate about contact. As originally modelled by Hodges, *emporia* were established by rulers in emergent kingdoms in the 7th and 8th centuries. Based on a system of gift-giving and reciprocity, with an economy embedded in social structures they used monopolistic gift-exchange to retain power and status, reward followers and build alliances (Hodges 1989). The last thirty years has transformed our knowledge of both the major *emporia* like Ipswich and Southampton, but more notably discovered many other smaller Middle Anglo-Saxon trading sites. Characterized as 'wiclets' by Hodges (2006, 68–70), they are still minimalized by him in terms of their economic impact. Perhaps the single most important element in this has been our increased understanding of coin use in this period. Not only has this provided the single most important contradiction of Hodges' more anthropological understanding of coinage as being socially embedded, it has revealed a significant number of coin-rich sites to have had similar economic trajectories to places like *Hamwic*, and several to have had regional, rather than merely local, economic importance in trade networks (Pestell 2011, 561–2; Naylor 2012). Equally important is the increasingly detailed picture we now have gold coin use in the preceding, pre-*emporia*, 6th and 7th centuries (cf. Scull *et al.* 2016). This is exactly that period when political elites were establishing themselves as kings over more defined territories with, according to Hodges' model, the social structures which *emporia* were subsequently developed to help maintain (Carver 2005, 497–502; Hodges 1989, 186–93).

Once thought of as 'special-purpose' money struck in limited amounts, the number of post-pseudo-Imperial gold *tremisses* now being recovered through metal-detection, and the number of dies they represent, demonstrate that their issues were far from limited or restricted. While undoubtedly still used for large-scale transactions, they increasingly indicate a monetized economy, albeit apparently unregulated. The earliest gold coinage in Anglo-Saxon England begins with imported types whose dating is difficult, including Byzantine, Frankish, Visigothic and Burgundian types. More important for our present concerns, the picture given by Rigold (1975) in his catalogue of the Sutton Hoo coin hoard saw Kent as the pre-eminent area for such coinage, apparently strengthening the case for contact between this area and the Merovingian kingdoms. The hoard of 37

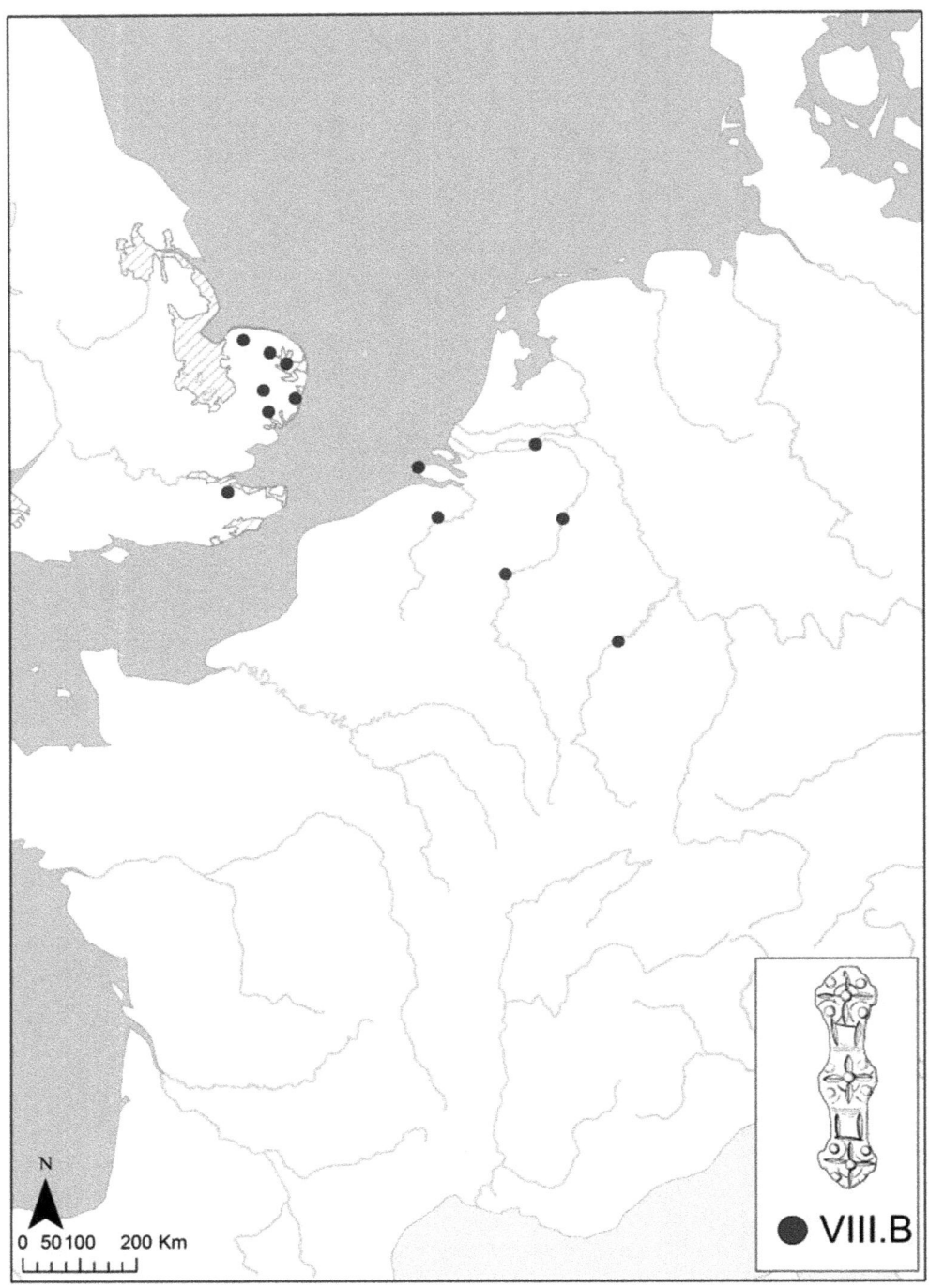

Fig. 10.8. Distribution of (above) Type VIII.B and (opposite) Type XII ansate brooches: generally and sub-types Ai–iii, after Weetch 2014, figs. 5.12 and 5.10. Copyright R. Weetch.

East Anglia, Frisia and Continental Connections

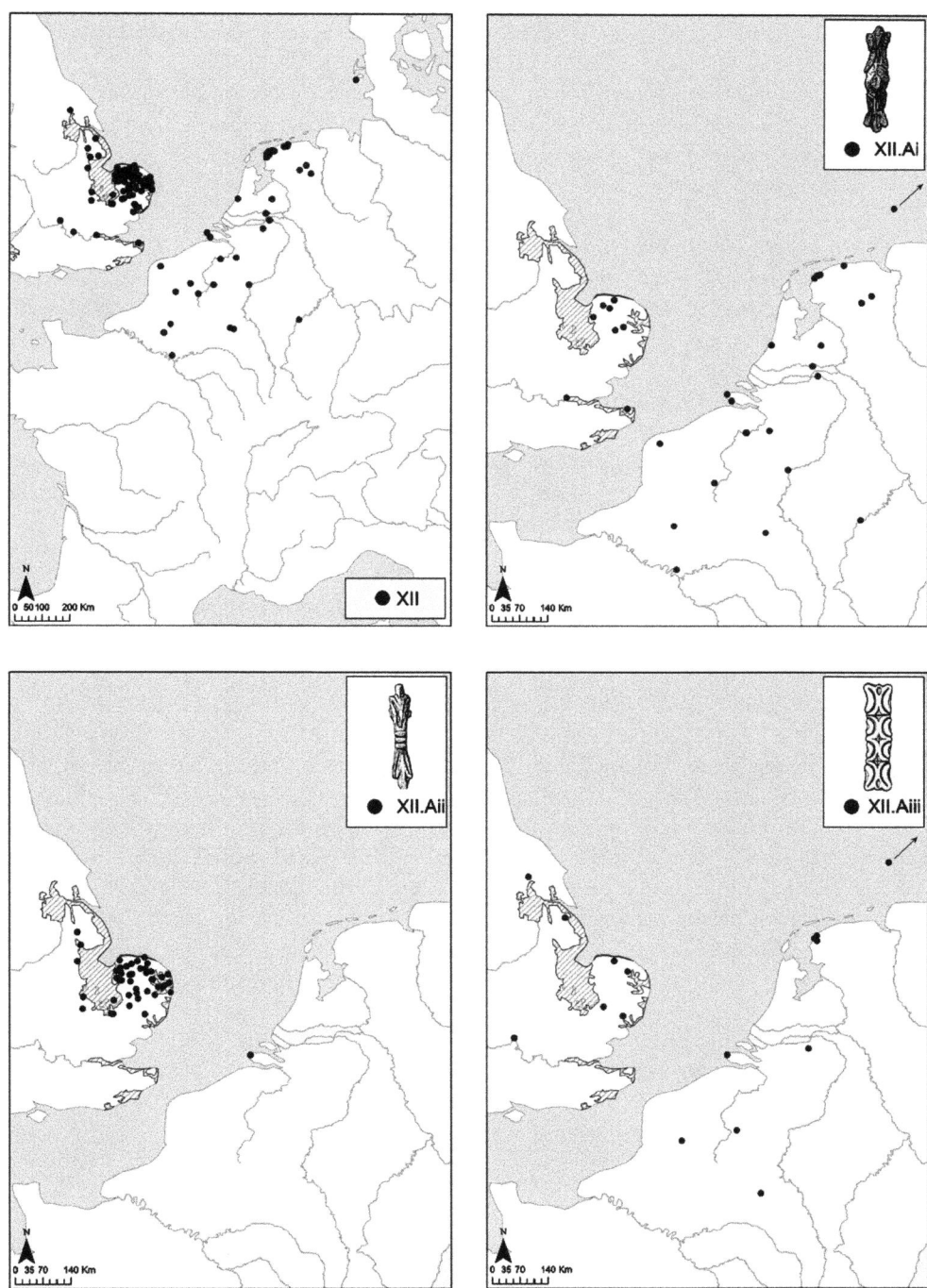

Merovingian *tremisses* in the Sutton Hoo ship burial was accommodated within this, being seen as specially selected and symbolic (Grierson 1970).

We can now see that there were also large numbers of gold coins present in Norfolk and Suffolk, as well as quantities in Yorkshire, Lincolnshire and Essex, including along the Thames valley. These indicate that gold coinage from northern France was circulating widely within the North Sea zone (Williams 2006, 170–1). Among these coins, the rise of mint-and-moneyer types allows us to see the increasing prominence of north Frankish areas such as Quentovic, but importantly also Dorestad, Huy, Maastricht and Cologne, as well as anonymous Frisian issues of 'Nietap' type. A spectacular demonstration of this, and an illustration that the Sutton Hoo coins were not a unique collection, is the discovery of another *tremissis* hoard from the kingdom of East Anglia. Found on the west Norfolk fen-edge near Swaffham, it comprises at least 57 continental *tremisses* and, remarkably, a crushed 6th-century bracteate.[10]

With a number of die-duplicates, the coins have a preponderance of issues from the Austrasian area of north and eastern Frankia, including die-identical examples from Mainz and Strasburg (two each) and Maastricht (three examples). It tends to suggest a hoard collected while travelling through this area and again illustrates the contact between East Anglia and the Low Countries.[11] Perhaps as interesting is the crushed bracteate. While the coin hoard has been well dispersed by ploughing, its recovery is from an area with few other finds. This, and the sheer rarity of gold bracteates in East Anglia (Behr and Pestell 2015), makes it a curious component of the hoard, being of much earlier (6th-century) date. Its presence perhaps recalls the Sutton Hoo hoard which includes three gold blanks and two ingots, and which led Williams to suggest that the hoard's total weight of 61.11g is equivalent to 48.12 *tremisses* or 16.04 *solidi*. He therefore concludes the ingots and blanks 'may have been included to make up a total weight' (Williams 2006, 177). He has further argued that this gold coinage was being used in the context of a wider bullion economy, in which *tremisses* acted as a weight standard. In support of this, he cites the presence of a *tremissis* from the Chipping Ongar 'hoard' of two coins; one of which had a plug of gold attached, which brought it up to 1.3 g (ibid., 182). Significantly, this is not a one-off occurrence, as two other examples have also now been found, again in East Anglia, at Beachamwell (Norfolk) and Rendlesham (Suffolk).[12]

East Anglia's reception and use of such gold coinage unsurprisingly led it to produce its own issues of *tremisses* (Marsden 2016), the international reach of which has recently been illustrated by the discovery of an example being found near Rouen.[13] East Anglia was a leading arena for both the circulation of gold coinage and thus high-value (and

---

[10] Understandably, this new hoard's findspot is not yet being disclosed. The site has been detected by different people over the years, making it likely that other finds of *tremisses* may have been made but not reported. The total of 57 known coins is therefore likely to be a minimum figure.

[11] Perhaps significantly, two coins (from Huy and Sion) die-link to the Sutton Hoo hoard. These die-linkages are the observation of my colleague Dr Adrian Marsden, who is publishing the hoard (Marsden in prep.).

[12] The *tremissis* from Beachamwell (NCM 2012.182) weighs 1.309 g while that from Rendlesham (EMC 2013.0198) is brought up to 1.23 g.

[13] My thanks to Adrian Marsden for making me aware of this. The coin, found in late 2015, is die-identical to another recovered from Thrandeston, Suffolk (EMC 2010.0008) of Marsden's die type 4G (Marsden 2016). Its pale gold colour suggests it is a late coin issue.

presumably high-volume) associated trade, with an economic focus on a par with Kent and the south coast. Equally important, such early trade centres are now being increasingly localized, with the identification of multiple-finds of gold coinage at certain sites, like Coddenham and Rendlesham, showing economic foci in the pre-*emporia* landscape.

Our picture of these trading sites becomes still more detailed, and nuanced, as we enter the period of early silver coinage or *sceattas*. Of particular importance are the so-called Series D and 'Porcupine' *sceattas*, categorized as Series E, with their highly degenerate designs derived from Roman busts. They have been found in large numbers in both England and Low Countries and while some are English imitations, it is clear that the majority are Frisian. A corpus of over 3,000 Series E *sceattas* has now been compiled by Op den Velde and Metcalf (2009 and 2010), and three phases of production identified. They suggest that nearly a thousand dies may have been used in the first phase, nearly 4,000 in the second and many fewer, perhaps only about 400 in the third. If a die could strike about 10,000 coins before needing replacement this allows for the production of about 50 million coins of porcupine-type alone (Op den Velde and Metcalf 2011, 104). Furthermore, it now seems that most porcupine *sceattas* were struck in the Rhine-mouth area, the bulk probably at Domburg and Dorestad, despite about four times as many being found in England compared to the Low Countries. The explanation for this disparity has been that the coins were essentially 'an export coinage, destined to pay for imported goods' (op den Velde and Metcalf 2011, 108).

Looking at the kingdom of East Anglia more specifically we may draw out certain elements in the use of coinage in more detail. Naismith (2013) used the 2,943 *sceattas* then recorded in England on the Corpus of Early Medieval Coin Finds (hereafter EMC),[14] of which 781 or 26.5% came from Norfolk and Suffolk. Of the coins from the two counties, some 224 (29.5%) were of Series D and E, compared to 190 (25%) of the local Series Q and R. Thus 'local' coinage was outnumbered in circulation by the number of imported coins, illustrating the active role of monetary exchange with, and economic impact of, the Continent. Equally telling is the dearth of English coinage on the Continent, only 84 coins, or 8%, of the 1,000-plus discovered at Domburg and Westenschouwen being English. Of these, only 6 were of East Anglian Series Q and R, while the local Series D and E represented 22% and 47% of coins found (Op den Velde and Klaasen 2004). These proportions have not changed fundamentally in East Anglia in the meantime and while some caution is necessary because the distribution also reflects the English lowland focus to metal-detecting, the numbers of *sceattas* do show a clear bias to the east coast and the North Sea littoral. At the centre of this is East Anglia, emphasizing its importance to this trading zone. Further still, there are concentrations of coinage, notably in south-east Suffolk and north-west Norfolk that seem to represent economically important areas within the kingdom (Metcalf 2001). The location of sites that have yielded above-average quantities of coins and often of other metalwork finds of 8th and 9th century date are the so-called 'productive' sites which are frequently difficult to interpret as they have been discovered by metal-detectorists rather than subjected to excavation (Ulmschneider and Pestell 2003; Davies 2010). They appear to represent a variety of functions, including ecclesiastical and secular centres as well as temporary markets or fairs (Pestell 2003).

[14] Online at www.fitzmuseum.cam.ac.uk/emc/.

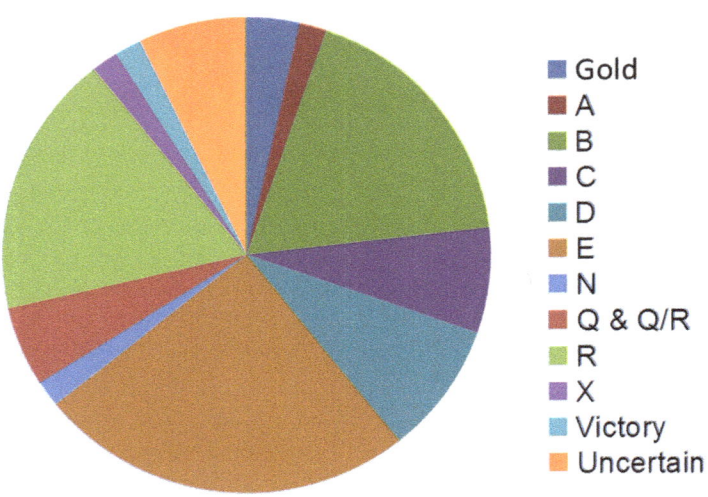

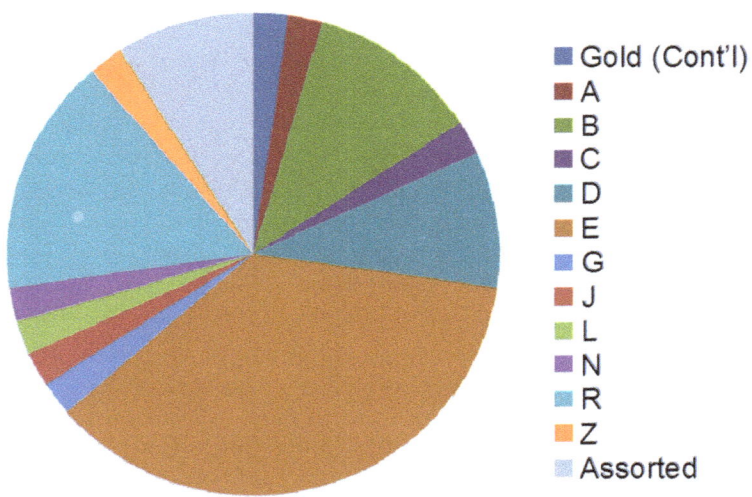

Fig. 10.9. Proportions of *sceattas* by series from Bawsey (above) and Caistor St Edmund (below).

In examining the coinage from some of these 'productive' sites, we can see distinct differences. For instance, Bawsey in north-west Norfolk has yielded over eighty *sceattas*, making it the most coin-rich site in Norfolk, and one of the largest in England. Various different *sceatt*-types have been found including, as we might expect, Series D and E, Series B, C and Q coins that may have been minted in Middle or East Anglia, and ten of Series R.[15] Looking at the overall proportions of coinage for Bawsey (Fig. 10.9a), the continental Series D and E account for 35%, higher than our rule-of-thumb average for the county. Even more striking is Caistor St Edmund near Norwich (Fig. 10.9b). Intensive metal-detecting has revealed another 'productive' site which is now the second-most prolific in Norfolk, with 43 recorded *sceattas*. The site lies, like classic *emporia* such as London and Rouen, outside the Roman town walls of the former *civitas* capital *Venta Icenorum* and would appear to be associated with a possible early-medieval estate centre, richly furnished 7th-century burials overlooking the site (Pestell 2011, 571–2; Penn 2000). Here, some 46.5% are of Series D and E, contrasting with 16.3% of Series R, whereas Bawsey's 24% is far closer to the expected level. Naturally, some variability between sites is only to be expected and the overall figures are not large enough to be statistically reliable. However, they may provide some commentary on the various redistributive functions of the sites, and their local or longer-distance connections. Perhaps also notable is that at Caistor we see a spike in its volume of lost coinage occurring about AD 700–20, which may suggest that it had two decades of booming trade, contrasting with the apparently more steady economy of Bawsey and other sites such as Barham in Suffolk (Pestell 2014, fig. 15). It is this rhythm of economic rise and fall that adds an interesting additional dimension to our understanding of the coinage and one which will repay further research in helping to interpret the nature of trading relationships with the Continent.

The decline of the *sceatt* coinage and Carolingian conquest of Frisia means that the role of international trade becomes harder to trace through coinage, and in particular to gain ideas of the volume of currency in use. In contrast to the mass of 8th-century continental *sceattas*, EMC records a modest 27 coins from Carolingian Frankia and the West Frankish kingdom between 768 and *c.* 877 contrasting with 69 coins from the period 584–750 for Merovingian Frankia.[16] It is also clear that new political controls associated with coin-use were being implemented. Naismith has pointed out that between *c.* 750/60 and 785, some 24% of southern English coinage was Carolingian, whereas a crackdown *c.* 785 led to foreign coins all but disappearing, so that *c.* 785–96, the native currency was about 99% English, and only marginally less *c.* 796–830 with 2.5% Carolingian coins (Naismith 2012, 205–8). While the total rises to about 10% *c.* 830–65, this period has even less certainty as many of the coins might well have arrived as a result of Viking losses rather than through the course of regular trade (ibid., 205–7).

Interestingly, of the 45 Carolingian coins recorded by EMC, by far the bulk belong to those of Louis the Pious (814–40), many of which are imitative examples of either

---

[15] There is also a claim that two gold coins had been found at Bawsey, suggesting use may go back to the second half of the seventh century. Certainly, gold coin-use also seems to date from *c.* 600 at the Suffolk sites of Rendlesham and possibly Coddenham. However, the gold coins at Bawsey were never seen and the veracity of the source, a detectorist convicted for illegal metal-detecting, is certainly questionable.

[16] EMC accessed March 2016.

Fig. 10.10. Ship penny of King Æthelstan of East Anglia (*c.* AD 825–45). Copyright Norwich Castle Museum and Art Gallery.

Anglo-Saxon or Frisian manufacture. Although a spread have been found running along the south and east coasts, once again the bulk of the finds has been made in East Anglia. Equally interestingly, the distribution of these coins is more widespread, unlike the earlier concentrations of *sceattas* to the north-west and south-east of the kingdom. They now appear to lie around Thetford and Ipswich, two of the Late Anglo-Saxon towns in the kingdom, perhaps indicating the growth of urbanism.

Perhaps the most succinct echo of the importance of European trade to the kingdom of East Anglia may be found in the unique coinage of its king, Æthelstan (*c.* 825–45). As so often for East Anglia, he is known principally from his extensive issues of coinage, with a variety of designs. Notably, one featured a ship (Archibald 1982; Williams 2010) (Fig. 10.10). The two known examples – from different dies – were both found in Norfolk, at West Harling, and near Norwich. They have the king's name and title surrounding the central ship design, which was unprecedented among English broad-flan pennies. It clearly imitates Carolingian 'ship' deniers which were minted in small numbers at Quentovic and Dorestad in the last years of Charlemagne and early years of Louis the Pious. Perhaps inevitably, they resemble most clearly the Dorestad type. The coin-type was not only a clear expression of Æthelstan's claim to kingship and independence from external overlordship, but consciously avoided Mercian coin design. Equally important, it surely acted as a statement reflecting East Anglia's links with the Continent, and presumably the importance of trade with it. If this seems to push the evidence too far, this continental contact was aped in another issue of Æthelstan, known this time from a lead trial-piece, using the Carolingian 'Temple' design, again known from deniers of

Louis.[17] Æthelstan was presumably allying himself with a continental ruler rather than his English contemporaries (and rivals).

Pottery

I shall end this brief survey by considering the role of pottery. So often ubiquitous on archaeological sites, it is perhaps surprising to find that very little of foreign manufacture appears in East Anglian archaeological assemblages. In the 7th century, imported wheel-turned Frankish vessels seem to have been accorded value as exotic goods, finding their way into a number of inhumation burials.[18] These pots were studied by Evison (1979) and found to have an overwhelming concentration in Kent, perhaps unsurprisingly given their Frankish origins. A number have been found in East Anglia, including the curious bottle found in the mound one ship burial from Sutton Hoo (Youngs 1983) and from the robbed grave 13 at Caistor-by-Norwich (Myres and Green 1973, 215 and

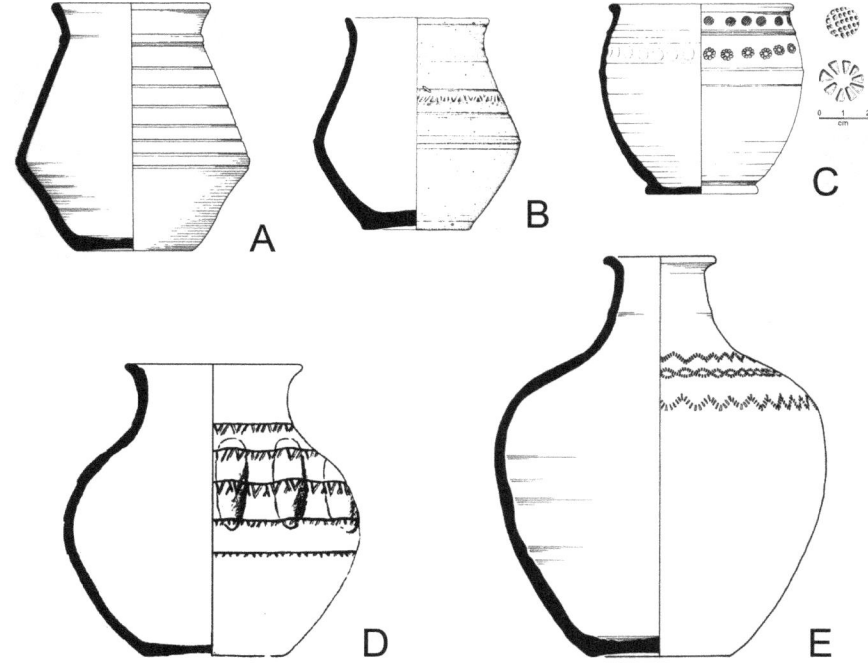

Fig. 10.11. Frankish vessels recovered from 7th-century East Anglian burials. (A) 'Near Diss'; (B) Bayfield; (C) Snettisham; (D) Caistor St Edmund; (E) Coddenham. Scale 1:4. Drawings A–C and E by Jason Gibbons, copyright Norfolk Historic Environment Service and (E) Suffolk County Council; (D) after Myres and Green 1973, Fig. 61 F, copyright Norfolk Museums Service.

---

[17] EMC 2000.0090.
[18] Alternatively, they held high-status goods, for instance wine or olive oil, none of which have yet been identified through residue analysis: Geake 1997, 90.

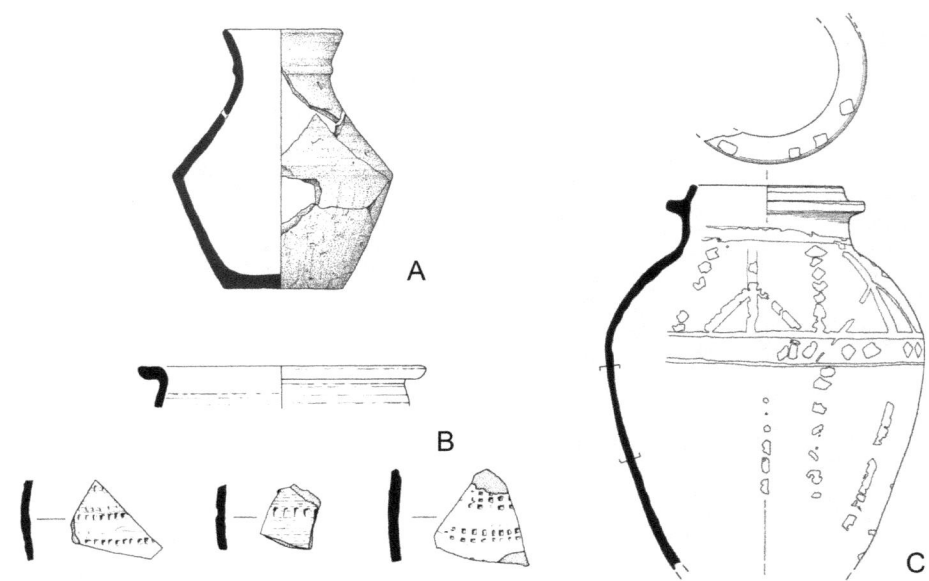

Fig. 10.12. Imported continental pottery found in East Anglia. Badorf Ware from (A) Bloodmoor Hill, Carlton Colville and (B) Fishergate, Norwich; (C) Tating Ware from Staunch Meadow, Brandon. Drawings copyright (A) Cambridge Archaeological Unit; (B) Norfolk Historic Environment Service; (C) Suffolk Archaeology Service.

223–4). More recently, three other high-status burials have been excavated in Norfolk including imported pots. One, from Bayfield, is of Evison's Group 1, dating to the first half of the 7th century and with a fabric pointing to a source in the Pas-de-Calais (Penn and Whitmore 2007, 219). The other two, from Snettisham and 'near Diss' are as yet unpublished; that from Snettisham (Fig. 10.11C) is an open bowl, showing some features of Evison's Group 3 bowls, and that from 'near Diss' (Fig. 10.11A) is a tall biconical bowl of Evison's Group 3b. Two further examples also probably derive from the Pas-de-Calais, excavated from graves in Coddenham and Hadleigh, Suffolk, and have fabric so similar they may be products of the same kiln-site and even cargo (Vince 2011, 75–7). Together, these examples suggest that their inclusion as grave-goods – whether or not they were included for containing something else of value – formed part of a defined set of object-types recognized as particularly appropriate to a well-furnished burial. Beyond issues of prestige this was equally likely a symbolic element indicative of cultural connections placing these 7th-century individuals in an international framework, by referencing Frankish material culture.

We may see a transition in the use of such imported pottery in burials, to its presence on settlement sites, at Bloodmoor Hill, Carlton Colville, on the Norfolk-Suffolk border. Here, 20 sherds were recovered, comprising 0.6% of all Anglo-Saxon pottery by weight. Eighteen of these were from one Merovingian biconical jar (Fig. 10.12A), probably northern French and of the same types as the earliest imports seen from *Lundenwic*. Two more sherds, one Rhenish of Walberberg type, the other of Huy type from the Meuse valley, appear to be of mid-7th- to early-8th-century date, preceding the use of Ipswich ware (Tipper 2009, 223–4).

By the early 8th century, East Angles had largely abandoned hand-made ceramics with the industrialized production of Ipswich-ware pottery, which appeared throughout the kingdom from *c.* 720 (Blinkhorn 2012). Despite this being the age of the *emporia*, the appearance of continental pottery remained restricted across the kingdom. At the high-status settlement of Brandon, for instance, extensive excavations yielded 21,502 Anglo-Saxon period sherds, yet of these only 76 (0.35%) were of imports, the bulk (20,406 or 95%) being Ipswich ware (Blinkhorn 2014, 149–50 and 157–9).[19] The manufacture of such a robust well-fired local ceramic, and the evident supply network allowing it to reach all corners of the kingdom, possibly made it less important or desirable to import pottery from elsewhere. However, the same lack of continental ceramics is true of other sites outside East Anglia, for instance the large finds assemblage from the high-status settlement at Flixborough, with only 51 sherds (0.98%) of the Middle Anglo-Saxon pottery (Young *et al.* 2009, 339 and 349–68).

At one level, this suggests that bulky continental ceramics were rarely traded and relatively unimportant. However, it may also lead us to question the use of such pottery. The Ipswich ware recovered at Flixborough is also relatively small in terms of the overall Middle Anglo-Saxon pottery assemblage, comprising 282 sherds or 5.4% of the total. This is one of the largest known collections outside the kingdom of East Anglia (only *Lundenwic* has produced more) and is one of the northernmost sites yielding the ware. Within the assemblage, the sherds are characteristically from large jars and pitchers; nearly a quarter (23.7%) of jars have a rim diameter of 161 mm or more, a higher proportion than in Ipswich, while pitchers, representing less than 5% of Ipswich ware vessels from East Anglian sites, make up a third of the assemblage from Flixborough (Young *et al.* 2009, 359). This may suggest that it is the contents of the pot which were more important than the vessel containing them.

In this light we may compare the evidence of pottery imports between Ipswich and elsewhere in the kingdom. Within the *emporium*, imports comprise a significant proportion of the total Middle Anglo-Saxon ceramic assemblage, of up to 15% (Wade 1988, 96). Although Ipswich was positioned midway between Quentovic and Dorestad, the majority of pottery is Rhenish rather than North French. Of these, Badorf ware (including Relief-Band Amphorae), is especially common with at least 130 vessels represented, although numerous other Rhenish types have also been identified including Walberberg, Hunneschans, Tating and Grey-gritted wares (Coutts 1991). The latter is interesting in that it is a far more utilitarian pottery-type, characteristic of the northern Netherlands coastal region, but has a minimum of 33 vessels represented at Ipswich. For Coutts, this type of pottery was 'probably … the personal cooking wares of Frisian traders in the North Sea *emporia*' (ibid., 17). Smaller quantities of various northern French wares were also recovered, including Black- and the less common Grey- and Brown-Burnished Wares, Greyware (of a type found at Quentovic) and La Londe Types I and II.

---

[19] There is a discrepancy between the 21,507 sherds stated by Blinkhorn at page 149 and the 21,502 in his table 1; I have taken table 1 as being the correct figure in that it is here broken down into its elements.

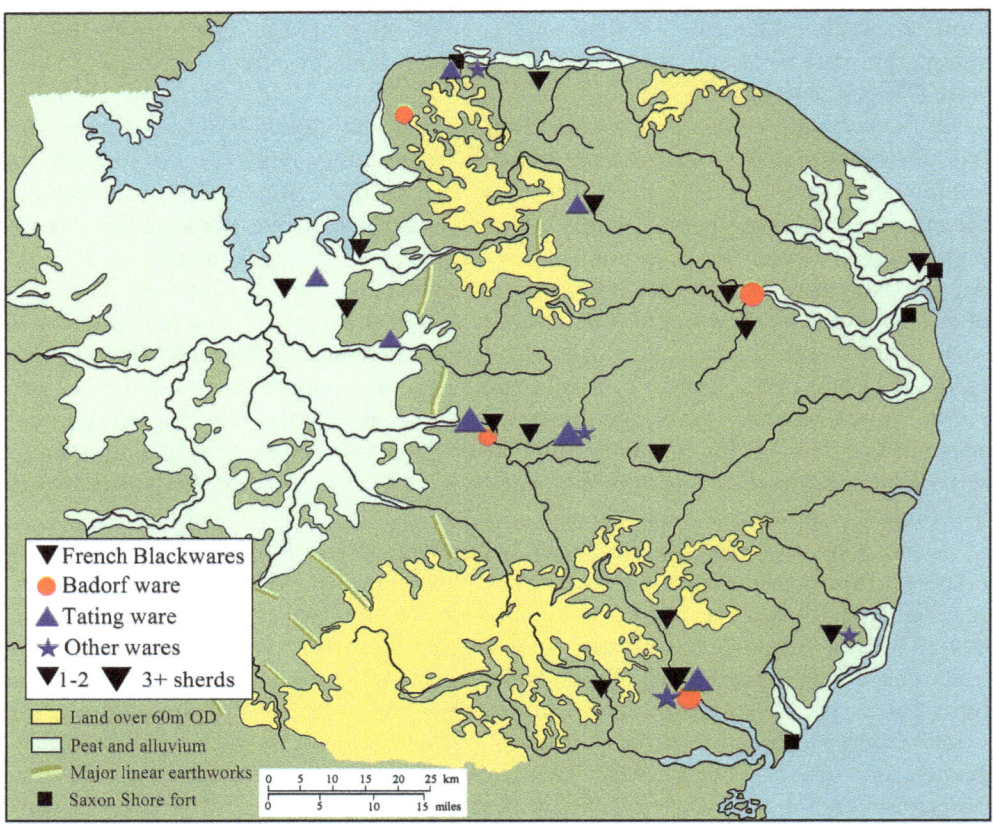

Fig. 10.13. The distribution of imported continental pottery within the Kingdom of East Anglia.

Two points are of particular note. First, the vessel forms of the continental imports do vary but many, especially among the majority Badorf wares, are from jars or spouted pitchers, just like the Ipswich ware at Flixborough. This suggests close links to the wine trade, with them acting as wine containers (Hodges 1989, 57–9). Frisian merchants have been closely associated with the wine trade, being important purchasers at the October fair of St Denis in Paris, 'the greatest wine market of Western Europe' (Verhulst 2002, 102). However, equally significant must have been German wine from Upper Franconia, a colony of Frisian merchants in Mainz being attested in the second half of the 9th century, while Rhenish oakwood and Alsace pinewood from casks have been excavated from Dorestad (ibid., 100). It seems possible at least that much of the Badorf ware in Ipswich may have been used to transport wine which was then sold on and redistributed throughout the kingdom and beyond.

Second, an increasingly diverse range of imported pottery has been revealed by excavation and fieldwalking in East Anglia (Fig. 10.13). Of this, the Rhenish material is clearly in the majority, presumably reflecting the importance of German products (Hodges 1989, 92–4), or perhaps alternatively, the goods largely offered up to this region by Frisian and other merchants. Not only is the range of material expanding, but the types of sites it is being found on. Tating ware, 'the finest pottery available in north-west Europe' (Hodges 1989, 59) was once associated with ecclesiastical use, and its occurrence at high-status and ecclesiastical sites (such as York, Winchester and the episcopal settlement of North Elmham in Norfolk) did nothing to dispel this. However, its discovery at sites like Middle Harling, West Dereham and Terrington St Clement in Norfolk suggest a more equivocal status; even at the wealthy settlement of Brandon the 27 sherds recovered appear to derive from one single vessel (Blinkhorn 2014, 158 and table 6.1). The issue is now how to explain this dichotomy between the presence of so much imported pottery in Ipswich and its limited yet varied appearance elsewhere in the countryside.

Conclusion

Despite the sparse documentary record attached to the kingdom of East Anglia, much can still be said about its social and economic contacts with the Continent between the 7th and 9th centuries. Indeed, perhaps the most significant feature of this *lacuna* after the events described in Bede's *Ecclesiastical History* is that the ongoing political contacts can only have become stronger given what archaeology is showing.

Perhaps most important, throughout the period East Anglia's long coastline and position on the eastern seaboard was crucial to its wealth, power and contacts. Its geographical position enabled it to be a direct participant in trade around the North Sea littoral while Ipswich's central position between Dorestad and Quentovic gave it an optimum location for drawing on both markets. In extending to the Wash, the kingdom had partial control over the outflow of the rivers Ouse and Nene, through which the midlands could be reached. This is probably one reason that Mercia was for so long in conflict with East Anglia, as these systems provided a major access route for continental trade and the exercise of taxation and tolls. The importance of the Wash area and fen-edges of west Norfolk and south Lincolnshire to early trade is demonstrated by the discovery of so many coin-rich sites here.

This maritime importance must also have been a key element in East Anglia's relationship with the Merovingian kingdoms. As we have seen, items of material culture such as pottery were clearly important in issues of status and identity when used in burial tableaux by many of the wealthiest in mid-7th century East Anglia, just as in Kent. Yet the role of Kent, so often seen as a Merovingian cultural bridgehead in England, and influential in the mediation of such continental fashions, perhaps need not have been such a unique power in this maritime world. It is perhaps ironic that it should be the burial of a ship at Sutton Hoo that Carver sees as a reaction to this Frankish, Christian, world (Carver 1998, 134–6; 2005, 501–2). The earlier aristocratic ship burial at Snape (*c.* 550; Filmer-Sankey and Pestell 2001) shows this was not unique and the presence of Merovingian coinage and pottery elsewhere in the kingdom, as both hoards and individual losses, shows that this was already a world with myriad cultural influences.

Perhaps as interesting is seeing the means by which such cultural influences were imported. Throughout this paper, the role of Frisian merchants has been implied, yet even the presumed foreigners found at Ipswich's Buttermarket cemetery could equally well have been Frankish from their objects. Only with the rise of the 8th-century *sceatt* coinage and its preponderance of Frisian issues is a more clear connection seen, maintained in the 9th century with the sharing of ansate brooch-types. Yet, we may also question what we hope to find. As the *sceattas* indicate, this was a currency for exporting items from England; it is only in Ipswich that we have substantial evidence of bulk-imported foreign commodities in Badorf and other wares – material that is conspicuously sparse in the wider kingdom. There are, perhaps, two issues.

First, the role of traders (in which 'Frisian' was perhaps a useful catch-all description) was often ghostly, as the middle-men need not have left their own mark but that of their cargoes. This would have become more acute as English coinage effectively came to exclude foreign issues in the later 8th and 9th centuries. Second, and more problematic, for all the apparently unregulated freedom of trade evidenced in the *sceatt* coinage and 'productive' sites, Ipswich remains the only source of its eponymous pottery, utilizing a network extensive and efficient enough to distribute it throughout the kingdom and make hand-made wares all but extinct. Despite this nexus, imported pottery at any time hardly made it beyond the wharves of the *emporium*. If the coinage from such sites as Bawsey and Caistor St Edmund does indicate their prominence in international trade, why are they not producing similar densities of imported pottery? Likewise, the emphasis that some scholars have recently placed upon coastal zones differing in character from areas inland (Loveluck and Tys 2006), with greater connectivity resulting in richer material culture, is certainly true of East Anglia as a whole. However, within the kingdom itself, different areas diverge in their wealth or evidence for continental contacts; the north-west of Norfolk, south-east of Suffolk and the region's fen-edge show a definite preference for coinage and materially rich sites that contrast surprisingly with, for instance, coastal north-east Norfolk with its rich soils. The shadow of social and political control still looms large as an issue.

If I conclude on such uncertainties, it is equally clear that we have come an enormous way in understanding the subtleties of East Anglia's – and Anglo-Saxon England's – relationships with its continental neighbours. We are now beginning to see a more nuanced picture in which personal contacts as much as wider social or cultural shifts may have played their part. As we refine our dating of these patterns still further, we may finally bring even clearer resolution to that picture.

Acknowledgements

I am grateful to a number of people for providing information and assistance in the preparation of this paper. My colleagues Andrew Rogerson and Steven Ashley have provided me with information on the burials from Snettisham and 'near Diss' and allowed me to reproduce elements of these graves in advance of their publication, as well as numerous line drawings by Jason Gibbons. Adrian Marsden has generously shared details of the new 'near Swaffham' *tremissis* hoard as well as debating coin finds from Norfolk with me. Rosie Weetch has kindly allowed me to reproduce two of her distribution maps, while Ian Wood, John Naylor and Gareth Williams kindly commented on an earlier draft. Discussions with them all have helped to shape my views expressed here, but naturally none of them are responsible for any mistakes that stubbornly remain. This paper is dedicated to the memory of my late father, a Norfolk European.

References

Published primary sources

Avitus of Vienne, *Selected Letters and Prose*, trans. D. Shanzer and Ian Wood, 2002. Translated Texts for Historians 38 (Liverpool).

Bede, *Historia Ecclesiastica Gentis Anglorum*. In Bertram Colgrave and Sir R. A. B. Mynors ed. and trans. 1969, *Bede's Ecclesiastical History of the English People* (Oxford).

Boniface, *The Letters of Saint Boniface*. Emerton, Ephraim 1973 (New York).

Eddius Stephanus, *Life of Bishop Wilfrid*, ed. Bertram Colgrave, 1927, *The Life of Bishop Wilfrid by Eddius Stephanus. Text, Translation and Notes* (Cambridge).

English Historical Documents. Whitelock, Dorothy ed. 1979, *English Historical Documents I c. 500–1042*, 2nd edn. (London).

Procopius, *Procopius' History of the Wars*, ed. H. B. Dewing, 1919. Loeb Classical Library 48 (London).

Vita Domnae Balthildis. Fouracre, Paul and Richard Gerberding, ed. 1996, *Late Merovingian France History and Hagiography 640–720*, Manchester Medieval Sources (Manchester), 97–132.

Secondary sources

Archibald, Marion 1982, 'A ship-type penny of Æthelstan I of East Anglia', *British Numismatic Journal* 52, 34–40.

Behr, Charlotte and Tim Pestell 2015, 'The bracteate hoard from Binham – an early Anglo-Saxon central place?', *Medieval Archaeology* 58, 44–77.

Birbeck, Vaughan, with Roland Smith, Phil Andrews and Nick Stoodley 2005, *The Origins of Mid-Saxon Southampton: Excavations at the Friends Provident St Mary's Stadium 1998–2000* (Salisbury).

Blinkhorn, Paul 2012, *The Ipswich Ware Project: Ceramics, Trade and Society in Middle Saxon England*, Medieval Pottery Research Group Occasional Paper 7 (London).

Blinkhorn, Paul 2014, 'Pottery'. In *Staunch Meadow, Brandon, Suffolk: A High Status Middle Saxon Settlement on the Fen Edge* East Anglian Archaeology 151, A. Tester, S. Anderson, I. Riddler and R. D. Carr (Bury St Edmunds), 149–66.

Bos, Jurjen M. 2007–8, 'Medieval brooches from the Dutch Province of Friesland (Frisia): a regional perspective on the Wijnaldum Brooches. Part II: disc brooches', *Palaeohistoria* 49–50, 709–93.

Bremmer, Rolf H. 1990, 'The nature of the evidence for a Frisian Participation in the *Adventus Saxonum*'. In *Britain 400–600: Language and History*, ed. A. Bammesberger and A. Wollmann (Heidelberg), 353–71.

Carver, Martin 1998, *Sutton Hoo Burial Ground of Kings?* (London).

Carver, Martin 2005, *Sutton Hoo. A Seventh-Century Princely Burial Ground and its Context*, Reports of the Research Committee of the Society of Antiquaries of London 69 (London).

Coutts, Catherine 1991, 'The pottery descriptions'. Unpublished typescript archived at http://archaeologydataservice.ac.uk/archives/view/ipswich_parent_2015/downloads.cfm, accessed March 2016.

Davies, Gareth 2010, 'Early medieval "Rural Centres" and West Norfolk: a growing picture of diversity, complexity and changing lifestyles', *Medieval Archaeology* 54, 89–122.

Eggenstein, Georg, Norbert Börste, Helge Zöller and Eva Zahn-Biemüller 2008, *Ein Weld in Bewegung: Unterwegs zu Zentren des frühen Mittelalters* (Berlin and Munich).

Es, Wim A. van 1990, 'Dorestad centred'. In *Medieval Archaeology in the Netherlands: Studies Presented to H. H. Van Regteren Altena*, Studies in Prae- En Protohistorie 4, ed. J. C. Besteman, J. M. Bos and H. A. Heidinga (Assen and Maastricht), 151–82.

Evison, Vera 1979, *A Corpus of Wheel-Thrown Pottery in Anglo-Saxon Graves* (London).

Filmer-Sankey, William, and Tim Pestell 2001, *Snape Anglo-Saxon Cemetery: Excavations and*

Surveys 1824–1992, East Anglian Archaeology 95 (Bury St Edmunds).
Fouracre, Paul 2015, 'Balthild and "her" seal ring: text and artefact'. In *Entre texte et histoire: Études d'histoire médiévale offertes au professeur Shoichi Sato*, ed. O. Kano and J. L. Lemaître (Paris), 129–42.
Garipzanov, Ildar H. 2009, 'Coins as symbols of early medieval "Staatlichkeit"'. In *Der frühmittelalterliche Staat – europäische Perspektiven* Österreichische Akademie der Wissenschaften Forschungen zur Geschichte des Mittelalters Band 16, ed. W. Pohl and V. Wieser (Vienna), 411–22.
Geake, Helen 1997, *The Use of Grave-Goods in Conversion-Period England, c. 600–850*, BAR British Series 261 (Oxford).
Grierson, Philip 1970, 'The purpose of the Sutton Hoo coins', *Antiquity* 44, 14–18.
Hines, John, and Alex Bayliss eds 2013, *Anglo-Saxon Graves and Grave Goods of the 6th and 7th Centuries AD: A Chronological Framework* (Leeds).
Hodges, Richard 1989, *Dark Age Economics*, 2nd edn (London).
Hodges, Richard 2006, '*Dark Age Economics* revisited'. In *Goodbye to the Vikings? Re-reading Early Medieval Archaeology*, ed. R. Hodges (London), 63–71.
Hoggett, Richard 2014, 'The mystery of the seven Anglo-Saxon *monasteria*', *Norfolk Archaeology* 46, 55–60.
Hübener, W. 1972, 'Gleicharmige Bügelfibeln der Merowingerzeit in Westeuropa', *Madriger Mitteilungen* 13, 211–44.
Knol, Egge 2009, 'Anglo-Saxon migration reflected in cemeteries in the northern Netherlands'. In *Foreigners in Early Medieval Europe Thirteen International Studies on Early Medieval Mobility*, Monographien des Römisch-Germanischen Zentralmuseums 78, ed. D. Quast (Mainz), 113–29.
Loveluck, Chris 2009, 'The dynamics of elite lifestyles in the rural world, AD 600–1150: archaeological perspectives from Northwest Europe'. In *La culture du Haut Moyen Age, une question d' élites*, ed. R. Bougard, R. Le Jan and R. Mckitterick (Turnhout), 139–70.
Loveluck, Chris, and Dries Tys 2006, 'Coastal societies, exchange and identity along the Channel and southern North Sea shores of Europe, AD 600–1000', *Journal of Maritime Archaeology* 1, 140–69.
Lucy, Sam 1998, *The Early Anglo-Saxon Cemeteries of East Yorkshire. An Analysis and Reinterpretation*, BAR British Series 272 (Oxford).
Marsden, Adrian 2016, 'East Anglia's earliest issues: the Trophy Type shillings', *Caesaromagus The Journal of the Essex Numismatic Society* 120, 50–9.
Martin, Toby 2015, *The Cruciform Brooch and Anglo-Saxon England* (Woodbridge).
Metcalf, Michael 2001, 'Determining the mint attribution of East Anglian sceattas through regression analysis', *British Numismatic Journal* 70, 1–11.
Metcalf, Michael 2011, 'English money, foreign money: the circulation of tremisses and sceattas in the East Midlands, and the monetary role of 'productive sites'. In *Studies in Early Medieval Coinage* 2, ed. T. Abramson (Woodbridge),13–46.
Myres, J. Nowell, and Barbara Green 1973, *The Anglo-Saxon Cemeteries of Caistor-by-Norwich and Markshall, Norfolk*, Reports of the Research Committee of the Society of Antiquaries of London 30 (London).
Naismith, Rory 2012, *Money and Power in Anglo-Saxon England: The Southern English Kingdoms 757–865* (Cambridge).
Naismith, Rory 2013, 'Coinage in pre-Viking East Anglia'. In *East Anglia and its North Sea World in the Middle Ages*, ed. D. Bates and R. Liddiard (Woodbridge), 137–51.
Naylor, John 2012, 'Coinage, trade and the origins of the English *emporia, c.* AD 650–750'. In *From One Sea to Another: Trade Centres in the European and Mediterranean Early Middle Ages*, ed. S. Gelichi and R. Hodges (Turnhout), 237–66.
Naylor, John 2015, 'The use of gold coinage in the 6th and 7th-century burials in England'. Unpublished paper presented at the XV International Numismatic Congress, Taormina (Italy), 23 September 2015.

Naylor, John 2016, 'Two coin pendants from an Anglo-Saxon burial near Diss, Norfolk', *Medieval Archaeology* 60(2), 360–2.

Nieuwhof, Annet 2013, 'Anglo-Saxon immigration or continuity? Ezinge and the coastal area of the northern Netherlands in the Migration Period', *Journal of Archaeology in the Low Countries* 5(1), 53–83.

Op den Velde, Wybrand, and C. J. F. Klaassen 2004, *Sceattas and Merovingian Deniers from Domburg and Western Schouwen* (Middelburg).

Op den Velde, Wybrand, and Michael Metcalf 2009–10, 'The monetary economy of the Netherlands c. 690–760 and the trade with England: a study of the 'porcupine' sceattas of Series E', *Jaarboek voor Munt- en Penningkunde*, 90–1.

Op den Velde, Wybrand, and Michael Metcalf 2011, 'Series E reconsidered'. In *Studies in Early Medieval Coinage 2*, ed. T. Abramson (Woodbridge), 104–10.

Pader, Ellen 1982, *Symbolism, Social Relations and the Interpretation of Mortuary Remains*, BAR British Series 130 (Oxford).

Penn, Kenneth 2000, *Excavations on the Norwich Southern Bypass 1989–91 Part II: The Anglo-Saxon Cemetery at Harford Farm, Caistor St Edmund*, East Anglian Archaeology 92 (Gressenhall).

Penn, Kenneth 2011, *The Anglo-Saxon Cemetery at Shrubland Hall Quarry, Coddenham, Suffolk*, East Anglian Archaeology 139 (Bury St Edmunds).

Penn, Kenneth, and David Whitmore 2007, 'A Seventh-Century burial at Bayfield', *Norfolk Archaeology* 45, 212–21.

Pestell, Tim 2003, 'The "afterlife" of "productive" sites in East Anglia'. In *Markets in Early Medieval Europe: Trading and 'Productive' Sites 650–850*, ed. T. Pestell and K. Ulmschneider (Bollington), 122–37.

Pestell, Tim 2004, *Landscapes of Monastic Foundation: The Establishment of Religious Houses in East Anglia c. 650–1200* (Woodbridge).

Pestell, Tim 2011, 'Markets, emporia, wics and "productive" sites: pre-Viking trade centres in Anglo-Saxon England'. In *The Oxford Handbook of Anglo-Saxon Archaeology*, ed. H. Hamerow, D. A. Hinton and S. Crawford (Oxford), 556–79.

Pestell, Tim 2012, 'Das Baldehildis-Siegel'. In *Königinnen der Merowinger Adelsgräber aus den Kirchen von Köln, Chelles und Frankfurt am Main*, ed. E. Wamers and P. Périn (Regensburg), 145–8.

Pestell, Tim 2014, 'Bawsey – A "productive" site in West Norfolk'. In *Landscape and Artefacts: Studies in East Anglian Archaeology Presented to Andrew Rogerson*, ed. S. Ashley and A. Marsden (Oxford), 139–65.

Rigold, Stuart 1975, 'The Sutton Hoo coins in the light of the contemporary background of coinage in England'. In *The Sutton Hoo Ship Burial I*, ed. R. L. S. Bruce-Mitford (London), 653–77.

Rogerson, Andrew, and Steven Ashley 2010, 'A selection of finds from Norfolk recorded in 2010 and earlier', *Norfolk Archaeology* 46(1), 121–35.

Rogerson, Andrew, and Steven Ashley 2011, 'A selection of finds from Norfolk recorded in 2011 and earlier', *Norfolk Archaeology* 46(2), 248–62.

Rogerson, Andrew, and Steven Ashley 2013, 'A selection of finds from Norfolk recorded in 2013 and earlier', *Norfolk Archaeology* 46(4), 554–68.

Scull, Christopher 2009, *Early Medieval (Late 5th – Early 8th Centuries AD) Cemeteries at Boss Hall and Buttermarket, Ipswich, Suffolk*, Society for Medieval Archaeology Monograph 27 (London).

Scull, Christopher 2011, 'Foreign identities in burials at seventh-century English emporia'. In *Studies in Anglo-Saxon Art and Archaeology: Papers in Honour of Martin G. Welch*, British Archaeological Reports British Series 527, ed. S. Brookes, S. Harrington and A. Reynolds (Oxford), 82–97.

Scull, Christopher 2012, 'The composite belt suite'. In *Lundenwic: Excavations in Middle Saxon London, 1987–2000* Museum of London Archaeology Monograph 63, ed. R. Cowie and L. Blackmore with A. Davis, J. Keily and K. Rielly (London), 284–6.

Scull, Christopher, Faye Minter and Judith Plouviez 2016, 'Social and economic complexity in early medieval England: a central place complex of the East Anglian kingdom at Rendlesham, Suffolk', *Antiquity* 90, 1594–612.

Stoodley, Nick 1999, *The Spindle and the Spear: A Critical Enquiry into the Construction and Meaning of Gender in the Early Anglo-Saxon Burial Rite*, BAR British Series 288 (Oxford).

Thomas, Gabor 2012, 'Carolingian culture in the North Sea world: rethinking the dynamics of personal adornment in Viking-age England', *European Journal of Archaeology* 15/3, 486–518.

Thörle, S. 2001, *Gleicharmige Bügelfibeln des Frühen Mittelalters* (Bonn).

Tipper, Jess 2009, 'Pottery'. In *The Anglo-Saxon Settlement and Cemetery at Bloodmoor Hill, Carleton Colville, Suffolk*, East Anglian Archaeology 131, ed. S. Lucy, J. Tipper and A. Dickens (Cambridge), 202–43.

Ulmschneider, Katharina, and Tim Pestell 2003, 'Introduction: Early medieval markets and "productive" sites'. In *Markets in Early Medieval Europe: Trading and 'Productive' Sites 650–850*, ed. T. Pestell and K. Ulmschneider (Bollington), 1–10.

Verhulst, Adriaan 2002, *The Carolingian Economy*, Cambridge Medieval Textbooks (Cambridge).

Vince, Alan 2011, 'Characterisation of wheel-thrown Anglo-Saxon vessels from Coddenham grave 24 and Hadleigh (HAD059)'. In *The Anglo-Saxon Cemetery at Shrubland Hall Quarry, Coddenham, Suffolk*, East Anglian Archaeology 139, ed. K. Penn (Bury St Edmunds), 74–7.

Wade, Keith 1988, 'Ipswich.' In *The Rebirth of Towns in the West AD 700–1050*, CBA Research Report 68, ed. R. Hodges and B. Hobley (London), 93–100.

Weetch, Rosie 2014, 'Brooches in Late Anglo-Saxon England within a North-West European Context', Unpublished Ph.D. Thesis, University of Reading.

Whitelock, Dorothy 1972, 'The pre-Viking Church in East Anglia', *Anglo-Saxon England* 1, 1–22.

Williams, Gareth 2006, 'The circulation and function of coinage in Conversion-period England, c. AD 580–675'. In *Coinage and History in the North Sea World c. 500–1250. Essays in Honour of Marion Archibald*, The Northern World 19, ed. B. Cook and G. Williams (Leiden), 145–92.

Williams, Gareth 2010, 'The influence of Dorestad coinage on coin design in England and Scandinavia'. In *Dorestad in an International Framework: New Research on Centres of Trade and Coinage in Carolingian Times*, ed. A. Willemsen and H. Kik (Turnhout), 105–11.

Williams, Gareth 2013, 'The circulation, minting and use of coins in East Anglia c. AD 580–675'. In *East Anglia and Its North Sea World in the Middle Ages*, ed. D. Bates and R. Liddiard (Woodbridge), 120–36.

Wood, Ian 1991, 'The Franks and Sutton Hoo'. In *People and Places in Northern Europe 500–1600 Essays in Honour of Peter Hayes Sawyer*, ed. I. Wood and N. Lund (Woodbridge), 1–14.

Wood, Ian 1992, 'Frankish hegemony in England'. In *The Age of Sutton Hoo*, ed. M. O. H. Carver (Woodbridge), 235–41.

Wood, Ian 1994, *The Merovingian Kingdoms 450–751* (London).

Wood, Ian 2016, *Fursey and his Brothers: Their Contribution to the Irish Legacy on the Continent*, Fursey Pilgrims Occasional Paper 9 (Lincoln).

Yorke, Barbara 1990, *Kings and Kingdoms of Early Anglo-Saxon England* (London).

Young, Jane and Alan Vince with Paul Blinkhorn 2009, 'The Anglo-Saxon pottery'. In *Life and Economy at Early Medieval Flixborough c. AD 600–1000 The Artefact Evidence*, Excavations at Flixborough 2, ed. D. H. Evans and C. Loveluck (Oxford), 339–401.

Youngs, Susan 1983, 'The pottery bottle'. In *The Sutton Hoo Ship Burial* 3, ed. R. Bruce-Mitford (London), 597–607.

11

A Comparison of the Injury Tariffs in the Early Kentish and the Frisian Law Codes

Han Nijdam

In fond memory of Lisi Oliver

This paper aims to compare the injury tariff found in the *Law of King Æthelberht* of Kent (the Kentish Law or *Ab*) dated *c*. AD 600 with the injury tariffs in the Frisian legal tradition. This tradition comprises both the injury tariffs in the *Lex Frisionum*, written mainly in Latin towards the end of the 8th century, and the tariffs written down in Old Frisian law manuscripts dating from the 13th to 15th centuries. Close cultural and linguistic connections have been observed between Anglo-Saxon England and Frisia. Furthermore, a sometimes exclusive relation between Kent and Frisia has been suggested. In this paper I scrutinize these connections with regard to injury tariffs. In addition, I look into the status of research and where the possibilities for future research lie. It will become clear that trying to find exclusive Anglo-Frisian parallels or even reconstruct an Anglo-Frisian proto-tariff is useful but also tantalizing: the goal seems within our reach but we never quite get there.

Honour and revenge

Injury tariffs are texts in which various types of possible injuries and harms that can be inflicted on a person are listed, accompanied by an amount of money which was due to the victim. Their nature and origins are discussed in more detail in the following section. Before discussing them, and why the Kentish and Frisian traditions deserve to be compared, however, the rationale behind injury tariffs needs to be addressed. Essentially, the goal of these texts was to make it possible to buy off revenge. They are a product of the institution of blood money (*wergild*: 'man price' in Germanic), allowing a killer to pay a certain amount in goods (money, valuables, land, cattle, houses) to the next of kin of the victim of a homicide. Paying blood money can obviate a blood feud in which many lives would be lost and which could disrupt a society for years (Netterström and Poulsen eds 2007). Combined with ritual acts and taking a certain amount of time (Miller 2006, 108), sometimes even as much as a year, the institution of *wergild* effectively makes it possible to restore peace between two families. Blood money is in use by various cultures all over the globe. Cultures, that is, 'of a type of egalitarian political society that rather strictly limits centralized authority, and in which honour is of high importance culturally' (Boehm 2007, 203).

Honour is a very important aspect of this 'game': it is important to the kin-group of the victim to guard the honour of their dead kinsman as well as their own, and that they come out of the process without any loss of honour and preferably even with honour gained (Nijdam 2008). Perhaps this whole 'honour game' is best described by William Miller (1990, 108–9) in his book on feuding in medieval Iceland:

> The skillful participant in exchange was the one who knew how to manipulate the multitude of signs that attended the classification of a transaction to the increase of his honor, not his net worth. The adept players in this game, that is, the honorable men and women, were those who knew whether and when to pay and to pay back, to give and to receive, or to take a thing and leave behind what they thought it was worth. Our cases suggest that they were more likely to exchange goods and services in the forums of dispute processing or in the festive hall, by compensation payment or gift, than in a marketplace or the countryside, by sale and purchase. And whether the exchange was to be by feud or feast was what they bargained over.

In general terms, there are certain aspects of the concept of honour that deserve closer consideration here. As noted, honour is all-important in cultures where *wergild* and compensation are used as a means by which honour that has been lost can be restored. These observations bring to light several aspects of what honour is. First of all, it has to do with being able to defend oneself from becoming a victim. A man of honour is not to be trodden upon (Bowman 2006). Secondly, honour is a form of capital, which can be gained and lost. This means that honour is quantifiable (Nijdam 2013). All Germanic societies had some form of social stratification. Men were not equal: there were freemen (the default), slaves, servants and noblemen. The *wergild* for each of those social strata differed: the *wergild* of a nobleman was usually two or three times that of a freeman (Hines 2013; Miller 2006, 109). In fact, the very notion that a sum of money (i.e. *wergild*) can somehow substitute a human person forms the root of quantifying honour (Miller 2006; Nijdam 2013). Characteristic of the androcentric character of the societies in question is the fact that the reference point for personal value in these codes is automatically male.

The last – and in this context perhaps most important – point is that honour is personal and is very much embodied. The core notion here is that honour starts at the physical body and that relations or possessions come to be incorporated by a person. This conglomerate of a man's physical body, his relations (i.e. his family and his servants) and possessions (money, lands, cattle, etc.) then forms the total sphere of someone's embodied honour. As I have tried to show previously (Nijdam 2008; 2010; 2013), damaging any of these things damages the person at the centre of the embodied honour-sphere. This damage will very probably feel 'painful' to a greater or lesser extent, hence leading to the urge to take revenge. And this model of embodied honour also makes it comprehensible how money or other goods can supplement the loss of honour in another area, such as the injuring of the physical body.

Injury tariffs

In injury tariffs, the human body is mapped and a selection of the injuries that one person can inflict upon another are listed together with the appropriate amount of compensation. These texts tend to expand over time, especially once written culture sets in. Tariffs often also include damage to someone's possessions or the people he is responsible for. In view of the all-importance of honour in societies where *wergild* functions – these have even been labelled 'economies of honour' (Miller 1990, 26–34) – it is more accurate to say that injury tariffs map embodied honour (Nijdam 2008; 2010; 2014a).

Within the Germanic sphere, injury tariffs form a part of the various law codes that were recorded in the Early Middle Ages upon the authority of the Merovingian, Carolingian and Anglo-Saxon kings. Collectively, they go by the name of *Leges Barbarorum* – the laws of the Germanic peoples. In most parts of Europe, this text genre gradually died out as a consequence of the growing central governments. In medieval Frisia, however, a different political situation arose. Here the various autonomous Frisian *terrae* or territories ruled themselves (Vries 2015). This led to continuity and the gradual further development of their indigenous law.

The Old Frisian vernacular compensation tariffs are found in manuscripts dating from the 13th century onwards. These tariffs – the oldest of which have been textually dated to the 11th century – can be seen as continuations of the injury tariffs in the *Lex Frisionum* (which will be treated in more detail below). The Old Frisian compensation tariffs list all kinds of damages of and injuries to a man and his belongings – his lands, house, wife, children, cattle, and servants. The tariffs also enumerate various insults.

The most archaic Old Frisian tariff, the *General Old East Frisian Compensation Tariff* (on which more below) forms a nice example of an injury tariff. I will give the first clauses of the version that can be found in the First Riustring Manuscript (*c.* 1300) (Buma and Ebel 1963, 58–60; the translation is mine):

1a.   Faxfanges bote fif skillinga and fiuwer panninga ieftha twene etha.
1b.   Dustslek alsa felo.
1c.   Blodilsa unblikande alsa felo.
1d.   Blikande blodrisne binna clathon tian skillinga and achta panninga ieftha twene etha.
1e.   Blikande blodrisne buta clathon en skilling and niugun enza ieftha thre etha.
1f.   Metedolch binna clathon tian skillinga ieftha fiuwer etha.
1g.   Metedolch buta clathon tian enza and achta panninga ieftha fif etha.
1h.   Thria lesoka an tha forhafde iahwelik fif skillinga.
1i.   Breskredene fiuwer enza.
1j.   Thrira bena breke twilif skillinga.
1k.   Thrira lithwega iahwelik en half pund buta ethe.
1l.   Thet haued thruchslein, thi thruchkeme there brinponna twilif skillinga.
1m. Thi inrene thes blodes alsa felo.
1n.   Helibreda fel twilif skillinga.
1o.   Haueddusinge sex and thritich skillinga.
1p.   Abel and inseptha tian skillinga buta ethe.
1q.   Hete and kalde tian skillinga, mith ethe to haldande.
1r.   Thera fif sinwerdena iahwelikes bote sex and thritich skillinga: *uisus, auditus, gustus, odoratus et tactus; sione, here, smek, hrene, fele.*

1a. The compensation for grabbing someone by the hair: five shillings and four pennies, or two oaths.
1b. A hard blow: the same amount.
1c. A bleeding wound that is invisible: the same amount.
1d. A bleeding wound that is visible but can be covered by clothing: ten shillings and eight pennies, or two oaths.
1e. A bleeding wound that is visible and can not be covered by clothing: one shilling and nine ounces, or three oaths.
1f. A measurable wound that can be covered by clothing: ten shillings, or four oaths.
1g. A measurable wound that can not be covered by clothing: ten ounces and eight pennies, or five oaths.
1h. Cutting through the three wrinkles in the forehead: each five shillings.
1i. Cutting through the eyebrow: four ounces.
1j. Three fractured bones: twelve shillings.
1k. Three wounds which cause synovial fluid to run out of a joint: each a half pound, without an oath.
1l. If the head has been cut and the skull penetrated: twelve shillings.
1m. If blood flows into the wound: the same amount.
1n. If the meninges have been cut: twelve shillings.
1o. Vertigo: thirty-six shillings.
1p. Scar tissue which protrudes or has sunken into the skin: ten shillings, without an oath.
1q. Sensitiveness to heat and cold: ten shillings, to be obtained by an oath.
1r. The compensation for each of the five senses: thirty-six shillings; *visus, auditus, gustus, odoratus et tactus*: sight, hearing, taste, smell and touch.

This Riustring version contains 99 items in total. I have reconstructed the original text of the *General Old East Frisian Compensation Tariff*, based on the five extant versions, to a text which consisted of 117 items (Nijdam 2008, 409–29). The other versions contain in the order of 130–40 clauses. It is important to pay attention to the number of items of these texts, because it seems that size does matter here, in the sense that it might inform us how these tariffs may have evolved. Injury tariffs have not been analysed in a detailed manner from this perspective, but it is not hard to reconstruct how the tariffs have grown from listing the *wergild* and the principal limbs and organs to be damaged and then going into ever more detail.

The tariff which was recorded in the early 20th century among the Kamba, a people in Kenya, certainly meets these criteria (Diamond 1971, 269; see Table 11.1). In 21 clauses, it lists the forms of homicide the Kamba distinguished, as well as the loss of the most important limbs: arms and fingers, legs and toes, ears, eyes, teeth, nose, testicles and penis. It furthermore makes a distinction between acts that were perpetrated intentionally and those that were done by accident. Because it spans several centuries, the Frisian tradition especially clearly shows how the injury tariffs grew and expanded over time in an effort to describe every possible injury. This development accelarated once writing had firmly established itself in medieval Frisia. This aspect of the evolution of this text genre is something to keep in mind in the analysis that is to follow.

Table 11.1. Injury tariff recorded among the Kamba (Kenya), early 20th-century.

1.	Murdering a man	14 cows, 1 bull
2.	Murdering a woman	7 cows, 1 bull
3.	Murdering a child	6 cows, 1 bull
4.	Homicide of a man	7 cows, 1 bull
5.	Homicide of a woman	4 cows, 1 bull
6.	Homicide of child	Dependent on the sex
7.	Loss of a finger	1 cow, 1 bull
8.	Loss of a toe	1 bull, 1 goat
9.	Loss of a leg or arm	7 cows, 1 bull
10.	Loss of both legs or arms	14 cows, 1 bull
11.	Loss of an ear	5 goats
12.	Loss of an ear (by accident)	2 goats
13.	Tearing out an ear	1 goat
14.	Loss of an eye	1 cow, 1 bull
15.	Loss of both eyes	14 cows, 1 bull
16.	Loss of a tooth	1 goat
17.	Loss of a tooth (by accident)	1 pot tembo (palm wine)
18.	Loss of the nose	1 cow, 1 bull
19.	Loss of a testicle	4 cows, 2 bulls
20.	Loss of both testicles	14 cows, 1 bull
21.	Loss of the penis	14 cows, 1 bull

In injury tariffs, the compensations for the principal limbs (arms, legs, hands, eyes, etc.) are most commonly fractions of a complete *wergild* or the total sum of money a person (again, male by default) was worth. In a Germanic context, a clear example of this is that the loss of a hand, an eye or a foot was usually set at half a *wergild* (Oliver 2011, 137–40). At the lower end of the scale, i.e. for minor damages, compensations were usually fixed amounts of money and thus unrecognizable as fractions of an original *wergild*, especially when a tariff tradition had gained some age. Tariffs never differentiate between the various social groups. They are based on the *wergild* of a freeman (Rubin 1996).

It is important to note that compensations could be added up when several injuries had occurred and that this might lead to a total sum that exceeded one *wergild*. A frequently quoted case can be found in the *Law of Æthelberht*: 'If a person damages the genital organ, let him pay with three person-prices' (Oliver 2002, 74–5; Miller 2006; Oliver 2014). Though not an example of how compensations could be stacked and thus exceed one *wergild*, it is an example of the fact that if a person lived, the compensation to be exacted could surpass that of one *wergild*. The reason for this was that if the victim died, guarding his honour was left to the next of kin who had to extract revenge on his behalf or accept *wergild*. If the victim lived, however, his honour was his own responsibility. He was the one who had to go on living with some serious form of disability or mutilation and still keep his honour at the same level it was before his injuries (Nijdam 2008, 135–6)

The oldest Kentish and Frisian law texts and their manuscripts

The *Law of Æthelberht* has only been handed down in one manuscript. This *Textus Roffensis* is a 12th–century compilation of law codes and charters. These law codes start with the *Law of Æthelberht* (c. AD 600) and continue through to texts dating from the reign of Henry I (1100–35) (Wormald 1999, 244–53). Various linguistic and orthographic features of the text make it very plausible, however, that the *Law of Æthelberht* is genuinely as old is it purports to be, i.e. the beginning of the 7th century (Oliver 2002, 20–5; Hough 2015). Furthermore, a few early-medieval writers mention the existence of the text, namely Bede in his *Historia Ecclesiastica Gentis Anglorum* (c. AD 731) and King Alfred (r. 871–99) in the introduction to his law code.

Table 11.2. The structure of the injury tariff in *Ab*.

33–7	HEAD
38–41	EAR
42–3	EYE
44–7	FACE
48–9	TEETH
50–2	ARM
53–9	HAND
60–3	On wounds and mutilations
64	GENITALS
65–7	LEG
67.1–68	On measuring wounds and on scars
69–71	FOOT

The *Law of Æthelberht* contains 83 clauses, several of which consist of more than one item.[20] In total then, the law text consists of 126 items. The actual injury tariff starts at *Ab* 33 and contains 60 items.[21] This means that the injury tariff makes up about half of

---

[20] I distinguish between clauses and items. One clause may contain one or more items, each item prototypically consisting of one type of wound and one compensation. Thus, the items are the actual building blocks and these are used to quantify the tariff material.

[21] There has been some debate on where the injury tariff actually begins, owing to the enigmatic character of *Ab* 32: *Gif man rihthamscyld þurh stinð, mid weorðe forgelde*, 'If a person pierces through the *rihthamscyld*, let him pay with its worth' (Oliver 2002, 70–1). Various scholars have discussed the *hapax legomenon*, *rihthamscyld* (most recently: Oliver 2002, 97–9; Ammon 2008; Hines 2013). I will not go into this problem too deeply here. Suffice it to say that the wording *mid weorðe forgelde*, 'let him pay with its worth', seems to point to an object that has been damaged, rather than any type of body part (Matthias Ammon proposes a translation 'female hymen'), because in the tariff section the formula is always to give a fixed price, followed by either *to bote*, 'as compensation', or *gebete*, 'let him compensate'. I agree with John Hines (2013, 401) that this wording might point to accidental damage. In my opinion, however, this also rules out any solution which involves unlawful entry into a house, unless this clause has gone astray and belongs to the cluster *Ab* 28/29. I am inclined though to agree with Lisi Oliver that this clause connects to the previous, *Ab* 31: 'If a freeman lies with a free man's wife, let him buy [him/her] off [with] his/her *wergild* and obtain another wife [for the husband] [with] his own money and bring her to the other man at home' (Oliver 2002, 69). Perhaps it will prove fruitful to think of a translation 'wedding-shield'? For Old Frisian a *hapax legomenon*, *aftswird*, 'wedding-sword',

the text. It is roughly structured according to the human anatomy, which it follows from head to toe. Its contents can be summarized as in Table 11.2.

It is interesting to note that only a few clauses cut through this neat structure: one on the shoulder (37) and one on the ribs (66). It is almost as if the author did not know where to put the clauses from the category CHEST/TORSO.

The *Lex Frisionum* is as distinctive as the *Law of Æthelberht*. What has come down to us is generally considered to be a draft that would have undergone some further editing before being formally accepted by Charlemagne, probably at the general diet in Aachen in 802 (Siems 1980, 10–18). Preponderantly on numismatical grounds, Dirk Jan Henstra dates the creation of the text between 785 and 794, since it shows a transition from gold-based to silver-based units of account. Thus, one finds amounts in *solidi* and *tremisses*, a paragraph which uses pounds and ounces *per veteres denarios*, 'in old money', one clause which mentions *denarii Fresionicis*, 'Frisian pennies', and finally a few clauses which mention amounts *novae monetae*, 'in new money'. All this leads Henstra to think the text was drafted before the monetary reform by Charlemagne in 793/794 (Henstra 2000, 70–1, 277–90; 2001).

There are no medieval manuscripts containing the *Lex Frisionum* known to us today. When Johannes Herold edited a collection of *Leges Barbarorum* in 1557, he had access to one of the rare manuscripts that were then around. The extensive study by Harald Siems (1980) of the *Lex Frisionum* has shown that there is no reason, however, to doubt the authenticity of the law code. First, a few early-medieval sources refer to 'the law of the Frisians'. Secondly, we know that there were at least two medieval manuscripts containing the *Lex* because they were referred to in later sources (Siems 1980, 49–57).

The fact that the *Lex Frisionum* we have at our disposal today is a draft version means it comes with several bonuses. First, there are a few clauses concerning the pre-Christian religion of the Frisians which would possibly have been edited out in a final version. One of these describes the penalty for someone who breaks into a pagan temple and steals the valuables inside it. One clause allows a mother to kill her newborn child, as long as it has not yet received nutrition. The reality of this is backed up by an episode from the 9th-century *Life of St Liudger*, where we find a heartbreaking story about the mother of Liudger, Liafburch, who was saved as a newborn infant from being killed by her own grandmother through the intervention of a neighbour who put some honey in the baby's mouth (Siems 1980, 334–8).

More important to the focus of the present discussion is the amount of injury tariffs the *Lex Frisionum* yields. The last paragraph (Tit. XXII) of the main text is titled *De dolg*, 'on wounds'. It contains an injury tariff which consists of 89 items (see Table 11.3). The core text of the *Lex Frisionum* is followed by the additions of two 'wise men' Wlemar and Saxmund. These *Additiones Sapientum* yield another ninety-nine tariff items. On closer inspection, many of these are recurrences of clauses already given in the main text. It is likely therefore, that the main text represents the tradition stemming from the region

has recently been rediscovered (Nijdam and Versloot 2012). Hilda Ellis Davidson (1960) described the ritual use of swords at weddings in medieval European societies. She also mentions that according to Tacitus together with the more heavily attested swords, shields too were sometimes part of the gift a bride received at her wedding. Since all explanations given so far have not been satisfying, this solution might prove to connect with other data in the future.

between the Rivers Vlie and Lauwers and the *Additiones Sapientum* that from the eastern part of Frisia (Nijdam 2008, 68). In all, the tariff material in the *Lex Frisionum* is massive compared to all the other *Leges Barbarorum*. As noted by Wormald (2003, 53) the Frisian tariff is not only the longest and most elaborate by itself, but it is further expanded in the *Additiones Sapientum*, adding even more material.

Table 11.3. The structure of the injury tariff in the *Lex Frisionum*, Tit. XXII.

1–18	HEAD
19–21	TEETH
22	Collarbone
23	Rib
24–44	ARM AND HAND
45–6	EYE
47–56	TORSO
57–9	PENIS AND TESTICLES
60–4	LEG AND FOOT
65	Hair pulling
66–70	Measuring wounds
71–4	Bone splinters protruding from a wound
75	How compensations for several wounds should be compiled into one compensation
76–9	Arm and leg, hand and foot lamed or severed
80–1	Protrusion of the long through a wound
82	Tying someone up
83	Throwing someone in the water
84–6	Piercing arm, hip, jaw, tongue, scrotum
87	Saving someone from drowning
88–9	Touching a woman in an indecent manner

In spite of the gap of 300–400 years between the *Lex Frisionum* and the Old Frisian compensation tariffs – the oldest of which have been textually dated to the 11th century (Johnston 2001) – it is clear that we are looking at the same legal tradition, which had continued and developed since its recording in the *Lex Frisionum*. We can tell that there is continuity by a number of clauses and especially vernacular terms that were already used in the *Lex Frisionum* and which we find in younger forms in the Old Frisian tariffs (see Table 11.4).

Table 11.4. Vernacular terms found in both the *Lex Frisionum* and the Old Frisian tariffs.

Lex Frisionum	Old Frisian Tariffs
sipido	inseptha
smelido	smelinge
liduwagi	lithwei
wlitivam	wlitewemmelse

The Old Frisian tariffs show clear signs of evolution since the *Lex Frisionum*. The oldest Old Frisian manuscripts stem from the eastern part of Frisia (between the Rivers Lauwers and Weser). They contain both a *General Old East Frisian Compensation Tariff* and various regional tariffs. The General Tariff is traditionaly dated to the 11th century, being one of the two oldest Old Frisian law texts. The various redactions in the 13th-century manuscripts support this date. The regional tariffs are *in statu nascendi* in the 13th century but have grown into adult texts in manuscripts stemming from the 15th century. In those younger manuscripts, the old *General Old East Frisian Compensation Tariff* has disappeared. Apparently, in pace with the growing autonomy of the various regions which took place during the 13th century, each region developed its own tariff. Some figures: the *General Old East Frisian Compensation Tariff* had an average of around 130 items. The oldest versions of the regional tariffs contained around seventy items in average, which is fewer than the two complete tariffs that survived in the *Lex Frisionum*. The youngest Old East Frisian tariffs contain around 200 items and slightly more than 400 respectively, making the latter the largest Old Frisian tariff.

West of the Lauwers (the province of Friesland in the Netherlands), a slightly different picture emerges. Here all surviving manuscripts stem from the 15th century. They all contain a large number of regional compensation tariffs. Most of these are rather small: around 130 items on average. One tradition – the *Bireknade Bota*, 'Calculated Compensations' – grew into a general West Frisian tariff and reached a size of around 300 items.

History of research

As stated earlier, blood money or *wergild* as a mechanism to buy off revenge is a universal phenomenon. It can be found all over the world. Combined with the renewed insight that there is such a thing as human universals and that humans are no *tabulae rasae*, to be instructed by the culture and language they are born into, this opens up new perspectives for the study of culture (Pinker 2002; Hanlon 2013). Within the context of research into the Germanic injury tariffs, this boils down to two things. In the first place, in the way they address violence, revenge and human anatomy, these tariffs contain much material that can be found in many cultures around the globe. Secondly, they can be seen as manifestations of a 'Germanic' culture. This has not been unproblematic in the past (Nijdam 2014b).

Before Patrick Wormald's (2003) article 'The *Leges Barbarorum*: law and ethnicity in the post-Roman West', research on the *Leges Barbarorum* had for decades focussed on the influence of Roman law. Wormald's paper marks the beginning of a different view on their 'Germanicness' (Wormald 2003, 30):

> there are two good reasons to think that the law brought to light in *Lex Salica* was that of a selfconsciously 'barbarian' culture. In the first place, its keynote is compensation paid to an injured by the injuring party, including the kin of each. The harmonics underlying that note are those of bloodfeud: if payment was not made by the perpetrator and/or his kin to the victim and/or his, then revenge would be taken on any of the former by any of the latter.

According to Wormald the injury tariffs form the very core of the *Leges Barbarorum* (Wormald 2003, 46):

> Most of these laws were at the outset [...] repositories of ancient traditions, which it is not misleading to call "Germanic". They are in fact among the best evidence we have for the stolidity of a Germanic culture.

The next milestone in analysing the injury tariffs was Lisi Oliver's *The Body Legal in Barbarian Law* (2011), in which all injury tariffs in the *Leges Barbarorum* are compared. Oliver used the human anatomy to structure her work into separate chapters on the head, the torso, arms and legs and the hands and feet. Her goal was not to reconstruct a proto-law or a proto-tariff. The enormous variation of patterns she found makes this impossible. This point will be further exemplified below when analysing the *Law of Æthelberht* and the Frisian tradition, but suffice it to say that the valuation of the various teeth, fingers and toes varied enormously in the various *Leges* (Oliver 2011, 137–64, 227–37). Almost the only consistent factors are the existence of *wergild* and the fact that in most *Leges Barbarorum* the hands, eyes and feet are valued at half a *wergild* each. This enormous variation in the various Germanic tariffs seem to be a confirmation of Wormald's idea that 'a tariff recognizable as one's own was perhaps itself an ethnic marker' (Wormald 2003, 41). In other words, it would seem that each Germanic tribe strove to create its own unique tariff.

There are good reasons to zoom in on the relationship between the Frisian and the Anglo-Saxon injury tariff traditions. First, if the various Germanic traditions on the injury tariffs are too disparate to be able to reconstruct anything proto-Germanic, our next best chance is to look at these two traditions, given everything we know about the close connections that have already been established for the Anglo-Frisian 'sphere'. Anglo-Saxon and Frisian are the most closely related Germanic dialects (Hines 1995; Stiles 1995); they share a common phase in the development of the runic alphabet (Parsons 1995); close archaeological connections have been established (Gerrets 1995) – in the latter case even more specifically between Kent and Frisia (Nicolay 2014, 250–61; Oliver 2014, 58–60).

Secondly, there are now several in-depth studies available which make it possible to compare these two traditions and which have already pointed at a closer connectedness within the Anglo-Frisian sphere. In 1973, Horst Haider Munske published an important study on Germanic legal terminology (Munske 1973). In this study, Munske analysed and mutually compared the Anglo-Saxon, Old Frisian and the Old High German legal terminologies. He found a number of archaic legal terms which were shared only by the Anglo-Saxon and the Frisian sources (Munske 1970; 1973). These will be discussed below. Patrick Wormald's 2003 article and especially its appendix, consisting of a table showing the types of wounds found in the various *Leges Barbarorum*, was a significant step forward in trying to fully get to grips with the material of the injury tariffs. Lisi Oliver's *The Body Legal in Barbarian Law* (2011) then made a huge leap forward, and with the help of her findings we can now begin to calibrate our understanding of this genre. The Old Frisian injury tariff tradition had been poorly studied until *Lichaam, eer en recht in middeleeuws Friesland* ('Body, Honour and Law in Medieval Frisia') appeared (Nijdam 2008). Although focusing on the later-medieval vernacular tradition, this did address the injury tariffs in the early-medieval *Lex Frisionum* and especially the continuity between those two traditions.

Lisi Oliver's analysis in *The Body Legal* and my own work on the Old Frisian tariffs have a few things in common. Independently of each other we discovered that it was important to analyse exactly how the various texts treated the human body and its structures. How were the fingers of the hands grouped and how were they valued? Which finger was most priced and why? How were the teeth grouped together and how were these categories valued in the tariffs? This way of looking at these texts uncovers an important layer by means of which one can – in a way of speaking – pick the brain of the culture in which they were written down. In this way the mental maps of the body of the Anglo-Saxons and Frisians are made explicit. We will see that these were not static: these maps are not some sort of unalterable DNA. What is unalterable is the anatomy of the human body: that is the true solid bedrock of this text tradition.

In what follows, this approach will be combined with Munske's insights concerning the legal terms that were shared only by the Anglo-Saxon and Frisian texts. Here I have chosen to compare the injury tariff in the *Law of Æthelberht*, referred to below as *Ab* when referring to particular parts of that text, with both the *Lex Frisionum* and the Old Frisian material in order to be able to compare the onset of the Anglo-Saxon tradition with the whole Frisian tradition. The idea behind it is to create a kind of lens to focus on every detail of *Ab*.

Analysing the Kentish and Frisian injury tariffs

Since the tariff in the *Law of Æthelberht* is essentially a simple text, which is concomitant with its date of origin, this makes it a good starting point to compare it to the *Lex Frisionum* and the Old Frisian tariffs. In what follows, I compare the two traditions on three aspects. Firstly, on the technical legal terms used: what do we find in *Ab* and how exclusively are these terms shared with the Frisian tradition? Secondly, I do this for the way the human body is treated, both in terms of the way the body is structured in the two traditions as in the terms for the body parts that are used. Thirdly, there are a few other technical aspects to be compared: ways of measuring wounds and building in categories to measure the severity of injuries.

Technical legal terms

The following list of technical terms concerning wounds and injuries can be extracted from *Ab*: *banes blice*, 'exposure of a bone' (34); *banes bite*, 'cutting of a bone' (35); *cearwund*, 'grievously wounded' (63.1); *dynt*, 'a blow' (61); *feaxfang*, 'hair pulling/seizing' (33); *gelæmed*, 'lamed / paralysed' (37); *healt*, 'lame / paralysed' (65.1); *hrif wund*, 'abdominal wound' (62); *sceard*, 'gashed' (41, 45); *spræc awyrd*, 'speech damaged' (49); *sweart*, 'black' (61.3); *wælt[-]wund*, 'welt-wound' (68); *wlitewamme*, 'disfigurement of the appearance' (60); *woh*, 'damaged' (43); *þirel*, 'pierced' (40, 46, 62.1). I will address those terms that have a parallel in the Frisian tradition.

The first term that shows an exclusive parallel in the Frisian material is *feaxfang*, 'hair pulling/seizing'. This is the first clause of the Kentish injury tariff and that of various Old Frisian tariffs as well, especially those from the area east of the Lauwers, among which is the oldest Old Frisian tariff, the *General Old East Frisian Compensation Tariff*, dating from the 11th century (Johnston 2001). The *Lex Frisionum*, however, does not start with a clause on grabbing someone by the hair, although the main text (Tit 22, §65) does include such a clause: *Si quis alium iratus per capillos comprehenderit, IIII solid(is) componat, et pro freda duobus solid(is) ad partem regis*, 'If someone grabs another man by the hair out of anger, let him pay 4 *solidi* and two *solidi* to the king for breaking the peace' (Eckhardt and Eckhardt 1982, 78). The vernacular term is one of the stronger arguments for a shared Anglo-Frisian tradition, since – as Munske pointed out – this term only appears in the Old English and in the Old Frisian corpora (Munske 1973, 208–9). Oliver's (2011, 108–11) analysis, however, shows that other *Leges Barbarorum* also contain clauses on seizing someone's hair but, because these were written in Latin, the vernacular terms are not provided.

In the second and the third clause of *Ab* (33 and 34), we encounter two related terms which describe what can happen when a weapon hits the skull of the victim: *banes blice*, 'exposure of the bone (of the skull)' and *banes bite*, 'cutting of the bone (of the skull)'. Munske (1973, 208) pointed to the fact that the latter term is also found in the Old Frisian material. It occurs once, as *benes biti*, in the *Riustring Compensation Tariff* (Buma and Ebel 1963, 70; Nijdam 2008, 430–9). This is a perfect example of what Munske had already concluded: that the oldest and most persuasive parallels between the Old English and Old Frisian legal terminology stem from the eastern part of medieval Frisia, between the Rivers Lauwers and Weser. The term *banes blice* is not found in Old Frisian, although the verb *blika*, 'to appear, to show, to be exposed' is used as a technical term in the Old Frisian compensation tariffs (cf. clauses 1c, 1d, 1e in the *General Old East Frisian Compensation Tariff* quoted earlier). This is, however, also the case in various other Germanic dialects and this is one of the many occasions where it is hard to draw a line between specific Anglo-Frisian relations and a more general Germanic pattern or stock of legal terms that are dependent of the state of the source material.

Two terms in *Ab* describe forms of paralysis: *gelæmed*, 'lamed' and *healt*, 'lame'. The last term has been identified by Munske (1973, 209) as a typical Anglo-Frisian parallel. Again, however, on closer inspection, this term occurs in other Germanic traditions as well. It is the more archaic of the two, which was gradually replaced by *lam-* 'lame' in the various traditions (Munske 1973, 250–1). Old Frisian retained forms with *halt* until the 14th century, which led to the following compounds: *griphalt*, 'grab-lame (not being able to grasp things)', *strikhalt*, 'walk-lame', *fothalt*, 'foot-lame', *strumphalt*, 'lame because of mutilation', *homerhalt*, 'hammer-lame (not being able to grasp a hammer)', *hexehalt*, 'knee-lame (as a consequence of cutting the hamstring)' (Hofmann and Popkema 2008, 170, 195, 202, 219, 469; Nijdam 2008, 207).

Another interesting term is *wlitewamme*, 'disfigurement of the appearance' (*Ab* 60), which is also found in the *Lex Frisionum* and copiously in the Old Frisian tradition. It stems from a verb **wemma-*, 'to damage'. In the Anglo-Saxon tradition, we encounter *gewemman* as verb and *ungewemmed* as adjective (Munske 1973, 77). For Old Frisian an adjective *wemmed* is attested and Old Frisian *wlitewlemmelsa* is encountered many times in the compensation tariffs. The latter term, however, again is not confined to the Anglo-Frisian sphere (Oliver 2011, 101–2).

For now, there are a two more terms which need to be discussed. First, the term *sceard*, 'gashed, slit' (*Ab* 41, 45) is used for describing a type of injury which can occur to nose and ears. The etymology of the word is visible in 'to shear', meaning 'to cut (with scissors)' (Boutkan and Siebinga 2005, 348). This is also found in the Old Frisian tradition, where compounds with -*skerdene* (or its metathesized form -*skredene*) are attested abundantly, such as *breskredene*, 'cutting the eyebrow', as attested earlier in the citation of the *General Old East Frisian Compensation Tariff*. In the *Riustring Compensation Tariff* we again find a curious parallel, where it is said that if *thi lippa twa eslain, thet hi half skerde se*, 'the lip [is] cut in two, so that it is half slit through'. Although, again, this legal term is found in a few other Germanic dialects, it does add a little weight to suspect some as of yet unexplainable Riustring/Kentish connection.

This illusive Riustring/Kentish connection also applies to *spræc awyrd*, 'speech impaired/damaged' (*Ab* 49), which again finds a neat exclusive parallel in the *Riustring Compensation Tariff*, where we encounter the compound *sprekwerdene*, 'impairment of speech'. An important aspect of this type of injury is its context. In other words: what is the cause of the impaired speech? In *Ab* it is a consequence of damage to the teeth. This is concomittant with a commentary that can be found in some Old Frisian tariffs, which state that of the four front teeth, *tha ura thwene waldath there spreze, tha nithera twene thes spedla*, 'the upper two govern the faculty of speech, the lower two the flow of saliva' (Nijdam 2008, 224). In various Old Frisian tariffs, we encounter another legal term, *wonspreke*, also meaning 'impairment of speech'. These damages are either caused by injuries to the lips, teeth or tongue. Lisi Oliver (2011, 96) incorrectly assumed that the *Lex Frisionum* and *Ab* run parallel at this point because in the *Lex Frisionum* speech impairment is listed as a consequence of hitting someone on the head, rendering the victim either deaf or dumb and not as a consequence of damage to the teeth, as is the case in *Ab*. The Old Frisian Riustring tradition does on the other hand show a nice parallel to *Ab*.

Partonomy and body parts

The legal terms used represent one layer of the tariffs that needs to be analysed. The second layer is that of the way the body is treated in terms of partonomy and anatomy. How is the human body structured by these texts and how are these structures assessed? Overviews exist of the way the hands and teeth were structured by the various tariffs and how the individual fingers and teeth were valued relatively to one another (Oliver 2011, 140–58; Nijdam 2008, 220–4). These structures will be reviewed here for the Anglo-Frisian traditions. It is important to note, however, that these structures are not to be viewed as revealing some sort of 'tariff DNA'. They turn out to be quite fluid and open to change and variation. This can be shown clearly by looking at the Frisian tradition, because it offers so much and it contains material from a span of several centuries (Nijdam 2008, 220–4; see also Table 11.5).

In general, *Ab* treats the body more or less from head to toe as do some but not all Old Frisian tariffs and the *Lex Frisionum*. Several of the other tariffs in the various *Leges Barbarorum* show this structure as well. *Ab* values the six principal body parts, i.e. hands, eyes and feet, at half a freeman's *wergild* each, which amounts to fifty shillings.

In *Ab* the compensations for the loss of the individual fingers neatly add up to 50 shillings (i.e. a half *wergild*), while there is no clause on the loss of the complete hand (Oliver 2011, 140–1). The thumb is valued highest, as is the case in all tariffs and all *Leges Barbarorum*. This is obviously due to the immense practical value of the thumb for gripping objects. In Table 11.6, I have plotted this out for *Ab* and for the *Lex Frisionum*. Because

Table 11.5. Groupings of fingers in the Old East Frisian tariffs. BHu = *Hunsingo Compensation Tariff*, BEm = *Emsingo Compensation Tariff*, BAg = *General Old East Frisian Compensation Tariff*, BRu = *Riustring Compensation Tariff*, BB = *Brokmer Compensation Tariff*.

Grouping of the digits	BHu	BEm	BAg	BRu	BB
1. Thumb; 2. Index finger + Middle finger; 3. Ring finger + Little finger. Each set is valued at ⅙ wergild	x	x	x		
1. Thumb; 2. 4 fingers. Each set is valued at ¼ wergild				x	x
1. Thumb + Little finger; 2. Index finger + Middle finger + Ring finger	x		x	x	

the latter also contains extra material in the form of the *Additiones Sapientum*, the *Lex* in fact yields two different schemata. In the first schema, stemming from the main text (Tit. XXII. *De dolg*), the thumb is valued highest. In *Ab* and in various of the Old East Frisian tariffs, the little finger is valued highest after the thumb and this is also concomitant with practical value of the little finger (Oliver 2011, 144). In the *Lex Frisionum*, however, in both tariffs found there, the ring finger is valued the highest after the thumb. The difference between the two tariffs is that in Tit. XXII, there is an extra compensation for the loss of the palm, adding up to forty-five *solidi* in total. In the *Additiones Sapientum* tariff, there is no extra compensation for the loss of the palm, but the thumb extracts half of the compensation for the loss of the hand, i.e. twenty-two and a half *solidi* and the fines for the rest of the fingers also add up to this amount, again giving a total of forty-five *solidi* for the loss of the hand.

Table 11.6. Compensations for hand and fingers in *Ab* and the *Lex Frisionum*.

	Ab.	*Lex Frisionum* 22	*Additiones Sapientum*
thumb	20	13	22.5
forefinger	9	7	6
middle finger	4	7	4.5
ring finger	6	8	7
little finger	11	6	5
palm	0	4	
TOTAL	50 shillings	45 *solidi*	45 *solidi*

Within the Old Frisian tradition, the Old East Frisian tariffs mostly value the thumb at one-third of the entire hand and then go on to group the four fingers in groups of two (forefinger + middle finger, ring finger + little finger) and valuate these groups at a third of a hand as well (Nijdam 2008, 220–4). The little finger is still valued highest after the thumb, which means that the ringfinger is allotted a relatively small fine. One Old East Frisian tariff values the thumb at half a hand and the four fingers together at the other half. In some tariffs, the three middle fingers of the hand are fined extra because of the 'blessing against the devil' one can perform with them. The Old West Frisian tariffs are less elaborate as far as the hand is concerned. One group has a declining sequence of 12 to 8 ounces for the loss of thumb to little finger. For this group of tariffs an older schema can be reconstructed where the loss of the thumb is valued at 12 ounces and the fingers each at 8 ounces.

In contrast with this enormous variation of schemata, there is a strong parallel between the Anglo-Saxon and the Frisian traditions where the lexicography of the fingers is concerned. Apart from the word for the thumb, which is common Germanic and can be found practically everywhere, both traditions have 'shooting finger' for the forefinger (OE *scytefinger*, OFris *skotfinger*); 'middle finger' (OE *middelfinger*, OFris *middelfinger*, but also *grate finger*, 'great finger'); 'gold finger' for the ring finger (OE *goldfinger*, OFris *goldfinger*); and 'little finger' (OE *lytla finger*, OFris *liteke finger*, but also *slutere*, 'the closer').

The way in which the teeth are categorized and valued is also very informative. Dentists group the teeth into incisors (the upper and lower four front teeth), canines, premolars and molars. Functionally the canines are valued the highest by dentists, followed by molars and incisors. Aesthetically the incisors come first, followed by canines and molars. The *Leges Barbarorum* show a plethora of valuations of the respective teeth (Oliver 2011, 102–7). *Ab* (48) distinguishes the four front teeth, which are valued at 6 shillings, the canines at 4, the premolar next to the canine at 3 shillings, and 'the others' at 1 shilling each. The *Lex Frisionum* (Tit. XXII, 19–21) distinguishes the incisors (at 2 *solidi*), the canines (at 3 *solidi*) and the molars (at 4 *solidi*). The *Additiones Sapientum* tariff (Tit. III, 36–8) groups and values the teeth in exactly the same way. The Old East Frisian tariffs also categorize the teeth in three groups: incisors, canines and molars. Some traditions however further group the incisors into two groups of four: the upper and lower two front teeth and the four teeth that are next to those (two in the upper jaw and two in the lower jaw). These four front teeth are valued the highest because of their visibility: the aesthetic valuation prevails in this case. As was the case with the fingers, the Old West Frisian traditions again are much more sober in this respect. They only distinguish between teeth and molars and value the former twice as high as the latter (Nijdam 2008, 224–5).

Finally, the third set of principal limbs, i.e. the feet, require our attention. The main text of the *Lex Frisionum* has a descending sequence of an 8 to 4 *solidi* compensation for the loss of the toes. These amounts add up to 30 *solidi*, being two-third of the 45 *solidi* for the loss of the entire foot. Together with compensation of 15 *solidi* for the rest of the foot, this again adds up to the 45 *solidi* we also encountered as the compensation for the loss of the hand. The *Additiones Sapientum* tariff (Tit. III, 1–4) yields a different picture. First, it is explicitly stated that the loss of the foot requires the same compensation of the hand. After that, the compensations for the individual toes are given: 11¼, 3, 2 2⅔, 2⅔, 2⅔, adding up to 22.25 *solidi*, which is almost half of the 45 *solidi* for the entire foot.

Implicitly then, the toes are valued at half the rate of the fingers, but the values of the individual toes do not follow that of the corresponding fingers. This, on the other hand, is exactly what happens in *Ab* (69–70). First the text gives the compensation for the loss of the entire foot (at half a *wergild* or fifty shillings) and then for the big toe. Then it proceeds thus: 'For each of the other toes let him pay half the amount already discussed for the fingers' (Oliver 2002, 77). This in fact leaves a quarter of a *wergild* unaccounted for: whereas the fingers add up to 50 shillings, the toes add up to only 25 shillings (see also: Oliver 2011, 161–2). Should the loss of the stump of the foot then exact the balance of 25 shillings, as the *Lex Frisionum* explicitly states?

In the Old Frisian tradition, the toes have been completely converted into the equivalents of the fingers. This was almost certainly enhanced by the fact that the six principal limbs were made into a separate category in the Old Frisian tariffs which were called the *sex litha*, 'the six limbs'. These became a kind of health check: a man was 'healthy' if his 'six limbs' were intact (Nijdam 2008, 219–20). This development also reinforced the complete alignment of hands and feet, to such an extent that some tariffs simply state: *Tha tana hagon alsa grate bote alsa tha fingra*, 'The toes exact the same compensations as the fingers', a statement which is remarkably similar to that in *Ab* quoted earlier (Nijdam 2008, 218).

Measuring mechanisms used in the tariffs

The third layer in the tariffs is that of the ways injuries are measured and categorized in order to establish their (relative) severity.

The first variable is that of visibility. As we saw earlier, an unblemished appearance was the ideal in an honour society. It is not surprising, then, that it was relevant whether wounds which could potentially leave scars were visible or not, in other words whether they could be covered by clothing or not (Nijdam 2008, 226; Oliver 2011, 165–7). Both *Ab* and the Old Frisian tariffs make the same distinction between wounds that are 'inside the clothes' (OE *binnan wædum*, OFris *binna klathum*) and those that are 'outside the clothes' (OE *buton wædum*, OFris *buta klathum*) (see the beginning of the *General Old East Frisian Compensation Tariff* cited earlier). The term *Ab* uses, *wæd*, 'clothing', is also found in Old Frisian (*wede*), but again the term is not confined to these two languages: it is attested for almost all Germanic dialects (Boutkan and Siebinga 2005, 433).

Secondly, tariffs frequently distinguish several degrees of severity of particular injuries. In *Ab* we encounter two kinds of *wlitewam*: *æt þam lærestan wlitewamme*, 'for the least disfigurement of the appearance', followed by *æt þam maran*, 'for the greater'. The compensations are three and six shillings respectively. In the Frisian tradition, both in the *Lex Frisionum* and in the Old Frisian tariffs, groups of three are very frequent. The Old Frisian tariffs frequently distinguish three degrees of an injury: the lowest (OFris *minnesta*), the middle (OFris *midlesta*) and the highest (OFris *hagesta*) degree (Nijdam 2008, 59–60).

The *Lex Frisionum* describes three wrinkles in the forehead that can be cut through and this clause can also be found in the Old Frisian tariffs, which add that no more than three wrinkles are to be compensated. The number three is in other words also used as a maximum (Nijdam 2008, 78). Since this is a clause that is absent in the other *Leges Barbarorum* and since it does reappear in the Old Frisian tariffs, this can be considered as one of the fingerprints of the Frisian tradition. I will return to this point in my conclusion.

Finally, the length of wounds was measured and compensated accordingly. In *Ab* (67), wounds are measured in inches: each inch exacts one shilling (Oliver 2002,76–7). In the *Lex Frisionum*, the main text and the *Additiones Sapientum* yield three systems of measuring wounds (Nijdam 2000; 2009, 51–2). The first two systems measure by means of the 'span' or the distance between the extended thumb and forefinger and the lengths of the knuckles of the fingers. The third system measures by means of inches, just as *Ab*. The *Additiones Sapientum* text adds that this system stems from the area between the rivers Sincfal and Vlie, the western part of Frisia. This system is also encountered in the Old Frisian tariffs. There, this unit is called *mete*, '(standard) measure' and it is described as the length of the upper knuckle of the thumb. This simple system of measuring with the help of standard units (inches/*mete*) seems to have won out over the two more intricate and inaccurate systems in the *Lex Frisionum*.

Conclusions

Some conclusions can now be drawn. Although *Ab* and the Frisian material look alike in some respects and share some legal terms (but almost never exclusively), they differ to such a degree that it is impossible to reconstruct an Anglo-Frisian proto-tariff. The two traditions show such divergence at the various levels studied here that it safer to assume that they both grew independently out of a common stock of terms and concepts that was shared throughout a large part of the Germanic world. In that respect, one keeps returning to Patrick Wormald's observation that 'a tariff recognizable as one's own was perhaps itself an ethnic marker' (Wormald 2003, 41).

We do not need to give up on the notion of an Anglo-Frisian or Ingvaeonic sphere entirely though. The two traditions do show a relative closeness to one another. The analysis undertaken here also confirmed the closer relationship between the Old East Frisian tradition and the Anglo-Saxon tradition Munske already pointed at. Not all of Munske's data could be used here though, since the analysis was confined to *Ab*. Oliver and Munske repeatedly found links between the laws of Wessex (Alfred and Ine) and the *Lex Frisionum* (Oliver 2011, 227–37). These parallels need to be studied closer in the way done here for *Ab*, i.e. combining the insights of Munske and Oliver.

That brings us to the question of where to go from here. Given the fact that these types of legal texts provide very important testimony to the cultures they represent, here are several things that should be studied more closely. In the first place, the studies by Munske, Oliver and myself should be converted into a database. This database would include vernacular terms, constructions, wound types, information on the human anatomy, and more. Next, we need to find the fingerprints or markers of the various individual tariff traditions. The clause on cutting through the wrinkles in the forehead which can only be found in the *Lex Frisionum* and then later again in the Old Frisian tariff tradition is a case in point. This will allow us to gain a better understanding of the character of the individual tariff traditions. The result of this enterprise would be an insight into one of the fundamental aspects of Germanic culture and would allow us to get a clearer view on which elements are universal, which common Germanic, and which make up the fingerprints of the cultural sphere around the North Sea.

References

Primary sources

Buma, Wybren J., and Wilhelm Ebel ed. 1963, *Das Rüstringer recht*, Altfriesische Rechtsquellen 1 (Göttingen).
Eckhardt, Karl A., and Albrecht Eckhardt ed. 1982, *Lex Frisionum*. Monumenta Germaniae Historica. Fontes iuris Germanici antiqui in usum scholarum separatim editi XII (Hannover).

Secondary sources

Ammon, Matthias 2008, 'Piercing the rihthamscyld – a New Reading of Æthelberht 32', *Quaestio Insularis* 9, 34–51.
Boehm, Christopher 2007, 'The natural history of blood revenge'. In *Feud in Medieval and Early Modern Europe*, ed. J. Büchert Netterström and B. Poulsen (Aarhus), 189–203.
Boutkan, Dirk, and Sjoerd Siebinga 2005, *Old Frisian Etymological Dictionary*, Leiden Indo-European Etymological Dictionary Series 1 (Leiden and Boston).
Bowman, James 2006, *Honor. A History* (New York).
Diamond, Arthur S. 1971, *Primitive Law, Past and Present* (London).
Ellis Davidson, Hilda R. 1960, 'The sword at the wedding', *Folklore* 71(1), 1–18.
Gerrets, Danny 1995, 'The Anglo-Frisian relationship seen from an archaeological point of view'. In *Friesische Studien II*. NOWELE Supplement Volume 12, ed. V. F. Faltings, A. G. H. Walker and O. Wilts (Odense), 119–28.
Hanlon, Gregory 2013, 'The decline of violence in the West: from cultural to post-cultural history', *English Historical Review* CXXVIII 531, 367–400.
Henstra, Dirk Jan 2000, *The Evolution of the Money Standard in Medieval Frisia. A Treatise on the History of the Systems of Money of Account in the Former Frisia (c. 600–c. 1500)* (Groningen). Accessed on 7 June 2016 via http://www.rug.nl/research/portal/publications/pub%2812414162-9f0b-431e-92f0-d0e8eb24bed5%29.html!null
Henstra, Dirk Jan 2001, 'Het probleem van de geldbedragen in de Lex Frisionum', *Jaarboek voor Munt- en Penningkunde* 88, 1–32.
Hines, John 1995, 'Focus and boundary in linguistic varieties in the North-West Germanic continuum'. In *Friesische Studien II*. NOWELE Supplement Volume 12, ed. V. F. Faltings, A. G. H. Walker and O. Wilts (Odense), 35–62.
Hines, John 2013, 'Social structures and social change in seventh-century England: the law codes and complementary sources', *Historical Research* 86, 366–407.
Hofmann, Dietrich, and AnneTjerk Popkema 2008, *Altfriesisches Handwörterbuch* (Heidelberg).
Hough, Carole 2015, 'The earliest English texts? The language of the Kentish laws reconsidered'. In *Textus Roffensis: Law, Language and Libraries in Early Medieval England*, ed. B. O'Brien and B. Bombi (Turnhout), 137–56.
Johnston, Thomas S. B. 2001, 'The Old Frisian law manuscripts and law texts'. In *Handbuch des Friesischen*, ed. H. H. Munske, N. Århammer, V. F. Faltings, J. F. Hoekstra, O. Vries, A. G. H. Walker and O. Witts (Tübingen), 571–86.
Jurasinski, Stefan 2006, *Ancient Privileges: Beowulf, Law and the Making of Germanic Antiquity* (Morgantown).
Miller, William I. 1990, *Bloodtaking and Peacemaking. Feud, Law, and Society in Saga Iceland* (Chicago and London).
Miller, William I. 2006, *Eye for an Eye* (Cambridge).
Munske, Horst Haider 1973, *Der germanische Rechtswortschatz im Bereich der Missetaten. Philologische und Sprachgeografische Untersuchungen. I Die Terminologie der älteren westgermanischen Rechtsquellen* (Berlin and New York).

Netterström, Jeppe Büchert, and Björn Poulsen ed. 2007, *Feud in Medieval and Early Modern Europe* (Aarhus).

Nicolay, Johan A. W. 2014, *The Splendour of Power. Early Medieval Kingship and the Use of Gold and Silver in the Southern North Sea Area (5th to 7th Century AD)*, Groningen Archaeological Studies 28 (Groningen).

Nijdam, Han 2000, 'Measuring wounds in the *Lex Frisionum* and the Old Frisian Registers of Fines'. In *Philologia Frisica Anno 1999. Lêzingen fan it fyftjinde Frysk filologekongres 8, 9 en 10 desimber 1999*, ed. P. Boersma, Ph.H. Breuker, L. G. Jansma and J. van der Vaart (Leeuwarden), 180–203.

Nijdam, Han 2008, *Lichaam, eer en recht in middeleeuws Friesland. Een studie naar de Oudfriese boeteregisters* (Hilversum).

Nijdam, Han 2009, 'Klinkende munten en klinkende botsplinters in de Oudfriese rechtsteksten: continuïteit, discontinuïteit, intertekstualiteit', *De Vrije Fries* 89, 45–66.

Nijdam, Han 2010, 'Belichaamde eer, wraak en vete. Een historisch- en cognitief-antropologische benadering', *Tijdschrift voor Geschiedenis* 123, 192–207.

Nijdam, Han 2013, 'Honour and shame embodied: the case of medieval Frisia'. In *Shame between Punishment and Penance. The Social Usages of Shame in the Middle Ages and Early Modern Times / La honte entre peine et pénitence – les usages sociaux de la honte au Moyen Âge et aux débuts de lépoque moderne*, Micrologus Library Vol. 111, ed. Bénédicte Sère and Jörg Wettlaufer (Firenze), 65–88.

Nijdam, Han 2014a, 'Compensating body and honor: the Old Frisian compensation tariffs'. In *Medicine and Law in the Middle Ages*. Medieval Law and its Practice 17, ed. W. J. Turner en S. M. Butler (Leiden and Boston 2014), 25–57.

Nijdam, Han 2014b, 'Indigenous or universal? A comparative perspective on medieval (Frisian) Compensation law'. In *How Nordic are the Nordic Laws? Ten Years After. Proceedings of the Tenth Carlsberg Conference on Medieval Legal History 2013*, ed. P. Andersen, K. Salonen, H. Sigh and H. Vogt (Copenhagen), 161–81.

Nijdam, Han, and Arjen Versloot 2012, 'Kodeks Siccama. Spoaren fan in ferdwûn Aldwestfrysk rjochtshânskrift', *Us Wurk* 61, 1–56.

Oliver, Lisi 2002, *The Beginnings of English Law* (Toronto, Buffalo, London).

Oliver, Lisi 2011, *The Body Legal in Barbarian Law* (Toronto, Buffalo, London).

Oliver, Lisi 2014, 'Genital mutilation in medieval Germanic law'. In *Capital and Corporal Punishment in Anglo-Saxon England*, ed. J. P. Gates and N. Marafioti (Woodbridge), 48–73.

Parsons, David 1996, 'The origins and chronology of the "Anglo-Frisian" additional runes'. In *Frisian Runes and Neighbouring Traditions*, Amsterdammer Beiträge zur älteren Germanistik 45, ed. A. Quak and T. Looijenga, 151–70.

Pinker, Steven 2002, *The Blank Slate: The Modern Denial of Human Nature* (London).

Rubin, Stanley 1996, 'The *bot*, or compensation in Anglo–Saxon law: a reassesment', *Journal of Legal History* 17(1), 144–54.

Siems, Harald 1980, *Studien zur Lex Frisionum* (Ebelsbach am Main).

Stiles, Patrick 1995, 'Remarks on the "Anglo-Frisian" thesis'. In *Handbuch des Friesischen*, ed. H. H. Munske, N. Århammer, V. F. Faltings, J. F. Hoekstra, O. Vries, A. G. H. Walker and O. Witts (Tübingen), 177–220.

Vries, Oebele 2015, 'Frisonica libertas: Frisian freedom as an instance of medieval liberty', *Journal of Medieval History* 2015, 1–20.

Wormald, Patrick 1999, *The Making of English Law: King Alfred to the Twelfth Century. Volume I. Legislation and Its Limits* (Oxford).

Wormald, Patrick 2003, 'The *Leges Barbarorum*: law and ethnicity in the post-Roman West'. In *Regna and Gentes. The Relationship between Late Antique and Early Medieval Peoples and Kingdoms in the Transformation of the Roman World*, The Transformation of the Roman World 1, ed. H.-W. Goetz, J. Jarnut and W. Pohl (Leiden and Boston), 21–53.

12

Cultural Contacts between the Western Baltic, the North Sea Region and Scandinavia

Attributing runic finds to runic traditions and corpora of the Early Viking Age

Christiane Zimmermann and Hauke Jöns

On the basis of the artefactual finds and structures, and based on contemporary or later written sources, early trading centres are generally conceived of as meeting places and melting pots of people from different cultures. A highly vivid sketch of the multicultural network of communication formed by the trading centres of a 'Northern Arc' ranging from the North Sea region to the eastern end of the Baltic and into Russia is drawn by Stéphane Lebecq (2007). In his overview, he touches on the exchange of goods from the 7th century through to the 9th, the different forms of economic enterprises in that period, and the impact of Viking expansionism. The jigsaw pieces of his panoramic picture are taken from chronicles, the historical accounts of Ohthere's and Wulfstan's voyages, and from archaeological excavations at the most prominent of these trading centres, including Dorestad, Hamwic, Ribe, Hedeby and Birka.

Interestingly, though, while drawing this picture, he never asks about the actual form of communication between the merchants and manufacturers coming from many different regions all over north-western Europe. This omission may be explained by the fact that, in most cases, neither the written sources which are drawn on to shed light on the political and religious history of these places nor the archaeological finds and structures provide any evidence of the languages and dialects spoken by the people living on these sites. The historical sources confine themselves to the most basic external information: thus Rimbert, describing the trading centre at Hedeby in his *Vita Anskarii* (ch. 24), only mentions 'the great variety of people from all over the world'. Adam of Bremen offers more detail in his description of Birka (*Gesta Hammaburgensis Ecclesiae Pontificum*, I.60). He explicitly mentions Danes, Northmen, Slavs and people from Samland (on the Baltic coast). Helmold of Bosau names not only Slavs as inhabitants of the Baltic trading centre of Jumne/Jomsburg but also a 'mixed population of Greeks and barbarians', together with – as he calls them – 'Saxons' (*Chronica Slavorum*, II.22).

These selective references show that the historical sources usually only give names of groups, tribes or peoples, or even stereotypical group-labels, such as 'barbarians' as opposed to Greeks. Ultimately one might wonder why some groups are named and others remain unnamed, such as the Frisians, who – judging by the basis of archaeological evidence – must have played an important role in supra-regional trade of that time. The goals and purposes of the writers, of their respective sponsors, and the literary and historical traditions they were drawing on, need to be taken into account to answer this question. Helmold's mention of 'Saxons' as the only specific group among the 'barbarians' might, for example, be readily explained by the fact that he himself was a Saxon historian. Most essential for the question at hand, however, is that no languages are mentioned in these sources, nor any of the problems intercultural communication might have caused. From the references to Danes, Northmen and Saxons one might deduce that a northern and a more western or North-Sea variant of the Germanic languages were spoken, varieties which would later be referred to as Old Norse, Old Saxon and Old Frisian. But this would imply identifying language-groups with the historical groups and peoples mentioned in the texts – something linguists usually try to avoid, as linguistic reality is rarely so simple.

Archaeological evidence, on the other hand, confirms and supplements the vague and sketchy picture in that the multiplicity of origins attested in the written sources seems to manifest itself in the cultural diversity of the material artefacts and structures of the early trading centres. Most of all the burial customs testify to the different cultural identities of the people living on these sites. Apart from the continuation of burial practices attested in the neighbourhood of the trading centres themselves, burial structures and grave goods at sites such as Groß Strömkendorf suggest the presence of burial communities from different regions of northern, eastern and western Europe, and thus echo the accounts of Rimbert, Adam and Helmold. But the archaeological remains also allow us to assume that the social groups represented by the respective burial traditions did not live side by side without social interaction. The frequent examples of new and hybrid forms of burial practice as well as settlement and buildings on the trading sites suggest that there were close contacts and social interaction between the people originating from different burial communities. The key question concerning the form of communication between these groups nevertheless remains.

For a linguist, the most obvious approach to the question of the linguistic milieu and the languages and dialects spoken at the trading centres of the 8th and 9th centuries would be to address and investigate the primary language sources.[1] For the period in question, though, linguistic evidence is scarce, and – if limited to evidence from comparable mixed language milieux – consists almost exclusively of runic evidence.[2]

---

[1] We shall refer to the period from the middle of the 8th up to the middle of the 9th century as the Early Viking Age.

[2] Manuscript evidence for the northern and western varieties of the Germanic languages starts only later – especially in the Scandinavian (c. 1180) and Frisian areas (c. 1200). It must also be borne in mind that the earliest manuscripts generally stem from scholarly contexts and thus have a completely different language context. They mostly consist of religious and law texts, which are in part versified

The total number of extant runic sources for the North Sea region, the adjacent Western Baltic area, and for Scandinavia in the Early Viking Age is – at only a rough estimate – no more than 200, and the number of runic objects recovered from trading sites adds up to no more than 30: including in both counts several objects which are difficult to date and might actually belong to the late 9th or 10th century. Most of these inscriptions are difficult to read and very seldom have they been satisfactorily interpreted. A more differentiated chronological distribution within the period in question has so far only been achieved for datable archaeological objects (cf. Imer 2007) – but, as some of these objects are merchandise or portable objects, their provenance is not necessarily identical with their find-spot and this could equally apply to the provenance of the runic inscriptions they bear. They thus will not necessarily provide evidence of the language and the linguistic milieu of the area they were found in (e.g. the Duesminde brooch, the Donzdorf brooch or the Hamwic bone). As a result it is almost impossible to come up with a synchronic linguistic context and setting for a new runic object recovered from one of these sites. With a second group comprising the early monumental rune-stones, however, the geographical provenance may be fairly certain – which again may allow for conclusions with regard to the language attested in the inscriptions they bear. The dating, however, is usually only secondary in these cases, achieved by means of comparison of rune-forms and linguistic features, and based upon assumptions about their development in time. A firm and reliable basis on which to characterize the linguistic milieu on the trading sites of the Early Viking Age is therefore elusive.

By default, regarding the primary linguistic sources, an alternative linguistic approach might be chosen:

1. Looking at the range of possible communication scenarios that have been established by previous theoretical and practical research on language contact and intercultural communication, and/or

2. Taking into account the later internal linguistic data of the languages and language varieties attested in the area under scrutiny, in this case the North and West Germanic languages and language varieties attested in manuscripts from about a century later and onwards.

In respect of point 1, on the basis of the results of previous theoretical and practical research on language contact and intercultural communication, six different communication scenarios can be differentiated in language contact-situations (Simensen 1994; Braunmüller 1995):

Type A: each party speaks her or his own language or language variety;

Type B: at least one of the speakers is bi- or multilingual and switches to the language of his or her partner in communication;

Type C: the participants in the communication act use a common regional or national standard;

Type D: some type of hybrid or pidgin language is used for communication;

Type E: the participants use a *lingua franca*;

and/or written and worded following specific scholarly models. This also holds true for most of the earliest manuscript evidence of Old Saxon and Old English language, which is dated to the late 8th and 9th century.

Type F: communication and exchange is achieved only via an interpreter.

In a related study on practical communication in Viking Age England and on the basis of the (lack of) evidence in the written sources, Matthew Townend (2002) concluded that, as there is no mention of interpreters in the texts, we have to accept that people somehow managed to understand each other using their respective mother tongues. This, however, presupposes a certain similarity between the languages involved.

The variety of Greek spoken at Jumne and the different varieties of the Slavonic languages were probably not mutually intelligible. With regard to the varieties of Slavonic and Germanic spoken by the Danes and Northmen in Birka, we might actually assume the existence of interpreters, as the old Scandinavian word for 'interpreter' is supposed to be a Slavonic loan word, i.e. *túlkr* (cf. Simenson 1994, 44).

In respect of point 2, the extant internal information on the languages and language structures of the varieties of early-medieval Germanic in northern and western Europe does seem to support this assumption. From comparative philology and historical reconstruction, most scholars now agree that there must have existed a certain degree of mutual intelligibility between North Germanic and most of the West Germanic varieties, at least up until or maybe even including the Viking Age. Although the earliest attested texts already document several separate innovations in all linguistic branches (i.e. phonological, morphological, syntactical and lexical innovations), many similarities remained. William G. Moulton (1988, 26) thus concluded his comparative study with the judgement that 'linguistically, there was indeed for many centuries a Germania that was unified at the core, with several particular branches. It was unified linguistically because many speakers of different dialects could, and did, easily learn how to talk with one another.' Townend (2002, 182) summarizes his linguistic comparison in quite a similar way: 'I would therefore conclude that the available evidence points fairly unequivocally to a situation of adequate mutual intelligibility between speakers of Norse and English in the Viking Age.' Michael Barnes, however (1993 and 2003), seems sceptical of the elaboracy of this 'semi-communication': 'The far-reaching structural and lexical similarities between Scandinavian on the one hand and Old Saxon, Old English and, as far as can be determined, Old Frisian on the other, seem likely to have made rudimentary communication possible without the need to resort to language learning, but it is hard to see how this can have risen much above the slow articulation of simple phrases accompanied by gesticulation.' (1993, 101). Keeping this caution in mind, it might still be quite safe to assume that the Germanic varieties of the 8th and early 9th centuries were still close enough that people of different language-groups could communicate with each other speaking their own variety, without using a *lingua franca* or an interpreter.

Thus, returning to the six different scenarios presented above, Type A seems to be the most probable. The trading centres were probably multilingual milieux in which most communication was performed using one's own vernacular language, although certain accommodation and levelling processes, including language simplification, are likely to have been involved. Once seasonal trade developed into the more permanent presence of merchants and manufacturers, closer cultural contacts may be assumed, including intermarriages between different language-groups. New forms of communication might have been the result of this, probably different degrees of bi- and multilingualism or even the formation of new sociolects of the languages in question, as has been suggested for

Birka and Hedeby, with idioms known as *Birkasvenska* or *Hedebynordiska* (cf. Johansson 2002, Widmark 1994). In acknowledging this scenario one may further deduce that more than one writing-system was known to the people living on these sites, i.e. different runic writing-systems and maybe even the roman script. In the period under consideration at least two runic writing-systems were in use:

1. The 16-character younger *fuþąrk* (with sub-systems differing in the shape of the characters: Barnes 2012, 61–2); the earliest attestation of this reduced writing-system is found on the Ribe cranium, dated AD 725–60 (Stoklund 2004; Svøsø 2013);

2. The 26/28-character, 'Anglo-Frisian' *fuþorc*, attested from the 5th century onwards (cf. Hines, and Waxenberger, this vol.).[3]

These two writing-systems originate from a single predecessor, the common Germanic older *fuþark*, the earliest records of which are dated to the 2nd century, and which was in use well into the 7th century (e.g. in the Stentoften and Björketorp inscriptions: cf. Krause 1966; Imer 2007, Catalogue; Schulte 2015). The development of its successors, the younger *fuþąrk* and the Anglo-Frisian *fuþorc*, did not result in completely altered character-forms. Several of the established graphic forms of the older *fuþark* remained, although some of them had changed sound-values as they formed part of a new writing-system. As a result, inscriptions written in one or the other rune-row by a Scandinavian, English or Frisian inscriber may not be distinguishable simply by the shape of the characters. If diagnostic runes are lacking and the meaning of the inscription and the etymology of the lexical items is not secure, the question of attributing the new inscription to either of the runic corpora may be impossible to solve.

The coexistence and the parallel use of two writing-systems may also imply that more than one inventory of character shapes could be drawn on to represent words and sounds in writing. The use of Scandinavian younger *fuþąrk* runes to write Latin or even Middle English texts is well attested (cf. the Bridekirk font: Barnes and Page 2006, 278–85). But even hybrid inscriptions with letters belonging to two different rune-rows have surfaced: the St Albans II bone from Hertfordshire attests Scandinavian and Anglo-Frisian runes side-by-side in **wufri(k)**, presumably a form of the common Old English personal name *Wulfric* (Barnes and Page 2006, 329). As the linguistic background of inscription, Barnes and Page assume a 'mixed cultural group'.

With regard to the form of communication, therefore, the initial picture of the life and communication on the Early Viking Age trading centres may be supplemented as follows. We most probably have to reckon with a linguistic milieu where different languages were spoken that were mutually intelligible. In this milieu more than one runic alphabet was probably known and could be drawn on when carving a new runic inscription. The contact of cultures, languages and writing-systems may even result in hybrid inscriptions with a mixed use of languages and rune-rows. All these data are crucial and have to be kept in mind when tackling the task of reading and interpreting a new runic inscription from one of these mixed cultural contexts we expect the trading centres to have been. The recently discovered comb fragment from the trading centre at Groß Strömkendorf is such a case in point.

---

[3] A later expansion to 31 characters seems to be a 'locally based' variety of this rune-row that was only used in the north of England (Barnes 2012, 40).

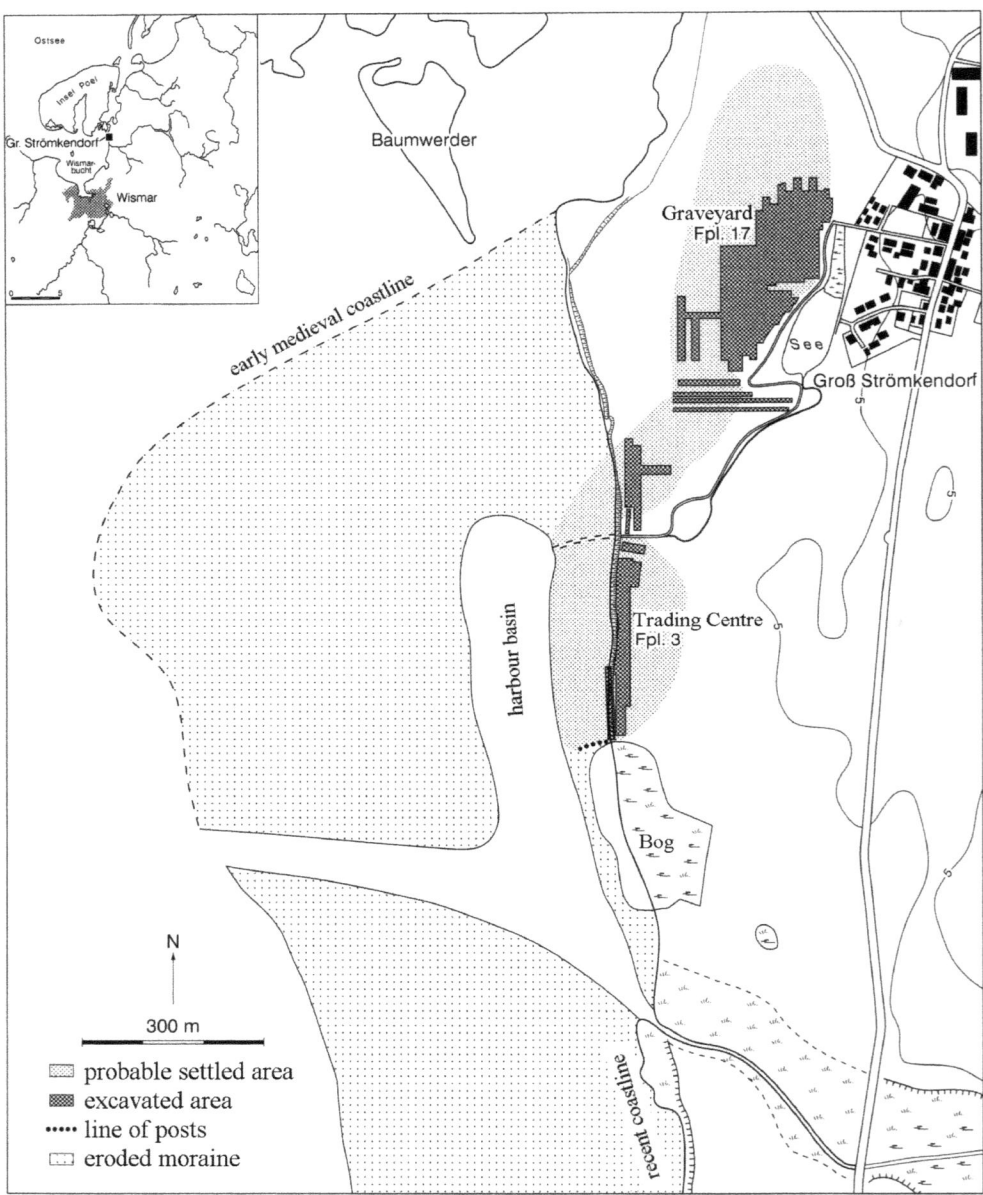

Fig. 12.1. Groß Strömkendorf. The map shows the extent of the settled area and the position of the trading centre, the graveyard and the harbour basin (after Schmölcke and Jöns 2011, fig. 1).

Groß Strömkendorf

The site of Groß Strömkendorf is situated on Wismar Bay in the south-western Baltic region. Our knowledge about this site derives mostly from interdisciplinary research carried out between 1988 and 1999 (summarized in Müller-Wille 2009). In the course of these investigations it was possible to prove that the site functioned as a trading centre from as early as the second quarter of the 8th to the early 9th century AD, benefiting from calm waters and a natural harbour protected by the island of Poel (Fig. 12.1). Historical sources indicate that the area was settled by the Obodrites, a Slavic tribal community that migrated into the south-western Baltic region in the second half of the 7th century (Jöns and Müller-Wille 2015). The Groß Strömkendorf site offered access to the maritime trade-routes between the Cimbrian Peninsula and the eastern Baltic (Bogucki 2004, 2012; Jöns 2009). The settled area covered more than 20 ha, including the trading area itself and its periphery together with a neighbouring cemetery. The remains of the harbour-basin, which are now submerged owing to a considerable rise in sea-level in the south-western Baltic, were also discovered and partly investigated (Jöns 2011). The investigations carried out so far give a vivid impression of the life here of people with different origins from all over Europe, and of the manifold contacts they had. In the following, only the most important results will be presented.

The cemetery

The cemetery was positioned at the northern periphery of the trading centre on a small hill. It has been fully excavated (Fig. 12.2); 242 graves of different character were investigated, indicating a burying population of varying origins and roots (Gerds 2015). Most of the deceased were cremated, and buried either in urns or small pits, or simply by spreading the ashes in ditches or on the ground-surface. Cremation graves of any kind have to be considered part of the funeral traditions of the western Slavs (Paddenberg 2000). One may therefore conclude that local Obodrite individuals were interred in these graves. However, a closer look at the cremation graves from Groß Strömkendorf reveals that 66% of them – 105 burials – were urn graves, which have hitherto been recorded only in small numbers from the early western Slavic settlement area and from southern Scandinavia. However, they were very common in the coastal areas of the North Sea during the 8th and 9th centuries (Gerds 2015, 62–4). Therefore, the common practice of urned cremation could be viewed as evidence of a large community rooted in the North Sea region. Further analyses of the graves showed that most of the urns were found on the western periphery of the cemetery, and that they were deposited in the final two decades before AD 800. Together with the known extension of the settlement area in this period, it is inferred that these graves indicate the arrival of people from the North Sea region, leading to a growth in population (Gerds 2015, 217–18).

There were also inhumation graves of varying character amongst the funeral traditions practised at Groß Strömkendorf. The majority of the deceased in these graves were buried without coffins in a supine position, but around 40% of both males and females lay in a crouched or contracted position. While burying the dead supine was common practice in Early Viking Age Scandinavia and in the areas west of the Elbe, burying in

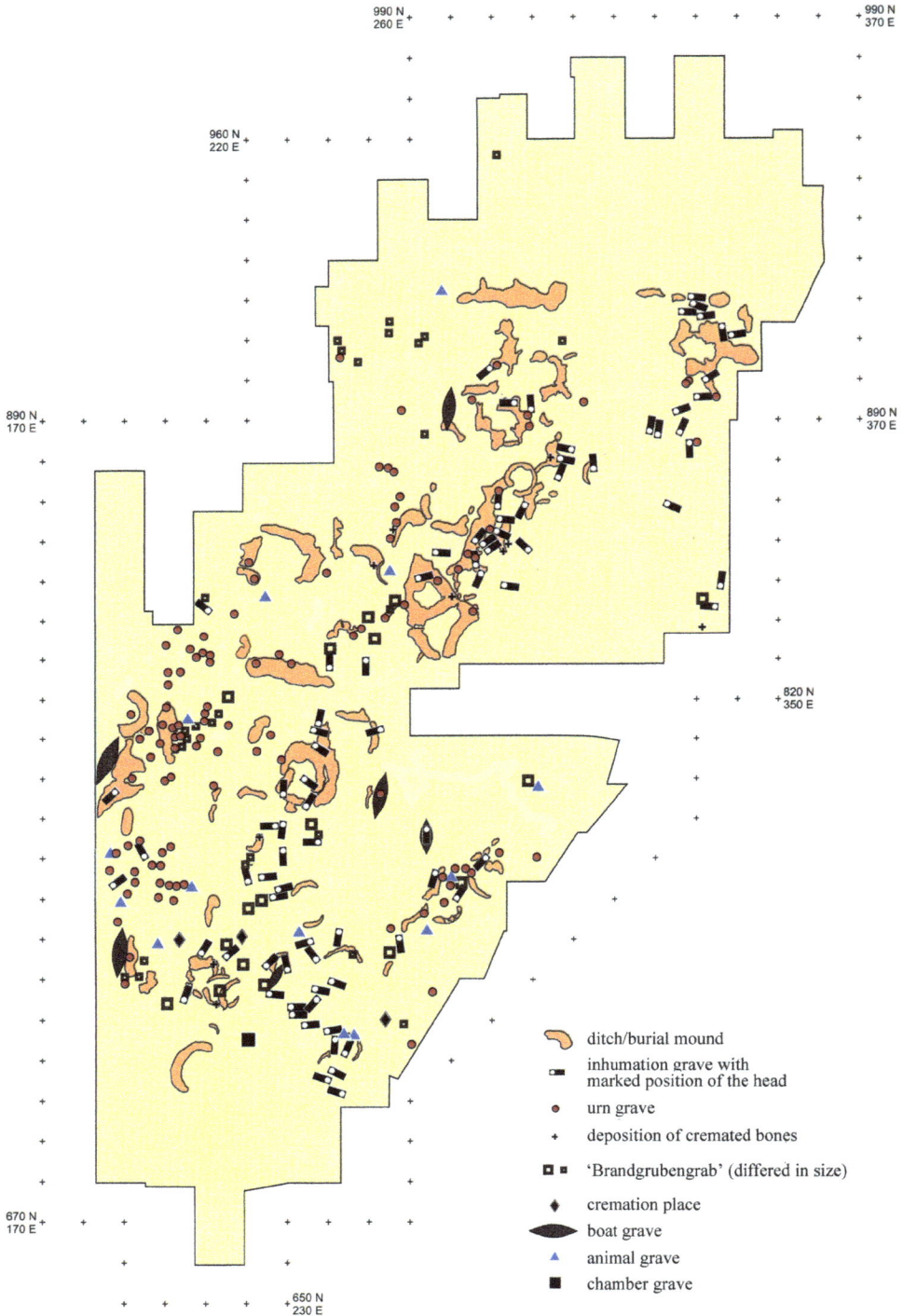

Fig. 12.2. Groß Strömkendorf. General plan of the graveyard (after Gerds 2015, Plan 1).

crouched or contracted positions was almost entirely restricted to southern Scandinavia. Clusters of such graves from the 8th and early 9th century are known particularly in Sjælland, Bornholm and Skåne (Jørgensen and Nørgaard Jørgensen 1997).

The evidence of six graves associated with boats is also of great interest, indicating that the community that buried these persons was familiar with Scandinavian burial customs (Müller-Wille 1995). A closer look into the distribution of contemporaneous burials of this type reveals that during the existence of the Groß Strömkendorf trading centre burials in occur were mostly in eastern Sweden, western Finland and Norway (Fig. 12.3; Gerds 2006). This may hint that groups from these areas were present in the Wismar Bay around AD 800 too.

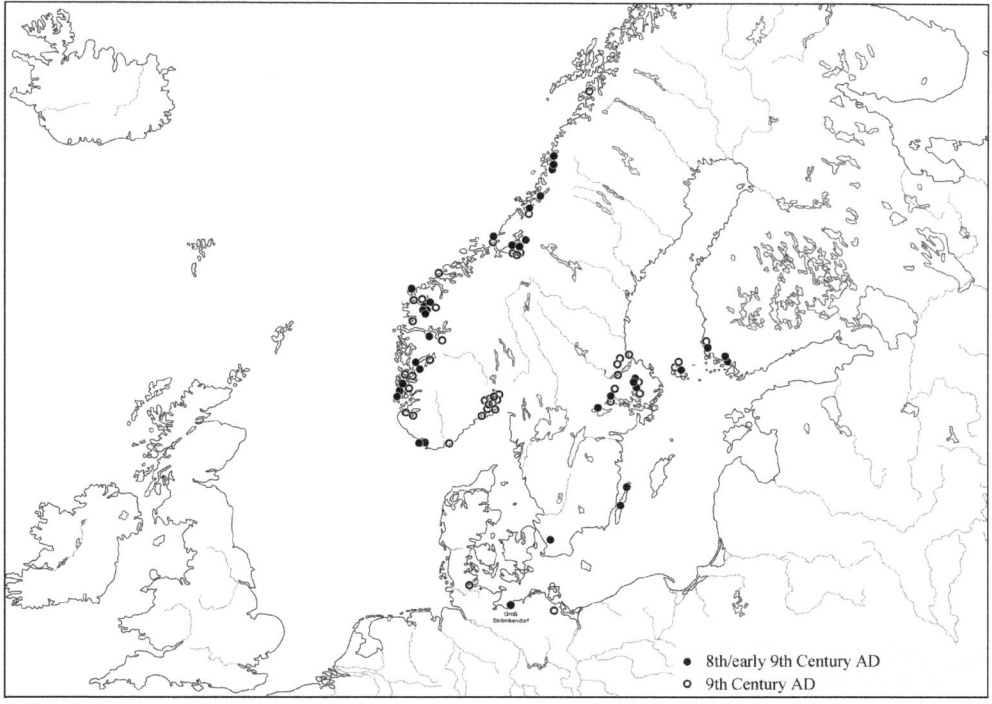

Fig. 12.3. Distribution of dated boat graves of the 8th and 9th centuries AD in northern Central Europe and Scandinavia (after Gerds 2015, fig. 21).

Last but not least, there were nine horse burials and five dog burials, dispersed throughout the cemetery. In a few cases these were combined with inhumation graves (dogs) or cremation graves (horses). In addition, eight depositions of horse and dog skulls, found in ditches around burial mounds or in inhumation graves, but also in boat graves, are remarkable. Animal graves and depositions of animal parts are undoubtedly foreign to the Slavic funeral tradition but find close parallels in some of the neighbouring areas (Fig. 12.4). Burials or depositions of horses and dogs of the 8th or early 9th century AD are well known from Saxon and Frisian territory in north-western Germany (Gerds 2013), but also at a few sites in southern Scandinavia and the eastern Baltic, especially in Lithuania (Bertašius and Daugnora 2001).

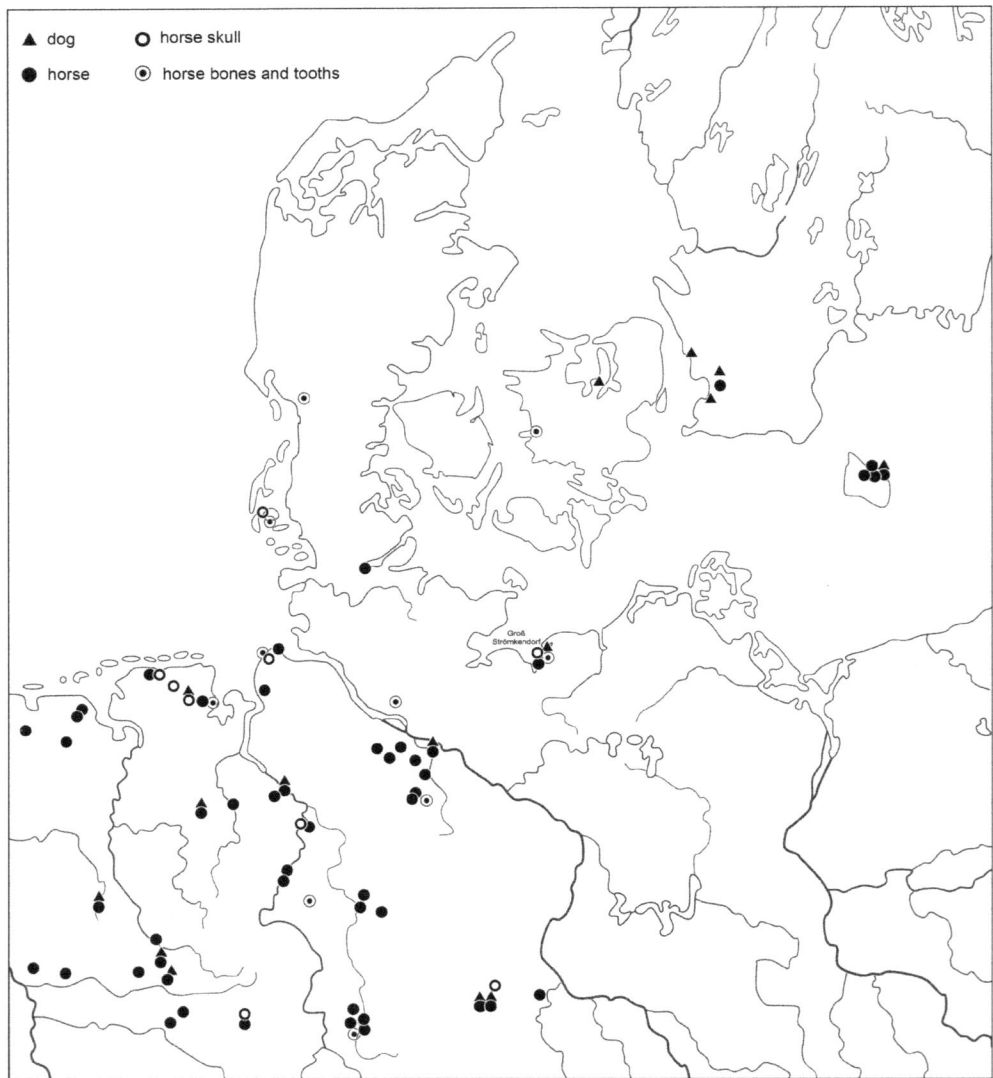

Fig. 12.4. Distribution of dated animal graves and depositions of animal bones of the 8th and 9th centuries AD in northern Central Europe and Scandinavia (after Gerds 2015, fig. 22).

To sum up, the graves at Groß Strömkendorf demonstrate that burial customs from several areas of the Baltic and North Sea areas were tolerated and practised in the same cemetery. It may be assumed that the population of Groß Strömkendorf not only had diverse roots, but formed a more or less symbiotic community.

The settlement and its character

This conclusion drawn from the cemetery evidence is corroborated by the fieldwork results from the settlement (Müller-Wille and Tummuscheit 2004). Owing to the restriction of the excavated area to a strip 25 m wide and 500 m long along the current shoreline, the characterization of the settlement is limited, although additional geomagnetic surveys at least mark out the overall distribution of deep dug features. Almost all buildings found so far were small *Grubenhäuser* combining Scandinavian lay-out and constructional details with stone-built hearths that may be considered common in the Slavic settled area along the upper reach of the Elbe in Thuringia and Saxony (Fig. 12.5; Tummuscheit 2011, 286–97). The *Grubenhäuser* were surrounded by pits and ditches of various function and often accompanied by wells. In numerous well-shafts, oak-built wooden facings have been preserved that allow dendrochronology to be used to reconstruct the development of the settlement at a very high resolution (Fig. 12.6). The datings indicate that the first buildings were constructed c. AD 730 at the latest. The site then was a rather unstructured *Grubenhaus* settlement spreading over areas along the shore and also covering the hill where the cemetery was later established.

The second phase of development took place between AD 760 and 770, when the settlement was reorganized and expanded. From then on, the settlement activities gravitated along the shore-line area in the vicinity of the harbour, while the neighbouring hill was reassigned to the aforementioned cemetery. In the settlement, a road-system and plot-boundaries were established. This spatial planning and the resulting lay-out of the settlement are reminiscent of the market area structure in Ribe (Feveile 2006, 71) or the Frisian trading *terps* such as Emden or Groothusen (Siegmüller and Jöns 2012; Eichfeld 2015).

Only a few years later, around 770, the inhabited area was further extended to the south. Here too, the layout of the site was shaped by rows of *Grubenhäuser*. According to the dendrochronological data, the last building activity at the site was in AD 811. By then the site had probably already lost its significance and in the following years it was abandoned.

Additional information about the dating of the site as well as the living conditions and the economic basis of the people of Groß Strömkendorf is provided by the detailed analyses of the numerous finds which were salvaged during the excavation. As all excavated layers were sifted through sieves of 4 mm aperture, large numbers of small objects such as glass beads, coins, amber fragments and fish bones were recovered (Schmölcke and Jöns 2013, 62). These small finds confirmed that craft and trade were Groß Strömkendorf's economic basis. Diverse production waste from metalworking as well as from the manufacture of bone, antler, amber and glass was found alongside typical commodities such as foreign pottery, rotary basalt querns, whetstone slate, sherds of glass vessels and glass and amber beads (see Müller-Wille 2009). This material underscores the economic significance of craft activities and the involvement of Groß Strömkendorf in communication and exchange with the eastern Baltic, Scandinavia, western Europe and the North Sea region.

There is similar evidence from a group of sites such as Menzlin, Ralswiek, Bardy-Świelubie and Truso/Janów Pomorski, which were established during the Early Middle

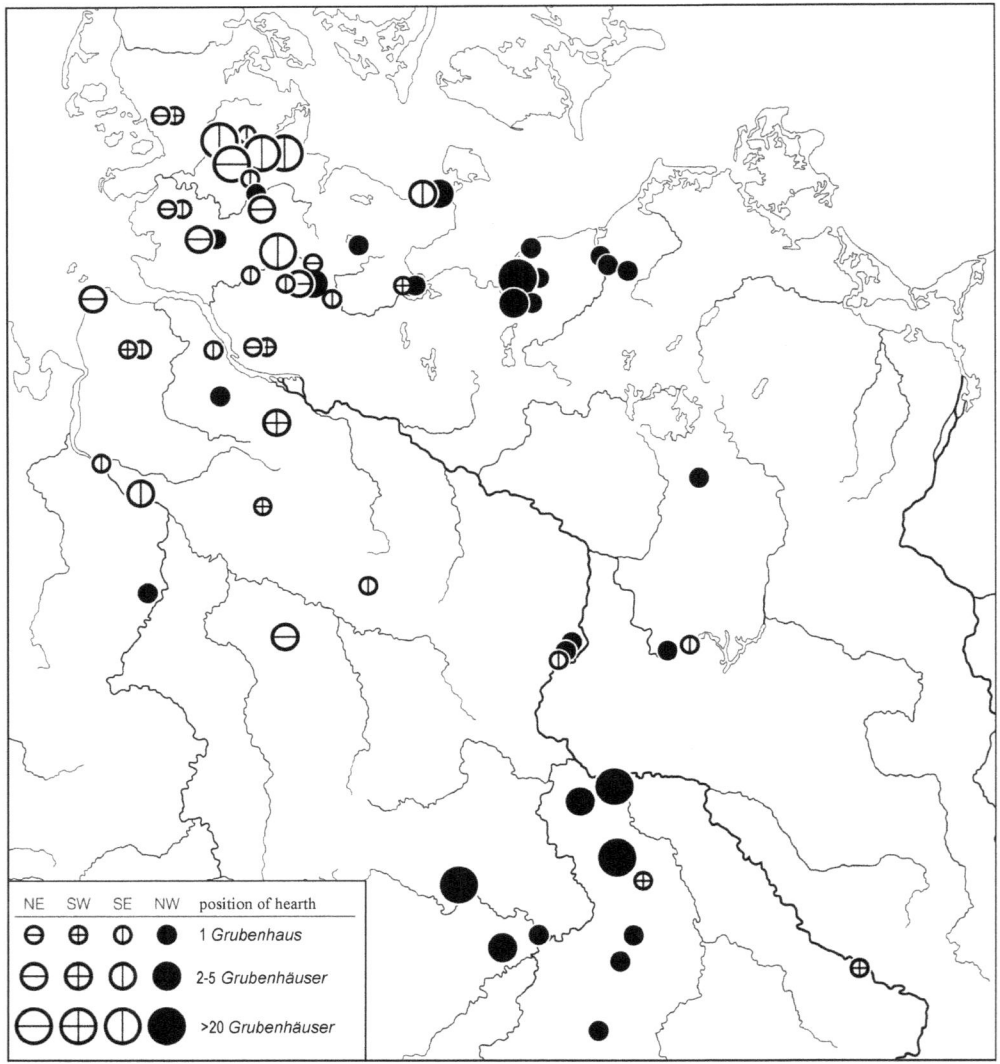

Fig. 12.5. Distribution of *Grubenhäuser* with stone-built hearths of the 8th–11th centuries AD, and their position in the house, in northern Central Europe (after Tummuscheit 2011, fig. 57).

Ages along the southern Baltic rim (Kleingärtner 2014; Karle *et al.* 2015 with refs.). As far as we currently know, none of these places had a predecessor in the Roman Iron Age or the Migration Period; in fact they have to be considered a result of interaction between communities of Scandinavian origin and Slavic people (Jöns and Müller-Wille 2015). Together with a large number of trading places identified along the Scandinavian coasts, they prove that the Slavic-settled area and southern Scandinavia became parts of a trading network at the beginning of the 8th century AD. This network emerged during the 7th and 8th centuries in the southern North Sea area, where it was based on specialized trading sites that offered favourable conditions for water and land transport, and

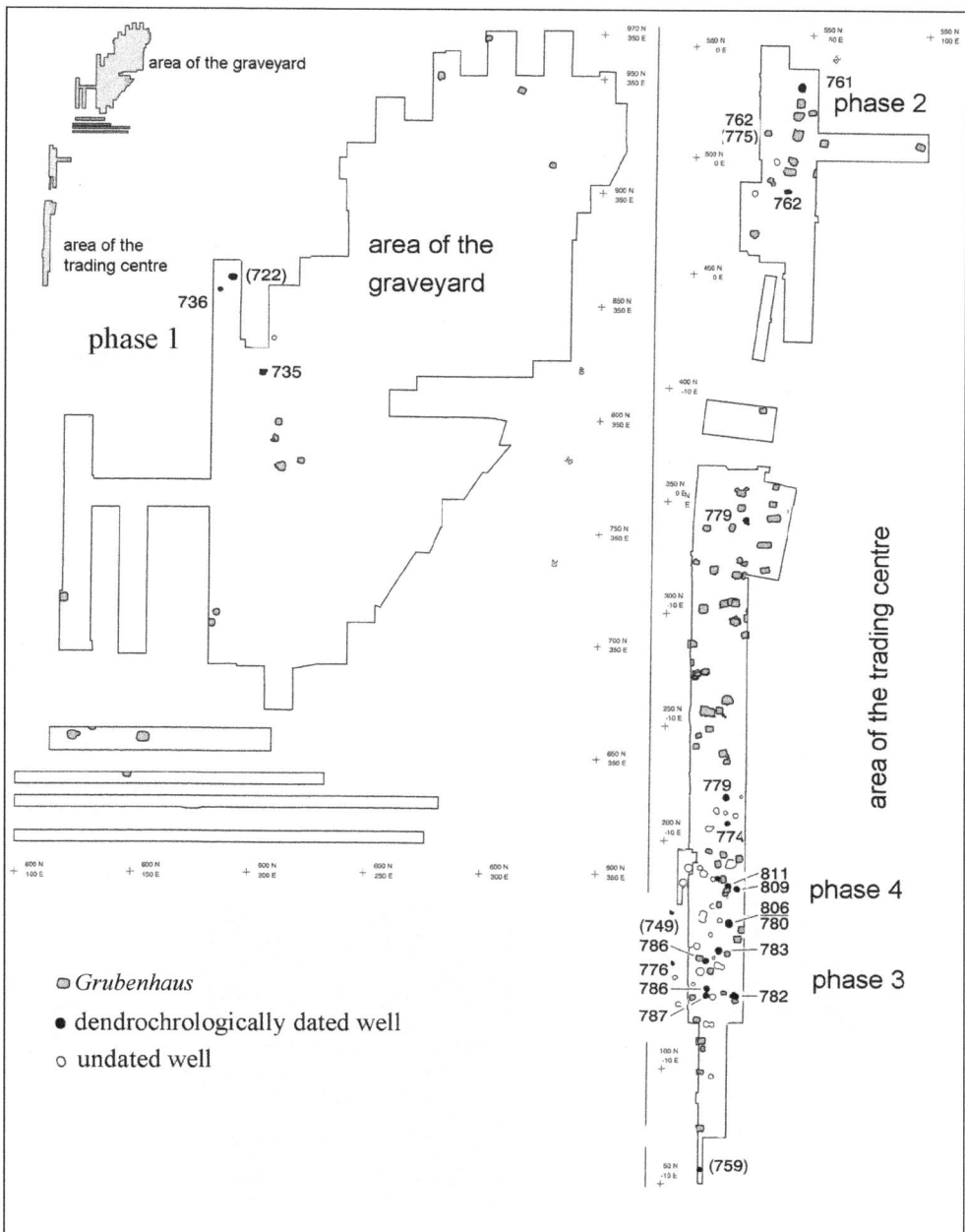

Fig. 12.6. Groß Strömkendorf. Development of the trading centre, based on the distribution of *Grubenhäuser* and dendrochronologically dated wells (after Tummuscheit 2011, figs. 4 and 103).

are referred to as *portus, emporia* or *vici* in contemporary written sources (Lebecq 1992).

For the southern Baltic Sea, evidence from written sources about the organization of trade and exchange is rare and concerns almost exclusively *emporia*, travel conditions and communication networks between the second half of the 9th and the 11th century AD (Kleingärtner 2014, 177–91). As a result of their political and economic significance, the famous *emporia* of Birka in Lake Mälaren and Hedeby at the tip of the Schlei fjord have attracted exceptional attention from the chroniclers of this period, so that the available information not only records military and political actions, but also indicates the presence of people of different origin in these places (Jankuhn 1984; Müller-Wille 2007).

The first of mention of Hedeby in the Frankish Annals of AD 804 indicates powerful initiatives by the Danish King Godfred to strengthen the position of Hedeby. Consequently, in 808 he led a force to the territory of the Slavic Obodrites and destroyed an *emporium* that was called Reric and probably located in Wismar Bay. This emporium was situated not far from the area of influence of the Carolingian Empire and must have been one of Hedeby's major competitors (Jöns 1999). According to the Annals, Godfred took merchants with him and brought them to Hedeby – which is called here by its Saxon name, *Sliasthorp*. One year later the Annals note that Godfred's men murdered Dražko, ruler of the Obodrites, at *Reric*. After this *Reric* is never mentioned again. The once-flourishing trading centre presumably no longer existed. Therefore the rise of Hedeby in the early 9th century AD was closely intertwined with the fate of *Reric* (Jöns 2009, 167–70).

Searching for the remains of *Reric* has been considered a desideratum of early-medieval archaeology and history for a long time (Jantzen and Schirren 1998). Especially in the 1980s, several scholars sought to locate the site, arguing more or less convincingly for sites such as Old Lübeck, Starigard Oldenburg and the hill-fort of Mecklenburg (Jöns 2009, 167–8 with refs.). But since the discovery in Groß Strömkendorf and the excavations described above, it is commonly accepted that this site is the emporium of *Reric*. The topographic setting, directly on the shore of Wismar Bay, using a natural harbour, the proven economic background and its estimated significance in its heyday around 800, and not least the evidence of a mixed population with communities from Scandinavia and the North Sea area, are strong arguments for this. Last but not least, the abandonment of the site at the beginning of the 9th century may be linked to the attack of Godfred and the relocation of the merchants as reported in the Frankish Annals (Jöns 1999). Finally, there is no other place in the Wismar Bay area that has produced a comparable range of finds and features.

The trading connections of *Reric*

To find out if *Reric*/Groß Strömkendorf might also have functioned as a bridge between the North Sea area and the Baltic area, as Hedeby did at least between the 9th and the 11th century AD, the foreign goods that undoubtedly originate from the North Sea area or which were probably distributed along the North Sea trade routes are of special interest.

Frisian Coarse Ware and *Muschelgrusware*, represented by 200 sherds, may be considered the result of Frisian influence in Groß Strömkendorf (Brorsson 2010). In addition, a small amount of Saxon pottery has been found; this was probably produced in the adjacent areas to the west (Brorsson and Jöns 2013). Another 300 sherds were identified as Merovingian Black ware, Tating ware, Mayen ware, Badorf ware and *Reliefbandamphora*; they originate from the area around Cologne, Bonn and Mayen. Also glass vessels – represented by 447 fragments of elongated palm cups (both with and without horizontal ribs), bowls and funnel beakers, together with ribbed and squat jars – may undoubtedly be considered as imports from the Frankish area. As Alexander Pöche has pointed out (2005), 30% of the sherds were decorated, mostly with applied trails, but also sherds with *reticella* or *in calmo* decoration were found. This composition is almost identical to the fragments of glass vessels of Phases B to D in Ribe. They are dated to the 8th century, with the percentage of decorated sherds ranging from 35% to 40% (Lund Feveile 2010, 201). This contrasts with the frequency of decoration on glass vessels from the 9th and 10th centuries, as the finds from the Phases E, F, G and H1 from Ribe or from Hedeby, with frequencies of decorated sherds of 15–20%, prove (Steppuhn 1998, 58).

Innumerable fragments of Mayen basalt querns, imported from the Rhine area, with a total weight of roughly 80 kg, were also recovered. Claus Feveile (2010, 142–5) has recently shown that fragments of basalt quernstones have been found in almost all excavations of Viking-period villages in the southern Danish North Sea area. Therefore, this material may be considered as the importation of everyday goods in this region. This differs from the Baltic area, where finds of querns made of basalt are still more or less restricted to trading sites and their surroundings (Kleingärtner 2014, 119–20, 124).

In the range of coins found so far, a strong western influence is visible. Although the excavations saw continuous water-sieving of the contents of the features, only nine coins were retrieved. This number has increased enormously over the last ten years, to more than a hundred, by the extensive use of metal-detectors in the area (Jöns 2015). The newly discovered coins are spread widely over the cemetery as well as the area along the present shore-line, indicating that the settlement continued over an area of at least another 10 ha to the east of the known site (Fig. 12.7). The majority of the coins (about 60) are Arabic dirhams, stressing the high significance of Islamic silver to Baltic trade in the Early Viking Age. Surprisingly, more than 30 Anglo-Frisian *sceattas* – representing the Wodan/Monster as well as the Porcupine type – have also been found, forming the largest collection of this type of coins for the whole of the Slavic-settled Baltic region (Fig. 12.8). Together with a small number of Frankish deniers, these coins indicate strong economic connections between Groß Strömkenorf and the Frankish and Frisian settled areas in the west, and especially the North Sea region.

The water-sieving that was carried out systematically during the excavations in Groß Strömkendorf also led to the salvaging of thousands of pieces of comb-making waste. The scientific analysis of this material has shown that the use of bone in comb-making was quite common. Although most combs in Groß Strömkendorf were made from red deer antler, similar to most of the other Baltic trading centres, goat and sheep horns were also used as raw material. In addition it has been observed that ribs and long bones from horses, cattle, goats and sheep were used for the comb-plates and the connecting plates. All this material was available locally. Neither from Hedeby nor from Ralswiek or Menzlin is so specific a selection known (Zimmermann and Jöns 2013). This choice of material gives Groß Strömkendorf an extraordinary position within the group of Baltic *emporia*, but it fits well with trading sites with comb-production along the southern North Sea coast. Especially in the Frisian clay district, bone was commonly used in the 8th century in the production of characteristically decorated plates for the front side of combs, as Tempel (1972) has pointed out. One reason could be that antler was rare in this district. But comb-making waste from Dutch and English sites also show the combined

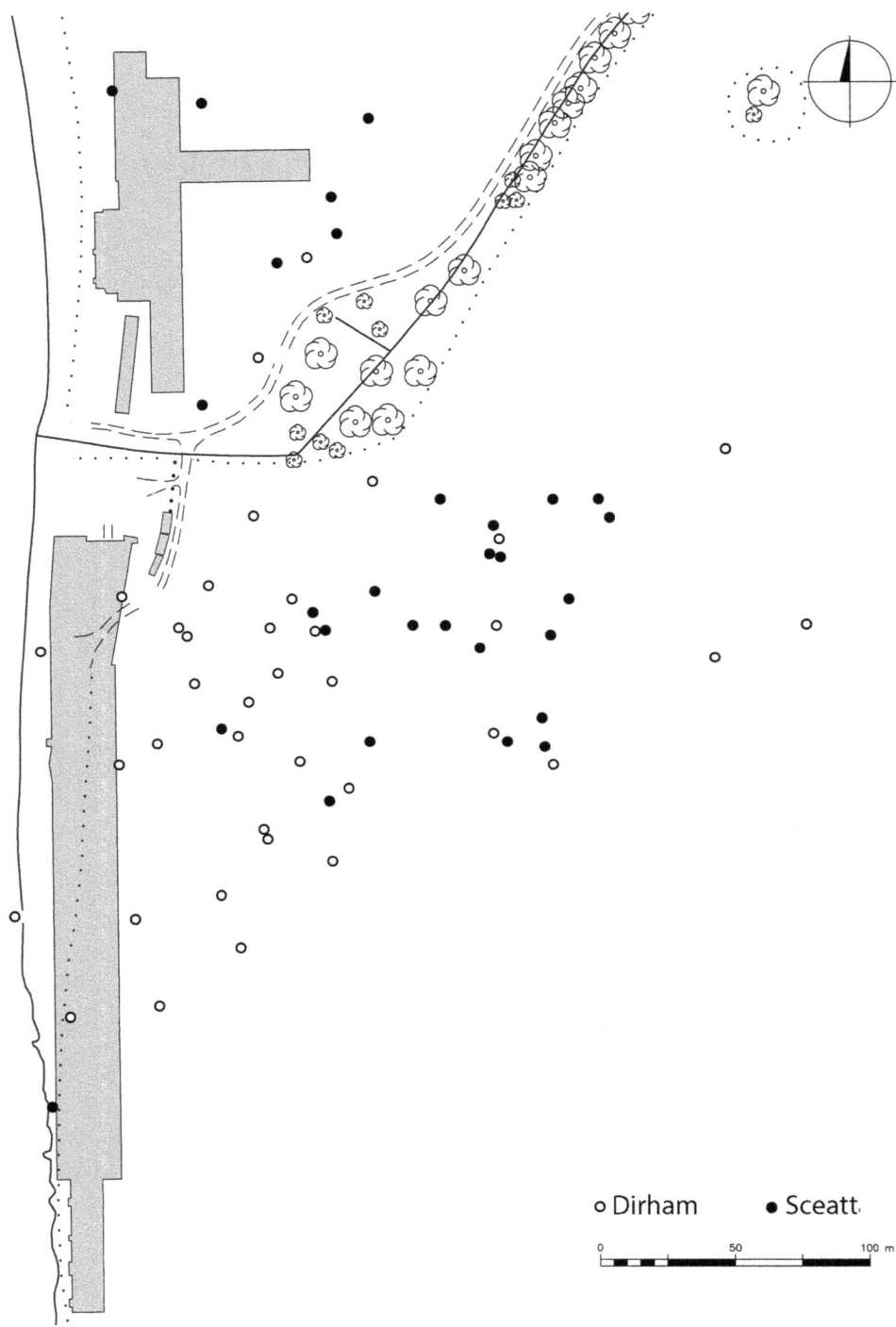

Fig. 12.7. Groß Strömkendorf. Distribution of dirhams and *sceattas* (after Jöns 2015, fig. 2).

Cultural Contacts between the Western Baltic, the North Sea Region and Scandinavia

use of antler and bone, although there was undoubtedly access to red deer and their antler. This is proven for Dorestad, and for Ribe, where ribs of horses and cows were often used. Like the comb-makers of Groß Strömkendorf, those of Ribe frequently used horn from sheep, cattle or goats, although antler was surely available in the required amount (Schmölcke and Jöns 2013; Zimmermann and Jöns 2013, 114).

Fig. 12.8. Groß Strömkendorf. *Sceattas* found during metal-detector surveys. (Photograph: Sabine Suhr, State Agency for Culture and Heritage Management, Schwerin).

A comb fragment with a runic inscription

Among the comb remains was a small bone fragment with a runic inscription. It was found in a workshop area where amber and iron had been worked and glass beads produced, and traces of comb-making were also found (Zimmermann and Jöns 2013, 112–14). It was found in the fill of a *Grubenhaus*, which from the dendrochronologically dated phasing was probably constructed in the years around AD 770. The comb fragment was found together with numerous potsherds, glass and amber beads and fragments of Frankish glass vessels, indicating that the *Grubenhaus* was abandoned in the two decades around the year 800. Osteological investigation of the object showed that it was made from the metapodium of a sheep or goat. The conclusion from this is that the fragment derives from a comb that was either produced in the North Sea region or was manufactured locally by a comb-maker who was used to working according to the comb-making traditions of the North Sea region (Zimmermann and Jöns 2013).

The fragment with the runic inscription was part of the connecting plate of a composite comb. In two places fractured drill-holes and saw traces prove that the moulding had actually been part of a complete comb. Four runic symbols are quite easily discernible on the otherwise undecorated surface of the fragment (Fig. 12.9). They were incised into the bone with a pointed object.

In trying to achieve a reading for a new runic inscription one usually attempts to reconcile the attested graphic forms with already known attestations of characters of

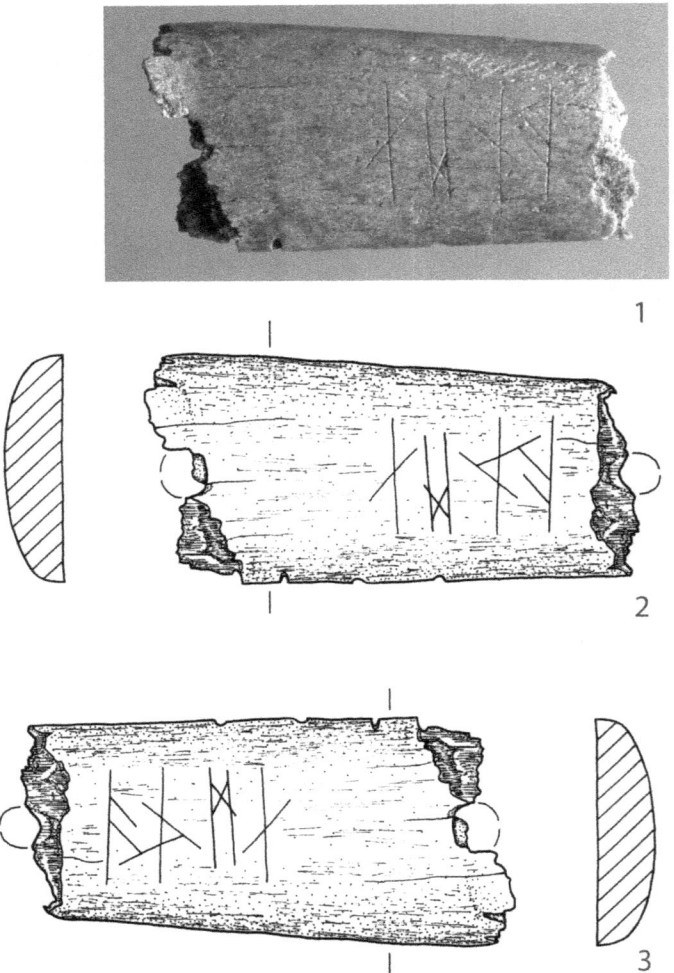

Fig. 12.9. Groß Strömkendorf. Fragment of a comb with a runic inscription.
1 Photograph, 2 drawing, 3 drawing (mirrored) (after Zimmermann and Jöns 2013, fig. 5).

the writing-system(s) in use. As pointed out above, the runic object stems from a multi-cultural context from around the year 800 or slightly earlier, a time at which at least two runic writing-systems are known to have been in use, the Early Viking Age varieties of the younger *fuþąrk* and the Anglo-Frisian *fuþorc*. Taking all the relevant contextual data into account the new inscription might prove to be a written form of Pre-Old Frisian, Old Saxon (or even Old English?) or of a variety of Common Scandinavian/Old Norse in either the Anglo-Frisian *fuþorc* or the younger *fuþąrk*.

As the identification of the runic characters and the writing-system should be the point of departure for a runological analysis, the graphic forms will be characterized first. Only at a second stage can the speech-sounds represented by the characters of the writing-system be determined. But even with only one runic system to refer to, a certain range of grapho-typological character-variation has to be taken into account. This character-variation could be idiosyncratic, but it may also have local, regional, social, or chronological significance; it might even be caused by the specifics of the writing material and surface. In individual cases the identification and attribution of one so far unknown variant can prove problematic, especially when dealing with genetically related systems with some identical graphic standard variants. Three of the four runes on the Groß Strömkendorf comb-fragment are particularly problematic.

Rune no. 1 (Fig. 12.10a)

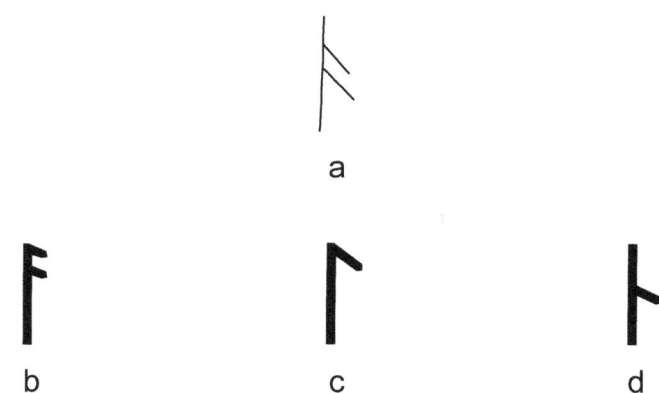

Fig. 12.10. a: Rune no. 1 in the Groß Strömkendorf comb inscription; b: older *fuþark ansuz*-rune; c: younger *fuþąrk* short-twig **l**; d: younger *fuþark* short-twig **n**.

On the grounds of formal characteristics, rune no. 1 can be identified as a realization of the so-called *ansuz* or (later, in the Anglo-Frisian *fuþorc*) *æsc* rune. It shows the significant diagnostic features, one stave with two parallel descending twigs going off to the right. In model rune-rows of the older *fuþark*, in the Early Viking Age variety of the younger *fuþąrk* and in the Anglo-Frisian *fuþorc* it is generally normalized as shown in Figure 12.10b.

Different variants of this rune are found in all rune-rows under consideration. The form attested here with the twigs branching off from the middle of the stave is as yet not attested as a variant in the Frisian or the OE runic corpus. Here, exclusively variants with branches joining directly or very close to the top of the vertical are in use.[4] The attested form is, however, quite a common variant in younger *fuþąrk* inscriptions of both the 'long-branch' and 'short-twig' varieties in the subsequent phases of the Viking Age (Barnes 2012, figs. 15–16).

---

[4] For the corpus of Frisian inscriptions, see Quak's overview (1991, 287–98), which consists of short descriptions and distributions of the attested runic characters, and the checklist of inscriptions in Looijenga (2003, 303–28) with normalized runic transcriptions of each runic legend, and the edition of the Frisian runic corpus known at the time by Giliberto (2000). For the Old English corpus a detailed graphemic study is currently being prepared for print (Waxenberger, forthcoming; cf. Waxenberger, this vol.; with grateful acknowledgement to Gaby Waxenberger for giving me access to these data and discussing the relevant details.)

In both the Scandinavian and the Anglo-Frisian writing-systems, however, the place where the twigs join the main stave has no distinguishing function, so the carver would not have to care about this feature when writing this rune. Even a very low position would not change the functional value as would be the case, say, for younger *fuþąrk* short-twig **l** and **n** (Fig. 12.10c–d). From a graphemic point of view either classification would thus be as probable as the other.

An identification of rune no. 1 as an Anglo-Frisian rune would result in a transliteration **æ**; if it is read as a Scandinavian rune, **ą** would be the most appropriate transliteration. But which of these would represent the most credible reading? Should one assume an idiosyncratic Anglo-Frisian variant or rather an – apparently – too early Scandinavian one? Before jumping to conclusions, the immediate graphic context, i.e. the accompanying symbols and their features, should be taken into account. However, on the basis of the extant written attestations and their often quite broad archaeological datings – the Elisenhof comb (AD 775–875) or the Haithabu stick 1 (AD 800–1000), which attest a similar variant, albeit in a distinct short-twig writing context (for the datings, see runer.ku.dk and Imer 2007, Catalogue) – the forms point rather towards the Scandinavian younger *fuþąrk*.

Rune no. 2 (Fig. 12.11a)

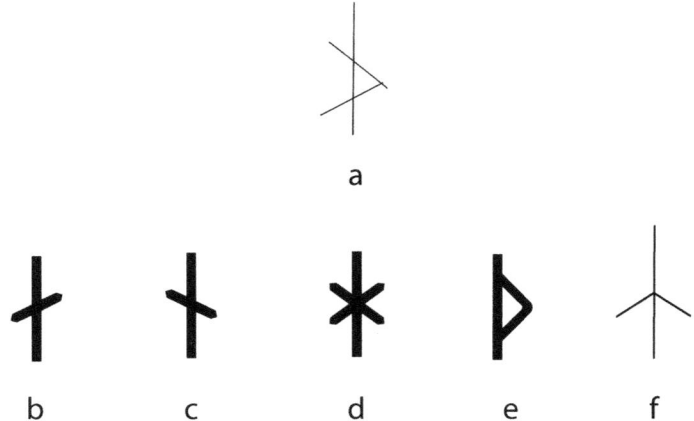

Fig. 12.11. a: Rune no. 2 in the Groß Strömkendorf comb inscription; b: younger *fuþąrk* long-branch **a**; c: long-branch **n**; d: the 'star' rune; e: the **þ** rune; f: bind-rune combining younger *fuþąrk* short-twig **a** and **n**.

The rune in question consists of a stave and two twigs. These twigs may be described as diagonal lines crossing the stave and running in opposite directions, one starting from the bottom (if read from left to right), the other running the other way, to meet and form a kind of angular pocket a few millimetres to the right of the main stave. Taking these main graphic features into account, several standard runic symbols may come to mind:

1. Scandinavian younger *fuþąrk* **a** (the common variant in the mid- and late Viking-Age long-branch set of this writing-system: Fig. 12.11b);
2. Scandinavian younger *fuþąrk* long-branch **n** and Anglo-Frisian **n** (Fig. 12.11c);

3. The 'star rune': Scandinavian younger *fuþąrk* **a** in the common variant of the Early Viking Age rune-row and Anglo-Frisian **j** (Fig. 12.11d);
4. Scandinavian younger *fuþąrk* **þ** and Anglo-Frisian **þ** (Fig. 12.11e).

The fact that the twigs cross the vertical at a considerable length renders the attested elements similar to long-branch variants of **a** and **n**; these would form a bind-rune **an** or **na** with both diagonal lines crossing the same stave. Although there are several **a-n** bind-runes attested in the Scandinavian runic corpus of the Viking Age (MacLeod 2002, 124–5 and table 15), none resembles this specimen; these later **an** bind-runes combine short twig rune-forms and thus show the form in Figure 12.11f (cf. MacLeod 2002, 127). Although long-branch **a** and **n** are also attested quite frequently as elements of bind-runes (MacLeod 2002, 126) they never occur in the combination **an**.

Alternatively, one might consider a correction of some kind. This cannot be ruled out, as there are several such instances in the Viking Age corpus of the younger *fuþąrk*, especially in connection with the runes **n** and **a**, the resulting graphic form often also resembling the star rune.

At the same time the star rune itself (Fig. 12.11c) is a possibility. Several graphic variants of this character, as on the Ribe cranium, document the crossing or contact of the two twigs a few millimetres to the right or left of the stave; a feature which is also very prominent in this case. The 'same' star rune – though with a different linguistic role – is also part of the Anglo-Frisian rune-row and attested several times in the Old English runic corpus; in all instances, however, the rune is executed very accurately, and it never shows the formal features documented here.

If, on the other hand, the focus of the analysis is directed to the fact that both diagonal lines meet at one point – one of the lines actually almost stops at this meeting point – to form a buckle or pocket, there is a fourth possible reading. This pocket may suggest that the inscriber actually intended a variant of the *þorn*-rune (Fig. 12.11d). Although the extent to which the diagonal lines cross and extend on the 'wrong' side of the stave is unprecedented in both the Scandinavian and the Anglo-Frisian corpora, the fact of the two twigs crossing the stave is itself attested several times. The closest example for comparison would again be the inscription on the Ribe cranium, where similar but not such extreme features are attested. An identification as either Scandinavian or Anglo-Frisian *þorn* would result in the transliteration **þ**.

Rune No. 3

This form is common in inscriptions in the Anglo-Frisian *fuþorc*, and also attested as a variant in Early Viking Age inscriptions in the younger *fuþąrk*; the most closely dated parallel is on the Ribe cranium. The transliteration is **m** for all the rune-rows in question.

Rune No. 4

Taken at face value, the fourth rune could be identified as a realization of the long-branch variant of the younger *fuþąrk* **a** rune (cf. above). Interestingly, however, the inscription Westeremden B of the Frisian corpus attests a similar form. But the reading and interpretation of that inscription are much disputed, as it shows many uncommon runic variants (Quak 1991, 293; Looijenga 2003, 312). It may be most advisable to leave this 'parallel' out of the discussion.

On the other hand, a reading as a reversed variant of **n** of either the younger Scandinavian *fuþąrk* or the Anglo-Frisian *fuþorc* cannot be entirely excluded. Reversed variants are still attested in several Scandinavian Viking Age inscriptions even though the direction of writing from left to right was becoming more and more conventional and the formerly quite common reversed variants were marginalized into rare exceptions. In the Anglo-Frisian corpus the new inscription on the Baconsthorpe tweezers confirms the existence of reversed variants for this corpus too – although still only as the exception to the rule (cf. Hines 2011, 285 for a possible explanation).

Altogether the scales lean rather towards a reading as Scandinavian long-branch **a** for rune no 4, and the most probable transliteration would thus be **a**.

Interpreting the inscription

Comparing the results of the discussion for each individual rune, a Scandinavian younger *fuþąrk* system as the background of the inscription seems the most plausible case, even if it cannot rest on specific, diagnostic features of the runic characters but rather on comparison with attested graphs in 'contemporary' inscriptions of the relevant runic corpora. At the same time, however, it has to be kept in mind that the number of contemporary inscriptions with graphic forms which have so far eluded a conclusive reading is almost as large as the number of inscriptions which have been read and were drawn upon for this analysis. This conclusion should therefore be treated with caution.

Nevertheless, even the presentation of a younger *fuþąrk* transliteration is not unequivocal. The available options are:

ą(na)ma [also ą(an)ma] – supposing a bind-rune
ą(n)ma or ą(a)ma – supposing a correction
ą(a)ma
ą(þ)ma

while a hypothetical Anglo-Frisian transliteration would most probably result in (æþ)m(n).[5] Taking only the closest parallels in contemporary inscriptions into account, ą(a)ma and ą(þ)ma would have to be chosen as the most probable transliterations, the focus of comparison being the Ribe cranium with its attested graphic variation (cf. Stoklund 2004).

The transliterations listed here do not, however, take possible hybridity into account, as on the St Albans II bone (above), where the transference of one or more characters from one writing-system to the other is attested. Classification as a hybrid inscription in this sense often only arises from a confrontation of the attributed language of an inscription with the features of the given graphic forms. In the case of the St. Albans II bone, the classification as hybrid – attesting the transfer of an Old English runic character **w** into the matrix of a Scandinavian writing-system – rests upon the interpretation of the runic sequence as the personal name *Wulfric*. This was also the case for the Ribe cranium

---

[5] The list of possibilities would be extended further if a reverse reading of the fourth rune as **n** were allowed for.

inscription, where some of the characters were 'identified' only after the inscription had been interpreted.

For the four-letter inscription from Groß Strömkendorf, however, there is no obvious interpretation such as the four-letter legends **kaba, kobu, kabu,** or **kabz** for 'comb' on the combs of Frienstedt (c. AD 300), Toornwerd (8th century), Oostum (8th/9th century) and Elisenhof (775–875) have offered.[6] As noted, the selection of a specific rune-row does not foreclose the choice of language. Even if the runes may be classified as most probably of Scandinavian provenance, the inscription may nevertheless prove to be a West Germanic text, be that Pre-Old Frisian, Old Saxon, or any other variety. Whichever language variety might be represented here, from the fact that there is some room left between the first and the last rune and the relevant fractured edges of the object, it is reasonably safe to assume that the written sequence is complete.

As language transcription and interpretation of a runic inscription are not solely dependent on the transliteration but also on orthographical norms of the writing-system in question the next step in the analysis is to consider orthographic rules which may be of relevance in the given graphemic context. It can in fact be observed that nasal consonants are very often omitted in writing if directly followed by homorganic obstruents. This rule was already observed in the older *fuþark*, as the inscription **kaba** on the Frienstedt comb, amongst others, proves. It is also attested for several of the Frisian inscriptions, e. g. **kabu** on the Oostum comb or **welad[u]** on the Schweindorf *solidus* (on the latter, see Hines, this vol.). In the Scandinavian younger *fuþąrk* it is still quite commonly observed (Williams 1994).

In this light, a transcription of the reading **ą(þ)ma** may result in a sequence *anþma*. This would also be very much in accordance with the fact that the *ansuz*-rune ą – which was originally restricted to nasalized contexts – occurs at the beginning of the sequence. In all other respects, though, a sequence *anþma* would prove very problematic. According to the established view of Old Scandinavian language development, the consonant cluster -*nþ*- would already have undergone assimilation and developed into -*nn*- by this period. For interpretation as *anþma* it has to be assumed that this development had not yet occurred. An alternative line of thought could start with the supposition of an 'irregular' use of the nasal ą-rune – which is indeed attested several times in the Scandinavian corpus (Williams 1990) – and lead to a transcription as *aþma*. As both *anþma* and *aþma*, however, seem to be quite uninterpretable sequences from a Scandinavian point of view a different perspective may be helpful.

From the point of view of North Sea Germanic language structures, the most probable transcriptions of the sequence **ą(þ)ma** could be *āþma* or *ą̄þma*, for we undoubtedly have to reckon with the loss of the nasal between vowel and homorganic fricative by the 8th century. The use of a Scandinavian nasal ą-rune would then be quite acceptable in this context, as the related lengthening and raising of [a] to [o:] in these phonetic environments very probably proceeded via intermediary stages of nasalized vowels [ã:] and [õ:] with an articulatory position somewhere between the [a:] and [o:] sounds. According to the established model of development of the North Sea Germanic languages, however, this process of nasalization and raising, as well as the subsequent phonemic

---

[6] I thank the RuneS research centre Eichstätt-München for providing the datings of the Oostum and Toornwerd inscriptions.

merger of /ɔ̄:/ and /o:/, seem to have been completed by the end of the 7th or beginning of the 8th century, at least in Old English (cf. Waxenberger, this vol.). However, the earliest runic attestations of Pre-Old Frisian, such as on the Arum yew-wood sword or the Rasquert sword-handle, point to a later date, somewhere near the end of the 8th century (Waxenberger, this vol.). Further evidence, as in the form **kabu** on the Oostum comb (*c.* 8th/9th century) in comparison to **kobu** on the Toornwerd comb (dated to the 8th century) suggests that the new sound could still rendered by an **a**-rune. This is also attested for Old Saxon, where the result(s) of this sound-change could be rendered by /â/ beside /ô/, as is shown by several attested Old Saxon nouns and names (Holthausen 1921, §§106 and 191; Gallée 1993, §§51 and 214).

Neither *āþma* nor *ą̄þma*, however, are attested lexemes or names in either of the languages under consideration here. Even as a short form of a personal name we may run into problems. We would have to assume a hypocoristic root *āþm-/ą̄þm-*, displaying a first element *āþ-/ą̄þ-*, and the initial consonant of a second name-element beginning with *m-*, such as *mund-, mar-* oder *mod-* (Förstemann 1966; Kaufmann 1968). Although Förstemann assumes the existence of this type of name together with the 'suffix' *-m-*, no such formation is attested in either the Scandinavian or the North Sea Germanic onomasticon. In addition, a complex consonant cluster like *-þm-* would be rather unusual in a hypocoristic name-formation.

As an appellative *āþma* or *ą̄þma* might be analysed as a derivative with the suffix *-ma-/-man-* (cf. Ahlsson 1960). As a productive formative this suffix is only attested in Frisian, although there may have existed some isolated formations in Swedish dialects too. Only very few older *-ma-/-man-* formations are common to both the North Germanic and West Germanic languages as part of the inherited Germanic lexicon. Amongst these old formations we find the word for breath, OE *ǣðm/ēðm*, OS *āðom*, Old East Frisian *ēthma* (< Gmc *ēthman-*) which can be derived from Germanic **ēðma-* or **ēþma-*, and which is also attested in an *n*-stem variant **ēðman-/*ēþman-*.[7] If we wanted to suggest that our inscription was somehow related to this noun, we would again have to ignore the fact that a Scandinavian nasal **ą** rune was used in the beginning of the inscription and work on the basis of a transcription *āþma* or even *ǣþma* (cf. also Zimmermann 2013, 371; Århammer 2012).

The alternative reading **ą(a)ma** might be considered to represent the short form of the personal name *Amma* f. or **Ammi* m.; the female variant of this hypocoristic formation is attested in the Scandinavian language corpus (cf. the sequence **amu** on rune-stone *Ög* 91) and interpreted as a short form of female names beginning in *Arn-* or *Am-* (Peterson 2007, s.v. *Amma*); a parallel formation for a presumed male counterpart **Ammi* may be attested in the short form *Abbi* on DR 143B, which is interpreted as hypocoristic form of, *inter alia, Ábjörn* (Peterson 2007, s.v. *Abbi*). It may also be the hypocoristic form of a West Germanic name on the basis of a first element *am(a/i)-* (v. the probable sequence **a(m) o** on the Gammertingen canister and the interpretation and etymology of the name in Nedoma 2004, 180–2). In both cases the **ą**-rune at the beginning of the sequence would have to be interpreted as some kind of preposition or adverb.

---

[7] For the Scandinavian languages, on the other hand, only the nouns *andi* and *önd* are attested, which go back to a dental derivation of the root *an-*, forming a Gmc *an-ð(a)-*, or *an-þ(a)-*, depending on the position of the stress.

A reading **ąnama**, on the other hand, could be interpreted as a combination of two names, a male name *Án* and a female name *Amma* (Peterson 2007, s.v. *Án* and *Amma*; Henrik Williams, pers. comm.), but the bind rune **na** would then form a word boundary which would be difficult to explain.

As neither graphotypological analysis nor the range of probable or possible transcriptions and linguistic interpretations produce conclusive results, the attribution of the Groß Strömkendorf inscription to one specific and well-defined corpus of runic inscriptions appears beyond reach. Amongst the criteria which have been employed to establish the different runic corpora set up in the last decades and centuries, three criteria emerge as the most common and frequently used: (1) geographical provenance; (2) language affiliation; and (3) diagnostic rune-forms and affiliation to specific rune-rows. Although it might be expected that only one of these criteria would be adhered to in establishing a corpus, the reality of the established corpora is quite the contrary. Usually, more than one or even all three criteria are used in combination, the order of reference being far from transparent. For the Danish, Norwegian, and Swedish corpora, the criteria are most exclusively geographic and linguistic: the modern – or, in the case of Denmark, the historical – borders and linguistic classification as Scandinavian (or Proto-Old Norse) were the basis for the inclusion of inscriptions (cf. *SRI*, *DR*, *NIæR* and *NIyR*). But late Medieval Latin inscriptions from the same find-spots and areas were also included in the corpora. And only in the context of the corpus of Norwegian inscriptions are the inscriptions in the 'older runes', i.e. in the older *fuþark*, signalled as a separate sub-group because of their use of a specific rune-row. The geographical criterion is also most prominent in Tineke Looijenga's recent 'checklist of runic inscriptions in or from the Netherlands' (2003, 303–28). Further criteria, however, which are inscribed in the preposition 'from' of the phrase 'from the Netherlands', are presumed diagnostic and specifically 'Frisian' rune forms, such as in the case of the inscription on the Amay comb from Belgium, and linguistic criteria as the 'Frisian' case ending -*u*, as in the inscription **æniwulufu** or **aniwulufu** on the Glasgow/Folkestone *tremisses* or the interpretation of **katæ** in the inscription on the Hamwic bone as a 'Frisian' lexeme and word for 'knuckle bone' (cf. OFris *kāte*, Hofmann 1976, 73–6; cf. Waxenberger, this vol.). Conversely, rune-forms and linguistic criteria are ignored – at least in the first step of drawing up the list – in favour of the geographical criterion, as with the Bergakker scabbard-mount, the Borgharen buckle, or the Wijnaldum B pendant and Wijnaldum A bone piece, none of which displays diagnostic Anglo-Frisian rune-forms or specifically 'Frisian' linguistic forms (for a critical appraisal of the different criteria used to delimitate the Frisian runic corpus v. Nielsen 1994 and 1996, and Giliberto 1998). These approaches result in double attributions, as in the case of the Borgharen buckle which, on the basis of linguistic criteria, is also counted among the South Germanic inscriptions in the older *fuþark* (cf. Waxenberger, this vol.).[8]

---

[8] The term 'South Germanic' is used for the long-established German term *Südgermanisch*, in consistency with the usage of the *Runische Schriftlichkeit* project of the Union of German Academies. It may be understood as denoting a field within Continental Germanic that was a 'Pre-' stage for Old High German, Langobardic and Old Saxon to some extent.

In addition to those cases where rune-rows and linguistic criteria suggest the attribution to two different corpora, as is also the case with the Bridekirk font, which presents a version of Middle English in Scandinavian runes, or with Latin inscriptions in runes as on the March plate, or in cases where runic graphs of different rows are used in a single inscription (the St Albans II bone), the attribution to a corpus has to proceed along a clean and transparent hierarchy of criteria. For all three inscriptions the most recent classifications rest – irrespective of the languages attested in the inscriptions – on specific forms and features of the runic graphs: thus the Bridekirk font and the St Albans II bone are classified as Scandinavian inscriptions (in the younger *fuþąrk*), whereas the March plate is grouped with the inscriptions displaying the Old English *fuþorc*. This may suggest that the third criterion, i.e. runological arguments relating to diagnostic runic/graphic forms and affiliation with specific rune-rows should be more prominent in the process of attribution of new finds to runic corpora and form the first step in the classificatory argumentation. But this presupposes a close study of the attested graph-forms and their distribution for the periods under investigation. As long as that study remains a desideratum, the attribution of new runic inscriptions which evade easy and obvious language interpretation, inscriptions which stem from multilingual contexts and are incised on portable objects – in short, a great number of the inscriptions from the Viking Age recovered from early trading centres – will remain open for discussion.

In the case of the Groß Strömkendorf comb fragment, the runological arguments point towards a classification as 'Scandinavian inscription of the Viking Age' – but so far no such corpus is in existence.[9] At the same time, an attribution to the Swedish, Danish or Norwegian rune corpus proves difficult, as the inscription was found outside the modern and historical borders of these states, and the linguistic attribution of the inscription is uncertain. Following the example of Barnes and Page (2006), the Groß Strömkendorf comb might on the other hand be classified as 'Scandinavian inscription on the Continent', although the term 'Continental Inscriptions' has so far been reserved for inscriptions in the older *fuþark* and thus from *c.* AD 200–700.[10] A widening of the scope of this term, however, and further sub-groupings on the basis of the particular set of characters, may shed further light on Scandinavian cultural impact during the Viking Age.

Even if the attribution to a specific runic corpus may still be open to debate, what remains are the significant features of the Groß Strömkendorf find as an inscribed bone-fragment which derives from a comb that was produced in the North Sea area or was manufactured by a comb-maker who was used to working according to the comb-making traditions of the North Sea area, an object that at the same time gives an inscription using characters which most probably are part of an Early Viking Age Scandinavian writing-system, the younger *fuþąrk*.

---

[9] In this case 'Scandinavian' only refers to the fact that a specifically Scandinavian set of graphs is employed in the inscription.
[10] In a few older publications the term extends to include some inscriptions which are currently grouped with the Frisian corpus.

References

Abbreviations

DR = *Danmarks runeindskrifter,* 3 vols: Text, Atlas, Registre, ed. Lis Jacobsen and Erik Moltke (Kopenhagen 1941–2).
NIyR = *Norges innskrifter med de yngre runer,* 6 vols to date, ed. Magnus Olsen *et al.* (Oslo 1941–).
NIæR = *Norges Indskrifter med de ældre Runer,* 3 vols, ed. Sophus Bugge *et al.* (Christiania 1891–1924).
Ög = *Östergötlands runinskrifter,* ed. Erik Brate, Sveriges runinskrifter 2 (Stockholm 1911–18).
SRI = *Sveriges runinskrifter,* 14 vols to date, ed. Kungl. Vitterhets Historie och Antikvitets Akademien (Stockholm 1900–).

Primary Sources

Adam von Bremen, 'Gesta Hammaburgensis Ecclesiae Pontificum'. In *Quellen des 9. und 11. Jahrhunderts zur Geschichte der Hamburgischen Kirche und des Reiches,* ed. W. Trillmich and R. Buchner 1961 (Darmstadt), 137–499.
Helmold von Bosau, 'Chronica Slavorum'. In *Ausgewählte Quellen zur deutschen Geschichte des Mittelalters,* ed. H. Stoob 2002 (Darmstadt).
Krause, Wolfgang, *Die Runeninschriften im älteren Futhark,* mit Beiträgen von Herbert Jankuhn 1966 (Göttingen).
Rimbert, 'Vita Anskarii'. In *Quellen des 9. und 11. Jahrhunderts zur Geschichte der Hamburgischen Kirche und des Reiches,* ed. W. Trillmich and R. Buchner 1961 (Darmstadt), 16–133.

Secondary sources

Ahlsson, Lars-Erik 1960, *Die altfriesischen Abstraktbildungen* (Uppsala).
Århammer, Nils 2012, 'Nochmals zu altrüstr. reth ''Rad'' und ēthma 'Atem' et cons', *Us Wurk* 61, 105–13.
Barnes, Michael P. 1993, 'Norse in the British Isles'. In *Viking Revaluations,* ed. A. Faulkes and R. Perkins (London), 65–84.
Barnes, Michael P. 2003, 'Languages and ethnic groups'. In *The Cambridge History of Scandinavia. Vol. 1: Prehistory to 1520,* ed. K. Helle (Cambridge), 94–102.
Barnes, Michael P. 2012, *Runes. A Handbook* (Woodbridge).
Barnes, Michael P., and Raymond I. Page 2006, *The Scandinavian Runic Inscriptions of Britain,* Runrön 19 (Uppsala).
Bertašius, Mindaugas, and Linas Daugnora 2001, 'Viking horse graves from Kaunas Region (Middle Lithuania)', *International Journal of Osteoarchaeology* 11, 387–99.
Bogucki, Mateusz 2004, 'Viking age ports of trade in Poland', *Estonian Journal of Archaeology/ Eesti Arheoloogia Ajakiri* 8 (2), 100–27.
Bogucki, Mateusz 2012, 'On Wulfstan's right hand – the Viking Age emporia in West Slav Lands'. In *From One Sea to Another. Trading Places in the European and Mediterranean Early Middle Ages,* ed. S. Gelichi and R. Hodges, Seminari internazionali del Centro Interuniversitario per la Storia e l'Archeologia dell'Alto Medioevo 3 (Turnhout), 81–109.
Braunmüller, Kurt 1995, 'Formen des Sprachkontakts und der Mehrsprachigkeit zur Hansezeit. Eine einführende Übersicht'. In *Niederdeutsch und die skandinavischen Sprachen II,* ed. K. Braunmüller (Heidelberg), 9–33.
Brorsson, Torbjörn 2010, *The Pottery from the Early Medieval Trading Site and Cemetery at Groß Strömkendorf, Lkr. Nordwestmecklenburg,* Forschungen zu Groß Strömkendorf 3. Frühmittelalterliche Archäologie zwischen Ostsee und Mittelmeer 1 (Wiesbaden).

Brorsson, Torbjörn, and Hauke Jöns 2010, 'Analyses of the ceramic material from the emporium reric near Groß Strömkendorf, Mecklenburg'. In *Naturwissenschaftliche Analysen vor- und frühgeschichtlicher Keramik 1. Methoden, Anwendungsbereiche, Auswertungsmöglichkeiten*, Universitätsforschungen zur Prähistorischen Archäologie 176, ed. B. Ramminger and O. Stilborg (Bonn), 75–86.

Feveile, Claus 2006, *Det ældste Ribe. Udgravninger på nordsiden af Ribe Å 1984–2000*, Ribe Studier 1.1. Jysk Arkæologisk Selskabs Skrifter 51 (Højbjerg).

Feveile, Claus 2010, 'Mayen lava quern stones from the Ribe excavations 1970–76'. In *Ribe excavations, 1970–76*, Vol. 6, Jutland Archaeological Society Publications 75, ed. C. Feveile (Moesgård), 133–56.

Eichfeld, Ingo 2015, 'Groothusen und Grimersum – Siedlung, Wirtschaft und Wasserwege im frühmittelalterlichen Ostfriesland', *Siedlungs- und Küstenforschung im südlichen Nordseegebiet* 38, 217–37.

Förstemann, E. 1966 [1901], *Altdeutsches Namenbuch. Bd. 1: Personennamen* (Bonn).

Gallée, J. H. 1993, *Altsächsische Grammatik* (Tübingen).

Gerds, Marcus 2006, 'Scandinavian burial rites on the southern Baltic coast. Boat graves in cemeteries of early medieval trading places'. In *Old Norse religion in long-term perspectives. Origins, changes, and interactions*, ed. A. Andrén, K. Jennbert and C. Raudvere, Vägar till Midgård 8 (Lund), 153–8.

Gerds, Marcus 2013, 'Tiergrab, Tierbeigabe, Tieropfer? Pferde und Hunde auf dem frühmittelalterlichen Bestattungsplatz von Groß Strömkendorf bei Wismar'. In *Kulturwandel im Spannungsfeld von Tradition und Innovation*, ed. S. Kleingärtner, U. Müller and J. Scheschkewitz, Festschrift für Michael Müller-Wille (Neumünster), 127–38.

Gerds, Marcus 2015, *Das Gräberfeld des frühmittelalterlichen Seehandelsplatzes von Groß Strömkendorf, Lkr. Nordwestmecklenburg*, Forschungen zu Groß Strömkendorf 5. Frühmittelalterliche Archäologie zwischen Ostsee und Mittelmeer 6 (Wiesbaden 2015).

Giliberto, Concetta 1998, 'The criteria for a Frisian runic corpus revisited', *Amsterdamer Beiträge zur älteren Germanistik* 49, 155–68.

Giliberto, Concetta 2000, *Le iscrizioni runiche sullo sfondo della cultura frisone altomedievale* (Göppingen).

Hines, John 2011, 'New light on literacy in eighth-century East Anglia: a runic inscription from Baconsthorpe, Norfolk', *Anglia* 129, 281–96.

Hofmann, Dietrich 1976, 'Eine friesische Ruineninschrift in England', *Us Wurk* 25, 73–6.

Holthausen, F. 1921, *Altsächsisches Elementarbuch* (Heidelberg).

Imer, Lisbeth M. 2007, *Runer og runeindskrifter. Kronologi, kontekst og funktion i Skandinaviens jernalder og vikingetid*, vol. 1: Tekst, vol 2: Katalog (Kopenhagen).

Jankuhn, Herbert 1984, 'Soziale Gliederung der Bevölkerung von Haithabu nach historischen Quellen'. In *Archäologische und naturwissenschaftliche Untersuchungen an Siedlungen im deutschen Küstengebiet 2: Handelsplätze des frühen und hohen Mittelalters*, ed. H. Jankuhn, K. Schietzel and J. Reichstein (Weinheim), 335–8.

Jantzen, Detlef, and Michael Schirren 1998, '„Rerik steht wieder auf' oder: „Die Lösung des Reric-Problems' im April 1938'. In *Studien zur Archäologie des Ostseeraumes. Von der Eisenzeit zum Mittelalter*, ed. A. Wesse, Festschrift für Michael Müller-Wille (Neumünster), 67–76.

Johansson, K. G. 2002, 'Birka-Hedeby tur och retur'. In *Svenska Språkets Historia i Östersjöområdet*, ed. S. Lagman et al. (Tartu), 13–24.

Jöns, Hauke 1999, 'War das „emporium Reric' der Vorläufer von Haithabu?', *Jahrbuch Bodendenkmalpflege Mecklenburg-Vorpommern* 47, 201–13.

Jöns, Hauke 2009, 'Ports and emporia of the southern coast: from Hedeby to Usedom and Wolin'. In *Wulfstan's Voyage. The Baltic Sea region in the Early Viking Age as seen from shipboard* (Conference Wismar 2004), ed. A. Englert and A. Trakadas, Maritime Culture of the North 2 (Roskilde), 160–81.

Jöns, Hauke 2011, 'Settlement development in the shadow of coastal changes – case studies from the Baltic rim'. In *The Baltic Sea Basin*, ed. J. Harff, S. Björck and P. Hoth (Berlin –Heidelberg), 301–36.

Jöns, Hauke 2015, 'Early medieval trading centres and transport systems between Dorestad, Ribe and Wolin: the latest results of the Priority Research Programme "Harbours from the Roman Iron Age to the Middle Ages"'. In *Small Things – Wide Horizons: Studies in Honour of Birgitta Hårdh*, ed. L. Larsson, F. Ekengren, B. Helgesson and B. Söderberg (Oxford), 245–52.

Jöns, Hauke, and Michael Müller-Wille 2015, 'The early phase of Slavic settlement in the south-western Baltic coastal area – current research in the area between the Bay of Kiel and the Oder River', *Archaeologia Polonia*, 48, 197–228.

Jørgensen, Lars, and Anne Nørgaard Jørgensen 1997, *Nørre Sándegård Vest. A Cemetery from the 6th–8th Centuries on Bornholm*, Nordiske Fortidsminder 14. Serie B (København).

Kaufmann, H. 1968, *Altdeutsche Personennamen*, Ergänzungsband (München–Hildesheim).

Karle, Martina, Sebastian Messal and Steffen Wolters 2015, 'Early medieval emporia and their ports in the south-western Baltic Sea', *Siedlungs- und Küstenforschung im südlichen Nordseegebiet* 38, 239–55.

Kleingärtner, Sunhild 2014, *Die frühe Phase der Urbanisierung an der südlichen Ostseeküste im ersten nachchristlichen Jahrhundert*, Studien zur Siedlungsgeschichte und Archäologie der Ostseegebiete 13 (Neumünster).

Lund Feveile, Lene 2010, 'Hulglasskår fra markedspladsen i Ribe, ASR 9 Posthuset'. In *Ribe excavations, 1970–76, Vol. 6*, ed. by C. Feveile, Jutland Archaeological Society Publications 75 (Moesgård), 195–277.

Lebecq, Stéphane 1992, 'The Frisian trade in the Dark Ages; a Frisian or a Frankish/Frisian trade?'. In *Rotterdam Papers VII*, ed. A. Carmiggelt (Rotterdam), 7–15.

Lebecq, Stéphane 2007, 'Communication and exchange in northwest Europe'. In *Ohthere's Voyages*, ed. J. Bately and A. Englert (Roskilde), 170–9.

Looijenga, Tineke 2003, *Texts & Contexts of the Oldest Runic Inscriptions* (Leiden).

MacLeod, Mindy 2002, *Bind-Runes: An Investigation of Ligatures in Runic Epigraphy*, Runrön 15 (Uppsala).

Moulton, W. G. 1988, 'Mutual intelligibility among speakers of early Germanic dialects'. In *Germania. Comparative Studies in Old Germanic Languages and Literatures*, ed. D. G. Calder and T. C. Christy (Wolfeboro, NH), 9–28.

Müller-Wille, Michael 1995, 'Boat-graves: old and new views'. In *The Ship as Symbol in Prehistoric and Medieval Scandinavia* (Congress Copenhagen 1994), ed. O. Crumlin-Pedersen and B. Munch Thye, Publications from the National Museum Studies in Archaeology & History 1 (Copenhagen), 101–10.

Müller-Wille, Michael 2007, 'Auf der Suche nach den Kirchen Ansgars. Ein archäologischer Beitrag zur karolingischen Mission im nördlichen Europa', *Questiones Medii Aevi Novae* 12, 253–91.

Müller-Wille, Michael 2009, 'Emporium reric'. In *Historia Archaeologic. Festschrift für Heiko Steuer zum 70. Geburtstag*, ed. S. Brather, D. Geuenich and C. Huth, Reallexikon der Germanischen Altertumskunde-Ergänzungsbände 70 (Berlin–New York), 451–71.

Müller-Wille, Michael, and Astrid Tummuscheit 2004, 'Viking-age proto-urban centres and their hinterlands: some examples from the Baltic area'. In *Land, sea and home*, ed. J. Hines, A. Lane and M. Redknap, Society of Medieval Archaeology Monograph 20 (Leeds), 27–39.

Nielsen, Hans Frede 1994, 'Ante-Old Frisian: A Review', *Nowele* 24, 91–136.

Nielsen, Hans Frede 1996, 'Developments in Frisian runology: a discussion of Düwel & Tempel's Runic Corpus from 1970'. In *Frisian Runes and Neighbouring Traditions*, ed. T. Looijenga and A. Quak, Amsterdamer Beiträge zur älteren Germanistik 45 (Amsterdam), 123–30.

Paddenberg, Dietlind 2000, 'Studien zu frühslawischen Bestattungssitten in Nordostdeutschland', *Offa* 57, 231–345.

Peterson, Lena 2007, *Nordiskt runnamnslexikon* (Uppsala).

Pöche, Alexander 2005, *Perlen, Trichtergläser, Tesserae. Spuren des Glashandels und Glashandwerks auf dem frühgeschichtlichen Handelsplatz von Groß Strömkendorf, Landkreis Nordwestmecklenburg*, Forschungen zu Groß Strömkendorf 2. Beiträge zur Ur- u. Frühgeschichte Mecklenburg-Vorpommern 44 (Lübstorf).

Quak, Arend 1991, 'Altfriesische und altenglische Runen'. In *Old English Runes and their Continental Background*, ed. A. Bammesberger (Heidelberg), 287–98.

Schmölcke, Ulrich, and Hauke Jöns 2013, 'Livestock in early medieval ports of trade on the Baltic Sea: The emporium Reric and other Northern German sites'. In *Landscapes and Societies in Medieval Europe East of the Elbe: Interactions between Environmental Settings and Cultural Transformations*, ed. S. Kleingartner, T. P. Newfield, S. Rossignol and D. Wehner, Papers in Medieval Studies 23 (Toronto), 54–72.

Schulte, Michael 2015, 'Die Blekinger Inschriften als Status- und Machtembleme – Ein kulturhistorischer Syntheseversuch. In *Archäologie und Runen. Fallstudien zu Inschriften im älteren Futhark*, ed. O. Grimm and A. Pesch, Schriften des Archäologischen Landesmuseums, Ergänzungsreihe vol. 11 (Schleswig), 175–94.

Siegmüller, Annette, and Hauke Jöns 2012, 'Ufermärkte, Wurten, Geestrandburgen – Herausbildung differenter Siedlungstypen im Küstengebiet in Abhängigkeit von der Paläotopographie im 1. Jahrtausend', *Archäologisches Korrespondenzblatt* 42, 573–90.

Simensen, Erik 1994, 'Språkkontakt over landegrenser. Munnleg kommunikasjon i mellomalderen', *Collegium Medievale* 7, 33–50.

Steppuhn, Peter 1998, *Die Glasfunde von Haithabu*, Berichte über die Ausgrabungen in Haithabu 32 (Neumünster).

Stoklund, Marie 2004, 'The runic inscription on the Ribe skull fragment'. In *Ribe Excavations 1970–76, Vol. 5*, Jysk Arkæologisk Selskabs skrifter 46 (Aarhus), 27–42.

Svøsø, Morten 2013, 'Om dateringen af Ribe runehjerneskallen', *Futhark: International Journal of runic Studies* 4, 173–6.

Tempel, Wolf-Dieter 1972, 'Unterschiede zwischen den Formen der Dreilagenkämme in Skandinavien und den friesischen Wurten des 8. bis 10. Jahrhunderts', *Archäologisches Korrespondenzblatt* 2, 57–9.

Townend, Matthew 2002, *Language and History in Viking Age England. Linguistic Relations between Speakers of Old Norse and Old English* (Turnhout).

Tummuscheit, Astrid 2011, *Die Baubefunde des frühmittelalterlichen Seehandelsplatzes von Groß Strömkendorf, Lkr. Nordwestmecklenburg*, Forschungen zu Groß Strömkendorf 4. Frühmittelalterliche Archäologie zwischen Ostsee und Mittelmeer 2 (Wiesbaden 2011).

Waxenberger, Gaby 2010, 'Towards a Phonology of Old English Runic Inscriptions and an Analysis of the Graphemes', unpublished Habilitationsschrift (München).

Widmark, G. 1994, 'Birkasvenskan – fanns den?', *Arkiv för Nordisk filologi* 109, 173–216.

Williams, Henrik 1990, *Åsrunan. Användning och ljudvärde i runsvenska steninskrifter*, Runrön 3 (Uppsala).

Williams, Henrik 1994, 'The non-representation of nasals before obstruents: spelling convention or phonetic analysis?'. In *Proceedings of the Third International Symposium on Runes and Runic Inscriptions*, ed. J. Knirk, Runrön 9 (Uppsala), 217–22.

Zimmermann, Christiane 2013, 'Cultures and languages in contact. Das Kammfragment von Groß Strömkendorf im Kontext von Schrift(en) und Sprache(n) auf frühmittelalterlichen Handelsplätzen'. In *Twenty-Nine Smiles for Alastair*, ed. J. Hoekstra (Kiel), 357–76.

Zimmermann, Christiane, and Hauke Jöns 2013, 'Ein Kammfragment mit Runeninschrift vom frühmittelalterlichen Handelsplatz Groß Strömkendorf, Nordwestmecklenburg'. In *Kulturwandel im Spannungsfeld von Tradition und Innovation*, ed. S. Kleingärtner, U. Müller and J. Scheschkewitz, Festschrift für Michael Müller-Wille (Neumünster), 107–25.

Index

Aachen 229
accent (linguistic) 44, 47, 50
Adam of Bremen 243, 244
Additiones Sapientum, see Lex Frisionum
Ælfwald, K. of East Anglia 198
Æthelberht, K. of Kent 223, 227, 228–9
Æthelric 197
Æthelstan, K. of East Anglia 212–13
Æthilberg 197
Alcuin 199
Aldgisl 12, 37, 55
Aldwulf, K. of East Anglia 197, 198
Alfred the Great, K. of Wessex 37–8, 228, 239
Alhheard, Bp 199
Andulfus 68
Angles, *Anglii* 2, 56, 87, 125, 173, 194–5
Anglian dialect 146
Anglo-Frisian language 18, 25–6, 27–30, 48, 51, 93, 97, 105, 128, 141, 179, 193, 232
Anglo-Saxon Chronicle(s), the 37–8
Anglo-Saxons 4, 12, 17, 37, 56, 62, 64, 67, 68, 76, 86, 89, 152, 178, 199
 Anglo-Saxon kingdoms 34
Anna, K. of East Anglia 197
Appollinarius, Bp 197
armring 19, 78–9
assembly site 158
Avitus, Bp 197

back-mutation (*a-* and *u-*mutation) 126
Balthild, Q. 197–8
Baltic Sea and zone 243, 245, 249, 251–7
Bardy-Świelubie 253
Barham 211
Barward 155
Batavians 55, 57, 66
Bawsey 210–11, 218
Bayfield 213–14
Beachamwell 208
beads 86
Bede 37, 55, 89, 193, 195, 197, 198, 217, 228
Beowulf 37, 38, 56
bind-runes 263
Birka 243, 246, 247, 256
Bloodmoor Hill, Carlton Colville 214–15

bog iron 154
Boniface, Bp/St 37, 198
Boructuari 2
Bracon Ash 202
bracteate(s) 64, 78–80, 81, 89, 141, 151–2, 165–7, 168, 208
Brandon 215, 217
breaking 49
British Celtic 45–6, 47, 50, 66
Brittenburg (*Lugdunum*) 59
brooches 61, 75, 76, 161, 202
 Achlum Type 81
 Anglo-Saxon 56, 68
 annular 35
 ansate 203–5, 218
 composite and plated disc 84, 195
 cruciform 35, 64–5
 disc-on-bow 85, 173
 equal-armed 64, 76–8, 87
 Domburg Type 35, 53, 65–6, 81
 keystone garnet disc 81, 85
 Jutlandic 89
 saint (*Heiligenfibeln*) 202
 saucer 64, 77, 87
 small long 35
 square-headed 81
 supporting-arm 64, 76
Bubo 12
buckle(s) 84, 85, 199
Byzantine Empire 89

Caistor St Edmund (= Caistor-by-Norwich) 198, 199, 210–11, 213–14, 218
Campine 174
Cananefates 10, 56, 66
Carolingian Empire 3, 17–18, 36, 68–9, 90, 174, 185, 211, 229, 256
Castrium-Oosterburt 59
Celtic languages 34, 44–7, 50–2, 66, 126
Chamavi 56
charcoal production 154
Charlemagne 12, 15, 55, 132, 212, 229
Charles the Fat 20
Charles Martel 90
Chauci 10–11

Childeric, K. 197
Chilperic, K. 68
Chipping Ongar 208
Christianity, see Church; conversion
Church, the 2, 17, 32, 34, 37, 57–8, 197–8
clay district (Frisia) 2, 257
Clovis II, K. of Neustria 197
Cnobheresburg 197
Coddenham 209, 214
coffins, oak log 36
coins, coinage 31–33, 36, 68, 76, 83, 116, 161, 167, 199, 205–13, 217–18, 253, 257
  runic 32
Cologne (Köln) 130, 208
comb(s) 32, 111, 265
comb-making 257, 259, 268
communication 28, 243
  semi-communication 246
convergence 32, 46, 50–1, 173–87
conversion 15, 26
Cornish 45–6
Corvey 142
craft-production 164, 166, 204, 253, 257, 259
Cultural Transmission Theory 183
Cuthwine, Bp 198–9

Dagobert I 195
Danes 2, 18, 55, 90, 243–4, 246
Danish 138
Danube, R. 57
deniers (*denarii*) 212–13, 229, 257
Denmark 19, 35
depopulation, see habitation hiatus
Dingen 155, 158
Dingerwerden 158
dirhams 19, 257–8
Diss 195–6
  'near Diss' 213–14
Domburg 3, 19, 58, 209
Dommoc 198
Dorestad 3, 6, 17, 18, 19, 36, 208, 209, 212, 215, 216, 217, 243, 259
Dorregeest 59
Dražko 256
Drenthe (prov.) 6, 18, 45, 46
dune belt (Frisia) 5–6, 58–9, 67
Dunum 9
Dutch 51–2, 126–8, 139, 142, 145
  See also Middle Dutch, Old Dutch

Eadburgh, Abbess 198
East Anglia 36, 81, 83, 85, 86, 87, 141, 173, 193–218
  See also Norfolk; Suffolk
East Germanic 97
Eastphalia 127–8, 131–2, 135–6, 140, 142–6
Echternach 37
Elbe, R. 57, 87, 125–6, 137–8, 140, 152, 160, 161, 168, 249, 253
Elbe-Weser area/region/triangle 64, 76, 87, 89, 150–2, 165, 168–9
Eligius of Noyon, St 57
elite networking 75
Elst 62
Emden 36, 253
Ems, R. 36, 44, 45, 46, 51, 135–6, 138
emporium/-a (trading sites) 19, 202, 205, 211, 215, 218, 243, 245, 247, 249, 253–7, 268
Engelum 64
Englum 64
England 15, 19, 25–38, 64, 68–9, 75–9, 85, 87, 97, 152, 157, 168, 173, 176, 182, 184, 193, 202, 209, 246
Engria 135
Eorconwald/Erchinoald 197
equestrian equipment 16, 90
Essen 128, 130–1, 136–7, 140, 141, 142, 146
Essex 81–2, 85, 86, 87
  East Saxon kingdom 193

Fallward 152, 155
Faremoutiers-en-Brie 197
farmhouses 9, 61–2, 65, 166, 176–8, 182–4, 186
farming, arable 9, 59
farming, livestock 6, 9, 59
Feddersen Wierde 152, 154–5, 158
Felix 195
final -*u* on *a*-stem nouns 32–3, 110–11, 121, 267
finger rings 86
First Riustring Manuscript 225–6, 234–5
Flanders 3, 57, 61, 66, 173–87
Flemings 27–8
Flixborough 215, 216
Flögeln-Dalem 177
Floris V, Count of Holland 55
Foillán 197
Forum Hadriani 59, 62
Franks 2, 4, 56, 66, 67, 68, 81–2, 83–6, 140, 194, 217, 257
  Frankish realm 12, 18, 27, 75, 81, 87, 89, 135, 140
Freckenhorst 138, 146

Fresiones occidentales 53
Friesland (prov.) 3, 9–10, 11, 15, 34, 53, 58, 61–2, 66, 68, 79, 81, 83, 85, 87, 97, 173, 174, 178, 182, 202, 231
Frisian kingdom 2–3, 12
Frisian language 27, 29, 44–7, 52, 55, 66–7, 126, 128, 136, 143
  See also Old Frisian
Frisiavones 2, 10, 56
Frisii 2, 10–11, 12, 44, 46
fronting 30–1, 48–9, 105–9, 112, 117, 141
Fulda 128, 130
Fursa 197
fuþark 30, 93, 101, 117, 247, 261, 265, 267
fuþą̊rk 247, 260–5, 268
fuþorc 30, 101, 247, 260–1, 264, 268

Garderen 62
Gaulish 44–6, 50
Geest 152, 154–61, 165, 168–9
Genesis (Old Saxon verse) 128, 142–3
Germanic consonant shift 45
Germanic language family 27, 28, 30, 44–52, 66, 93, 96, 111, 112, 116, 125–6, 138, 223, 234–5, 238, 244, 266
Gesta Fresonum 29
glass vessels 16, 90, 199, 253, 256–7, 259
Godfred, K. of Denmark 256
Godfrid 20
Goeree 59
gold 31, 65, 68, 75–6, 78–80, 81, 83–6, 89, 152, 159, 195, 197–8, 205, 208–9, 229, 237
Gothic 116
Greek 246
Greeks 244
Gregory of Tours 58
Groningen (prov.) 3, 10, 11, 15, 18, 53, 58, 61–2, 64, 68, 97
Groothusen 253
Groß Strömkendorf (*Reric*) 244–68
Grubenhaus/-häuser 164, 165, 166, 255, 259
Grutte Pier 28
Gudendorf-Köstersweg 159–64, 166, 168

habitation hiatus 11, 34, 58–61, 126
Hadleigh 214
Halberstadt 130, 136
Halle 130
hanging bowl 85, 118
Hedeby 243, 247, 256, 257
Heidenschanze (Sievern) 156–8, 160, 164, 168

Heidenstadt (Sievern) 156, 157–9, 168
Heliand 128, 141–6
Helmold of Bosau 243–4
Hereswith 197
Heruli 57
Hogebeintum 10, 85
Holland 3, 5, 58, 67, 69, 127, 140
  North Holland 3, 15, 18, 53, 58–9, 65–9, 177–8
  South Holland 3, 9, 15, 17, 53, 59, 61, 66, 68–9
Honorius, Ab. of Canterbury 195
honour 224, 227, 238
horse burial 251
hunting 6
Huy 208
  Huy pottery 215
Hygelac (*Chochilaicus*) 37

IJ, R. 67
IJssel, R. 59
i-mutation (*i*-umlaut) 32, 49, 50, 96, 101, 117, 126, 132, 136–8, 142–3, 144–5
Indo-European/Proto-Indo-European (IE/PIE) 45, 112
Ingvaeonic 66, 128, 132, 179, 239
  See also North Sea Germanic
Ipswich (*Gypeswic*) 36, 205, 212, 215, 217–18
  Boss Hall cemetery 195–6
  Buttermarket cemetery 199, 217
  See also pottery, Ipswich Ware
Ireland 19, 20

Johannes de Beke 55
Jumne (Jomsburg) 244, 246
Junius, Franciscus *filius* 27–8
Justinian, Emperor 56
Jutland 35, 36

Kamba, the 226–7
Katwijk 6, 55, 68, 85
  -Zanderij 64
Kelling 202
Kent 79, 81, 83–6, 87, 89, 173, 205, 213, 217, 223, 232, 235
Kloosterwijtwerd 15–16
koiné, koineization 179–82, 183, 185–6

labio-velar mutation 49
Lagny-sur-Marne 197
Langenacker (Sievern) 155–6, 157
language contact 245–6

language shift 44, 46
language simplification 246
language spread 43
Latin 32, 44, 52, 96, 97, 113, 234, 247, 267, 268
Lauwers, R. 3, 230, 231, 234
law-codes 18, 20, 223–39
Laws of Æthelberht (Ab) 228–9, 232–9
Laws, Old Frisian 20, 25–6, 38, 223–39
Leges Barbarorum 225, 229–30, 231–2, 234, 235, 237
Leiderdorp 62
Lek, R. 59
lenition 45, 47
Lex Frisionum 3, 12, 53, 65, 68, 96, 223, 225, 229–39
  Additiones Sapientum 229–30, 236–7, 239
Liafbruch 229
Lippe, R. 136
Liudger 12, 15–16, 229
London (*Lundenwic*) 37, 202, 211, 214, 215
Louis the Pious 211, 212
Low Franconian 67, 135, 138, 144, 145, 179
see also Old Low Franconian
Low German, 127–8, 132–3, 142
  See also Middle Low German
Lull, Abb. 199
Lundeborg 155

Maas, R., see Meuse
Maastricht 208
Magdeburg 127, 130, 136, 140
Mainz 208, 216
Malorix 11, 44, 45
Martham 202
Mecklenburg hill-fort 256
Medemblik 36, 58
Meinsuit 15
Menzlin 253, 257
Mercia 90, 217
Merovingian Period, the 17, 62, 29, 86
Merseburg 127, 136, 142
  Merseburg Glosses 132, 142
metathesis 144
Meuse (Maas), R. and estuary 17, 45, 58–9, 62, 68, 135, 140
Middle Dutch 27
Middle English 28–30, 96, 109, 247, 268
Middle Harling 217
Middle High German 29
Middle Low German 111
Migration Period, the 26, 34, 53, 58, 61, 66–7, 76, 86–7, 125–6, 152, 155, 159, 161, 165, 166–7, 168–9, 173, 178, 179, 193, 195, 254
Mischsprache 126
monophthongization
  Germanic *ai 30–1, 48–9, 105–9, 116–17, 142
  Germanic *au 32, 48, 107–9, 142
Mucking 182
Münster (city) 15
  diocese 134

nasalization (velarization) and raising of Germanic *a* 30–1, 101, 109, 141, 265
neckring 78–9, 152
Niedersachsen (Lower Saxony) 3, 17, 35, 37, 53, 166, 253
Norfolk 79, 87, 193–5, 202, 209, 218
  See also East Anglia
North Albingia 137–8
North Frisia 53
North Germanic 47–8, 144, 245–6, 266
North Sea, the 2, 4, 5, 17, 20, 66–7, 87, 90, 125–6, 132, 136, 140, 146, 152, 165, 168, 173–4, 176, 178–9, 182–7, 193, 194–5, 208, 209, 215, 217, 239, 243, 245, 249, 252, 253–4, 257, 259, 268
North Sea Germanic (NSGmc) 48, 66–7, 125–40, 141, 143, 144, 145, 146, 179, 184, 185, 265–6
  See also Ingvaeonic
Northmen 243–4, 246
Nydam Style 78

Obodrites 249, 256
Oegstgeest-Nieuw Rhijngest 62, 85
Oer-IJ, R. 58
Ohthere 243
Old Dutch 127–8
Old English (and Pre-Old English) (OE) 28, 32, 61, 93–8, 101–12, 116, 118, 120–1, 125–7, 134, 141, 143, 145–6, 179, 184, 234, 246, 260, 263, 266
Old Frisian (and Pre-Old Frisian) (OFris) 18, 28, 46–7, 50–1, 66, 96–7, 1, 101, 104–5, 111–13, 116, 118, 120–1, 125–7, 132–4, 141–6, 179, 184, 225, 234, 237, 244, 246, 260, 265–6
Old High German (OHG) 97, 111, 126–8, 142–3, 146
Old Irish 44–5
Old Low Franconian (OLF) 66, 97, 126–8, 131, 142–6
Old Lübeck 256

Old Norse (ON) 113, 126, 244, 246
Old Rhine, R. and estuary 58–9, 64, 67–8
Old Saxon (OS) 28, 66, 111, 125–46, 179, 244, 246, 260, 265–6
Oosterbeintum 12
Oostergo 3, 11, 18
Oosterlauwers 3
Oostvoorne 59
Orosius, *Historia* 37, 55
Osnabrück 127, 135
Ostfriesland (East Friesland) 3, 9, 18, 53, 90, 97, 137
Oudenburg 174

Paderborn 146, 202
palatalization 28, 49, 51, 138–9
peatlands, peat bog (Frisia) 6, 9, 58–9, 67, 131, 134–5, 140
pin(s) 86
place-names 45–6, 59–61, 64, 136–9, 158
Pliny the Elder 2, 10
Postwick 197–8
pottery 61, 164, 165, 174, 182, 183, 184, 186, 199, 213–18, 253, 256
  Angelsaksisch 26, 34, 53, 55–6, 62–5, 68
  Anglo-Saxon 152
  Badorf ware 215–16, 218, 256
  Frankish 55, 62–4, 66, 213–15
  Frisian 256
  Hessens-Schortens ware 174
  Ipswich ware 215–16, 218
  Mayen ware 256
  Muschelgrusware 256
  organic-tempered 174–6
  sand-tempered 184–5
  Saxon 256
  Tating ware 215, 217, 256
  Tritsum ware 174
pre-Christian religion 229
Prittlewell 85
Procopius 2, 26, 56–7, 194
Proto-Germanic (PGmc) 46–7, 51, 111, 112, 133, 136, 141–4
Ptolemy 10

Quentovic 208, 212, 215, 217

Radbod 12, 55
Radigis 57, 194
Rædwald, K. of East Anglia 195
Ralswiek 253, 257
Rendlesham 208–9

Reric 256
Rhenen 62, 82
Rhine, R. and delta/estuary 2, 3, 6, 11, 37, 44, 45, 46, 51, 53, 57, 59, 62, 135–6, 138, 140, 152, 173–4,178, 184, 194, 196, 209, 257
Rhineland 202, 216
Ribe 36, 243, 247, 253, 257, 259
Rijnsburg 3, 55, 68, 85
  -de Hoorn 62
Rimbert 243, 244
Rodulf 18, 20
Roksem 177
Rouen 211
rune-forms
  āc-rune 31–2, 101, 103–4, 107, 110–16, 117, 120–1, 141
  æsc-rune 107, 117
  *ansuz-rune 30, 101, 105, 117, 261, 265
  ċen-rune 102, 117–19, 121
  hæġel-rune 117–20, 121
  ōs-rune 30–2, 101–5, 107, 121, 141
  ōþil-rune 32, 101, 104, 121
  'star'-rune 262–3
  þorn-rune 263
runes 244–5
  Anglo-Frisian 30–2, 232, 247, 262–3
  Anglo-Saxon 26, 26, 93–122
  Frisian 18
  long-branch 261, 264
  short-twig 261–3
  See also bind-runes; coinage, runic; fuþark; fuþąrk; fuþorc; rune-forms; runic inscriptions
runic inscriptions
  Amay comb 31, 9, 267
  Arum yew-wood sword 104–5, 113, 121, 266
  Baconsthorpe tweezers 264
  Bergakker scabbard-mount 97, 267
  Borgharen 97, 104, 121, 267
  Björketorp stone 247
  Brandon antler handle 104
  Bridekirk font 247, 268
  Chessell Down scabbard mouth-piece 102–3, 117
  Cleatham hanging-bowl 118
  Donzdorf brooch 245
  Duesminde brooch 245
  Elisenhof comb 262, 265
  Franks Casket 32
  Frienstedt comb 111, 265
  Gammertingen canister 266

Glasgow/Folkestone *tremissis* 97, 111, 116–17, 267
Groß Strömkendorf comb 247, 259–68
Haithabu stick 262
Harford Farm, Caistor-by-Norwich, brooch 32, 93, 104, 116, 120
Harlingen *solidus* 31, 33, 116, 118, 121
Lindisfarne stone 104
March plate 268
Oostum comb 110, 111, 113, 121, 265–6
Rasquert sword-grip 105, 266
Ribe cranium 247, 263, 264
St Albans bone 247, 264, 268
Sandwich stone 118
Schweindorf *solidus* 31, 32–3, 97, 110–11, 265
Selsey gold fragments 116
skanomodu *solidus* 31–2, 97, 101–2, 109, 110–11, 116, 117, 121–2, 142
Southampton/*Hamwic* bone 97, 110, 111–13, 121, 245, 267
Stentoften stone 247
Toornwerd comb 105, 110, 111, 113, 265–6
Undley bracteate 101, 141
Westeremden A weaving-sword 97, 113
Westeremden B yew-wood stick 97, 263–4
Whitby comb 32, 104
Wijnaldum A bone 267
Wijnaldum B gold pendant 118, 267

Saaksum 64
Sachsendingen 158
Sæthryth 197
St Denis, Paris 216
saltmarsh 6, 9, 58, 174
Samland 243
Sassenheim 64
Saxmund 229
Saxons 2, 4, 55, 56–7, 64, 66, 76–8, 87, 90, 125, 127, 132, 197, 244, 251
Scandinavia 4, 15, 20, 78–80, 84, 87, 89, 90, 150, 152, 155, 165, 168, 245, 249, 251, 253–4, 264, 265
sceatt/-as 32, 36, 173, 209–11, 217–18, 257–8
Scheldt, R. and basin 3, 174, 176, 183
seal matrix 197–8
seax 16, 202
shield boss 16, 202
ship(s), boats 38, 152, 212, 251
Sievern 79, 87, 89, 152–9, 160, 165–6, 168
Sigeberht, K. of East Anglia 195, 197
Sigibert II, K. of Austrasia and Burgundy 195

Sigibert III, K. of Austrasia 195–6
silver 19, 65, 75–8, 81–2, 85, 86, 87, 89, 161, 209, 229, 257
Sincfal, R. 239
skimmer, sieve 81
Slavonic language 246
Slavs 55, 136, 243–4, 251, 253–4, 256, 257
Snape 89, 217
Snettisham 213–14
solidus/-i 31–3, 83, 152, 195, 229, 234, 236, 237
    See also runic inscriptions, **skanomodu**
Solleveld 9, 62
South Germanic (*Südgermanisch*) 267 and note
Southampton (*Hamwic*) 36, 202, 205, 243
spearhead 199, 202
Spieka-Knill 165–7, 168
Sprachbund 29, 127
Starigard Oldenburg 256
Strasburg 208
Straubing 128, 145–6
Style I 75, 81
Style II 84–5
Suebi 58, 68
Suevi 57–8
Suffolk 193, 209, 211, 218
    See also East Anglia
Sutton Hoo 85, 89, 205, 208, 213, 217
Swaffham 208
sword, sword-fittings 16, 81, 85

Tacitus, *Germania* 2, 10, 11, 66
Tassilo Chalice Style 202–3
terp district 3, 6, 9–10, 11–12, 53, 55, 58, 61–2, 65, 67, 68
Terrington St Clement 217
Texel 6, 18, 19, 20, 58, 65
Textus Roffensis 228
Thames Valley 174
Thetford 212
Theudebert I, K. 57, 194
Theudechild 57
Thuringia 253
Thuringians 57
Tidfirth, Bp 199
Tiel 19
trade and exchange 75, 205, 209–13, 216–18, 244–7, 253, 257
trading sites, *see* emporium/-a
tremissis/-es 32, 36, 83, 205, 208, 229
Truchtlaching 203
Truso (Janów Pomorski) 253
Twente (prov.) 45, 46

Usquert 16
Utrecht 11, 37, 55, 67, 68, 85

Valkenburg (*Praetorium Agrippinae*) 17, 59
Vecht, R. 58, 68
velarization, *see* nasalization
Venantius Fortunatus 2, 68
Verritus 11, 44, 45
Vikings, Viking Age/Period, the 1, 17–19, 34, 38, 58, 125, 193, 211, 243, 245–7, 249, 257, 260–1, 263–4, 268
Vlie, R. 3, 61, 65, 76, 90, 230, 239
Voorburg 59

Waal, R. 45
Wadden Sea 6, 15
Wageningen 62
Walichrum 19, 58
Warni 2, 57, 173, 194
weaponry 90
Welsh 45–6
Werden 15, 128, 130–1, 138, 140, 141, 142, 143, 144
wergild 223–6, 231–2, 235, 238
Weser, R. and estuary 12, 17, 57, 87, 135–6, 137–8, 140, 152, 157, 168, 231, 234
West Dereham 217

West Germanic (WGmc) 34, 47–8, 97, 105, 111, 126–7, 134, 136, 138, 144, 179, 245–6, 265, 266
West Harling 212
Westenschouwen 209
Westergo 3, 11, 18, 64, 79, 81, 87
Westerklief 19
Westerlauwers 3
Westfalen (Westphalia) 36, 128, 131–2, 135, 142, 146
Widsith 37, 38
Wieringen 6, 18
Wieuwerd 85
Wijnaldum 3, 68, 85, 118, 202
 -Tjitsma 81
Wilfrid, Bp 37
Wilten/Wiltenberg 55
Winchester 217
Wlemar 229
Wulfstan 243

York 217

Zandstraat, the 174
Zeeland 3, 55, 58, 66
Zeeuwen 57
Zwin, R. 3, 12, 17